# THE HISTORY OF POLICING IN NORTH WALES

# The History of Policing in North Wales

by

H. Kenneth Birch

First edition: 2008

© Text: H. Kenneth Birch

Copyright © by Llygad Gwalch 2008
All rights reserved. No part of this publication may be reproduced,
stored in a retrieval system, or transmitted in any form or by
any means, electronic, electrostatic, magnetic tape, mechanical,
photocopying, recording, or otherwise, without prior
permission of the authors of the works herein.

ISBN: 978-1-84524-071-4

Cover design: Sian Parri

First published in 2008 by
Llygad Gwalch, Ysgubor Plas, Llwyndyrys,
Pwllheli, Gwynedd LL53 6NG
☎ 01758 750432   📠 01758 750438
✉ llyfrau@carreg-gwalch.com   Web site: www.carreg-gwalch.com

*I dedicate this book to my grandsons,*
*William and Elliot*

This history is written as a tribute to the countless numbers of police officers who, for the better part of 160 years have steadfastly upheld and maintained law and order in the towns and villages of north Wales. It is an interesting story, strong in tradition, courage, and at times, personal sacrifice, and one enriched by many excellent officers, some of whom have served, and are still serving with great distinction. Therefore, it is appropriate that as the millennium has passed and before memories fade, their work and achievements are recorded for posterity.

H.K.B.

# The Author

Henry Kenneth Birch was born in Everton, Liverpool in 1924, later moving with his parents to Manchester where he spent his childhood. Following his father's death he moved with his mother to Bethel and later to nearby Caernarfon. He served with distinction in the Royal Navy during the Second World War. Post demobilisation led to some three years at Talgarth Sanatorium. Subsequently he proceeded to Coleg Harlech, and later graduated at the universities of Wales (BA honours History, MA, PhD, Diploma in Social Science) and Hull (BPhil in Criminology).

Dr Birch worked initially as a civilian in the fingerprints section of the Cardiff CID. After a brief period as a schoolteacher at Pelsall in the Midlands, he was appointed lecturer at Chester College of Further Education where he taught police cadets among others. During his retirement he lectured regularly to police officers at the North Wales Police Headquarters in Colwyn Bay. Chief Constable David Owen, CBE, QPM, appointed him official historian of the North Wales Police in 1991. He was awarded his doctorate posthumously by the University of Wales in 2002 for a thesis on which this book is based. (In 1980 he was awarded his MA degree for a thesis on 'The Merioneth Police 1856-1950'.)

From 1964 until his death in December 2000, he lived with his wife at Aberdyfi. He served as Vice-Chairman of the Merioneth Historical and Record Society between 1986-2000.

# Contents

| | |
|---|---:|
| Foreword | 8 |
| Acknowledgements | 10 |
| Introduction | 12 |
| Chapter I:<br>The Social and Economic Conditions in North Wales, 1800-40 | 25 |
| Chapter II:<br>Crime and the Denbighshire Constabulary, 1840-57 | 62 |
| Chapter III:<br>The County Police, 1856-75 | 85 |
| Chapter IV:<br>A Time of Consolidation, 1876-88 | 143 |
| Chapter V:<br>Professionalism, Communications and Stability | 174 |
| Chapter VI:<br>Social Conflict and Mutual Aid, 1886-1911 | 204 |
| Chapter VII:<br>The First World War, 1914-18 | 238 |
| Chapter VIII:<br>The Inter-war Years, 1918-39 | 252 |
| Chapter IX:<br>The Second World War, 1939-45 | 276 |
| Chapter X:<br>Amalgamations and the Gwynedd Constabulary, 1945-74 | 295 |
| Chapter XI:<br>The North Wales Police, 1974-2000 | 326 |
| Conclusion | 361 |
| Bibliography | 371 |
| Index | 380 |

# Foreword

It is with a sense of pride that I put pen to paper to write a foreword to this book which charts the history of the police in north Wales over the last 150 years.

It can but be a matter of great regret that the author, Henry Kenneth Birch, did not live to see his work published. When I appointed him in 1991 as the official historian for the North Wales Police I was confident he would discharge his responsibilities with diligence. This book is clear evidence that my confidence was not misplaced.

Two dominant themes emerge from this work – the recurring nature of police work which grows in intensity with the passage of time and secondly the ever present question of control of the police service.

It is clear that the introduction of the motor car brought the motorist into contact with the judicial system. In the early days great efforts were made by the police to reduce accidents and control speed. To deflect the charge of harassment the chief constable of the day very wisely decreed that officers should 'behave respectfully to those to whom they believed had committed an offence'. Such a sentiment would clearly find a place in present day traffic enforcement which could be considered to border on the obsessional.

The steady increase in violence has seen the police service move from the concept of the parish constable to a highly organised and effective team, capable of dealing with extremes of violence and disorder. It is clear that this move was not of the service's making but merely a response to the ever declining social mores of our society.

The changing face of police accountability, from the standing joint police committees to the police authority, together with the ever increasing role of the Home Office is clearly to be seen. It is interesting to note the amalgamations which took place over the years. They were based on a common sense approach and generally had the support of the local Committee, and the public at large. The Police Act 1964 created the tripartite approach which provided a sensible and workable balance, provided all three parties confined themselves to their responsibilities.

The more recent proposals for amalgamations were clear evidence of one party outstripping its responsibilities by continuing with its proposals for an all Wales police force in the face of outright opposition. The proposals were based on the pretext of greater co-operation. Anyone with an iota of police knowledge or experience would have immediately realised the futility of such a proposal. The only benefit, if benefit be the appropriate word, would be the handing of power and control to the Centre.

Fortunately, common sense appears to have won the day. History clearly shows that amalgamations based on sound practical principles will be accepted whilst fanciful ideas divorced from the practicalities of service to the community are bound to founder. It is vitally important for the well-being of any society that the balance of control remains with each party exercising responsibilities commensurate with their role.

The rural nature of north Wales has played a prominent part in the gradual development of the North Wales Police Service. Its strength lies in its identification with the community it serves and the perception of the distancing of the Service from the people will work to its disadvantage.

The last 150 years has seen great changes in society, as evidenced by Dr Birch, and in considering the future there is a need to have regard to the strong traditions of the police service which this work has underlined. Ignoring these traditions will, in the long-term, neither benefit the North Wales Police Service, or the society it is here to serve.

David Owen, C.B.E., Q.P.M.
Chief Constable,
North Wales Police, 1982-94.

# Acknowledgements

In conducting this research I became increasingly aware that I owed a debt of gratitude to a great number of people. I am deeply indebted to Chief Superintendent Elfed Roberts of the North Wales Police who suggested that I should undertake this research; to the late Professor David J.V. Jones for his early words of encouragement, and to Professors Geraint H. Jenkins, Aled G. Jones and Ieuan Gwynedd Jones for continuing that encouragement. I also wish to acknowledge the tremendous assistance afforded to me over the years by the staff of the National Library of Wales and of the Hugh Owen Library, Aberystwyth; the Librarian and staff of the Commissioners' Library, New Scotland Yard; the editor and staff of the *Police Review*; the archivists and staff at the Caernarfon, Cardiff, Dolgellau, Hawarden, Llangefni and Rhuthun Record Offices, and also to Mr Arwyn Lloyd Hughes, Llandaff, friend and former County Archivist of Merioneth. Collectively, they made this research that much easier by their extensive knowledge and expertise. Much of the material contained in this work would not have been possible had it not been for the early foresight of the late Sir William Jones Williams, Chief Constable of the Caernarfonshire and later Gwynedd Constabulary, who recognised the importance of preserving police records, a policy that over the years has been continued by his successors, Sir Phillip Myers, Mr David Owen and Mr Michael Argent. One must also acknowledge those who, over the years filled the gaps in this work, for they played a vital role. They brought clarity where there had been obscurity and light where there had been darkness. In particular I wish to thank Mrs Margaret Baxter, Needham Market, Suffolk, Mr Roger Atkins, Abergavenny, and Mr John Tecwyn Owen, Penrhyn Bay, who generously provided me with important information on the Denbighshire, Flintshire and North Wales Police respectively. I have also been fortunate in receiving valuable information from a number of police officers, in particular Larry Davies, Trevor Edwards, Phil Hare, Frazer Jones, Gwyn Jones, Barry Madden, Mike Maidstone, R.B. Thomas, William Thomas, Peter Williams and all the staff at the Force Press Office, Colwyn Bay. Also, I have a very deep sense of gratitude to Dr Paul O'Leary of the Department of Welsh History, University of Wales, Aberystwyth, for his constant encouragement, patience and invaluable guidance; he has been, at all times, a tremendous source of inspiration. Finally, I wish to thank my family, in particular my wife, Hefin, who, over the years, has been a tower of strength. Without her faith and understanding I doubt whether this research would ever have seen the light of day.

# Introduction

Ever since the 1970s, it has been fashionable for a number of leading historians to write about the police. Such interest in the service might well arise as a result of a greater readiness in Britain today to examine afresh, the situations and institutions which all too often in the past have been taken for granted. Certainly, before the middle of the twentieth century, the police, as one of these institutions, was largely informed 'by a Whig view which saw history in relatively simple terms of progress and presupposed the emergence of a broad consensus in politics and society from the Victorian period'.[1] Such history was written by former civil servants or policemen who tended to accept the observations of 'the early nineteenth century reformers who believed the old parochial system of policing was, at best inefficient, and second, that England at the close of the eighteenth and beginning of the nineteenth century was faced with a serious increase in crime and disorder'.[2] In this interpretation, the police were acknowledged as being an obvious answer to a problem: they reduced acts of criminality and public disorder and therefore were seen as playing an important role in the emergence of the country's consensual society.[3]

However, as Clive Emsley further explains, there is an alternative view, although it is one examined from the opposite end of the political spectrum. Advocates of this approach, whilst accepting the police were the best answer to a problem, took the view that it was not crime and disorder, but rather the growth of an industrial society with its ruling classes ever anxious to safeguard their position and power to exert discipline on the new industrial working-class, that was the true underlying factor in this interpretation of events. If then, one accepts this alternative view as having some validity, then the consensus within 'Victorian society similarly owes much to the new policemen, and to the truncheon'.[4] It is an observation that receives much support from the historian Robert D. Storch, who labelled the police as 'domestic missionaries' intent on imposing forms of social control on the workers.[5] This idea by Storch that the police should be viewed as having the potential to use force, was one that would have received little sympathy among the more traditional historians of the English police.[6]

With such conflicting views on the police, it is appropriate at this time, to ask the important and somewhat intriguing question of the true position of the police in today's society, which, over the past 160 years, the period covered in this book, has constantly been in the throes of change. Certainly, on the evidence that is available to researchers such as myself, it soon became evident that there was not a simple answer. In an attempt to throw some light on the question, an article in a leading newspaper, written nearly thirty years ago, claimed, that in any society under pressure 'it is the forces trying to sustain the structure that bear the strain. Inevitably, the police will be thrust into the front line, seen on the one hand as a repressive force out to crush the democratic will, and on the other as going soft at the edges and failing to carry out their duty to protect the public'.[7] Such an observation is as true today as in the day it was written. Therefore, a much greater understanding of the dilemma thus posed, is one that urgently calls for even more research.

Jane Morgan, for example, in her valuable work on industrial strikes between 1900-39 was quick to recognise that between the late nineteenth century and the 1930s there came into being a number of 'crucial changes, still only imperfectly understood in the evolution of the British police'.[8] It was a period when there emerged a police force more clearly nationalised in the face of large-scale industrial disorder, and certainly one that was more answerable to 'edicts of central government, and free from local or national democratic accountability'.[9] There was, at the time, a noticeable extension in the powers conferred upon the police, particularly during periods of unrest. It was the significance of these changes that eventually led a number of distinguished historians, in a diversity of disciplines, to examine afresh the function and role of the police in England and Wales. Sociologists, criminologists, lawyers, political commentators and social theorists, have all expressed views, many of which even today, are judged contentious.

In addition to the informative works of Clive Emsley and Jane Morgan, other distinguished historians who have made a valuable contribution to the study of the police are Robert Reiner, Charles Reith, Michael Banton, Roger Geary, David J.V. Jones, T.A. Critchley, David Ascoli and Ben Whitaker. High-ranking police officers like Robert Mark, David McNee and John Alderson have also added their considerable weight to the discussion. In his analysis of the police, for example, Robert Reiner acknowledged that they came into being against a background of stiff opposition from a wide variety of political interests and philosophies.[10] With the passage of time, however, this opposition began to wane, particularly among the upper and middle classes. Time did little to dispel the deep-seated resentment of the working-class that on occasion surfaced in the form of sporadic physical violence which was 'symbolised by a stream of derogatory epithets for the new police: "Crushers", "Peel's Bloody Gang", "Blue Locusts", "Jenny Darbies", "Raw Lobsters" and "Blue Drones"'.[11] Yet, by the 1950s the police had become not merely accepted, but lionised by the broad spectrum of opinion. In no other country has the police force been so much a symbol of national pride.[12] A similar accolade to that observed by Reiner, although written some seventy years earlier, appeared in the editorial column of *The Times* in 1908 which claimed 'the policeman in London is not merely guardian of the peace, he is the best friend of a mass of people who have no other counsellor or protector'.[13] It was a statement that drew an angry reaction from among those holding revisionist beliefs, claiming instead that whilst such opinions on the police might well have applied to the upper or middle classes, they played little or no part in the experience of the underclass, 'nor in fact by the working class generally'.[14]

Whatever the rights or wrongs of such views, we are still no nearer to answering the question of the role of the police in today's society. In attempting to provide an answer, Sir Robert Mark, former Commissioner of the Metropolitan Police, claimed that within Great Britain the police represented government by consent.[15] He added that they were, on the whole, few in numbers and for the most part unarmed.[16] Sir Robert went on to emphasise 'that the police play no part in determining guilt or punishment and our accountability to the courts both criminal and civil, to local police authorities, to Parliament and to public opinion is unsurpassed anywhere in the world'.[17] Furthermore, 'whilst the police place great importance on their constitutional freedom the significance of their accountability should not be overlooked as a counter-balance to any improper use of it'.[18]

Agreeing with Sir Robert's views, Lord Scarman in his report on the riots in Brixton in 1981, laid great emphasis on the main principles governing the policing of a free society, which he contended was 'consent and balance on the one hand, independence and accountability on the other'.[19] What, in effect, he was illustrating, was the fact that if the police wished to secure the consent of the community which they 'needed to support their operations, they had to strike an acceptable balance between the freedom to operate without political or other constraints, and their alternate liability to the consent of the community'.[20] Such words brought sharply into focus the important functions of the police, as defined by Charles Rowan and Richard Mayne on the founding of the Metropolitan Police in 1829 – the prevention of crime, the protection of life and property and the preservation of public tranquillity.[21] As Jane Morgan observes, 'the conflict that can arise between the duty of the police to maintain order and their duty to enforce the law, and the priority which must be given to the former have long been recognised by the police themselves'.[22] The fact was clearly illustrated during the miners' strike in 1984-85, as 'was the inherent complexity of reconciling the principles of independence and public accountability'.[23] Although it is recognised that police freedom is vital, there are, nevertheless, limitations on the powers exercised by the police.

On the question of accountability and the consent of the community, David Taylor in his important *The New Police* emphasises that 'the idea of the police being servants of the community was always central to the thinking of nineteenth century police reformers'.[24] Even the retention of the historic title of constable was crucial in this respect for it did much to foster the idea that the new police after 1829 were, like the old constables, equally accountable and therefore under the control of those they served, and as such, drew their legitimacy from the people.[25] This was an observation that was in keeping with the works of such orthodox historians as Charles Reith, T.A. Critchley and David Ascoli, but certainly not one that was acceptable to revisionist writers such as Storch and Foster who rejected any suggestion that the people ever controlled the police, and pointed instead to the influence of the middle classes in the early years, particularly those residing in the boroughs.[26]

According to Storch, the introduction of a modern policing system, particularly in the industrial centres of northern England, stemmed from a realisation by the influential classes, that the time had arrived to create a professional, bureaucratically organised, lever of urban discipline and 'permanently introduce it into the heart of working-class communities'.[27] To revisionist thinkers like Storch, the introduction of the police was a significant extension into 'hitherto geographically peripheral areas of both the moral and political authority of the state'.[28] Their coming was viewed as symptomatic of the profound changes that were occurring in society which in turn revealed a widening gulf in class relations in the first half of the nineteenth century. It was also a period when both the actions and the murmurings of discontent emitted by the urban masses began to alarm the authorities.[29]

Yet, despite what many regard as the obvious reasons for the establishment of the new police, there are other relevant factors that we cannot ignore when conducting research. For example, over the years historians studying the police, public order and the criminal law have concentrated their attention on the role of the police 'in the repression of crime, public disorder and popular political movements, or have studied the police from the point of view of social administration'.[30] However, on closer examination, we discern that the police had a much broader mission. The crucial reason for the introduction of the new police was not simply to control crime, impose moral discipline or curb rioting *per se*.[31] It was, as Reiner explains, 'the need for a force which could stabilise relations between conflicting social classes as far as this was possible'.[32] In effect, the new police were given a free hand in controlling and regulating all facets of working-class lives.[33] Taking the revisionist view, the underlying motive for the establishment of the new police was the maintenance of the order required by the capitalist class, 'with the control of crime, riot, political dissidence and public morality being separate subsidiary facets of this overall mission'.[34] The work of the new police was not easy, and in the early years they confronted a number of serious problems, many of which were intractable and this led some police authorities to question their effectiveness in certain areas. Nevertheless, despite the difficulties, the nineteenth century 'saw the forging of a modern and generally effective technique of order-keeping: the installation of the eyes and ears of ruling elites in the very centres of working-class life'.[35]

If, as Storch and Foster record, the middle classes did exert influence on policing matters, particularly in the boroughs, then their research findings are supported by the actions of the Greater London Council in the late 1970s. Writing in his memoirs about his time as Commissioner of the Metropolitan Police, Sir David McNee, referring specifically to the question of accountability, made reference to the events in July 1978, when the Marshall Inquiry Report sponsored by the GLC was published.[36] The Report which was sent to the Commissioner was accompanied by a letter from Sir James Swaffield, chief executive of the GLC which indicated that his chairman, Sir Horace Cutler, was seeking a meeting between the council, the Commissioner and the Home Secretary, to discuss that part of the report which suggested that 'closer links should be established through a police committee, which would approve the force budget and have a voice in the appointment of the Commissioner, but not the operational control of the force'.[37] Sir David, however, had on a number of occasions suggested to the Home Secretary that there should be formal arrangements for regular consultation between the Home Office, the Commissioner and the London boroughs but he could not see any valid reason for allowing the GLC to join the Home Secretary as part of the Police Authority.[38]

Even Lord Scarman in his report on the Brixton disorders which was often critical of the police, never called for a change in the 'position of the Home Secretary as the Police Authority for the force'.[39] In fact, it was Lord Scarman's recommendations on the way future consultations with the police should be conducted, that angered left-wing politicians like Ken Livingstone and Paul Boateng, for they fell far short of what they considered as their ultimate objective – which was that the police were made to be more accountable for their actions. According to them, and they made no secret of it in their manifesto 'a labour controlled GLC would invite boroughs to join them in establishing a police committee to monitor the work of the force as a prelude to their gaining power to control the police.[40] The manifesto made it crystal clear that a Labour controlled GLC would campaign vigorously for a police authority that would consist solely of elected members of the council and London boroughs, who would have overall control of the Metropolitan and City of London Police. Such a body would be vested with the power to appoint all officers to the rank of chief superintendent and above, scrutinise the day to day affairs of the force and where it was necessary, allocate resources to the various police functions.[41]

Understandably, none of the proposals contained in the manifesto were welcomed by Sir David McNee who responded frostily. In fact, he had to declare that police officers often told him that, in their view, only the Conservative government of the day stood in the way of bringing about the changes required. Indeed, in their view, a return to power of a Socialist or even a Liberal government would lead inevitably to the proposals contained in the manifesto becoming a reality.[42] According to Sir David, any outside control over such important issues as promotion and resources, would place operational policing directly into the hands of a political authority 'which precisely was what the Police Act of 1964 sought to avoid, and for a very good reason'.[43] However, whether those same officers today, if a Conservative government was elected, would feel equally secure and comfortable is now very much debatable. At the last Conservative party conference in the summer of 1999, the now disgraced Lord Archer, speaking to delegates then, as the prospective candidate for the office of mayor of London, on the subject of law and order, declared that, if and when he became mayor, there would be fundamental changes in the way the capital was policed. For example, on the question of racism, if the new commissioner, Mr John Stevens, who succeeded Sir Paul Condon in January 2000, failed to address the problem to the satisfaction of all concerned, then he might well be removed. As for crime, he would call upon the commissioner, not merely to produce an annual, monthly or weekly report – but a daily one, so that the performance of the police could be continually assessed. In many respects, the type of police accountability that Lord Archer was seeking was not too dissimilar to that proposed by Ken Livingstone and Paul Boateng in their manifesto twenty-one years earlier.

The question that now immediately springs to mind is that of, why accountability by the police had become such an important issue by the 1970s? In order to answer this, one must inevitably return to the events occurring in Britain during the late 1950s and early 1960s. According to Michael Banton, it was becoming noticeable by 1958 that 'there were distinct signs emerging that tension between the police and the public was on the increase, this was reflected both in the mass media and in various departments of government'.[44] Certainly, at the time, there was widespread anxiety expressed about the amount of crime committed, and, commenting on the situation, Leon Radzinowicz described the statistics as 'grim and relentless in their ascending monotony'.[45] In addition to the worrying trend in crime, the 1950s was a time when deference generally was on the decline, and it became noticeable that there was a much greater willingness by the public to protest and question authority. The emergence of CND, the Aldermallston marches and the violent confrontations between rioters and police at Notting Hill and Nottingham in 1958, were clear evidence that certain sections of society were no longer willing to remain silent and passive on issues they believed were of paramount importance.[46] However, serious as all these events were, it was a series of scandals within the police itself, which involved officers at the highest level, that undermined public confidence in the service and raised, once more, important questions about police integrity and accountability. The mid-1950s saw the dismissal from the service of five chief constables, those in command at Blackpool, Brighton, Cardigan, Southend and Worcester, for offences that ranged from gross maladministration to conspiracy, theft and dishonesty, in that order.[47] It was an intolerable position that called for immediate action by the Home Secretary, and in November 1959, he duly announced that there was to be a Royal Commission 'to review the constitutional position of the police'.[48]

From the outset, it soon became evident that the Commission was not concerned with police efficiency, or crime, or the shortage of police officers. It had nothing to do, as had the Desborough and Oaksey Committees, with questions of pay and recruitment or conditions of service.[49] Neither was it like the Royal Commission of 1929 which had examined police powers and procedures. In effect, there was no disguising the fact that, basically, what the Royal Commission was seeking, was a way in which the police could be controlled, particularly when things went wrong, and in a manner that would not only be acceptable to Parliament, but would also redefine the constitutional position of the police in its relationship with the State.[50] The question of controlling the police was something that had occupied the minds of respective Home Secretaries over a number of years, and in many ways the Royal Commission's recommendations, which resulted in the Police Act of 1964, had never allowed them such a golden opportunity of achieving this objective.

However, the hopes of many were to be dashed when the Commission's proposals on accountability and complaints and their implementation in the Police Act 1964, 'were widely seen as vague, confused and contradictory'.[51] What it accomplished was to clearly strengthen the hands of the Home Office and the chief constables at the expense of local authorities.[52] Indeed, since the passing of the 1964 Police Act many observers believe, and to some extent rightly so, that it has left police authorities completely powerless.[53] Certainly, on the evidence available, the passing of the 1964 Police Act did little to clarify the position of the police and their accountability to the public they serve. Even today, it appears to be an area that continues to be shrouded in some form of mystique. As for corruption in the police structure, this seems to have continued unabated and becomes clearly evident after 1969, when a whole series of scandals at New Scotland Yard came to light and as a consequence, sent shock waves throughout the country.[54] The corrupt practices which were uncovered, included deals by detectives to cover up serious crimes, the setting up of criminals as *agents provocateurs*, perjury and the planting of evidence. What was even more shocking, was the revelation 'of the systematic, institutionalised and widespread network of corruption; the so-called 'firm within a firm'.[55] Confirmation that this was all too true, came when the initial investigation by the Yard itself, met with obstruction, leaks and the disappearance of essential documents.[56] Even a later investigation by one of the most senior and respected Inspectors of Constabulary (crime), Frank Williamson, ended in failure and, frustrated, 'he resigned prematurely, in disgust at his experiences'.[57] It was at this stage that the Home Secretary, Reginald Maudling, appointed Robert Mark as Commissioner. He had served as assistant commissioner since 1967. Immediately on his appointment he introduced reforms, which it was anticipated, would eradicate the cancer at the Yard as a price for its continued independence. It was as a direct result of these reforms, that during Mark's tenure of office at the Yard, some 500 officers left the force, many voluntarily, in anticipation of being investigated.[58]

In addition to police corruption, another area that was causing the public to become concerned, was that of social discontent. Nowhere was this concern better illustrated than in the miners' strike of 1984-85, when it was believed by many observers, particularly those on the left, that the police were far from attaining Scarman's ideals.[59] For example, for its part, the government made little attempt to conceal the fact that its ultimate goal was that of defeating the miners. As one Labour editor wrote, some months into the strike, 'for the government and Mrs Thatcher the strike has become a political battle she dare not lose as she looks over her shoulder to see what happened to Mr Heath ten years earlier'.[60] It was a strike that threw new meaning and light on the degree of centralisation under which the police conducted their operations and raised all the fundamental questions of police practice at times of a national emergency, and the principles of democratic accountability, either at local or national level. The tactics employed, particularly by chief constables in the mining and other areas, certainly illustrated what many had always believed which was that chief constables paid little, if any, real attention to what their local police committees said. From purely a policing point of view, Parliament 'could exercise little control over the determination of police policy'.[61] The Home Office on the other hand, always appeared most reluctant to answer any questions that might place them in a compromising position. With the local police committees seemingly ignored at times like this, there emerges a picture of growing police autonomy, which in turn, sees the police becoming more independent in their own disciplinary and bureaucratic controls which were often mediated behind the closed doors of the Home Office. What is becoming very plain is that since the miners' strike, centralisation has continued to expand, and this constantly raises questions about police accountability. There still appears no satisfactory answer, but one thing is certain and that is that developments after the strike have, as Reiner points out, reduced the role of local police authorities to virtual insignificance.[62] If this is true, and all the evidence so far, indicates that it is, then accountability has become even more illusive and consequently, the position is somewhat alarming, with the spectre of a police state awaiting in the wings.

There is little doubt that as political, industrial and racial tensions rise, the police more or less automatically become the focus of political controversy, centred upon their control and accountability.[63] If we focus our attention on the many racial issues which have surfaced over recent years – the events at Brixton are just one instance where the police came under severe criticism for their handling of events. Although Lord Scarman denied that the police were racist, he found that racial prejudice did manifest itself occasionally in the behaviour of a few officers on the streets.[64] Lord Scarman's views, however, were not compatible with the MacPherson Report of 1999, which branded the police as being institutionally racist[65] a fact, that later, Sir Paul Condon, Commissioner of the Metropolitan Police, was to vehemently deny. Commenting on the failure of the Metropolitan Police to act on the recommendations contained in the reports, and there were over seventy of them, led Michael Mansfield QC, to accuse them of total inertia.[66] In this instance, the criticism was unfair, for since the publication of the report, the Metropolitan Police have organised a department under the supervision of the Deputy Assistant Commissioner, John Grieve, to ensure that racial attacks and accusations of prejudice are properly investigated. Such a move is looked upon as a start, certainly in the sphere of race relations, for it allows a degree of accountability to be exercised by the police.

Finally, although there is still a long way to go, there is much that police historians like myself can accomplish. For example, and here I must concur with the findings of Jane Morgan, so much fundamental historical data has remained unexamined, material that is of vital importance when one attempts to throw some light on the issue that has bedevilled historians so long – the true role and accountability of the police.

---

[1] Clive Emsley, *The English Police*, 2nd. edition (London, 1996), p.4.

[2] Ibid.

[3] Ibid.

[4] Ibid.

[5] Robert D. Storch, 'The policeman as domestic missionary, urban discipline and popular culture in Northern England, 1850-1880', *Journal of Social History*, 9 (1976), pp.481-519. Also consult Jane Morgan, *Conflict and Order, the Police and Labour Disputes in England and Wales 1900-1939*, (Oxford, 1987), p.6.

[6] Clive Emsley, op. cit, pp.3-4.

[7] *The Guardian*, 5 November 1971. Also read William Purcell, *British Police in a Changing Society*, (London, 1974), p. xvii.

[8] Jane Morgan, op. cit., p.3.

[9] Ibid., and also Sir Edward Troup, 'Police administration local and national', *Police Journal*, 1, (1928), p.5.

[10] Robert Reiner, *The Politics of the Police*, 2nd. edition (London, 1992), p.57.

[11] Ibid., also Robert D. Storch, ' "The plague of blue locusts": police reform and popular resistance in Northern England 1840-1857', *International Review of Social History 20* (1975), pp.61-90.

[12] Ibid., in making what many will regard as a sweeping statement, Reiner does acknowledge that some other police forces have equal claims to a commanding place in their country's popular culture, for example, the Federal Bureau of Investigation in America and the Canadian Mounted Police (the Mounties) in Canada. Scotland Yard plays the same role in British popular mythology, but the mundane 'Bobby' is also a cornerstone of national pride, unmatched by the treatment of any other country's routine patrol force.

[13] *The Times*, 24 December 1908 also T.A. Critchley, *A History of Police in England and Wales*, 2nd. edition (London, 1978), p.326, who claimed that 'The police are a body who, though distinctive in their character from all others, as the members of any public service must necessarily be, are yet related to the people whom they serve by ties of intimate personal association which are not to be found in any other country in the world'.

[14] R. Roberts, *The Classic Slum*, (London, 1973), p.100.

[15] Sir Robert Mark, *Policing a Perplexed Society*, (London, 1977), p.23 – abstracted from a lecture he delivered to the convocation of the University of Leicester in March 1976.

[16] Ibid., on the question of being unarmed, read Gerry Northam, *Shooting in the Dark, Riot Police in Britain*, (London, 1988), and Robert W. Gould and Michael J. Waldren, *London's Unarmed Police*, (London, 1986).
[17] Ibid., p.24.
[18] Ibid., p.25.
[19] Lord Scarman, *The Scarman Report – the Brixton Disorders 10-12 April 1981*, (London, 1981), p.102.
[20] Jane Morgan, op. cit., p.1.
[21] Charles Reith, *The Blind Eye of History – A Study of the Present Police Era*, (London, 1952), pp.154-67. Also David Ascoli, *The Queen's Peace – The Origins and Development of the Metropolitan Police 1829-1979*, (London, 1979), pp.86-7, and W.L. Melville Lee, *A History of Police in England*, (London, 1901), Sir John Moylan, *Scotland Yard and the Metropolitan Police*, (London, 1929).
[22] Jane Morgan, op. cit., p.1.
[23] Ibid.
[24] David Taylor, *The New Police in Nineteenth Century England – Crime, Conflict and Control*, (Manchester, 1997), p.77.
[25] Ibid.
[26] R.D. Storch, op. cit., pp.61-90, and the informative study by J. Foster, *Class Struggle and the Industrial Revolution*, (London, 1977). Consult also the contribution by T. Jefferson and R. Grimshaw, *Controlling the Constable*, (London, 1984).
[27] Ibid., p.61.
[28] Ibid.
[29] Ibid., p.62.
[30] R.D. Storch, 'The policeman as domestic missionary: urban discipline and popular culture in Northern England, 1850-1880', *Journal of Social History*, 9 (1976), p.481.
[31] Robert Reiner, op. cit., p.30.
[32] Ibid.
[33] M. Brogden, *The Police – Autonomy and Consent*, (London and New York, 1982), pp.53-71 and *Police Review*, 22 April 1983. For an insight into how the working man viewed the police read S. Reynolds and B. and T. Woolley, *Seems So! A Working Class View of Politics*, (London, 1911), pp.86-7.
[34] Robert Reiner, op. cit., p.31.
[35] R.D. Storch, p.496.
[36] Sir David McNee, *McNee's Law*, (London, 1983), p.228.
[37] Ibid.
[38] Ibid.
[39] Ibid.
[40] Ibid.
[41] Ibid., p.230.

[42] Ibid.

[43] Ibid.

[44] Michael Banton, *The Policeman in the Community*, (London, 1964), p. ix.

[45] Leon Radziniwicz and Joan King, *The Growth of Crime – the International Experience*, (Pelican Books, 1979), p.15, and Anthony Martiensson, *Crime and the Public*, (Penguin, 1951).

[46] Robert Reiner, op. cit., p.58.

[47] James Morton, *Bent Coppers*, (London, 1993), pp.90-127, also Clive Emsley, op. cit., pp.171-2. In the case of the Chief Constable of Worcester, he was charged with paying for his daughter's wedding out of police funds. Brighton's Chief Constable, successfully appealed in 1963 to the House of Lords on the grounds that the Watch Committee in dismissing him had not informed him of the charges he was to face. As a result of the decision by the House of Lords, the Chief Constable was able to retrieve his pension of £20 per week.

[48] T.A. Critchley, *A History of Police in England and Wales*, 2nd. edition (London, 1978), p.274.

[49] Ibid.

[50] Ibid.

[51] Ben Whitaker, *The Police*, (Penguin, 1964), pp.134-53.

[52] Michael Banton, op. cit., p.262.

[53] L. Lea and J. Young, *What is to be done about Law and Order – Crisis in the Eighties*. (Penguin Books, 1984), p.257.

[54] Sir Robert Mark, *In the Office of Constable*, (London, 1975), pp.94-109.

[55] Robert Reiner, op. cit., p.78-9.

[56] Ibid.

[57] Ibid.

[58] Ibid.

[59] Jane Morgan, op. cit. p.2.

[60] *The Times*, 29 March 1985.

[61] Jane Morgan, op. cit., p.2.

[62] Robert Reiner, op. cit. p.239.

[63] Sir Robert Mark, op. cit. p.284.

[64] Lord Scarman, op. cit. p.198.

[65] *Sunday Express*, 20 February 2000. See also *Police Review*, 18 February 2000.

[66] Ibid., Michael Mansfield, QC, represents the family of Stephen Lawrence, a young black teenager murdered in a racist attack, to which at first, the Metropolitan Police paid little investigative attention.

## Chapter I

# The Social and Economic Conditions in North Wales, 1800-40

If one is to appreciate and understand how, and why, the police forces in north Wales came into being then an examination, albeit brief, must be made of the social and economic conditions prevailing in the first half of the nineteenth century. Certainly, at this time, Wales was predominantly an agricultural country and was sparsely populated. As early as 1770 it was estimated that the population of Wales as a whole was about 500,000, a figure that had increased to 1,163,000 by 1851.[1] An indication of the increase in the population of the counties of north Wales between 1801-51 is illustrated below.[2]

Table 1.1.
Population Increase 1801-51

|  | 1801 | 1811 | 1821 | 1831 | 1841 | 1851 |
|---|---|---|---|---|---|---|
| Anglesey | 33,806 | 37,045 | 45,063 | 48,325 | 50,891 | 57,327 |
| Caernarfonshire | 41,521 | 49,655 | 58,099 | 66,818 | 81,093 | 87,870 |
| Denbighshire | 60,299 | 64,249 | 76,428 | 82,665 | 88,478 | 92,583 |
| Flintshire | 39,469 | 45,937 | 53,893 | 60,244 | 66,919 | 68,156 |
| Merioneth | 29,506 | 30,850 | 34,382 | 25,315 | 39,332 | 38,843 |

During the course of the nineteenth century, however, the pattern and movement of the population in Wales was to change significantly. From the figure of 587,000 it was to rise to over 2,019,000 by 1901.[3] In effect, the balance between the north and the south, and the urban and rural areas was completely transformed. The county of Glamorgan alone was to see its population treble between 1801-51 and within a further fifty years it was to increase fivefold to nearly one and a quarter million.[4] This figure was actually double the population for the whole of Wales in 1811. Significantly, the contrast between urban and rural counties becomes illuminating. In Anglesey during the first half of the nineteenth century the population rose from 33,000 to 57,000 yet by 1911 it registered but 50,000. Undoubtedly the main cause of these changes was the growth of industrialisation. As Wales became industrialised it also became urbanized as more of the population left their rural areas to reside in the towns. The effect of such changes was immense. The rapid increase in the population alone was to alter the very fabric of the nation. The increased investment in capital and the creation of an enlarged workforce automatically meant larger towns. This was, periodically, to place tremendous strain on local resources and government and on the forces of law and order, as well as on other institutions and a completely different pattern of social and political life becomes apparent. Wales entered the nineteenth century with certain specific disadvantages. Many of the counties, particularly in north Wales, were still isolated because of their geographical position and the appalling condition of the roads. The absence of important financial centres also contributed to the late transition to industrialisation, therefore retarding economic growth. However, such a situation had to change – the growth of industries in England was ultimately to have its effect on industry in Wales. The new industrial population in England called for additional food supplies and this placed a heavy demand on Wales which was still largely an agricultural nation. Although somewhat primitive in its methods of farming, it was also hindered by bad roads upon which to transport produce to an ever-growing market. It therefore became essential that if the needs of industry and agriculture were to be fully met, vital improvements were needed in communication and transport which, when they came, inevitably led to further changes.

As one writer explained, the industrialisation of Wales and a revolution in transport went hand in hand.[5] Certainly in the late eighteenth century and even at the beginning of the nineteenth, the condition of the roads was atrocious. When Arthur Young visited France in 1787 he found circulation stagnant on excellent roads.[6] If he had visited north Wales at the same time he would have seen a fast increasing traffic on the untracked heaths and narrow lanes.[7] Change, when it came, was as a direct result of the extension into Wales of turnpike trusts. The system which had many imperfections and one that in later years was to provoke so much anger and distress, at least provided Wales with a long awaited opportunity to expand industrially. It must always be borne in mind, however, that at no time did the trusts control more than one fifth of the roads in Wales.[8] Therefore, even with the introduction of trusts, many poor roads and steep gradients still existed thus impeding the progress of communities, particularly in the upland areas, from enjoying the prosperity being experienced elsewhere. Nevertheless, with the gradual improvement in the condition of the roads, the transportation of agricultural produce and manufactured goods continued to increase and as a consequence became more readily available in the expanding industrial townships, whose inhabitants were becoming much more demanding and discerning in their expectations and choice of merchandise. Many of the earliest turnpike acts to be introduced into the counties of north Wales were instituted between 1757-59. They were established originally to deal with what was then the principle route to Ireland – through Flintshire and along the coasts of Denbighshire and Caernarfonshire towards Holyhead. Later, in 1765, a further act brought the last stretch of the Holyhead Road under trust control.[9] Similar acts at this time also began the process of expanding reasonably maintained roads into the mining areas that were being opened to traffic in Flintshire and Denbighshire. As the eighteenth century drew to a close, numerous additional acts were passed which provided for the appointment of Commissioners or Trustees who were empowered to maintain and repair existing roads – such a development gave birth to a new occupation – the road engineer.[10] During the first thirty years of the nineteenth century we see the introduction of turnpikes penetrating deeper into the very heart of Snowdonia. Trusts were being established from Corwen to Llanrwst and down the Conwy valley to Conwy itself. Later still, the Caernarfonshire turnpike was extended through Caernarfon and Pwllheli and consequently opened up the remoter area of Llŷn. Eventually, trusts were extended into Merioneth – so the two southernmost and most mountainous counties in north Wales, Caernarfonshire and Merioneth were opened up to travellers. The Snowdonia range and Cadair Idris which dominated Merioneth, stood like gigantic sentinels guarding what many visitors viewed as the most breathtaking scenery in Wales.[11]

Despite this apparent progress in communications, one serious problem in north Wales remained, and it was one of great concern to the Post Office. Over several decades they had experienced constant difficulties in the delivery of mail to Ireland. In desperation, and eager to find a solution, officials of the Post Office appealed to Parliament asking for the setting up of a parliamentary committee to examine the whole question of the conditions of the London-Holyhead Road. That such a committee was appointed in 1810 and that Parliament intervened in the matter, was a clear indication of the importance they attached to commercial expansion at this time. A year later in 1811 a thorough survey was made of the whole of this important route by Thomas Telford, who was recognised as a brilliant engineer. Later, when the Government received his report and recommendations it acted quickly and appointed ten Parliamentary Commissioners who were to be ably advised and assisted by Telford in upgrading the Holyhead Road. The Commissioners were given exceptional powers and had the authority to deal firmly and swiftly with trusts on the route who were either obstructive or reluctant to accept any form of change. As a result of their investigation an act was passed in 1819 which authorized the building of a bridge over the Menai Strait. Two years later it was agreed that a similar construction should be built to span the River Conwy. As a further measure of control a new Shrewsbury-Holyhead Turnpike was established by an Act of Parliament; its terms of reference were, that a completely new road should be built across Anglesey and this resulted in the old Anglesey trust being dissolved in 1823.

However, if Telford was to succeed in his assignment two very important engineering feats had to be accomplished – the bridging of the Menai Strait near Bangor and the River Conwy at Conwy. As early as 1783-85 a number of plans had been submitted, one suggesting an embankment and a wooden drawbridge as a solution.[12] Another in 1801 by John Rennie who was of the opinion that a cast iron bridge with three arches would suffice.[13] A plan, incidentally not too dissimilar to Telford's later design. This plan although widely welcomed in Bangor and Beaumaris drew strong opposition from the commercial interests in Caernarfon who feared a loss in trade and in this they were aided by the influential figure of Assheton Smith, who, throughout, was fiercely critical of Telford's ideas. That Telford succeeded in what many considered was impossible, was seen in 1826 when both suspension bridges were opened amidst great excitement and acclaim. By 1830, the reconstruction of the Holyhead Road was more or less complete and its contribution to the prosperity of north Wales was considerable. Not only did it 'promote inland trade in five of the six North

Wales counties, but it influenced other turnpike trusts by giving them a model of scientific road making and management'.[14] Ten years later, in 1840, the Royal Commission on the State of the Roads was able to report favourably on almost all the turnpike trusts in north Wales. The trusts, when closely examined, covered a considerable distance of over 1,200 miles – of this the Holyhead Road accounted for nearly 107, Caernarfonshire for 160, Denbighshire and Flintshire for nearly 400. Anglesey accounted for only four miles, apart from the Holyhead Trust.[15]

Road improvement was ultimately to lead to quicker and more reliable stagecoach services being introduced. As early as 1784, on the advice of John Palmer of Bath, the Royal Mail was carried for the first time by stagecoach from Bristol to London.[16] His belief in the use of stagecoaches was that they would be quicker and, being armed, safer than the postal deliveries previously undertaken by post-boys on horseback.[17] In such a belief he was enthusiastically supported by Thomas Hosker of the Post Office who used his authority to acquire a more efficient and acceptable postal service.[18] Each year saw more coaching companies being established and it was estimated at one period that over 3,000 stagecoaches were running on the various routes in England and Wales. Yet, despite what appeared such an excellent service many travellers found Wales not so well furnished with stagecoaches as other parts of the kingdom.[19] Stagecoach companies began to compete often aggressively, with one another as to who could travel the fastest, safest, and most cheaply.

Certainly, the early years of the nineteenth century saw the beginning of the coaching age in Wales. One of the earliest pioneers of stagecoaching was the landlord of the White Lion Hotel in Chester who as early as 1776 put a 'flying post chaise' on the road to carry passengers daily, Sunday excepted, to Holyhead for a fee of two guineas each.[20] Three years later, Robert Lawrence, the innkeeper of the Raven and Bell at Shrewsbury began a rival service – his coaches running daily to Holyhead via Wrexham and Mold.[21] It was he who eventually displayed great initiative when collaborating with other metropolitan inns and was able to provide passengers with a coaching service all the way from London. Later, a coaching service was again established from Chester, to tackle the new but difficult Penmaenmawr road, which ran through Caernarfonshire to Holyhead – a route that contained within it many turnpike trusts, therefore making the journey somewhat expensive for the stagecoach proprietors wishing to extend their services into Caernarfonshire and Anglesey. It was a time when counties to the north were also to benefit from a rapidly expanding coaching service. By 1812 Denbighshire and Flintshire had services which operated three days a week from Chester to Mold, Ruthin and Denbigh. Such pioneering work made it clear to observers that the long isolation of counties like Caernarfonshire and Anglesey was now coming to an end. That complete isolation was to be something of the past was clearly demonstrated in 1816 when the first stagecoach service into Merioneth undoubtedly helped to demolish the barrier which had isolated the county from the rest of the country for so long.[22] Initially operating between Barmouth and Corwen the service enabled travellers to connect with coaches plying the Holyhead route. Later, an additional service, enabled travellers to connect with coaches running between Dolgellau and Mallwyd, which was timed to link up with coaches running between Shrewsbury and Aberystwyth. In Caernarfonshire, a coaching service to accommodate the 'Gentlemen and Clergy of Lleyn and Eifionydd began between Bangor, Caernarfon and Pwllheli in 1822'.[23] Five years later a twice weekly coach service operated out of Welshpool and Newtown to Machynlleth, Aberdyfi and Tywyn along a newly made coastal road. Earlier in 1823, a daily Royal Mail service was introduced between Shrewsbury, Welshpool and Newtown which by 1840 had been extended to include towns like Machynlleth and Aberystwyth into receiving regular postal deliveries.

It was the coming of the railway in the 1830s that saw what many viewed as the golden age of coaching start to decline. Clearly too, the advent of the railway was also responsible for the gradual demise of the turnpike trusts. As one writer aptly explained 'it was the smoke rising above the Stockton and Darlington line in 1825 that first signalled the doom of the trusts'.[24] However, there is ample evidence that several turnpikes remained in existence well into the second half of the nineteenth century. Certainly, as late as 1862 a number of them were auctioned to the highest bidder at the Angel Inn, Dolgellau.[25] In Caernarfonshire, turnpike gates did not entirely disappear until 1890 whilst in Anglesey they were to remain for a further five years – the last survivors of all.[26] In the early years of the coming of the railways, coaching companies had experienced the futility of attempting to compete by reducing fares, but it was clear from the outset that rail travel was quicker, and much more comfortable, especially during inclement weather. Therefore it was inevitable, that faced with such obvious difficulties, coaching proprietors and those in charge of turnpike trusts were eventually to accept defeat. Furthermore, if additional confirmation was needed that the days of coaching were numbered, it came in 1842 when the 'wonder coach' which had done so much to increase the rate of travel on the Holyhead Road gave up the struggle after a gallant race with a train.[27] For many, a journey by stagecoach had never been one viewed with enthusiasm. Indeed, for some travellers it had been a dreadful experience, with one passenger 'describing the journey as fearing for his life – finishing the journey bruised, tired and shaken to pieces'.[28] Nevertheless, despite its shortcomings, the stagecoach had over the years provided a valuable service. It had enabled people to travel more extensively, providing them with access to communities that hitherto had been completely insular. Commerce, too, had been substantially stimulated by the stagecoach, for many of the passengers were often commercial travellers suitably excited at the prospect of introducing their latest wares to markets further afield. The era of the stagecoach had also provided essential employment – for coach drivers, innkeepers, blacksmiths, ostlers, grooms and wheelwrights.[29] Certainly, between 1810-30 the stagecoach had enjoyed a period of unrivalled prosperity, but with the coming of the steam locomotive with all its potential, there came into being a whole new dimension and meaning to travel and industrial expansion.

It is important when examining the industrialisation of north Wales in the nineteenth century not to overlook the significance of canals as well as shipping and shipbuilding. It was during the period between 1780-1800 that the greater part of the canal system of Great Britain came into existence.[30] In mid and north Wales the building of canals was on a more limited scale. The steep gradients and the general topography of the area made canal building a daunting prospect. Nevertheless, north Wales possessed two important canals, the Ellesmere and the Montgomeryshire, which were built in stages between 1779-1819. The Ellesmere was used extensively over the years for the transportation of freight from the ironworks at Brymbo and Bersham as well as coal from the nearby collieries at Ffrwd and Talwern. The Montgomeryshire canal system, unlike that of Ellesmere, did not pass through areas of heavy industrialisation. Beginning in the southern part of Denbighshire it proceeded westwards crossing the River Vyrnwy via Telford's famous aqueduct at Chirk *en route* to the Severn valley where it connected with the woollen towns of Welshpool and Newtown.

Although much coal was carried along this route the main traffic was that of grain and dairy produce, commodities that were considered essential for the rapidly expanding industrial cities to the north such as Liverpool and Manchester. However, with the development of a rail network in the 1840s the canal system of trading began to falter. In comparison with the railway, canals were slow and expensive. Yet, it should be recognised that canals like the Ellesmere and Montgomeryshire had played a crucial role in the economic development of north Wales. They had been the arteries along which had flowed the coal, iron and steel, so much the life-blood of industrialisation.[31]

As for shipbuilding – between 1800-50 many ports along the north Wales coast were to experience periods of prosperity. In Merioneth, for example, the port of Barmouth was involved in the shipment of Welsh Webs, long lengths of coarse woollen cloth, coastwise to London, Liverpool and Chester.[32] It is also recorded that Welsh Webs were shipped to places as far afield as Spain, Portugal and South America.[33] Slate too, from the quarries of Caernarfonshire and Merioneth was exported in large quantities. In 1825, over 12,000 tons were shipped abroad from Porthmadog, a figure that increased to 100,000 tons by 1867.[34] Slate was also sent from Bangor and Porthmadog to North and South America and in the 1850s to Australia when the cities of Melbourne and Sydney expanded during the 'Age of Gold'.[35]

Shipbuilding also played a vital role in the economic development of the maritime trade in north Wales. Between 1769-1840 sixty-one ships, mainly sloops, were built on the River Dyfi.[36] At nearby Pwllheli over 300 vessels left the blocks between 1786-1836.[37] In Anglesey, many of the vessels built were mainly for fishing and the coastal trade and there is little doubt that shipbuilding in the county was stimulated by the development of the Amlwch copper mines and the Caernarfonshire slate quarries. Compared with ports like Caernarfon, Port Dinorwic, Nefyn, Pwllheli and Porthmadog, however, shipbuilding in Anglesey was on a smaller scale.[38] Certainly, during the first half of the nineteenth century, shipbuilding had been a major provider of employment for thousands of workers. Within the many maritime communities along the coast at this time there emerged a strong reservoir of skills and expertise – with occupations such as ships' carpenters, shipwrights, nailers, rope-makers, sail-makers and, of course, the mariners themselves.[39] The shipbuilding industry was to continue well into the last quarter of the century. At places like

*Capt. David White Griffiths, Chief Constable, Anglesey Constabulary 1857-76.*

*William Hughes (Constable of Pwllheli Borough Police 1869-79 – First Borough Police in the United Kingdom)*

*Capt. George W. Bulkeley Hughes, Chief Constable, Anglesey Constabulary 1877*

*Lanarkshire-born Chief Constable Major T. J. Leadbetter (Denbighshire Constabulary), Wrexham, 1878-1912*

*Wrexham District (Denbighshire Constabulary) Summary Pay Sheet for May 1874, showing Wrexham policing costs for one month.*

CHIEF CONSTABLE'S OFFICE,

DOLGELLEY,

*20th July, 1901.*

# Merionethshire Police Pay.

The Secretary of State for the Home Department having by letter dated 19th July, 1901, approved of the following Scale of Pay to the Members of the Merioneth County Police Force as detailed in the Schedule below, namely:—

|  | On appointment. | After 1 Year's Service. | After 2 Year's Service. | After 4 Year's Service. | After 6 Year's Service. | After 7 Year's Service. | After 8 Year's Service. | Maximum Rate of Pay per Annum. |
|---|---|---|---|---|---|---|---|---|
|  | £ s. d. | £ s. d. | £ s. d. | £ s. d. | £ s. d. | £ s. d. | £ s. d. | £ s. d. |
| Constables per week... | 1 4 0 | 1 5 0 | 1 6 0 | 1 7 6 | 1 8 0 | 1 9 0 | 1 10 0 | 78 4 3 |
| Sergeants per week ... | 1 11 6 |  | 1 12 8 | 1 13 10 | 1 15 0 |  |  | 91 5 0 |
| Inspectors per annum.. | 100 0 0 |  | 105 0 0 | 110 0 0 | 115 0 0 |  | 120 0 0 | 120 0 0 |
| Superintendents do... | 135 0 0 |  | 145 0 0 | 155 0 0 |  |  | 165 0 0 | 165 0 0 |

## Revised Scale of Pay for Constables only.

------------

The Merionethshire Standing Joint Police Committee have on the 31st December, 1907, adopted a revised Scale of Pay for Constables appointed on the strength of the Force after the 25th December, 1907, and the Home Secretary having by letter dated 24th January, 1908, approved of the Scale as detailed in the Schedule below.

|  | On Appointment. | After 1 Year's Service. | After 3 Year's Service. | After 6 Year's Service. | After 7 Year's Service. | After 8 Year's Service. | After 10 Year's Service. | Maximum Rate of Pay per Annum. |
|---|---|---|---|---|---|---|---|---|
|  | £ s. d. | £ s. d. | £ s. d. | £ s. d. | £ s. d. | £ s. d. | £ s. d. | £ s. d. |
| Constables per week .. | 1 4 0 | 1 5 0 | 1 6 0 | 1 7 6 | 1 8 0 | 1 9 0 | 1 10 0 | 78 4 3 |

That the Members of the Force who do not occupy County Lock-up Houses be paid 1/2 per week in addition to the sums mentioned in the above Scales and that Sergeants not provided with Houses in like manner be allowed 2/4 per Week in addition to the sums mentioned in the above Scale, if the Chief Constable shall so think fit.

That the Chief Constable be and he is hereby empowered to place a Constable or Sergeant upon a higher rate of Pay in anticipation of his length of Service for Meritorious Conduct.

**THOMAS JONES,**
CHIEF CONSTABLE.

Dolgelley : Printed by Edward Williams, Victoria Printing Works.

*Merioneth Police Pay Scale, 20 July, 1901.*

*Mold Division of the Flintshire Constabulary, 1890s.*

*Flintshire Constabulary officers attending Investiture at Caernarfon Castle, 1911.*

*Chief Constable Lewis Protheroe and officers of Anglesey Constabulary being recipients of the Coronation Medal (King George V), 1912.*

*PC Williams (Abergynolwyn) dressed to catch bakers selling underweight bread.*

*Chief Constable Thomas Jones (Merioneth Constabulary)*

*Group of policemen in Caernarfon Castle with Superintendent/Deputy Chief Constable Samuel Thomas Harris (1855-1936) c. 1890*

*A group of Caernarfonshire police in the castle c. 1890*

PC 11 Oliver Cromwell Davies (Merioneth Constabulary) at Prisoner of War Camp at Fron-goch, Bala, 1914-18. (Courtesy of Gwynedd Archives Service)

PC 11 Oliver Cromwell Davies (Merioneth Constabulary) at Prisoner of War Camp at Fron-goch, 1914-18.

PC 14 Charles Ashton (Merioneth Constabulary) – known as 'The Literary Policeman'.

Prisoners flanked by Merioneth Constabulary escort on steps of Blaenau Ffestiniog Police Station, 1910.

*Officers stand outside Blaenau Ffestiniog Police Station in 1910.*

*Sgt. David Williams (Denbighshire Constabulary) with sons (Back left: PC Thomas Williams – Denbighshire Constabulary; Back right: Arthur Howell Williams – Merioneth Constabulary, and Back centre: PC Alun Williams – Shropshire Constabulary; ancestors of the late PC Kenneth Williams (North Wales Police/Penrhos Nature Reserve) – a family who served the Police Service for almost 150 years.*

*Merioneth Constabulary, Dolgellau, 1912*
*(Courtesy of Gwynedd Archives Service)*

*PC Arthur Howell Williams (Merioneth Constabulary) with dog 'Earl'
at Abergynolwyn, circa 1915.*

*Officers of Merioneth Constabulary escort at funeral of one Dr Roberts of Isallt, Blaenau Ffestiniog, circa 1920s. (Courtesy of Gwynedd Archives Service)*

*PC 69 Nevil J. V. Davies (left) and PC 127 William Henry Jones (Denbighshire Constabulary), Wrexham, 1936.*

*Winston Churchill with Det. Ch. Insp. Humphrey Jones outside St George's Hotel in pre-war Llandudno, circa 1938.*

*Caernarfonshire Police, inspected within the castle walls, 1929*

*A group of Caernarfonshire police in front of the old gaol*

*Group of Flintshire Constabulary Motorcyclists Government Inspection, Rhyl, 1930s.*

*PC 7 John Marshall Jones (Flintshire Constabulary) on motorcycle patrol circa 1930s.*

*THETIS submarine immediately following beaching at Moelfre Bay on 3 September, 1939 (day World War II was declared). Vessel sank Liverpool Bay, 1 June, 1939, with loss of 101 lives.*

*PC 41 Hugh Richard Pritchard (centre) (Anglesey Constabulary – later PC 196 North Wales Police) with two of the four survivors of the crew of submarine THETIS. Survivors: Leading Stoker Walter Arnold (right) and passenger Frank Shaw (left). Capt. H. P. K. Oram, RN and Lt. F. G. Woods were the other survivors.*

*PC 7 John Marshall Jones (Flintshire Constabulary) with patrol car circa 1930s.*

*Members of the Denbighshire Constabulary Civil Defence team circa 1937. Sgt. Tom Roberts is seated centre front.*

*Anglesey Constabulary Reunion Dinner held on 29 October, 1949.*

*WPC Elizabeth (Betty) Trivett (uniform) at Wrexham with friend circa 1940.*

*Ch. Supt. Nevil John Volander Davies.*

*Wrexham Borough (Denbighshire Constabulary)
Special Constables 1942.*

*Home Secretary and Minister for Welsh Affairs,
Rt. Hon. Sir David Maxwell Fyfe, accompanied by the
Chief Constable of Gwynedd (three counties), Lt. Col. William Jones
Williams and Supt. Griff Roberts, DCC, on the official opening of the
Police Headquarters at Maesincla, Caernarfon, in 1953.
Right: Sgt. Walter Williams and PC G. V. Roberts.*

Aberdyfi and in particular Derwenlas, the boom years in shipbuilding were between 1840-80, although with the coming of the railway between Machynlleth and Aberystwyth in 1863-64 shipbuilding at Derwenlas began to decline. At Pwllheli, shipbuilding ceased in 1878 and at Nefyn and Aberdyfi in 1880.[40]

It was the opening of the Stockton to Darlington line in 1825 and that of the Liverpool to Manchester in 1830 that ushered in the railway age, although in north Wales the main thrust of railway development did not occur until after 1850 – not that the coming of the railway was universally welcomed. In the more rural areas of north Wales the advent of a railway often aroused anger, and at times stiff opposition, and was viewed as an unwanted intrusion. Many landowners also expressed their concern and were vociferous in opposition, believing that the possibility of steel rails being placed across their estates was an encroachment that might well infringe their rights. In fact, such was their influence, that in 1818 when a bill to promote railways was presented to Parliament it was rejected. Nevertheless, despite opposition, railway development particularly between 1843-48 was to increase rapidly.

It was the passing in 1844 of a Railway Act, instigated by Gladstone, that eventually gave impetus to rail expansion in north Wales. After much pressure from Irish members of Parliament who demanded a speedier postal link with Ireland, work began on the Chester to Holyhead line in November 1845.[41] The line was completed in four years, and Irish mails were taken for the first time all the way to Holyhead on 18 June 1849.[42] Hailed as a great feat of engineering, it incorporated the work of Robert Stephenson's tubular bridges which crossed the River Conwy and Menai Strait respectively. Construction of the line created employment for thousands of navvies, many of them Irish, who were driven to seek work in Wales and elsewhere, as a direct consequence of the appalling conditions which existed in Ireland in the 1840s. Arriving in Wales though did not guarantee them a better life, or even a more peaceful one. For example, in a dispute with 300 Welshmen in May 1846 a number of Irish navvies were driven from working on the line at Penmaenmawr.[43] Yet, despite disputes such as this, which were a frequent occurrence, rail expansion into other areas of north Wales gained momentum. In 1852 the line from Bangor was extended to Caernarfon, and it was proposed at the time that a railtrack to Ffestiniog should also be laid; this however was not achieved until 1874.[44] Further expansion occurred in

1867 when a line from Caernarfon was linked to Pwllheli and eventually Barmouth. The expansion of railtrack in the north however was not matched by development in mid-Wales, which meant that the counties of Montgomeryshire and Merioneth were to remain for some little time outside the main tracks. It was not until the early 1860s, when a line from Shrewsbury was linked to the Cambrian Coast, that the population residing in the southern half of Merioneth received the beneficial effects of rail expansion. Undoubtedly, as the years progressed the expansion of the railways was clearly acknowledged as being central to industrial development, and as such, was eventually to lead to a complete transformation of the economic and social life of Wales.

The first half of the nineteenth century was a period that was dominated by social agitation. Yet, despite this, there seemed no apparent solution to an agonising problem. Many felt that the key to the whole problem lay in political reform, particularly in the House of Commons. It was true that by 1815, and after the cessation of the war with France, a feeling grew, that Parliament was unbalanced in its composition and generally unrepresentative of the population. In short, the electoral system, which had remained unchanged for centuries was now no longer acceptable to large sections of the population who clamoured for a more democratic approach by government. During this period, the general administration of the counties in north Wales was firmly in the grip of the gentry. Sitting as magistrates in quarter sessions they assumed responsibility for a variety of day-to-day affairs. As justices of the peace they wore the mantle, when called upon, of 'a police chief, a tax assessor, magistrate, road-surveyor, a recruiting officer, a censor, inquisitor, and a licensor'.[45] Understandably, the office of justice of the peace was not one that was popular. It was sought by many, simply as a means of acquiring prestige and local influence rather than from any genuine desire on their part to serve the community. Interestingly, many of the most active magistrates were clergymen. Frequently, many of the decisions reached by magistrates were debatable and this created much distress among those who believed that in their case there had been a serious miscarriage of justice. Yet, for those unjustly treated there was little opportunity to gain any form of redress for what was so often a genuine grievance. Any appeal to Parliament was looked upon as a fruitless exercise, for this was merely appealing to those who regarded as their priority the protection of their own class – the landed proprietors. As one historian explained 'politics, whether at national or local level, was to remain well into the 1850s, the preserve of the gentry and landed proprietors'.[46] Therefore, the privileged positions of families like the Penrhyns of Caernarfonshire and the Bulkeleys of Anglesey placed them in a small but elite group. Life generally for the ordinary people in the middle of the nineteenth century was often hard and unrewarding and their plight was highlighted to some degree in the Poor Law Amendment Act of 1834. Introduced primarily as a piece of legislation that hopefully would solve some of the social problems then in existence, it was seen by many as somewhat severe in its recommendations, and even more so in its findings. For example, the Poor Law Commissioners were convinced that all poverty was caused by laziness and this view not only caused dismay but widespread anger. Such a view did not take into account the problems created by industrialisation, the growth in population, or of the decline in the domestic industries. In many ways, the Act introduced as a measure to treat poverty, left much to be desired. Yet, despite its many shortcomings the Act acknowledged that for many, wages had scarcely risen for a quarter of a century and the average family survived on the minimum of food – generally a diet of potatoes, oatmeal, milk, and little else.[47]

The agrarian decline in Wales had been gathering pace for a number of years and for those engaged in the industry the outlook was extremely bleak. Adding to what was already a distressing picture, the passing of the Corn Laws in 1815 did little, if anything, to alleviate the position. Perhaps a true measure of the real state of the industry came in a speech from the throne in 1816 when it was declared that 'the manufacture, commerce and reserve of the United Kingdom were in a flourishing condition' – the omission of agriculture was significant.[48] Much of the distress in agriculture at this time could be rightly blamed on a series of bad harvests which followed the ending of the Napoleonic wars in 1815, which in turn sent the price of food rising to a point which few people could reach. Even farmers themselves, in many instances, were compelled to sell livestock at a low price in order to pay their rents and feed and clothe their families.[49] As if to inflame the situation even further, the labour market became flooded with ex-soldiers returning from the wars with France, with one estimate putting the figure as high as a quarter of a million.[50] Many drifted in north Wales adding to a labour force clearly demoralised and smarting under the Speenhamland system of poor relief and the viciousness of the game laws which were a cause of perpetual friction.[51] This observation, no matter how repugnant, was all too familiar a picture in the eighteenth and nineteenth centuries. Therefore, in examining the position of agriculture, one has to conclude that bad harvests, a tithe system which was burdensome, particularly after the Act of 1836, the enclosure of commons, the raising of rents without consultation or justification, along with a continual rise in unemployment, was setting the scene for widespread discontent and confrontation. Inevitably, this situation must have alarmed the authorities, as well as sending an unwelcome coldness coursing through the veins of the landowners.[52]

Workers in the woollen industry, like those in agriculture were also experiencing difficulties. Their industry was in decline and the reasons for the deterioration had been evident for some years and this was the transition from domestic hand loom weaving to power loom weaving in the factories outside Wales. Such changes in the methods used in the manufacturing of woollen goods was to lead to thousands of hand-loom weavers in counties like Merioneth, Montgomeryshire and Denbighshire to become displaced, thus joining the already saturated ranks of the unemployed. Over the centuries there had scarcely been a parish in mid and north Wales without its spinners, carders, weavers and fullers.[53] It was therefore, not surprising that families, particularly in the winter months, would spend long evenings carding, spinning, dyeing and weaving.[54] If confirmation was needed that the manufacture of woollens had been a great industry it came in 1797, when a writer maintained 'that it was seldom among the lower classes that a Welshman wears a coat that is not made in the principality. Yet, within fifty years this ceased to be true, for Yorkshire woollens sold in fairs and shops were ousting the native homespun'.[55] Certainly, the absence of machinery and the lack of capital investment were factors largely responsible for the eventual decline of the industry in north Wales. Occasionally, some machinery would be purchased in an attempt to revitalise an ailing industry, but all too often it was bought cheaply and was already outmoded and discarded by an English mill.[56] That the writing was on the wall for the woollen industry was seen in 1831 when it was noted that many weavers were drifting away to seek other employment. This movement of workers, combined with an apparent reluctance to accept change, helped considerably in determining the price counties in north Wales would pay for their lack of initiative. When power looms were eventually introduced into Montgomeryshire in the middle of the nineteenth century, it was too little and too late. Those engaged in the woollen industry had simply failed to recognise the tremendous changes that were taking place, and had tended for far too long to cling to the old traditional ways and work practises. This tendency to ignore change and progress inevitably meant that when the industry in Wales finally decided to become competitive it was already much too late. Woollen centres like Bala and Dolgellau found that they could not compete on equal terms with their larger counterparts in Yorkshire, such as Halifax and Dewsbury, who already had the advantage of modern machinery and the necessary expertise. It was this type of competition which Wales could not match that finally led to the demise of the Welsh woollen industry. Although, it has to be recorded, that on a very limited scale, the production of woollen goods continued to be produced in Anglesey as late as 1901,[57] and in Caernarfonshire too, a few mills were still operating up until the First World War.[58] The decline both in the woollen industry and that of agriculture was to lead to many workers abandoning their homes in the faint hope that they might find employment elsewhere. Such action on their part was to generate considerable alarm amongst the authorities in north Wales. Over the years it had been widely recognised that life for the farmer and his labourers had been extremely difficult. Working as many of them did, often from dawn to dusk, on land they could never own, inevitably led to tension and bitterness. Little wonder, living under such conditions with the ever present reminder of their subjection to the landowners, that an atmosphere of complete and utter despair would be created. Therefore, it was in no way surprising that sooner or later some form of protest would erupt against a system that was clearly and completely indifferent to their needs.

An early indication that the patience of the ordinary people was beginning to wear thin came when a series of food riots occurred firstly at Ffestiniog, and later at Amlwch, in 1815 and 1817 respectively.[59] In the 1820s one sees incendiarism being used more frequently as a means of protest. Indeed in 1827 a woman was executed for setting alight a haystack in Montgomeryshire.[60] In Merioneth, too, property was often subjected to attacks of arson.[61] There was trouble amongst the miners at Rhosllannerchrugog in December 1830, which led to a company of the Denbighshire Yeomanry being sent to quell the disturbance and at one point they were ordered to fire to disperse an unruly crowd. There is little doubt that by the 1830s, the signs of general unrest were growing daily more ominous, and this was particularly true in the areas around the coalfields of Denbighshire and Flintshire.[62]

It was during the mid 1830s and as a direct result of the failure of the Reform Bill of 1832, to grant the vote to all male adults, that Chartism emerged as a powerful force. Chartism was undoubtedly a great class movement, caused by the differences, accentuated by the Reform Bill, between the wealthy middle class and the proletariat. The 'People's Charter' drawn up in 1838 incorporated six main points – the main objectives being, that every adult man must be given the right to vote, and that vote was to be by ballot, thus removing the dangers of bribery and intimidation. In short, the aim of the Charter was to make Parliament representative of the people and not of class. Chartism appealed to many in Wales, especially in the flannel districts bordering Merioneth. Support was also strong in places like Wrexham and Ruabon, and in 1838 a Chartist meeting at Newtown attracted between 3,000 and 5,000 people. What the authorities feared was that amongst the Chartists were many ex-soldiers, who had been taught to fight, and drill and use arms.[63]

Throughout north Wales hundreds of people travelled around seeking any kind of assistance that was available and pauperism was widespread. In the five northern counties in 1846 almost 10 per cent of the population was in receipt of poor relief. This figure was 1.4 per cent more than the figure for south Wales and 1.2 per cent more than in England and Wales as a whole.[64] Many of those who had drifted out of Wales in an unsuccessful search for work often returned even more bitter and disillusioned, for by the 1830s and 1840s pauperism was being recognised as a national problem. Surprisingly, however, despite the number of paupers in north Wales the amount spent on relief by the authorities was less in 1846 than it had been in 1831. For example, the expenditure per head of population had gone down by at least half in every county except Caernarfonshire and Anglesey. Certainly, the overall picture was extremely depressing for the destitute.[65]

With the onset of unemployment and pauperism the incidence of drunkenness and crime began to rise, causing concern throughout north Wales. The appearance in Dolgellau of young people drunk in the street was one that could be mirrored in many other towns at this time.[66] However, apart from the problems already mentioned, the authorities were experiencing difficulties of another kind but equally serious. The increase in the population, particularly in the towns, posed very serious problems in the sphere of public health. The standard of housing was generally poor, builders were often unscrupulous and out to make quick profits. Edwin Chadwick's report 'The Sanitary Conditions of the Labouring Classes' graphically detailed the inadequate system of drainage and sewerage disposal. Even where they existed they were all too often incapable of dealing with the large volume of effluent. Diseases were prevalent everywhere and did not differentiate between rich and poor. Diphtheria and scarlet fever killed many children each year. In the cholera epidemic in 1832, thirty people died in Caernarfon and eighteen in Flint. When a further outbreak occurred in 1849 the death toll in north Wales was higher, with towns like Holyhead and Holywell losing forty-two and forty-six people respectively. It was, to say the least, a most alarming and frightening situation.[67]

Wherever one turned it was a picture of utter despair and misery. The answer for many was in religion and in nonconformity in particular. It was also a time when the masses were becoming politically conscious and in Wales in particular, the political alignment was determined to a large extent by the spirit of nonconformity. Therefore, religious differences allied themselves with social and economic differences, to separate still further the largely anglicised establishment from most of the ordinary people. In Wales, nonconformity seemed almost synonymous with the working-classes and, fired by political speeches and the literature urging reform, gave a moral and religious fervour to the pursuit of social and economic justice. This rift, between the establishment and the people, was further widened when the *Report of the Commissioners on Education in Wales* was published in 1847 (known as the 'Blue Books'). In the Report, the Commissioners were highly critical of the language, the religion, and the morals of the people. The Welsh were portrayed, as ill-educated, poor, dirty, unchaste and potentially rebellious, and much of the blame for their plight was put on the Welsh language and nonconformity.[68] Such findings were not only widely denounced but created also a great wave of anger throughout the whole of Wales. That such feelings were not to be short-lived was illustrated in the late 1850s when Michael D. Jones, speaking about the clergy of the established church, referred to them as 'officers of the aristocracy generally appointed and promoted by them and saw them as spiritual constables or police in black instead of blue clothes'.[69]

Thus, the picture of north Wales in the middle of the nineteenth century was one of a steadily deteriorating situation in the social fabric – near destitution with its attendant evils of pauperism and alcoholism being widely prevalent. Throughout the five counties there was an embittered workforce, devoid of hope and cynical in its general attitude towards authority.[70] Adding to what was already a depressing scene, there was a spiralling in the growth of crime, assisted in part by the emergence of the 'travelling criminal', one of the less desirable consequences of the improvement in the means of communication. The sole responsibility for the maintenance of law and order at this time, rested on the shoulders of the magistrates, aided by parish constables – who had long outlived their usefulness. Visitors to Britain in the early years of the century continually expressed surprise on hearing that there was no professionally trained police force. Not even the magnitude of the Gordon Riots in 1780, in which at least 700 people died on the streets of London, stirred the government to take action and reform the antiquated policing system.[71]

It would seem, therefore, that apart from the formation of the Thames River Police in 1800 under Patrick Colquhoun, England and Wales entered the nineteenth century under the old inefficient arrangements. A succession of parliamentary committees meeting in 1812, 1816, 1818 and 1822 all concluded that to introduce any form of professional policing would be totally incompatible with British justice.[72] Many of the witnesses appearing before these committees believed that a great deal of the crime committed stemmed from the poorer sections of society and saw petty offences as giving the greatest cause for concern, since in their opinion, the more serious criminal acts, like highway robbery were steadily declining.[73] Yet, despite this reluctance by the authorities to face reality, it was widely acknowledged that any disturbance out of the ordinary could only be settled with the aid of the military. Nowhere was this better illustrated than in the Corn Riots of 1816 and the infamous Peterloo Riots of 1819 when a detachment of the Manchester Yeomanry made a savage attack on a political gathering, killing eleven people and injuring over 500 more.[74]

In retrospect, it seems somewhat strange that in spite of widespread agitation and confrontation, the authorities still appeared incapable of appreciating that a trained and disciplined police force would be better equipped to deal with civil disorders than the military. Even the financial loss through theft each year was seemingly preferred to the cost of instituting a regular police force. However, change came in 1822 with the appointment of Sir Robert Peel as Home Secretary. At first, Peel was not keen to commit his reputation too swiftly to so controversial a measure as police reform, although there is little doubt that it was something that he dearly wished to achieve. In February 1828 he moved for the appointment of an inquiry into the state of the police in the metropolis. In July of the same year the committee reported on its findings, and amongst those presenting evidence was Edwin Chadwick, who with Bentham and Colquhoun, made up the trinity of Utilitarians whose school of thought finally reconciled the English ideal of liberty with the French idea of police.[75] The report of the committee gave Peel all he wanted; it also satisfied the wishes of the Utilitarians in that it recognised the primary importance of the preventive nature of police work.[76]

In April 1829, Peel introduced into Parliament his bill for the improvement of the police in the metropolis, and in many ways the timing could not have been more opportune. He had the full support of the Duke of Wellington, who, ever since Peterloo had favoured entrusting the maintenance of law and order to professional police rather than soldiers.[77] Influential public opinion too, had been impressed by the writings of Bentham and Colquhoun, and confidence in the system of parish constables was slowly being eroded. Added to this, political opposition by this time had been partially conciliated. So on 29 July 1829, Robert Peel, who sought 'to teach people that liberty does not consist in having one's home robbed by organised gangs of thieves', saw his bill become law.[78] Its passing established the Metropolitan Police, which in later years served as a role model for other forces.[79] Indeed, between 1835-40, a number of provincial towns in England and Wales sought not only advice but assistance and expertise from officers in the Metropolitan Police.[80]

The 1830s was certainly a time when crime in many areas was escalating at an alarming rate. It was, in part at least, in a move to remedy this deteriorating situation, that the 1835 Municipal Corporations Act, encouraged boroughs to establish their own police forces – a welcome development, even though the Act was primarily concerned with Local Government reform, rather than with actual police efficiency. One has to recognise, however, that a few boroughs did possess a fairly disciplined and efficient police system prior to 1835; what was apparently lacking was an absence of any degree of uniformity.[81] Incidentally, of the 178 boroughs mentioned in the Act, only about a hundred Watch Committees could claim to have established a police force by 1838 and even by the early 1850s there were still at least six that remained unpoliced.[82] Later, in 1839, a further piece of legislation permitted counties, if they so wished, to establish constabularies.[83] In north Wales only the authorities in Denbighshire took full advantage of the Act. It was therefore, against this background of economic and social change, industrial expansion and political ferment that the Denbighshire Constabulary came into being in 1840.

---

[1] John Davies, *A History of Wales*, (Harmondsworth, 1993), p.319.

[2] John Williams, *Digest of Welsh Historical Statistics*, vol.1 (Cardiff, 1985), p.7.

[3] Gareth E. Jones, *Modern Wales – A Concise History*, 2nd. edition, (Cambridge, 1984), p.151.

[4] Ibid.

[5] Ibid, p.176.

[6] A.H. Dodd, *The Industrial Revolution in North Wales*, (Cardiff, 1951), p.89.

[7] *North Wales Gazette*, 17 May 1810. Letter which describes road conditions fifty years earlier.

[8] David Williams, *A History of Modern Wales*, (London, 1951), p.193.

[9] A.H. Dodd, op. cit., p.92.

[10] Ibid., pp. 89-101.

[11] A. Morris, *Merionethshire*, (Cambridge, 1915), p.4.

[12] A.H. Dodd, *A History of Caernarvonshire 1284-1900* (Denbigh, 1968), p.268.

[13] *North Wales Gazette*, 23 August 1810.

[14] A.H. Dodd, *Industrial Revolution in North Wales*, op. cit., p.96.

[15] Ibid.

[16] Edward Royle, *Modern Britain – A Social History*, (London, 1987), p.9. See also W.T. Jackman, *The Development of Transportation in Modern England*, 2nd. edition, (London, 1962), p.213.

[17] David Taylor, *Mastering Economic and Social History*, (London, 1988), p.130.

[18] Ibid.

[19] A.H. Dodd, *The Industrial Revolution in North Wales*, op. cit., p.100.

[20] Ibid., p.97.

[21] Ibid., pp.97-8.

[22] Ibid.

[23] Ibid., p.99.

[24] W.M. Stern, *Britain Yesterday and Today*, (London, 1962), p.133.

[25] Hugh J. Owen, *The Treasures of the Mawddach*, (Bala, 1950), p.56.

[26] A.H. Dodd, *A History of Caernarvonshire*, op. cit., p.270.

[27] A.H. Dodd, *The Industrial Revolution in North Wales*, op. cit., p.101, - the wonder coach was the first to travel a hundred miles in a day.

[28] D. Taylor, op. cit., pp.124-5.

[29] Ibid., p.130.

[30] A.H. Dodd, *Industrial Revolution in North Wales*, op. cit., pp.101-10.

[31] Ibid.

[32] Lewis Lloyd, *Sails on the Mawddach*, (Caernarfon, 1981), p.7.

[33] A.H. Dodd, op. cit., p.121.

[34] D.W. Morgan, *Brief Glory*, (Liverpool, 1948), pp.113-14.

[35] Lewis Lloyd, *The Port of Caernarfon 1793-1900*, (Caernarfon, 1989), p.35.

[36] D.W. Morgan, op. cit., pp.102-6.

[37] Aled Eames, *Ships and Seamen of Gwynedd*, (Gwynedd Archives Service, 1976), p.1.

[38] David Thomas, 'Anglesey shipbuilding down to 1840', *Transactions of the Anglesey Antiquarian Society and Field Club*, (1932), pp.107-9.

[39] G.H. Jenkins, *The Foundations of Modern Wales*, (Oxford, 1993), p.275.

[40] Lewis Lloyd, op. cit., p.46.

[41] D.G. Evans, *A History of Wales 1815-1906*, (Cardiff, 1989), p.40.

[42] A.H. Dodd, *Industrial Revolution in North Wales*, op. cit., pp.113-16.

[43] For an excellent background on this period see Paul O'Leary, 'Anti-Irish riots in Wales, 1826-1882', *Llafur*, 5 (4), (1991), pp.27-36. See also T. Coleman, *The Railway Navvies*, (London, 1981), p.24.

[44] A.H. Dodd, *Industrial Revolution in North Wales*, op. cit., pp.116-17.

[45] G.H. Jenkins, op. cit., p.166.

[46] I.G. Jones, 'Merioneth politics in mid-nineteenth century – the politics of a rural economy', *Journal of the Merioneth Historical and Record Society*, V (IV), 1968, pp.273-326.

[47] A.H. Dodd, *Industrial Revolution in North Wales*, op. cit., p.352.

[48] A. Radford, *The Economic History of England, 1760-1860*, 2nd. edition (London, 1960), p.109.

[49] D. Taylor, op. cit., pp.222-3.

[50] Ibid.

[51] R. Tames, *Economy and Society in Nineteenth Century Britain*, (London, 1972), p.62. Also consult D. Gareth Evans, op. cit., pp.1-14, and the excellent study on agriculture by David W. Howell, *Land and People in Nineteenth Century Wales*, (London, 1978).

[52] Gareth E. Jones, op. cit., p.160.

[53] G.H. Jenkins, op. cit., p.120.

[54] Ibid.

[55] A.H. Dodd, *Industrial Revolution in North Wales*, op. cit., p.272.

[56] H. Evans, *Gorse Glen*, (Liverpool, 1948), p.95.

[57] J.G. Jenkins, 'Rural industry in Anglesey', *Transactions of the Anglesey Antiquarian Society and Field Club*, (1967), pp.52-3.

[58] D.G. Evans, op. cit., p.176. In fact a number of mills overcame the difficulties of the 1920s and remained open until 1938.

[59] David J.V. Jones, *Before Rebecca – Popular Protests in Wales 1793-1835*, (London, 1973), p.69, and *Chester Chronicle*, 21 February 1817.

[60] Ibid., pp.58-9, and *North Wales Gazette*, 12 April 1827.

[61] *North Wales Chronicle*, 31 January 1828.

[62] David J.V. Jones, op. cit., p.118. This confrontation became known as the 'battle of Gutter Hill'.

[63] D.G. Evans, op. cit., pp.146-8. Also John Davies, op. cit., pp.375-8, and A.H. Dodd, *A History of Caernarvonshire*, op. cit., p.333. Consult also David J.V. Jones, *Chartism and Chartists*, (London, 1975).

[64] Sir Thomas Phillips, *Wales: The Language, Social Conditions, Moral Character and Religious Opinions of the People, Considered in their Relation to Education*, (London, 1849), pp.580-1.

[65] Ibid.

[66] B. Parry-Jones, 'The journals of H.J. Reveley (1812-1889) of Bryn-y-gwin, Dolgellau', *Journal of the Merioneth Historical and Record Society*, vi (iii), 1971, p.276.

[67] D.G. Evans, op. cit., pp.47-51. For an excellent account on public health see I.G. Jones, *Mid-Victorian Wales – The Observers and the Observed*, (Cardiff, 1992), pp.24-53. A general account of cholera can be seen in G. Penrhyn Jones, 'Cholera in Wales', *National Library of Wales Journal* X(3), 1958, pp.281-300.

[68] D.G. Evans, op. cit., p.126.

[69] I.G. Jones, 'Merioneth politics in mid-nineteenth century – the politics of a rural economy', *Journal Merioneth Historical and Record Society*, v (iv), 1968, p.318.

[70] W.R. Lambert, *Drink and Sobriety in Victorian Wales 1820-1895*, (Cardiff, 1983), p.47. Also P. P. 1847 xvii, pp.286, 351 and 478-85, and D.G. Evans, op. cit., pp.53-8.

[71] C. Hibbert, *King Mob*, (London, 1958), p.131.

[72] T.A. Critchley, op. cit., p.46.

[73] PP, 1816 (510) v, *Report on the State of the Police Metropolis*, pp.29, 143-4.

[74] R.J. Morris, 'Clubs, societies and associations' in F.M.L. Thompson, (ed.), *The Cambridge Social History of Britain 1750-1950*, 3 (Cambridge, 1993), p.405. In this work there is an interesting account of nineteenth century crime by V.A.C. Gatrell, chapter 5, pp.243-310. There is a graphic account of the Peterloo Riots and a list of the victims in Eric J. Hewitt, *A History of Policing Manchester*, (Manchester, 1979), pp.32-6.

[75] T.A. Critchley, op. cit., p.49.

[76] PP, (1828), vol. vi, Police of the Metropolis.

[77] Peel and Wellington gave their reasons for reform, 1829. Speeches on the Metropolis Police Bill, House of Commons, 15 April 1829, and House of Lords, 5 June 1829. Hansard Parliamentary Debates, 2nd. series, 1829, cols. 868, 880-1, 1750-1.

[78] 10 Geo. iv, c.44.

[79] T.A. Critchley, op. cit., p.50, where he states that 'Although, one has to applaud the work and tenacity of Sir Robert Peel in the field of police reform, it is regrettable, as one writer suggests "that in harvesting the corn he failed to acknowledge his debt to those who had long prepared the way. Henry and John Fielding, who sowed the seed three quarters of a century earlier, Patrick Colquhoun, who raised the crop, and Bentham who tilled the soil in which it grew".'

[80] W.L. Melville Lee, *A History of the Police in England*, (London, 1901), pp.256-59. See also Charles Reith, op. cit., pp.195-6, in which he states that the passing of the 1835 Act was to lead to a number of London policemen, of all ranks, being sent to more than 200 provincial centres in response to direct requests, thereby providing the borough forces with a unifying system of organisation, principles and values as exhibited by the Metropolitan Police. Much of this early training was based on the original Scotland Yard *Handbook of General Instructions* which became, to a greater or lesser extent, the basis of organisation for all the borough forces in England and Wales.

[81] Clive Emsley, *Crime and Society in England 1750-1900*, pp.180-1. For a view of crime prior to 1750 see J.A. Sharpe, *Crime in Early Modern England 1550-1750*, (London, 1984).

[82] Ibid., in which he cites Jenifer Hart, 'Reform of the borough police, 1835-1856'. *English Historical Review*, LXX (1955), pp. 411-27. The following is a list of Welsh borough forces (1829-1969). Brecon 1829-89; Carmarthen 1831-1944; Haverfordwest 1833-89; Beaumaris 1836-60; Flint 1836-64; Neath 1836-1947; Newport 1836-1967; Monmouth 1836-81; Swansea 1836-1969; Tenby 1840-89; Pembroke 1856-58; Kidwelly 1857-58; Pwllheli 1857-79; Merthyr Tydfil 1908-69; Denbigh 1854-8; Welshpool ?-1857. For an excellent account of the formation and amalgamation of the county, city and borough forces in England and Wales see M.B. Taylor and V.L. Wilkinson, *Badges of Office*, (Henley-on-Thames, 1989).

[83] T.A. Critchley, op. cit., pp.85-8.

## Chapter II

# Crime and the Denbighshire Constabulary, 1840-57

If crime was causing concern in England, then the authorities in Wales were no less anxious about the rising tide of criminal activity which was being experienced in the various counties. The enclosure riots in north Wales early in the nineteenth century saw Dragoons being called upon to quell disturbances at Aberdaron in 1805 and later in 1809 at Llanddeiniolen. These were early examples of the readiness of the magistrates when faced with serious unrest to call for military aid.[1] In 1816, as a result of low wages and conditions of employment colliers went on strike at Mold, and to restore order, cavalry was used to disperse the mob.[2] Strikes were common occurrences in Wales, particularly when employers attempted to lengthen the hours of work, as seen when miners rioted at Halkyn in 1822. A more serious situation occurred at Llanddulas in 1829 when fusiliers from Chester were brought in to confront and contain the rebellious limestone quarrymen who were strongly opposed to the enclosure of common land.[3] But strikes were not confined to north Wales. In the south Wales coalfields there were claims in the 1820s, that power was falling into the hands of the 'Scotch Cattle', an illegal terrorist organisation, and in the 1830s, again in the south, there was a daring attempt at revolution with the Merthyr and Newport Risings. As Dr David J.V. Jones rightly claimed, such events were proof, if proof was needed, 'that beneath the apparently quiet surface of Welsh life dangerous forces were at work'.[4]

Certainly, in the larger towns, there was a growing awareness by the magistrates that crime was reaching an unprecedented level. There were numerous instances of armed robbery, of thefts from shops and houses, and pickpocketing had become a lucrative way of life for many criminals.[5] In fact, throughout the 1820s and 1830s there were frequent reports of organised gangs visiting fairs at such places as Wrexham and Llangollen where they deftly relieved unsuspecting persons of their purses and wallets. With crime so prevalent in parts of north Wales there is little wonder that the prison population was constantly rising. That such was the case, is illustrated in the returns for the Ruthin county gaol and house of correction for the period 1827-34 which clearly indicate that the numbers being admitted each year were on the increase. For example, 82 people were admitted in 1827; 94 in 1830; 129 in 1832; and 150 in 1834.[6] Street violence was frequently observed in many of the towns, and particularly at weekends, at places like Bagillt in Flintshire and Rhosymedre in Denbighshire. At Barmouth, constant brawling in the streets led the inhabitants there to call for a more efficient policing system as well as more lock-ups.[7] Similarly, in Bangor and Tywyn and other coastal towns along the north Wales coast, residents feared that the incidents of bad behaviour would drive away many tourists and called on the police to remove drunken seamen, prostitutes, vagrants and navvies to areas less conspicuous.[8] In fact, most of the hostility and violence experienced by the authorities arose as a consequence of enforcing legislative measures which were largely unpopular, like the new licensing laws or the Poor Law Act of 1834.

Crime and the methods of containment were always factors that were high on the agenda whenever and wherever magistrates met. However, in the 1830s their attention was to become focused on an issue which not only threatened the general maintenance of law and order, but the stability of government itself. Their concern was centred on the widespread discontent and rioting by those who continually demanded political reform. As early as 1831 many towns in Wales had experienced spasmodic disturbances, including that of the Merthyr Rising, which was regarded by many as a determined attempt to by-pass the polite politics of the Westminster elite.[9] The situation became even more explosive when those who had agitated and had fought so tenaciously for political reform were to find that with the passing of the Reform Bill of 1832 they had achieved virtually nothing.[10] With feelings of anger, frustration, even betrayal, they became the backbone of the Chartist movement, the main channel for the unrest which was sweeping through the industrial communities of England and Wales between 1836-42.[11] Yet, despite the seriousness of the situation during the Chartist era, the government never found it necessary to introduce repressive legislation. 'The law, as it at present stands' said Earl Grey, 'has been found by active magistrates, who exerted themselves properly, to be sufficiently powerful to put down disturbances'.[12] The statement was to be proved correct in November 1839 by the severity shown by the authorities during the Newport insurrection, an incident described as the high point of physical force Chartism, and the scene of the bloodiest battle in mainland Britain during the nineteenth century.[13]

The problems experienced in Newport left the government with painful memories. That lessons had been learned was to be seen when correspondence from the Home Office, particularly during the Rebecca Riots of 1839-44, made it plain that government action in the future would only sanction police and military assistance in times of unrest, if in turn, those responsible for the local forces of law and order had made some provision to reform themselves.[14] It was in order to assist counties in England and Wales to establish a competent policing system that the Rural Police Act of 1839 – known as the 'Permissive Act' – came into being on receiving the Royal Assent on 27 August 1839.[15] Still fearing further outbreaks of disorder and sedition, magistrates in several Welsh counties were quick to take full advantage of the opportunities afforded by the Act. With its passing, magistrates could determine whether or not they wished to establish a constabulary. It was also left to their discretion on the actual size of the force, although it was stipulated that the ratio was to be no more than one police officer for every thousand inhabitants. Magistrates were also given the authority to appoint their new chief constable, and if the situation warranted it, to dismiss him. Unlike their counterparts in the boroughs, chief constables in the counties also had absolute power in appointing their subordinates.[16] It was the duty of the Home Secretary to formulate the rules and regulations concerning management, clothing and pay, but apart from this involvement there was to be no direction from the centre.

However, even before the 1839 Act had actually received the Royal Assent, a notice in a newspaper laid down further conditions which magistrates were expected to consider and adhere to if they wished to establish a county constabulary:[17]

a. All rules to be revised by the Secretary of State.

b. Chief constable to appoint and dismiss petty constables.
c. Constables to have the authority of special constables under 1 and 2. Will. iv c.41.
d. Chief constable to attend Quarter Sessions and make quarterly reports to the justices on the state of the police.
e. There were to be allowances for necessary expenses incurred in the apprehension of offenders, and in the execution of the duties of the constables under the Act.
f. Constables could be appointed for separate divisions if the magistrates did not think it proper to appoint them for a whole county.
g. Expenses to be defrayed out of the county rates.
h. Regulations as to the county rate, to apply to the increased rates levied for the police.
i. Treasurer to keep separate accounts of the police rates.

In north Wales only the magistrates in Denbighshire showed any real interest in the establishment of a county force. The remaining counties were seemingly content in retaining the old inefficient methods of policing, which in their view was far cheaper to operate. An indication of Denbighshire's serious intention to adopt the Act was seen in April 1840, when at a meeting of magistrates sitting in quarter sessions, the chairman, Mr John Heaton, said that consideration had now to be given to the formation of a constabulary. It appeared that at an earlier meeting most magistrates had strongly favoured a constabulary force, although a final decision on the matter had been left in abeyance. However, it was now time to make that decision, and this evoked protest from Major Yale who strongly objected to the Act on the grounds of expenditure. Other speakers were much more supportive, the Lord Lieutenant, R.M. Biddulph, Esq. spoke in favour of the Bill believing that the protection of property was well worth the extra expense.[18] After a ballot it was decided by seventeen votes to four that the Act of 1839 should be adopted and applied to the whole of the county.[19] As a result of the decision, the clerk of the peace was authorized to send a letter immediately to the Secretary of State, stating that, magistrates sitting in quarter sessions had agreed to adopt the Rural Constabulary Act of 1839.[20] It was also resolved at the meeting that in addition to a chief constable whose salary was to be £250 per annum, there should also be three superintendents at a £100 each per annum. The new constabulary was also to have twenty-four constables, of whom three were to receive 18s per week, and the other twenty-one, 15s per week, with all officers being supplied with clothing and accoutrements.[21] Later, in correspondence with the clerk of the peace, magistrates made it known that it was their firm intention to appoint a chief constable at the next sitting of the quarter sessions which were to be held at Ruthin on 1 May 1840.

The number of applicants for the position of chief constable is unknown, but since it was probably viewed by many as a prestigious position, it is likely that it would have attracted a substantial number. Whatever the figure, a short list of three candidates was drawn up. In the voting that followed, Major Miles Wynne obtained eighteen votes, whilst Lieutenant Lawson and Mr John Denman received seven votes each. Unfortunately, when Major Wynne's name was submitted for approval to the Secretary of State it was rejected on the grounds that the candidate was over age. Somewhat surprised by the decision, the magistrates were forced to reconsider the position and eventually chose Mr John Denman to be the first chief constable of Denbighshire.[22] On appointment Mr Denman was thirty-eight years of age and the eldest son of the Reverend John Denman, rector of Llandegla and the vicar of Llanarmon (1820-31). At the time of his appointment, the new chief constable was residing at Glanrafon, Llanfair Dyffryn Clwyd, near Ruthin. Little is known about his early background except that he had a reputation of being an excellent horseman. The area to be policed by the new constabulary was quite extensive, stretching from the valleys of the Dee, Ceiriog and the Tanat in the east, across the Clwydian hills, and the Hiraethog to the Vale of Conwy and the seaboard in the west. At the time of Mr Denman's appointment, the horse was regarded as the monarch of the highway, and was one of the reasons why, in the chief constable's remuneration, there was always provision made for a horse and forage. Indeed, a horse was essential in a county where communication between one district and another was so poor. An example of how bad communication was, is seen at a later date, when magistrates sitting at quarter sessions, discussed the delay which took place before the chief constable received news at Ruthin of riotous behaviour at Hafod colliery, Ruabon.[23]

When the Denbighshire constabulary was formed, certain areas within the county were already in a state of unrest. In the eastern parts of Denbighshire, the hundreds of Bromfield and Chirk were in an unsettled state owing to the closure of blast furnaces and the trade depression at the coalmines. This resulted in hundreds of unemployed and starving colliers roaming the countryside, which posed a constant threat to all who stood in their way.[24] Certainly, the newly appointed constables had a most difficult time, and being few in number met much opposition. In the more rural areas of the county they were looked upon as being unnecessary and a burden on the rates. In fact, in the parish of Llanfair Dyffryn Clwyd, a meeting on 11 December 1840, which was mainly attended by farmers and local inhabitants, decided to send a petition to the chairman of the next quarter sessions protesting against the Rural Police Act on the grounds of cost. They felt crime was rare and that the five parish constables were quite adequate.[25] Yet, a little earlier, a petition by residents of Dolgellau, had been presented to the magistrates in Merioneth, asking for a rural police force to be established, as there had been numerous robberies in the area and no one had been arrested for the offences.[26] Such conflicting views as those expressed by residents in Denbighshire and Merioneth must have made it difficult for authorities to assess the real state of opinion in support of a rural constabulary. Not that Denbighshire was alone at this time in being criticised for having a constabulary. As early as 1841 there was a growing body of opinion from all over the country that rural policing was becoming far too expensive.[27] It was to meet such criticism, that the Home Office became actively engaged in assisting counties like Denbighshire to get their new forces off to a successful start during the early stages of the Act of 1839 becoming operative. That this was certainly the case, is seen in the correspondence contained in the Home Office County Constabulary letter-book, particularly for the period October 1839 and May 1840.[28] During this time Lord Normanby, who succeeded Lord Russell as Home Secretary in August 1839, frequently issued guidelines and advice to all who sought his assistance.

However, it was the magistrates who probably required some assistance and guidance in Denbighshire. In a newspaper article they had been subjected to serious criticism over the manner in which they went about appointing senior officers to the force. It seems that several Tory magistrates had met at the County Hall in Ruthin on 9 June 1840 for the sole purpose of appointing three superintendents. There were, apparently, a number of suitable candidates, some of whom were serving officers in cities like Liverpool, Manchester and Birmingham and possessed a great deal of experience in police duties. However, those considered the least efficient, but commanded the greatest favour, were the ones who were successful. One of those favoured, but not appointed, had only one hand, and the writer went on to ask whether the Secretary of State would ever have allowed such an appointment, since he had objected to Major Wynne becoming chief constable on the grounds that he was seven years over the age limit. The magistrates, in their defence, claimed that their decision was based purely on some candidates being unable to speak Welsh. Yet, officers with wide experience in Liverpool were actually Welshmen and fully conversant with the language. The writer concluded 'that it was all a Tory plot, the elections were rigged, and the magistrates only met to make the workings of the Act look good'.[29] Confirmation that such comments were not mere pique came a little later when a writer in a similar vein and signing himself 'A ratepayer', went on to say 'that a well established and regulated police force would be beneficial, particularly since the population was rapidly increasing in parts of North Wales. However, although such a force required expenditure and rightly so, he did not think it should be spent to provide out of county funds and maintenance for the scapegoat sons and dependants of some lay or clerical squireens, whose dissolute conduct and irregular habits render them fitter to be placed under the surveillance of a police force, than persons proper to hold any command in one. The establishment of a county police should not be available for such scandalous jobbery as has been too often witnessed in selecting men to fill lucrative offices connected with county business'.[30]

On assuming command Mr Denman had first to familiarise himself with the men under his command and acquaint them with their many and varied duties. Of the officers themselves and their early background and ages, very little is known. A report some years later suggested that the average age of men joining the police during this period was twenty-six years.[31] Most recruits, it seems, came from the labouring classes, were mainly unskilled, and but for the police, might otherwise have looked to the 'field or factory or colliery for a life-time's drudgery, and whose fathers haunted by memories of the hungry forties, would pull every string in the parish to get their sons into secure employment'.[32] It was no easy job. Officers were expected to work upwards of twelve hours per day, seven days a week, and walk in all weather, perhaps as much as twenty miles in a single day when duty called; it was certainly not a calling for the faint-hearted.

At first, the chief constable encountered some difficulty in placing his men in the various stations due to the fact that no uniforms or accoutrements had been provided for them. It was however, a problem soon resolved and within a short space of time every officer had been equipped and was on patrol in various parts of the county. Superintendent Nicholls was appointed to take charge of the Llanrwst division, with Superintendent Kyffin taking command at Ruthin.[33] Turning his attention to administrative details, the chief constable then requested the court to name the sum to be retained from each constable's pay as a contribution towards the superannuation fund and the sum to be retained when an officer was sick.[34] In a further move, in which he believed police efficiency could be improved, the chief constable in his report to the quarter sessions asked for an orderly – in this he probably meant clerk – to be appointed and placed in the Ruthin office. The task of the person appointed would simply be to collate information on crime and criminal activity, which could then be conveyed quickly to officers in other parts of the county. He believed that such a scheme would greatly increase the detection rate, and was one that had been proved extremely successful by forces in other parts of the country.[35] Whether this appointment was ever made is difficult to ascertain. What can be said, is that in a letter dated 29 June 1841 he was able to inform the magistrates that information was now being supplied constantly to his office in Ruthin on the state of unrest by hundreds of colliers who had been discharged from their work at the British Ironwork Company's works at Cefn Mawr. He was also in a position to give names and details of speakers attending meetings in the area, five of whom came from Manchester. So it would appear that some kind of criminal intelligence system was operative at this time.[36]

The new chief constable appeared to lose little time in attempting to rectify what he considered weaknesses in the system of law enforcement within the county. It was one thing to establish a constabulary, but it was another matter entirely, as to where the police were to accommodate their prisoners. Throughout the county there was a serious shortage of suitable lock-ups. Magistrates meeting at Wrexham on 21 November 1839 unanimously agreed that the Bridewell in the town was completely unsuitable and needed to be replaced. As Wrexham was the largest town in the county and the most populous, it was understandable that its crime rate was higher than elsewhere in the county, yet, secure accommodation was minimal.[37] Places like Chirk, Llanrwst, Pentrefoelas and Cerrigydrudion also lacked suitable lock-ups, in fact, those arrested for offences in the latter place, had to be escorted fourteen miles in order to be placed in a cell.[38] The escorting of prisoners was a time-consuming duty, and one that frequently took officers away from their stations, allowing no doubt, some criminal acts to be committed during their absence. A typical example of the time and distance involved in such escort duty was seen when Constable David Davies of Llangollen received £1.6s for escorting two prisoners, John Williams and William Harris, both charged with felony, to the gaol in Ruthin, a distance of twenty-one miles. That the prisoners did not go hungry during their journey is seen in the bill, which included a sum of 5s for ten meals at 6d each.[39] Sometimes an officer had to go much further than twenty-one miles, as on the occasion when Constable William Jones and his wife travelled from Chirk to London to bring back Elizabeth Lovett or Levitt who had been charged with a felony.[40]

On occasion it was the police officers themselves who stood in front of the magistrates charged with an offence. At Wrexham early in June 1842, Superintendent Mostyn was fined £1.10s for an assault on a respectable shopkeeper and farmer.[41] At the same court, Constable Icke was charged with kicking a pregnant woman, causing her to lapse into premature labour, a claim a surgeon was to refute. Nevertheless, the magistrates were of the opinion that the constable had acted a little too officiously. As this was not the first time that he had behaved in such a manner, he received a caution and warned as to his future conduct.[42] That Superintendent Mostyn was not the most popular officer in Denbighshire was seen a little later, when a newspaper commenting on his departure from the town stated 'that things had changed for the better and the inhabitants of Wrexham were now much more willing to contribute towards the continuance of the police force than previously had been the case'.[43] Sometimes, disputes involving the police were settled out of court, as when Inspector Cunnah attacked Superintendent Nicholls and had to be forcibly restrained before serious injury could be inflicted on the officer. Whatever caused the attack, which apparently was unprovoked, is unknown. However, Inspector Cunnah was back on duty a few days later as if nothing untoward had taken place.[44] As for Superintendent Nicholls, he was to resign in September 1845, his position at Llanrwst being taken by Sergeant Edward Evans, who was promoted inspector. Being of a lower rank than his predecessor, his appointment saved the county £25 per annum.[45]

However, if some officers behaved in a manner which

brought discredit upon the service, there were others, who, in at least the chief constable's opinion, were worthy of some recognition for their devotion to duty. In his report dated 10 March 1845 he begged the attention of the magistrates to reward the following officers 'for their steadiness and general good conduct'.[46] Accepting the chief constable's recommendation, the magistrates ordered that the following officers should be rewarded as follows: Inspector Edwards of Wrexham and Inspector Robinson of Denbigh should receive 10s each; Constables Thomas Hughes, Llanrwst; William Lloyd, Llanfair Talhaearn; John Peters, Cerrigydrudion; William Peters, Holt; Mathias Rowlands, Wrexham; John Parry, Llangollen; William Jones, Abergele; William Jones, Chirk; were all to receive 5s each. A year later the chief constable made a similar request, this time for two inspectors and eight constables to be rewarded for their services, although it is not known whether on this occasion his request was granted.[47] In his report of 10 March 1845 the chief constable was also pleased to inform the magistrates that all under his command were working well. The numbers of those wishing to join the force had also increased, although he found it regrettable that so few were fluent in Welsh. As a further move to improve efficiency and promote more professionalism within the force, Mr Denman purchased a number of legal books from Russell and Prince's booksellers in Chester at a cost of £25.8s, in the firm belief that such a purchase would substantially assist his officers to have a better understanding of the law.[48] The chief constable could also claim that by the middle of the 1840s the force was better equipped. Certainly, new clothing and accoutrements for the men, although expensive, were frequently provided.[49]

Yet, despite the improvement in the force's discipline and performance it was to be constantly criticised. Calls for the entire force to be abolished came from a number of communities within the county. In the press, too, numerous letters called for the force to be disbanded, with many of those writing of their disapproval expressing derogatory comments. One writer from Ruthin called the police 'the scum of the county'.[50] As early as December 1842, the ratepayers of the parish of Ruabon sent a petition to the magistrates calling for the dismissal of the county police force.[51] A similar petition, this time from Llanfair, near Ruthin, also called for the force to be abolished on the grounds it was worse than useless.[52] Equally, in the eyes of those living in the parish of Llanfair Dyffryn Clwyd, the coming of the police force had caused more discontent and agitation throughout the county, than any other subject within living memory.[53] With such views being so openly and widely expressed, it is hardly surprising, that a determined attempt to abolish the Denbighshire constabulary was made at the autumn meeting of quarter sessions held at the County Hall in Denbigh in 1844. On the actual question of disbanding the force, the magistrates were almost equally divided. Colonel Yale, always critical of the force, demanded its abolition on the grounds of expense, the annual cost of the police being £2,000 and according to him the county was already £5,000 in debt. In order to bolster his argument, he claimed that the county of Denbighshire was reasonably peaceful and bordered by Welsh counties in which no police force existed. His view had the full support of Mr Townshend Mainwaring, MP of Galltfaenan and Marchwiel Hall, who claimed he was one of the first to vote for a county constabulary 'but had now become converted to the opinion it was quite unnecessary and wholly inefficient.[54] Colonel Yale then moved, and Mr Mainwaring seconded, a resolution which called for a report to be submitted to the Secretary of State calling for the force to be discontinued from 8 May 1845. There were however, magistrates present who took the opposite view, that the force should be retained at all costs. Mr Myddleton Biddulph, of Chirk Castle, maintained that the presence of the police was essential in the hundreds of Bromfield and Chirk. In this he had the support of Dr F.J. Hughes, chairman of the Wrexham petty sessions, who believed that Wrexham would not be so peaceful if the force was abolished. When the resolution was finally put to the court, thirteen magistrates voted for the force to be abolished, with twelve voting for its retention. Since an Act of Parliament required a majority of three fourths, the resolution was lost.[55]

Whatever the feelings of the chief constable, or of the men themselves, of the remarks made against them, (often so disparaging), they continued to do their duty. Crime was still being committed and that the police in the county had been vigilant, despite being accused otherwise, was seen in the chief constable's report to the quarter sessions dated 2 July 1844, in which he records the number of prisoners tried since the force was established:[56]

| Oct. 1841-42 | 91 |
| Oct. 1842-43 | 96 |
| Oct. 1843-44 | 85 |
| Oct. 1844-45 | 65 |

In the same report the chief constable also stated that since the establishment of the force in 1840, sixty-three officers had been dismissed, forty-one of these for drunkenness. Such dismissals clearly indicated that as far as possible, discipline within the force was being maintained, and where officers were neglectful of duty, there was no hesitation in terminating their employment. As officers either left the force, or were dismissed, it created a recruitment problem for the chief constable. In his report to the quarter sessions dated 4 January 1848, he reported the difficulties encountered when trying to recruit Welsh officers. Out of every ten applicants to join the force, only one came from a Welshman, thus leaving him with little alternative but to appoint English applicants.[57] That the force was more or less equally divided between Welsh and English officers is seen in his report dated 27 June 1848, in which he lists the force as having an establishment of thirty officers, twenty-seven constables and three inspectors, thirteen of whom were Welsh, thirteen were English and four were Irish. It is rather interesting, that a Welsh police force like Denbighshire, found little difficulty in recruiting able English officers, whereas the chief constable of Lancashire, Captain Woodford, found the opposite to be true. Most English applicants wishing to join his force, were more often than not, unable to read or write. In his experience, it was the Irish applicants who were by far the best, for he was not aware of a single instance of an Irishman applying to join who could not read and write.[58]

In a report to the quarter sessions dated 20 October 1846, the chief constable reported a decrease in crime and believed this was due to two important factors. Firstly, the building of the railway had provided employment for many within the county, thereby reducing those crimes associated with unemployment and poverty. Secondly, those known to the police for their criminality now had their movements more closely observed and reported.[59] A year later, in a report dated 19 October 1847 the chief constable blamed the railway for the rise in crime, for its coming he believed now enabled those with criminal intentions to enter and leave the county more easily, thereby creating for the police a new form of criminal activity – that of the travelling criminal.[60]

The abolition of the police force, a subject never far away from some people's minds, was again to be raised in 1849, this time with more determination by those who were foiled by their defeat in 1844. Their opportunity to call for the force to be disbanded arose as a result of a spate of robberies in the

Wrexham area, which caused much local anger, and led to a public meeting being held at the Lion Hotel, where it was decided that a further meeting should be arranged, this time in the Town Hall with the chief constable in attendance. In many ways, his meeting with members of the public proved more like an inquisition. Questioned at length on his policing policies, he admitted that he knew of the robberies and the concern it caused, but in many instances the crimes were reported long after the offences had been committed, and therefore there was little the police could do. Several at the meeting accused Mr Denman of spending far too much time in the Vale of Clwyd and in so doing, distancing himself from the areas of crime, a claim he firmly denied. When accused of not visiting or inspecting his men he retorted 'that after consultation with other chief constables at various dinners in London, they did not do so either'.[61] There was also a complaint by many at the meeting that the men appointed to the force lacked tact, intelligence and experience. But in reply to this criticism, the chief constable stated 'that if the calibre of the men was poor, so too were their wages – at 16s.6d per week you could not get good men for that'.[62] However, if the wages of the officers in Denbighshire were low, as the chief constable believed they were, then Colonel Yale, comparing their pay with other county forces like Gloucestershire, was of the opinion they should be reduced even further.[63]

Despite the mounting criticism of the police, the chief constable and his officers continued to perform their duties. Early in 1850, the chief constable located two constables to new stations, Constable Edward Pugh was moved from Eglwysbach to Llansanffraid, Glan Conwy, and Constable David Davies from Mochdre to Colwyn.[64] As these changes were taking place, magistrates elsewhere were beginning to dismantle the force, announcing that it was their intention to remove constables since they were no longer needed. Furthermore, they also called for the services of the chief constable to be dispensed with.[65] As if to introduce some finality into the proceedings, Colonel Yale, presented yet another petition, this time on behalf of the Wrexham Union, which called for the abolition of the constabulary in its present form from 1 January 1851, when a new and remodelled force would be established. In presenting the petition, Colonel Yale wished it to be placed on record that in seeking the abolition of the force, he had nothing against the chief constable personally or indeed of his officers.[66] Later, and as if to justify the actions of the magistrates in dismissing Mr

Denman, the chairman of the quarter sessions, Mr Thomas Hughes of Ystrad, Denbigh, stated 'we did away with the chief constable simply to save expense'.[67] So it was, that after years of campaigning, often quite vociferously, those who wished for the ending of the Denbighshire Constabulary had finally achieved their goal. For many in the county however, it was a sad occasion. The decision to abolish the force, they believed, was something the county would later regret. If, as Mr Thomas Hughes suggested, finance was a consideration in abolishing the force and its chief constable, then it was a claim that the Ruthin Board of Guardians viewed with some scepticism. They were of the opinion that after all the discussion about disbanding the force, the saving with the new constabulary would be approximately £200 per annum, and that, according to them, would soon be spent elsewhere.[68] Confirmation that the old force had not been too expensive to administer was seen in a bill presented by Superintendent Bradshaw to the quarter sessions in which he stated the cost of the constabulary in the Llanrwst area for the period 1 January to 11 February 1851:

| Supt. | John Bradshaw, Llanrwst | £9.16s |
| P.C.3 | David Davies, Colwyn | £4.19s |
| P.C.6 | Thomas Fudge, Llansannan | £4.19s |
| P.C.11 | John Peters, Cerrigydrudion | £4.19s |
| P.C.12 | Edward Pugh, Llanrwst | £4.19s |
| P.C.17 | Joseph Howell, Abergele | £4.19s |

If one adds to the above total £2.5s.3d for off-beat and other expenses, the total came to £36.16s.3d; all officers also paid 2s each to the superannuation fund.[69]

When the magistrates met at the County Hall in Ruthin on 20 January 1851, their main priority was to formulate a policy for the new force and the number of officers such a force would eventually require. Not every magistrate present at the meeting was entirely happy with the situation and several expressed the opinion that the old force should have been retained and even questioned the legality of the measures leading up to its removal.[70] That they were not alone in feeling that the old constabulary should have been retained was seen in the Wrexham area, when a petition was raised calling for the restoration of the force. Alarmed at such a prospect, those fiercely opposed to such a return, appointed a town crier to tour the area cautioning people not to sign.[71] At a meeting held on 20 January, the magistrates decided that in reorganising the force, the county would be better served if it was divided into two districts, with a superintendent being appointed for each. Therefore, as a result of Mr Denman's departure, control of the new force was to be firmly placed in the hands of two superintendents. Magistrates then turned their attention to recruitment and the number of officers they believed would be required for the new constabulary. As a result of much discussion it was decided that twenty-three officers would, in their opinion, be a sufficient number to police the county, fourteen of those appointed to be stationed in the Wrexham district, with the remaining nine being assigned to the town of Denbigh.[72] Having finalised the new arrangements, the magistrates then had the proposed changes communicated to the Home Secretary for approval, which they later received. The first senior officer to be appointed was Superintendent George Mark King, a most experienced police officer who had served in Leeds and London, and on his appointment he assumed command at Wrexham.[73] A little later, Superintendent John Bradshaw, also widely experienced, having served with the Metropolitan Police, was appointed to take charge at Denbigh.[74]

The Magistrates again turned their attention to recruitment, and placed a notice in a newspaper inviting applications for four posts of constable, at a wage of 18s per week, exclusive of uniform – applicants had to be under thirty-five years of age, at least 5' 7" in height, with the ability to read and write and keep records. It was also deemed as essential that all applicants should be fluent in the Welsh language.[75] That four officers with the necessary qualifications were appointed is seen in a bill showing the cost of swearing in the officers as 4s. Those appointed to the new force were William Pattison, John Rafferty, Joseph Jones and William Jones.[76] A further bill, this time for 7s, was submitted by Mr James Rees, printer and proprietor of the *Caernarvon and Denbigh Herald*, for an advertisement placed in the newspaper by Superintendent King, again seeking applicants to join the force[77]. One of the first duties of Superintendent Bradshaw on assuming office was to procure uniforms for his men, and the following articles of clothing were requested for the Denbigh division: one greatcoat, twenty pairs of trousers, twenty pairs of boots, twenty pairs of gloves (white buckskin), ten hats, ten dress-coats, and ten stocks.[78]

Within a few months of taking office Superintendent King submitted to the quarter sessions a report in which he expressed concern at the lack of suitable lock-ups in the county. The report, which called for urgent action by the magistrates to remedy this deficit also included for their information a list of where, in the county, stocks were available for those so punished for minor offences. Stocks, according to his survey were in place at Cerrigydrudion, Denbigh, Eglwysbach, Llanbedr, Llanrwst and Ruthin. In the parishes of Llanfair Dyffryn Clwyd, Llandyrnog, Llangwyfan and Llanddulas only the remains of stocks were visible, and the report concluded that twenty-six parishes had never had stocks.[79] That stocks were occasionally used, was seen on 26 September 1848, when David and William Hughes, who were convicted of being drunk, found themselves placed in the stocks at Denbigh for six hours.[80] Although in Denbighshire there appears no evidence to suggest that police officers were ever placed in stocks, they were from time to time either fined or dismissed for drunkenness. Constable Thomas Fudge was fined 5s in 1852 for appearing at headquarters in a drunken and abusive state,[81] whilst Constable William Rhodes was fined and reprimanded for being drunk in charge of a prisoner in 1853.[82]

The Wrexham area in particular, at this time, was notorious for its criminal element and had the reputation of harbouring criminals who were being sought elsewhere by the police. At certain times of the year, like that of the May fairs, criminal gangs from Liverpool, Manchester, Shrewsbury and other large towns would move into the area in the hope of some rich pickings. It was in order to contain such activity that the more affluent inhabitants in Wrexham sometimes raised money by private subscription to employ detectives from Liverpool, often dressed as hawkers, who would then freely mingle with the criminal fraternity in the hope of apprehending those committing crimes. In general, the idea was not a success. As records show, such surveillance work rarely produced an arrest.[83] Commenting on crime in the Wrexham area, Superintendent King in his report to the quarter sessions, maintained that despite the growth in population, the number of police officers stationed in the town was the same as in 1840 when the constabulary was established. In his opinion, the appointment of at least three more police officers was necessary if crime at its present level was to be controlled.[84] In his plea for more officers, the superintendent had the support of Mr John Heaton, chairman of the quarter sessions, and also that of Mr Townshend-Mainwaring. The latter, who had voted so consistently to abolish the old force, was now calling for greater efficiency by the present police, stating that he wished it placed on record that his house had been burgled and one of his bailiffs nearly killed.[85]

The cost of administering the new force was a factor the magistrates never allowed the police to forget. When they met in quarter sessions at Ruthin in January 1852, they resolved that no more than 2d per meal for three meals, or 3d per meal for two meals, be allowed per day for any prisoner when in the custody of the police. Following this resolution, Superintendent King directed that when a prisoner was detained in a lock-up for one night or more and needed refreshment, he must, if he had the means, be made to pay for it himself, but if he was unable to pay, he had to be supplied with food at a cost not exceeding 6d over a twenty-four hour period.[86] That few could afford to pay for their own food, is seen in a survey conducted between 1852-53 in which 177 of the 295 prisoners in police custody were unemployed, with the remainder on wages that averaged 12s per week.[87]

Despite constant calls by the magistrates for police prudence, Superintendent King continued to ask for more lock-ups to be built, and in reporting to the magistrates requesting such action, he informed them that the total cost of the constabulary for the year ending 31 December 1853 was £1,219.19s.7d, making Denbighshire the cheapest police force in the country apart from Bedfordshire.[88] Calls for less expenditure, however, were not something Superintendent Bradshaw had in mind when he reported to the magistrates that the cost of keeping his horse had become far too expensive and to such a degree that the family income had to be reduced as a consequence. He also claimed in his report that he felt he was entitled to an increase in pay, since the area under his command was larger than the one in Wrexham, yet, the superintendent there, with allowances earned £80 per annum more than he did.[89] In his report, Superintendent Bradshaw also informed the magistrates that he was shortly to lose one of his officers to the Borough of Denbigh as a result of the authorities there establishing their own police force from 1 April 1854.[90]

Whether the authorities in Denbigh Borough were disillusioned with the services provided by the new force is not clear. What can be stated is that despite the reorganisation of the force, and the division of the county into two districts for police purposes, criticism of the service continued unabated. Mr R. Humphrey Jones, Willow Hall, Wrexham, writing to a newspaper about the situation in the town, labelled the police 'lamentable, apathetic and disgraceful' as regards their efficiency. Such comments did little for police morale.[91] Such comments as these were not confined to officers in Denbighshire. In other areas also, there was a growing dissatisfaction with the existing police arrangements. The failure generally of counties like those in north Wales, apart from Denbighshire, to adopt the Act of 1839 was beginning to be noticed and expressed by a number of leading figures. Sir Richard Bulkeley, chairman of the Anglesey quarter sessions, believed that the adoption of the County Constabulary Act ought to be compulsory, and went on to say 'crime concerns not merely a parish, or a county, but the nation itself, and the efforts for its extirpation should be national also'.[92]

The failure of the counties to adopt the legislation of 1839, and later the Parish Constables Act of 1842 (described by one writer as 'a gallant effort to put life into the old constabulary'),[93] resulted in the Home Office assuming what can only be described as a *laisser-faire* attitude over the next ten years, to matters appertaining to the police. The situation was not helped by the indifference shown by many magistrates in north Wales who, largely untroubled by the crime and unrest experienced in the cities, had a tendency to shrug off ideas that called for any reform in the sphere of policing. Indeed, for many magistrates the very idea of change was something they viewed as abhorrent. In general they seemed unable to appreciate that the arrangements for policing in the early years of the nineteenth century were no longer appropriate for the 1840s and 1850s.

Times and events were, however, against those who opposed change. The voices of powerful figures like that of Sir Richard Bulkeley, did not go unheeded in the corridors of power. In 1853, a Select Committee on Policing met to examine ways in which the system could be improved generally.[94] Members of the committee had several important advantages over those who had sat on previous police bodies. For example, twenty-five years had passed since the passing of Peel's Bill, and this gave members an opportunity to assess the successes and failures of all previous police systems. What they discovered was not entirely unexpected. The system of policing generally was somewhat haphazard and all too often mismanaged. In some areas, and the counties of north Wales apart from Denbighshire were no exception, lack of foresight and concern for the level of rates, stifled any serious demand for the establishment of a really efficient police force.

When the report of the Select Committee was eventually published it listed eight points as to why a police system so successful in some areas had not been more widely adopted. They were also of the opinion that the 1839 Permissive Act had failed to provide a general and uniform constabulary force, so vital for the prevention of crime and the security of property. Where the Act had been adopted, they found the results extremely advantageous, and confirmation of this could not have come from a better source – the older criminals themselves, 'for they never mentioned the old police except with contempt and derision until, indeed, the establishment of the New Police, whereupon they spoke with affection for the old system'.[95] Certainly, one of the most significant factors to emerge from the report was, that in the opinion of the committee, central government should make a contribution towards an improved and extended system of policing, although it was made clear that in doing so there was to be no interference with local management, a point the magistrates in the counties of north Wales welcomed.

Following the findings of the Select Committee, Palmerston introduced a Bill in 1856 for the improvement of rural policing. It was for some a contentious issue, particularly for members representing boroughs, who believed that its implementation would allow the powers of the counties to supersede those of the boroughs. On the second reading of the Bill, Palmerston still insisted that the smaller boroughs should amalgamate with the counties – this did eventually happen, but not before another hundred years had elapsed. The Bill finally reached the statute book on 21 July 1856, thus bringing to the fore a notable experiment in reconciling the principle of central supervision with local management in a politically acceptable form.[96] In the history of the police it was a historic day, for so successful was the new pattern of administration contained in the County and Borough Police Act of 1856, that it was to survive in its original form for more than a century.

For the counties in north Wales it was the end of an era, the final breaking of a chain that had linked county policing to the parish constable system. The words uttered by Robert Peel in the House of Commons in February 1828 had at last been heeded. On that occasion, he addressed his remarks to those living in rural areas, saying, 'Why, I ask, should we entrust a grocer, or any other tradesman, however respectable, with the direction and management of a police force for 5,000 or 6,000 inhabitants? Why should such a person, unpaid and unrewarded, be taken from his usual avocations and called upon to perform the laborious duties of a night constable?'[97] The counties of north Wales, like so many rural areas throughout the country, had attempted to cling far too long to their old traditions and perhaps, the coming of improved communications had been the first intimation that counties, sooner or later, would have to adjust to new ideas and adopt arrangements more in keeping with a changing world.

In Denbighshire, the only county in north Wales to have adopted the legislation of 1839, the County and Borough Police Act was to have a very significant effect. When the justices met in quarter sessions at Ruthin in October 1856, the chairman informed them that the police force which they had divided into two districts now had to be consolidated and placed under the command of one chief constable. The two superintendents, formerly in charge of the Wrexham and Denbigh districts, were to be notified that on the appointment of a chief constable, their services would no longer be required, unless of course they obtained positions in the new constabulary.

Thus ended the many decades of arguments which had always followed any attempt to relive the counties of the old parish constable system. No words on the subject were more prophetic than those of Mr Rice, chairman of the Select Committee which laid the foundations of the 1856 Act. He stated that the time would shortly arrive when Parliament 'would reflect with surprise and astonishment that it had been seriously debated whether they should have throughout the country a uniform system of police, subject entirely to local management, or whether to continue the present isolated, disjointed and absurdly anomalous system, which was useless to the country at large'.[98]

---

[1] M. Arris, J. Latham, and J. Pott, *Crime and Punishment – A Welsh Perspective – Nineteenth Century Crime and Protest*, (Caernarfon, 1987), p.6.

[2] D. Gareth Evans, *A History of Wales 1815-1906*, (Cardiff, 1989), p.131.

[3] Merfyn Jones, 'Rural and industrial protest in north Wales', in T. Herbert and Gareth Elwyn Jones (eds.), *People and Protest: Wales 1815-1880*, (Cardiff, 1988), p.170.

[4] David J.V. Jones, 'Scotch Cattle and Chartism', in T. Herbert and Gareth Elwyn Jones (eds), *People and Protest: Wales 1815-1880*, (Cardiff, 1988), p.139.

[5] David J.V. Jones, *Crime in Nineteenth Century Wales*, (Cardiff, 1992), pp.125-6.

[6] See PP, 1837 xxxii Reports of the Inspectors of Prisons, North Wales, p.60. Also David J.V. Jones, op. cit., p.34. For a brief but nevertheless useful account of the workings of the Poor Law Act see J.D. Marshall, *The Old Poor Law 1795-1834*, 2nd. edition, (London, 1985).

[7] David J.V. Jones, op. cit., p.92.
[8] Ibid.
[9] Ibid., p.101. Also Gwyn A. Williams, *The Merthyr Rising*, (Cardiff, 1988), an excellent account of the events at Merthyr Tydfil in 1831.
[10] John Davies, *A History of Wales*, (London, 1993), p.375.
[11] Ibid.
[12] David Williams, *Keeping the Peace – The Police and Public Order*, (London, 1967), p.13.
[13] David J.V. Jones, op. cit., p.101. See also by the same author, *The Last Rising*, (Oxford, 1985).
[14] Ibid., p.205. See S. Palmer, *Police and Protest in England and Ireland, 1780-1850*, (Cambridge, 1988).
[15] The Rural Constabulary Act, 1839 (2 and 3 Vict., c.93).
[16] Clive Emsley, *Policing and its Context 1750-1870*, (London, 1983), pp.70-71.
[17] *CDH*, 24 August 1839.
[18] *NWC*, 14 April 1840.
[19] G. Lerry, 'The policemen of Denbighshire', *Transactions of the Denbighshire Historical Society*, 2 (1953), p.108.
[20] DQS Rolls, Easter, 1840. See also Returns of Police Establishments in each county or division of a county PP, vol.xxxii (1842).
[21] Ibid., those in attendance at the historic meeting of quarter sessions on 7 April 1840 included the following magistrates: John Heaton, Chairman; R. Middleton Biddulph Dungannon; R.H. Cunliffe; T.P. Jones-Parry R.N.; H.W. Meredith; F.I. Hughes; J. Ablett; B. Clough; R.M. Lloyd; Townsend-Mainwaring; T.G. Roberts; R. Miles Wynne; G. Naylor; E. Thelwall; F. Owen; J. Williams. Other Welsh counties that formed constabularies under the Act of 1839 were Montgomeryshire, 1840; Glamorgan, 1841; Carmarthenshire, 1843; Cardiganshire, 1844.
[22] G. Lerry, op. cit., p.108.
[23] Ibid., 109.
[24] Ibid.
[25] *CDH*, 19 December 1840.
[26] Ibid., 17 October 1840.
[27] T.A. Critchley, op. cit., p.89.
[28] HO, 65/4.
[29] *CDH*, 20 June 1840.
[30] Ibid., 3 October 1840.
[31] PP, 1877 vol. xv, Report of Select Committee on Police Superannuation Funds and Minutes of Evidence.
[32] T.A. Critchley, op. cit., p.145.
[33] DQS Rolls, (Michaelmas, 1840) Q S D/ S R/507.
[34] Ibid.
[35] Ibid.

[36] DQS Rolls, (Trinity 1841) D/QSD/SR/510.
[37] DQS Rolls, (Epiphany, 1840) QSD/SR/504.
[38] DQS Rolls, (Trinity, 1840) QSD/SR/506. See also *CDH*, 28 March 1846.
[39] DQS Rolls, (Epiphany, 1840) QSD/SR/504.
[40] DQS Rolls, (Epiphany, 1846) D/QSD/SR/529. Included in this bill, which in total came to £13.19s is the sum of £3.15s, being the cost of accommodation for the officer and his wife during their five-day stay in London.
[41] *CDH*, 25 June 1842.
[42] Ibid.
[43] Ibid., 12 October 1844.
[44] Ibid., 24 September 1844.
[45] DQS Rolls, (Michaelmas, 1845) QSD/SR/527.
[46] DQS Rolls, (Epiphany, 1846) QSD/SR/525.
[47] DQS Rolls, (Epiphany, 1846) DQSD/SR/528.
[48] DQS Rolls, (Epiphany, 1845) QSD/SR/525.
[49] See appendix, i for details of the cost and type of clothing and accoutrements ordered at this time.
[50] *CDH*, 12 October 1844.
[51] *NWC*, 13 December 1842.
[52] *CDH*, 2 March 1844.
[53] Ibid., 26 June 1844.
[54] G. Lerry, op. cit., p.110.
[55] Ibid., p.111. The magistrates, voting to abolish the force were: The Rev. E. Thelwell; Wilson Jones; W. Parry Yale; John Williams, M.D.; Rev. E. Evans; George Griffiths; Townshend Mainwaring, M.P.; T.P. Jones-Parry; J. Ll. Wynne; J. Price; Rev. J.F. Roberts; H. Ll. Williams, M.D.; B.W. Wynne. Those voting against the abolition of the force: Rev. R. Newsome; Joseph Ablett; John Heaton (Chairman); Geo. Naylor; F.J. Hughes, M.D.; Thomas Fitzhugh; W. Hanmer; Rev. T.G. Roberts; R.M. Biddulph (Lord Lieutenant); J.J. Ffoulks; Thomas Downward and J.W. Watling.
[56] DQS Rolls, (Trinity, 1844) QSD/SR/522.
[57] DQS Rolls, (Epiphany, 1848) QSD/SR/536.
[58] *Liverpool Mercury*, 17 July 1840.
[59] DQS Rolls, (Michaelmas, 1846) D/QSD/SR/531.
[60] DQS Rolls, (Michaelmas, 1847) D/QSD/SR/535.
[61] *CDH*, 5 May 1849.
[62] Ibid.
[63] Ibid., 5 January, 1850.
[64] DQS Rolls, (Epiphany, 1850) QDS/SR/545.
[65] Ibid., Magistrates calling for the dismissal of the chief constable were: John Williams; Thomas Hughes; Henry Sandbach; John Maddocks and B.

Wynne – in so doing they were adhering to the procedure as laid down in the Acts 2 and 3 Vict, C 93 and 4 Vict C 88.

[66] *CDH*, 19 October 1850.
[67] G. Lerry, op. cit., p.115.
[68] *CDH*, 25 January 1851.
[69] DQS Rolls, (Epiphany, 1851) QSD/SR/549.
[70] *CDH*, 4 January 1851.
[71] Ibid., 22 February 1851.
[72] Ibid., 4 January 1851.
[73] Ibid., 29 March 1851.
[74] G. Lerry, op. cit., p.115.
[75] *CDH*, 5 April 1851.
[76] DQS Rolls, (Epiphany, 1852) QSD/SR/552.
[77] DQS Rolls (Trinity, 1852) QSD/SR/553.
[78] DQS Rolls (Trinity, 1851) QSD/SR/550.
[79] DQS Rolls, (Epiphany, 1853) QSD/SR/555.
[80] DQS Rolls, (Michaelmas, 1848) QSD/SR/539.
[81] DQS Rolls, (Trinity, 1852) QSD/SR/553.
[82] DQS Rolls, (Michaelmas, 1853) QSD/SR/558.
[83] DQS Rolls, (Trinity, 1852) QSD/SR/553.
[84] Ibid.
[85] *CDH*, 3 July 1852.
[86] G. Lerry, op. cit., p.116.
[87] DQS Rolls, (Epiphany, 1854) QDS/SR/559. Of the 295 prisoners, 95 males and 36 females could neither read nor write. The survey also indicated that of the total number, 195 came from Wales, 67 from England, 26 from Ireland, 3 from Scotland and 4 were from abroad.
[88] DQS Rolls, (Epiphany, 1854) QSD/SR.561.
[89] DQS Rolls, (Trinity, 1854) QSD/SR.561.
[90] DQS Rolls, (Epiphany 1854) QSD/SR/560.
[91] G. Lerry, op. cit., p.116.
[92] *CDH*, 30 October 1852.
[93] F.W. Maitland, *Justice and Police*, (London, 1885), p.106.
[94] PP, 1852-3 vol. xxxvi Report of Select Committee on Police.
[95] P. Collins, *Dickens and Crime*, (London, 1962), pp.200-1.
[96] T.A. Critchley, op. cit., p.116.
[97] Ibid., p.48, in which he cites Hansard's Parliamentary Debates, N.S., vol. xviii, 28 February 1828, cols 784-816.
[98] Hansard's Parliamentary Debates, 3rd Ser., vol. cxl (10 March 1856) col.2, 181.

Chapter III

# The County Police, 1856-75

The passing of the County and Borough Police Act of 1856 created a pattern of police administration that was to continue for more than a century.[1] In Wales, the Act was a particularly important piece of legislation, especially in the north, where the counties of Caernarfonshire, Merioneth, Anglesey and Flintshire had all declined to adopt the earlier County Police Act of 1839 which permitted authorities, if they so desired, to establish a constabulary force where none had previously existed.[2] Under the new Act, magistrates were not only compelled to establish a constabulary, but also had to adhere strictly to the specific rules and regulations embodied in the legislation.[3] In addition, and as a further move to introduce a more professional approach to policing generally, the government announced that it was to appoint two Inspectors of Constabulary who would be invested with the power to inspect every force on an annual basis.[4]

Two clauses in the new legislation were of specific significance. The first required the authorities in every county to be fully responsible for the building and maintenance of an adequate number of police stations and cells in which to accommodate those arrested. Certainly, the lack of suitable places in which to secure those apprehended had imposed a serious restriction on the efficiency of the police in the past.[5] Secondly, under the new Act the government decreed that in future it would contribute out of central funds to each local authority, a quarter of their expenditure on police pay and clothing.[6] Furthermore, such payment, which was a completely new departure in the sphere of police finance, could only be paid if the forces inspected by the new inspectorate were certified as being efficient. Interestingly, boroughs with a population of less than 5,000 inhabitants were excluded from the structure of annual inspection and grant-aid because it was hoped that sooner, rather than later, the small borough would eventually amalgamate with the respective county forces. In northern Wales, however, the boroughs of Denbigh, Beaumaris, Flint and Pwllheli were to retain their independence until 1858, 1861, 1864 and 1879 respectively.[7] As a further measure, which it was hoped would lead to a more centralised system of policing it became compulsory for chief constables to submit each year to the Home Office not only the report of the inspectorate but also an annual return of the crimes committed within each county. Such figures had been requested earlier under the Municipal Corporations Act of 1835, but it was only after 1856 that annual crime rates were forwarded to the Home Office on a regular basis.[8]

(Plate 1)
William Hughes,
Constable of Pwllheli, 1869-79

Immediately on receipt of a letter from the Home Secretary which clearly outlined the County and Borough Police Act of 1856, magistrates in all the northern Wales counties met in quarter sessions to deliberate its implications. Many magistrates, although fully aware that they had little alternative but to accept the Act, nevertheless gave it a guarded reception, still fearing a loss of personal status and power in their relationship with the police. Indeed, nowhere was suspicion of the government's intentions more deeply rooted than in Merioneth, where several of the magistrates considered the proposals completely preposterous. In many ways their fears mirrored what magistrates in other Welsh counties felt, namely that government interference in local affairs would only lead in the years ahead to even more intervention. Many magistrates were of the opinion that there was no convincing argument for abandoning the traditional institution of the parish constable because it was cheap, and as far as they were concerned completely satisfactory.[9] Similar concern was also being voiced by magistrates in England, especially amongst those representing the boroughs. Such was their opposition to the Bill that on the 20 February 1856 a number of mayors assembled in a hotel in London which was close to the Old Palace Yard.[10] Later their numbers were swelled when several MPs and other influential people joined them bringing the total number of those present to more than a hundred.[11] Chairing the meeting the Lord Mayor of York attacked the Bill calling it 'dangerous and unconstitutional'.[12] Later, at a meeting with Sir George Grey, the magistrates, again led by the mayor called for the Bill to be withdrawn, claiming it to be 'an inroad on the principles of self government, serious in itself, and still more serious as a platform for further agression'.[13] Even in the House of Commons there were a number of members who believed passionately that the passing of the Bill would soon lead to the country being overrun by 20,000 armed policemen many of whom might be 'Irishmen or foreigners'.[14] They also held the view that if the Bill was passed it would make the Home Secretary a second Fouché with spies all over the kingdom.[15]

Yet, despite such outcries the Home Secretary was heartened by the growing support for his measures from those who advocated the importance of a constabulary. A writer in one newspaper commenting on the attitude of the magistrates in Merioneth who opposed the Bill, went on to accuse them of being painfully slow, saying 'it is useless and weak on the part of these gentlemen who are opposed to the establishment of a police force, to simply refer to the calendars as indicative of the paucity of crime. It is not likely that they will record a crime of which they have taken no cognizance'. In order to illustrate further what he considered to be the true position, the writer went on to relate 'that crime in Merioneth was on the increase and in the neighbourhood of Corris and Minffordd [near Tal-y-llyn] in particular, great numbers of sheep were being driven off the farms and sold in the different markets in the south'.[16] Support for the Home Secretary also came from Lord Newborough of Caernarfonshire, who on addressing the quarter sessions stated that it was essential to establish a constabulary, as failure to do so would see counties like Caernarfonshire 'infested by rogues and vagabonds'.[17] As in Caernarfonshire, magistrates in Anglesey were equally supportive of the Bill although they wished to emphasise at the outset that in creating a constabulary they 'were determined that it should be established at the smallest cost possible'.[18]

However, despite the mixed reception for the Bill, authorities in Wales were generally less hostile to change than many of their counterparts in England. Denbighshire had established a constabulary in 1840 as had Montgomeryshire which was followed a year later by the establishment of the Glamorgan force. In 1843 and 1844 respectively, the magistrates in the counties of Carmarthen and Cardigan also agreed to the establishment of a paid constabulary. The number of officers enrolled into the various forces varied but the figure generally was that of between eighteen and fifty-seven men each.[19] The alacrity with which the authorities established their forces was due in no small measure to their general fear of disorder and sedition, to an unacceptable level of crime, and by what was perceived as a serious threat to law and order by the influx of Irish immigrants and vagrants.[20] Even in the counties that saw little, if any, compelling reason to form a police force, the authorities attempted some improvement in their policing arrangements by introducing a system of appointing paid superintending police officers to oversee the work of the parish constables. Such an arrangement was undertaken by the magistrates in Anglesey, Caernarfonshire, Flintshire, Radnorshire, Pembrokeshire and Monmouthshire. It was looked upon as a bold initiative and one David Jones claims it was an experiment that in time became much praised.[21]

Therefore, in accepting so many changes it became quite clear that long before the compulsory County and Borough Police Act of 1856, the authorities in some parts of Wales had long prepared the basis for the eventual introduction of a professional policing system. This fact probably explains why Welsh MPs remained generally muted in their opposition to the Act when it finally came to be passed. Many English members were also at this time becoming much more amenable and generally accepted that change was inevitable in view of the events both at home and abroad which in turn, were beginning to create for the authorities a number of difficulties. The Crimean War, for example, had seen a number of military garrisons at home depleted of troops and as a consequence the army was no longer in a position to assist local government in times of civil unrest. A further problem for the authorities, again as a direct result of the war and its ending in 1856, was the return on being demobilised of thousands of 'rude and licentious soldiery'.[22] In addition and as if to add to the government's ever growing problems, the virtual end of transportation in 1853, meant that the public had become extremely alarmed by the prospect of having to accept into their midst those criminals who previously could have been conveniently shipped off to the antipodes, but now, having served a period in prison, could be released into society on a 'ticket of leave'.[23] Bearing all these factors in mind, it therefore comes as no surprise that when the Bill was presented to

Parliament, the scale of support which it received from across the political spectrum clearly illustrated that the more informed sections of society 'were now fully supportive of the idea of uniformed bureaucratic police organisations based on the traditional local government units of county and borough'.[24] Finally, with the passing of the Act in 1856, which incidentally came more than a century after Henry Fielding had taken up his appointment in Bow Street, the whole of England and Wales had at last agreed to the establishment of a paid police force.[25]

It was perhaps, only natural that the impending formation of a police force in each of the counties of north Wales would create concern in some quarters as to the effect such an innovation would eventually have on the county rates. However, once the Secretary of State had agreed in principle to the various proposals submitted by the clerks of the peace on behalf of the magistrates sitting in quarter sessions, it then became necessary for each county to advertise for suitable persons to command the new forces. This was to lead, over a period of some weeks, to a number of notices appearing in the press inviting those with the appropriate qualifications, and background, to apply to the county of their choice for the position of chief constable.[26] Although little is known about the personal background of most candidates, it comes as no surprise that with the ending of the Crimean War in 1856 many of those applying were former army officers who possibly viewed the prospect of becoming a chief constable as opening up a totally new career. It was also obvious that such a position would draw applications from among those who viewed the post as affording the opportunity of mixing socially with the gentry, since so many of the latter also sat as magistrates. In many quarters, army officers were looked upon favourably, as they were considered already trained for the job and accustomed to commanding men, for the new constabularies were often seen more as army battalions. This view probably stemmed from the fact that in the first half of the nineteenth century soldiers had often been called upon to maintain law and order, and therefore, there was little in the minds of many to distinguish between a civil force and a military one. In some instances, however, the most unlikely candidates sought the position of chief constable, as in Caernarfonshire, when a farmer in support of his application declared 'I do not pretend to any knowledge of the duties, but trust by zealous attention to surmount all difficulties that may arise from inexperience'.[27]

From the outset, it became clear that the new police

authorities, (watch committees in the towns, and justices in the counties), were seeking different kinds of men to command their respective forces. Certainly, it was only the large and prosperous cities that could afford the kind of salaries that would attract the most suitable candidates. In Liverpool, for example, the largest force outside London, with an establishment of 956 officers the salary offered to the successful candidate was £650 per annum, while at Manchester with a complement of 554 the salary was £100 per annum less.[28] In the counties the situation was completely different, and under Lord Normanby's rules the permissible salary allowed to the chief constables was within the range of £250 to £400 per annum. Some counties like Lancashire and Gloucestershire paid the maximum salary, whereas in north Wales, magistrates opted for the minimum of £250 per annum, apart from Flintshire which paid £275.[29] It was also noticeable that in the early appointments the authorities, particularly in the boroughs, tended to favour as their chief police officers men with former police experience, and it was often the practice to appoint those who had previously served with the Metropolitan Police. Such appointments brought with them the experience and traditions of the Metropolitan force, which undoubtedly helped set and develop common standards everywhere.[30] The county authorities, on the other hand, adopted a different policy. As far as the justices were concerned, former police experience counted for little. They were much more concerned with social acceptability, and where possible, preferred to appoint men with sound local connections, especially if this could be coupled with a military background. This was a policy that was to continue in some county constabularies until the outbreak of the Second World War.[31]

Yet, even before the first chief constable in north Wales was appointed under the Act of 1856, controversy raged in two counties, Caernarfonshire and Merioneth, as to the necessity for the successful applicant to be fluent in Welsh. Several of the magistrates were of the firm belief that such a qualification was completely unnecessary. In Merioneth, where feelings on the subject had been running high, a magistrate stated that he failed entirely to see the relevance of Welsh as a qualification and declared 'it was no more necessary for a chief constable to speak Welsh in this country than a knowledge of the Indian language was to an officer in the civil service in that country'.[32] Feelings on the subject of the Welsh language were equally strong in Caernarfonshire. Magistrates there had decided that a knowledge of the Welsh language was not indispensable.[33] This view was to create much criticism throughout the county. In the correspondence column of a newspaper, one signing himself 'A Caernarfonshire Ratepayer' expressed concern 'that in a county so Welsh in character the magistrates had excluded from the short list of seven every Welshman'.[34] What was interesting, however, in the short list drawn up by the magistrates was that all the candidates were experienced police officers.[35] Later and after mounting pressure to change their policy, the magistrates decided by twenty-eight votes to six to declare that a knowledge of the Welsh language was indispensable and this ultimately led to a completely new short list being compiled.[36]

The first of the chief constables to be appointed in north Wales was Mr Peter Browne, who assumed command of the Flintshire constabulary on 15 January 1857.[37] Little is known of his early background; a newspaper reporting the appointment stated that 'he was born and bred among the hills of Wales, was Welsh speaking and conversant with the manners and customs of the Welsh'.[38] In Caernarfonshire, magistrates sitting in quarter sessions on 7 April 1857 chose as their chief constable Thomas Parr Williams Ellis, of Glasfryn, a member of one of the oldest Caernarfonshire county families, who for a time had also served as a lieutenant in the Merioneth militia.[39] As far as the magistrates were concerned he was a most suitable choice. He was a local man, from a good family, and he could speak Welsh. In addition, although possessing very little police experience it was to his credit that in order to familiarise himself with certain aspects of police work he had spent some time at the office of the chief constable of Cambridgeshire.[40] On 3 March 1857 Anglesey magistrates chose as their chief constable Captain David White Griffiths, who, at the time of his appointment was living in Guernsey. He too, came from an old Caernarfonshire family and prior to assuming command held a commission as captain in the East Kent militia, and for a time served with the regiment on garrison duty at Malta during the Crimean War.[41] In Merioneth, Hywel Hedd Lloyd Clough, of Bala, was elected chief constable on 21 January 1857. Although little is known about his life, he was, when appointed, thirty-four years of age and a nephew of Mr R.W. Price of Rhiwlas, a member of an old county family. He had, it seems, resided in the county for some seventeen years during which time he had served with the local militia.[42]

It was, however, the forthcoming appointment of the chief constable of Denbighshire that caused the greatest interest and upon which much attention was focussed. For some months prior to the actual appointment, rumour had been freely circulating in the county that the favourite for the position was the former head of the old force, Mr John Denman. The likelihood of such an appointment being made was enough to make one writer from Ruthin declare: 'I cannot believe it possible a majority of the county magistrates numbering such names as are seen in the roll for Denbighshire will outrage public propriety by countenancing the selection of a man in every way so unsuitable for the head of the police service in so populous and spirited a county as this'.[43] Further criticism came from Llanrwst when a correspondent there declared, it would be 'a heavy blow if the leading houses forced Mr Denman again upon us'.[44] Yet, such scathing comments did little to diminish the spirits of those who openly supported the former chief constable. One such supporter states, 'that for ten years he had discharged his duties of office in a most satisfactory and exemplary manner' and went on to add 'whenever there was a case of any importance, even if on the limits, or at the most distant part of the county, there was Mr Denman active and ready'.[45] That the former chief constable also had the support of the magistracy, was seen when on the 8 January 1857, more than half of the magistrates sitting at the quarter sessions in Ruthin voted for his appointment, subject to the usual approval by the Home Secretary.[46] However, on being informed of the appointment and after consulting with law officers of the Crown, the Home Secretary had to refuse the nomination on the grounds that under the Act of 1856 Mr Denman's age precluded him from taking office and therefore a new election had to take place. Such was the support and determination of those supporting the former chief constable, that a petition which contained several signatures from ratepayers in Ruthin and Denbigh was submitted to the Home Secretary asking that the matter be reconsidered. That their plea did not fall on deaf ears was seen in the communication from Sir George Grey, which stated that he was willing in the circumstances to modify the rules. In the subsequent election which was held on 17 February 1857, Mr Denman, was once again unanimously elected to be the Chief Constable of Denbighshire.[47] His appointment, which was later confirmed by the Home Secretary, brought to an end what had been a long and contentious issue.

The immediate problem facing the newly appointed chief constables in north Wales was that of recruiting suitable men to be constables. Urgent consideration had also to be given to where such constables, when appointed, were to be positioned and what numbers were required if law and order was to be efficiently maintained. It was certainly no easy task, but any county that so desired, could call upon the services of one of the newly appointed Inspectors of Constabulary to advise and assist them when deciding on the type of force they required.[48] The responsibility for the inspection of forces in the Midlands and north Wales fell to Major-General Cartwright, and one of the first counties to seek his advice was Merioneth.[49] There, the magistrates had decided that ten police officers would be a sufficient number to police the county. However, at the first meeting between Major-General Cartwright and the magistrates, which was held at the adjourned quarter sessions in Bala in March 1857, it was generally agreed that the county merited more than the number originally suggested and that nineteen officers would be a more appropriate figure if Merioneth was to be effectively policed.[50] Furthermore, it was agreed that when officers were eventually appointed, they should be designated to the following stations – Dolgellau was to have two sergeants, one to act as clerk to the chief constable, and one constable; Bala was assigned an inspector and one constable; Corwen, one sergeant and one constable; Ffestiniog, one sergeant and one constable, while the stations at Llandrillo, Penrhyndeudraeth, Trawsfynydd, Harlech, Barmouth, Tywyn, Aberdyfi, Abergynolwyn and Dinas Mawddwy were each to be given one constable.

Throughout the early months of 1857 similar meetings to those held in Merioneth took place in all the other counties in north Wales. These meetings with the Inspectorate, in which ideas were frequently exchanged, led to every county, by June, reaching an agreement on the number of officers each authority required, if law and order was to be adequately maintained.

**Number of Police Officers in North Wales, 1857[51]**

|  | CC. | Supt. | Insp. | Sgts. | Cons. | Total |
| --- | --- | --- | --- | --- | --- | --- |
| Anglesey | 1 | – | 2 | 4 | 9 | 16 |
| Caernarfonshire | 1 | – | 4 | 4 | 28 | 37 |
| Denbighshire | 1 | 2 | 4 | 4 | 35 | 46 |
| Flintshire | 1 | 2 | – | 3 | 20 | 26 |
| Merioneth | 1 | – | 1 | 4 | 13 | 19 |

With the required strength of each force now finalised, magistrates were in a position to place suitable advertisements in the press inviting applications from those with the appropriate qualifications to apply for the posts of police constables,[52] one of the requirements being an ability to read and write and speak English and Welsh.[53]

The scale of pay in 1857 for those successful in their application to join one of the county forces in north Wales was as follows:

**Pay Scales for Police Officers in North Wales, 1857** [54]

|  | CC. | Supt. | Insp. | Sgts. | Cons. |
|---|---|---|---|---|---|
| Anglesey | £250 p.a. | – | £65 p.a. | 19s p.w. | 15s p.w. |
| Caernarfonshire | £250 p.a. | – | £65 p.a. | 23s p.w. | 16-19s p.w. |
| Denbighshire | £250 p.a. | £100 p.a. | £75 p.a. | 23s p.w. | 16-19s p.w. |
| Flintshire | £250 p.a. | £75 p.a. | – | 21s p.w. | 18s p.w. |
| Merioneth | £250 p.a. | – | £70 p.a. | 21s p.w. | 16-18s p.w. |

The variation in the rates of pay for constables, was due to the fact that the rank was divided into three classes, with officers being able to move from one class to another on promotion, with a subsequent increase in pay within the range laid down. In the early years, this type of classification created much bitterness, for far too often, little attention was given to such details as a man's length of service, or indeed his ability to do the job. Obviously, many officers grew increasingly despondent with a system they viewed as unjust and consequently left the service. It is at this point that the value of the Inspectorate was seen, for Major-General Cartwright constantly urged the magistrates throughout north Wales, that any advancement within the rank of constable should in the future depend on efficiency rather than on a vacancy occurring within the force. His sound advice eventually led to a much fairer system, with the magistrates, certainly in Caernarfonshire in 1861, agreeing that in future the chief constable should be allowed at his own discretion 'to place men in the grade of constable commensurate with their efficiency'.[55]

It is difficult to ascertain with any degree of certainty the background of those recruited by the police in north Wales in 1857. Little is known, for example, about their marital status, their standard of education, former employment, or age on joining.[56] Though on the question of age, there is evidence to suggest that the most common experience over the country as a whole, was for men to join between the ages of twenty and twenty-five, with those joining the Borough forces being slightly older.[57] It has also been claimed from contemporary evidence that many of those who were recruited into the police in the 1850s and 1860s, actually came from agricultural backgrounds and this observation was probably true.[58] As Carolyn Steedman stated 'the experience of seeing young men go off to try to be a policeman was evidently a common sight in some country areas'.[59] Certainly, of the eight men recruited into the Caernarfonshire constabulary at the Town Hall, Pwllheli, on the 3 June 1857, seven would have conformed to this latter observation.[60] However, it is likely that many more men from the agricultural areas applied to become policemen than were actually accepted. It has always to be recognised that acceptance into the police at this time was very much determined by the strictness with which the Home Office ruling on literacy being an essential requirement was applied by magistrates.[61] There is no evidence to suggest that magistrates in north Wales did other than conform to the Home Office guidelines.

Once enrolled, the newly recruited police officers found themselves embarking on a way of life that was not only different, but also extremely hard. Subjected to a severe disciplinary code of practice that county chief constables constantly enforced, officers were either fined, reduced in rank or class or even dismissed for the most trifling offences.[62] There was no right of appeal at this time and any officer who had the courage to speak out on an issue that he considered unfair, could soon find himself facing instant dismissal, much to the disgust of his fellow-officers.[63] Every officer was expected to work at least ten hours a day, seven days a week, for a weekly wage that was barely above subsistence level, especially if he was married. At this time there was no Police Federation in existence to protect and promote the interests of policemen. In fact, apart from Lord Normanby's rules and regulations on the respective rates of pay in the counties and the boroughs, the general conditions of service under which officers worked was ultimately left to the discretion of the local authority. During these early years all patrolling was done on foot and constables would frequently be expected to walk upwards of fifteen to twenty miles in a single day, in all weathers, upon roads that were so rough and uneven they resembled little more than cart tracks. That officers did traverse such distances when duty called, was seen when a constable stationed in Aberdyfi walked to Machynlleth in the neighbouring county of Montgomeryshire, a distance of ten miles, to detain and arrest a married woman who had eloped with a lodger, taking with her the property of her husband.[64] With officers expected to walk such distances in the course of their daily duties, it was understandable that as early as 1857, the chief constable of Merioneth should issue an order informing his men, that in future they would receive 2s a month for the purchase of their own footwear whenever necessary.[65]

Despite the apparent hardships experienced by the early constables, service with the police had certain advantages. Those appointed to the office of constable, for instance, must have felt they had finally achieved some measure of security, as well as respectability. There was also the opportunity for those officers with ambition and ability, to gain, given time, even further advancement within the service. In addition, officers could look forward to a small pension, a privilege shared by few other workers. Constables paid into a superannuation fund and could expect to receive a pension after serving fifteen years or more in the county force.[66] No superannuation would be paid to a police officer who was under sixty years of age, unless he was leaving the force on medical grounds. This system however, had certain drawbacks which over the years created much bitterness, not only among officers in north Wales but throughout the police service. The mere fact that a man had to make compulsory payments to a superannuation fund did not guarantee the receipt of a pension or a gratuity on leaving the force, even though he may have completed many years in the service.[67] In effect, the money was payable only on the recommendation of the chief constable and could be withheld if he or the magistrates thought fit. Indeed in Denbighshire, when Sergeant David Davies retired in 1870 after twenty-five years and three months service, several magistrates questioned the amount of pension he should receive as he was the owner of some private property. This led to one magistrate, a Mr Chambers, to declare, that an officer's private affairs should in no way prejudice the amount of pension payable to him. After much discussion, it was agreed that Sergeant Davies should be awarded a pension of £42 per annum which in effect amounted to two thirds of his pay.[68] Yet, despite, at times, the attempts to deny police officers certain rights, the police service for many, seemed an attractive proposition. This fact is borne out by the figures for recruitment in the early 1850s. In 1851 the number of officers serving in the various counties in England and Wales was 3,005. By September 1857, this figure, helped no doubt with the passing of the Act of 1856, had risen to 7,200.[69]

Expenditure on the police was always high on the agenda whenever magistrates in north Wales met in quarter sessions. The provision of clothing for the new recruits, for example, meant that tenders had to be placed in a number of newspapers calling upon clothiers and others to supply suitable uniforms and accoutrements for the newly established forces. A typical notice was that inserted by the magistrates in Flintshire which

PC 65 Evans (Caernarfonshire Constabulary) at Capel Curig 1950.

(Left) Chief Constable Lt. Col. Sir William Jones Williams, KCVO, OBE, QPM, BSc, LlB (left) on his retirement 30 September, 1970 at Caernarfon, with successor, Deputy Chief Constable Philip Myers (later Sir Philip Myers) with Police Authority Chairman Armon Ellis and Haydn Rees (Clerk to the Police Authority).

Flintshire Constabulary officers who attended Coronation of HM The Queen in 1953.

*Officers and men of the Merioneth Constabulary led by Chief Constable Richard Jones; and his son, Deputy Chief Constable Howell Odwyn Jones pose before amalgamation with Anglesey and Caernarfonshire Constabularies on 1 October, 1950.*
*(Courtesy of Gwynedd Archives Service)*

*Denbigh Police Ball mid-1950s at Denbigh Hospital.*

*The Gwynedd Constabulary Caernarfon Division soccer team at Llandudno circa 1955.*

*Mr Tarry, Her Majesty's Inspector of Constabularies on government inspection of Denbighshire Constabulary at Wrexham circa 1950s, accompanied by Supt. Owen Jones, DCC speaking to PC 93 Roberts (Glynceiriog).*

*Sgt. 69 Nevil J. V. Davies (Denbighshire Constabulary) directing traffic in Market Street, Abergele, 1955.*

*Taking a break whilst searching for a Missing Person in Ruabon area circa 1961. L-R. – PC 110 Tom Hughes, PC 78 Griff Thomas, PC 165 Ivor Jones and Sgt. 69 Nevil John Volander Davies (Denbighshire Constabulary).*

*Wrexham Drama Group (Denbighshire Constabulary) circa 1957.
Back row: Gwyn Trivett, Lloyd Hughes, Maurice J. Jones
and Cyril Edwards.*

*Parade along High Street, Wrexham, circa 1950s.*

*Wrexham (Denbighshire Constabulary) Drama Group at Church Hall, Wrexham, 1956.*

*Detectives (left to right) Gwyn Trivett, Charles E. Matthews and Glyn Hughes (Denbighshire Constabulary), Wrexham, 1950s.*

*Sgt. Gwyn Trivett (Denbighshire Constabulary) at scene of fire in Ivy Street, Colwyn Bay, circa 1962.*

*PC 41 Hugh Richard Pritchard (Gwynedd Constabulary)
at Eisteddfod Môn, Bodedern, 1960.*

*Motorcyclist PC 54 Dennis Davies (Denbighshire Constabulary) on
duty in High Street, Wrexham, escorting Armistice Parade, 1964.*

*Inspector Nevil John Volander Davies and PC 87 William Fowles, Wrexham, circa 1963 (Denbighshire Constabulary).*

*L-R. – Det. Insp. Emyr Jones, D/Ch Supt. John Hughes (last day of service) and Det. Supt. Reg Davies (Scotland Yard) in Holyhead, March 1969, during the Valley Murder enquiry.*

*Sgt. Gwyn Trivett (Denbighshire Constabulary) with Special Constable in Station Road, Colwyn Bay, circa 1965.*

*Denbighshire Constabulary Cricket XI circa 1960.*

*HMI Inspector 1960s at Flint Police Station. Chief Constable Atkins and DCC Ben Williams.*

*Staff at Denbighshire Constabulary Headquarters,
Ruthin 1966
(Chief Constable Walter Stansfield seated front centre).*

*Officers of the Gwynedd Constabulary escort a vehicle through protestors
at Tryweryn.*

*HMI Inspector 1960s at Flint Police Station. Chief Constable Atkins and DCC Ben Williams.*

*Traffic Dept. Flintshire Constabulary parade for HMI inspection.*

PC 148 Meirion Owen cycles on Llandudno Pier, 1964.

The Duke of Edinburgh speaks to Ch. Supt. H. Stanley Edwards and Supt. Nevil J. V. Davies, circa 1973.

PC Ken Williams (Gwynedd Constabulary/North Wales Police) at Penrhos Nature Reserve, Anglesey, mid 1970s.

*L-R. – Ch/Insp. Bill Griffiths, Det. Sgt. 518 Charles E. Matthews, Arthur Rowlands, G.C. and Ch/Insp. Hugh Davies at Wrexham Racecourse Ground early 1970s.*

*Senior Officers at Glan-y-Don, Colwyn Bay, circa 1974. L-R. – Nevil J. V. Davies, Maurice J. Jones, William Thomas, W. R. T. Griffiths, Margaret Whitehead, H. Stanley Edwards, Islwyn Jones.*

*Foreign visitors with Gwynedd Constabulary (five Counties) tent at Llangollen International Eisteddfod circa 1970. Supt. N. J. V. Davies (far left).*

*Rt. Hon. Robert Carr, MP (Secretary of State for the Home Office) with Chief Constable Philip A. Myers, QPM (later Sir Philip Myers), opening the new Police Headquarters at Glan-y-don, Colwyn Bay, on 9 October, 1973.*

*Det. Ch. Supt. R. Eric Evans (right) leads CID contingent on the occasion of North Wales Police being bestowed the Freedom of the Borough of Wrexham in 1978.*

*Staff Divisional Office, Llandudno, early 1970s.
L-R. – PC John Poyser, PC Hefin Jones, Ch. Insp. Northcott, Ch. Supt. H. Stanley Edwards, PC Alun Jones, Sgt. 435 R. J. Griffith, PC Ken Davies.*

*PC 276 Bob Jones and WPC 1150 Phyllis Jones (now Longson), Operations Room, Colwyn Bay circa 1977.*

*WPC 1150 Phyllis Jones (now Longson) speaks to Sgt. John Phillips at Conwy Carnival, circa Summer 1978.*

called for the following clothing to be provided. Each of the two superintendents were to be issued with a frockcoat of superior cloth with braid, one pair of trousers, again of superior cloth, and one belt. The three sergeants and twenty constables were each to be provided with one greatcoat with cape, two frockcoats with collar badges of white metal bearing the 'Prince of Wales' Feathers' and the words 'Flintshire Constabulary', two pairs of trousers, one hat, and one stock. The sergeants' frockcoats were to have chevrons placed on the right sleeve.[70] Meanwhile, Anglesey, in addition to clothing, the chief constable was authorised to obtain for his force, sixteen pairs of handcuffs, sixteen pairs of single handcuffs, sixteen staffs and sixteen cutlasses. As for the chief constable, he was authorised to wear any uniform he thought fit, complete with the addition of a sword.[71] In Denbighshire, however, although magistrates provided their officers with uniforms, it was felt that the two superintendents should purchase their own, and awarded them £7 each for this purpose.[72] That the expenditure on clothing was increasing was seen in Caernarfonshire, when in the year ending September 1860, the cost of providing uniforms and accoutrements amounted to £206.2s.[73]

A matter which was to prove of even greater concern for magistrates in the early years, was the expenditure incurred in providing adequate police stations and lock-ups throughout the counties of north Wales. Nevertheless, an example of determination, despite the cost, to provide such police stations and lock-ups as quickly as possible was seen in Merioneth, where the magistrates sitting in quarter sessions agreed to the immediate purchase of two sites at Penrhyndeudraeth and Barmouth.[74] It was agreed that the eventual cost of building a police station and lock-up at Penrhyndeudraeth should not exceed £400.[75] At nearby Dolgellau, a site was purchased for £500 with an additional sum of £645 being authorised for the eventual erection of a police station.[76] That such acquisitions were necessary, and that the shortage of suitable lock-ups was creating concern, was later clearly demonstrated, in a plea from the ratepayers in Aberdyfi when they wrote of their dissatisfaction with the existing police arrangements for holding those they arrested. It was as a direct result of this plea that a suitable site was eventually purchased from a Mr Hughes of Gogarth for the sum of £80.[77] Magistrates in Anglesey at this time also experienced an alarming rise in police expenditure although they realised that if the police were to retain their efficiency such expense was inevitable.[78] Alterations to the police station at Holyhead in 1859 amounted to £55, with an additional £84 being spent some three years later when extra cells were attached to the original building. Sites were also purchased and lock-ups built at Llanfechell, Malltraeth and Pentraeth. Later in 1864, the Venerable Archdeacon Jones received £180 for premises he owned at Bodedern although another three years elapsed before the building was finally converted into a police station at a further cost of £90.[79] Similarly, in 1866 a new police station was erected at Aberffraw for £287.[80] At Menai Bridge police station, which incidentally had been connected with a gas supply in 1865, the cost of an additional room for the use of the visiting magistrates amounted to £242.10s.[81] Even more costly, was the building of a police station at Llannerch-y-medd which amounted to £787.[82] Even this large sum was increased when substantial alterations and additions to the county gaol at Beaumaris in 1867 came to £1,895, a figure that within a year had risen to £2,404.[83]

The provision of additional police stations and lock-ups was not an issue confined solely to magistrates in Merioneth and Anglesey. In Flintshire, Mr Browne, the chief constable, was constantly urging magistrates sitting in quarter sessions, to improve the standard of police buildings throughout the county. One of his main concerns, particularly in the early years, centred on the condition of the police stations at Holywell, Rhyl, Hawarden and Hanmer, which he considered too small and needing to be enlarged at some considerable expense if they were to become functional.[84] On the question of expenditure, a problem surfaced in 1865 when a letter from Mr Ellis Byton, Town Clerk of Flint, claimed that the forthcoming amalgamation of the Borough, with that of the county in no way obliged the ratepayers in Flint to pay the same contribution towards the building and repair of police stations and lock-ups as those paying rates in the county.[85] However, after months of negotiations, and even an appeal to the Home Secretary, the matter was finally resolved when the authorities in the Borough decided against their original objection, much to the relief of the county magistrates, no doubt.[86]

In Denbighshire, magistrates faced a different problem regarding expenditure. Unlike the other authorities in north Wales they already possessed a number of police stations and lock-ups as a direct result of the earlier establishment of the Denbighshire Constabulary in 1840. Therefore, much of their early expenditure was incurred, not as a result of building new police stations but in renovating many of the old, for example at Ruthin, Llanrwst, Denbigh, Mochdre, Llangollen and

Llansantffraid.[87] However in 1858, as a result of its damp condition a new police station and lock-up was proposed for Cerrigydrudion at an estimated cost of £500.[88] How really secure it was became questionable in 1867, when a prisoner escaped from one of the cells due to a faulty lock. On being asked to comment on such a lapse of security, the chief constable stated he had no idea why it had happened, 'but he would never enter a lock-up again without first examining all the locks'.[89]

Like their counterparts in other counties of north Wales, magistrates in Caernarfonshire also found themselves embarking on what, at times, was to become an extensive building programme. The lock-up at Glan Conwy, for instance, which had been described as unfit for man or beast was to be demolished and completely rebuilt.[90] A similar call, this time to demolish the gaol at Caernarfon was made by Dr Watkin Roberts, who claimed the building had been condemned even before the cholera outbreaks in 1832 and 1833, and there had been rarely a time since, that it was completely free of fever.[91] Notices also appeared in the press in 1862 which called upon local builders to submit tenders for the renovation of the old police station in the town and thereafter to keep it in good repair for a minimum of seven years.[92] It was, however, a proposal by the town council of Pwllheli that caused some consternation among magistrates when in 1870, it was suggested that the county should seriously consider building a new police station in the town, although it was stressed that in no circumstances would the local ratepayers contribute towards the renovation of the building. On reading the town council's proposal, Lord Newborough retorted 'that it was one of the most impudent proposals that he had ever seen'.[93] What, no doubt, by the late 1860s had assisted every authority in north Wales when examining police expenditure, was the vision and wisdom of those magistrates who, as early as 1858, had appointed at each meeting of quarter sessions a sub-committee of justices to deal specifically with police accounts.[94] Certainly, expenditure on the police had been considerable, yet, such sub-committees ensured to the best of their ability that in no county had it been excessive.

If magistrates in north Wales were concerned about expenditure, then the police officers themselves were equally anxious about what they saw as an increase in their daily duties. It was not just the extra work that made so many of them disgruntled, it was also the additional restrictions that chief constables placed on their private lives. It was common practice for chief constables to make enquiries about the background and character of those constables who wished to marry. On one occasion in Flintshire, Mr Browne, the chief constable, even fined an officer 2s 6d for getting married without his permission.[95] A further example of Mr Browne's determination to stamp his authority on the force, was seen when he discouraged his officers from reading the *Police Service Advertiser*, a publication he viewed as 'nourishing a spirit of discontent and insubordination'.[96] Strong on discipline, Mr Browne, was probably reflecting views that other chief constables in north Wales could easily identify with. In short, chief constables in the 1860s expected from their officers almost submissive obedience, in the genuine belief that without it 'there could be no discipline and without discipline no efficiency'.[97] At this time, too, the wives of officers on occasion, were to feel, like their husbands that their lives were also somewhat restricted. For example, a married officer would be expected to encourage his wife to undertake certain ancillary duties, such as cleaning the police station and cells, and when required, lighting the fires and sometimes even providing food for the prisoners. In Merioneth, any wife who agreed to undertake such work was paid the princely sum of 10d a week for doing so.[98]

In the early years police officers throughout north Wales became increasingly responsible for a number of additional duties. They became, for example, inspectors of weights and measures, assistant relieving officers for vagrants, as well as inspectors of common lodging houses. As early as November 1857, officers in Caernarfonshire were appointed inspectors of weights and measures at Caernarfon, Bangor, Conwy, Nefyn and Porthmadog.[99] Later, in Anglesey in 1861, Inspectors Edward Owen and Robert Williams not only found themselves responsible for the inspection of lodging houses, but the sergeants and constables they supervised also acted as their assistants.[100] There were two main reasons for imposing such extraneous duties on the police. Firstly, it was considered that they could do the work more efficiently, and secondly, and possibly more importantly from the magistrates point of view, they were cheaper than those who had formerly undertaken these tasks.[101] In addition to the duties already mentioned, there were other equally irksome tasks which the police were expected to perform. The listing of names and addresses of all dog owners on an officers beat which later had to be submitted to the magistrates sitting in quarter sessions, was a task the police found tiresome.[102] An even more burdensome task, was the recording in a book, of every visit and every person an officer saw on his daily tour of duty. When visiting farms, officers had to obtain a certificate of attendance which noted the time and date of the visit and which had to be signed by the farmer, a procedure most policemen found time-consuming.[103] Not that the recording of an officer's visit was confined only to constables and sergeants. On one occasion, even a chief constable was asked to record where he visited in the county and whom he saw and spoke to. The case in question concerned Mr John Denman, chief constable of Denbighshire, who, at the quarter sessions in 1868, was asked by Colonel Biddulph how often he visited various parts of the county adding that in future such visits should be recorded. In reply, the chief constable stated he would be happy to conform with such a request, but he was the oldest chief constable in the country and felt that such an imposition should not be placed upon him, declaring that no other chief officer in England and Wales would be bound in this manner. However, his plea in no way swayed Colonel Biddulph, who stated that in future, the chief constable should conform to the suggestion.[104] Such administrative duties as those imposed on the police at this time had the full support of Major-General Cartwright, his dictum being that the more an officer was used in this way, the better policeman he would eventually become.[105] It was to ensure that his officers could deal more effectively with difficulties that might arise, that Mr Clough, chief constable of Merioneth, provided at numerous police stations in the county, copies of *Snowden's Police Constable's Guide for 1862*.[106] A similar guide was also issued by the chief constable in Flintshire, in an effort to improve the efficiency of officers when dealing with administrative duties.[107]

Undoubtedly, the many extraneous duties, coupled with the restrictions placed on their private lives, was, for a number of officers in north Wales too much to bear and in the 1860s men resigned in large numbers. In Caernarfonshire, a comparatively small force, it was estimated that at least ten officers each year resigned mainly as a result of what they considered was a poor rate of pay for the duties involved.[108] Indeed, it was the large number of officers leaving the Caernarfonshire constabulary that prompted the chief constable to proclaim that the cost of altering or providing new uniforms, which was expensive, should in future be borne, not by the ratepayers, but by those officers leaving the service.[109] In addition, to the large number of men resigning, many officers at this time were dismissed for a variety of disciplinary offences, such as the gross neglect of duty, insubordination, and not infrequently for drunkenness itself. Although it is virtually impossible to ascertain the actual number of men dismissed for drunkenness, the newspapers for the period 1857-80 do indicate that every force in north Wales had within its ranks officers, who on occasion were prone to overindulge.[110] As early at September 1857, Constable Evan Jones of the Flintshire constabulary was dismissed for being drunk and absconding from his station without permission.[111] On another occasion, a constable, again in Flintshire, allowed a prisoner to get drunk with him, which resulted in them both being taken into custody at Flint.[112] Not that drunkenness was confined to officers serving in Flintshire. In a newspaper report in 1870, magistrates sitting at the Denbighshire quarter sessions questioned whether three officers, Superintendent Pugh, Inspector Paterson and Sergeant Davies were deserving of a pension on their retirement as they were all more or less known to be strongly addicted to drink. Speaking in particular on the position of Sergeant Davies, one of the magistrates, Mr Mainwaring, reported that the sergeant was seventy-six years of age and had been a member of the force for twenty-five years and in his opinion, 'he ought to have been got rid of ten years ago'.[113] Commenting even further, he went on to explain that 'he was puzzled as to how the sergeant at 51 years of age and a former publican, had been allowed in the first place to join the Denbighshire constabulary. Forgetting his previous occupation, his age alone one might have thought, would have been a sufficient bar to him ever wielding a policeman's staff'.[114] During the early years a number of officers serving in the Caernarfonshire constabulary also faced charges of drinking too much and not always that wisely.[115] As for Merioneth and Anglesey, although there is little evidence of similar misconduct by officers it cannot be entirely ruled out that when the opportunity arose some officers drank quite heavily.

What was the position of the officers in north Wales who, despite the many resignations and dismissals, were nevertheless, still prepared to continue with their duties? No doubt the answer is to be found in the mid-1860s when an increasing professional awareness among the rank and file 'was given a centralised medium through the creation of the weekly *Police Service Advertiser*'.[116] At first, the paper contained general news stories as well as items of particular interest to police officers, but after a year it began to concentrate solely on police matters.

The paper began to introduce legal notes, including answers to questions about the law and police procedure. Eventually, a reader's column was introduced which contained letters that debated such topics as the arming of the police, the rights of policemen to vote, on the unfairness of superiors as well as conditions of service and promotion by merit. In many ways, the paper was partisan in that it provided its own offices at which representatives from forces throughout England and Wales could meet in order to discuss matters of mutual concern, such as the problems that faced poorly paid policemen and their families. It allowed officers, for example, to compare their working conditions with those of other workers whose wives could, for instance, keep a shop or some other kind of business, whereas a constable often on a smaller salary and working longer hours was unable to receive similar assistance 'which a careful and economical help-mate might be in a position to afford him'.[117]

Although policemen were generally from below the artisan class, the professional policeman in the middle of the nineteenth century saw himself as having risen to a position of respectability, with the hopes of rising further through hard work, dedication and sobriety. In short, the policeman was expected 'to bring satisfactory testimonials, write a good hand, be of a certain height, and able to withstand all the temptations to which he is continually exposed'.[118] In becoming professional, the police began to see themselves as experts in their field. Indeed, as experts in policing, senior police officers often called for changes in the law. The 1860s was also a period when many chief constables were frequently in contact with the Home Office, calling for greater powers of search and arrest for their officers, particularly in cases where poaching was suspected.[119]

How did the communities in which the police served react to the presence of a professional police force and what types of crime did officers in north Wales most frequently encounter in these early years? Most of the offences committed at this time, which will be examined in more detail later, were concerned with petty thefts, vandalism, vagrancy, poaching, drunkenness and on occasion public disorder. Yet, from the outset, despite such offences, the early police officers were viewed in certain quarters as being quite unnecessary. Speaking to members of the Bangor and Beaumaris Union on 19 May 1858, the Reverend T.J. Williams was extremely critical of the money spent on the police in Caernarfonshire, saying 'the police may be of service in the manufacturing and other populous districts in England, but in Wales, where the people are proverbially quiet their services are not required, and it is a wasteful expense to keep the police strutting around the county with nothing to do'.[120] That the cost of policing continued to cause concern throughout the 1860s was seen in 1868, when once again a gentleman of the cloth, this time the Reverend J. Morgan of Llandudno stated, that he was not too happy with the police rate of 3½d in the pound. Claiming he had made a study of the police rates in all the counties in north Wales he then compared the expenditure incurred in Caernarfonshire with that of Denbighshire and produced the following figures:

### Expenditure from Police Rates in Caernarfonshire and Denbighshire, 1868

|  | Caernarfonshire | Denbighshire |
|---|---|---|
| No. of officers | 56 | 59 |
| Force maintenance | £5,263.3s.3½d | £4,611.12s.7d |
| Cost of clothing | £500.18s.2d | £386. 3s.0d |
| Oil used | £35.13s.0d | £14.13s.0d |

In his questioning of the police rate, the Reverend Morgan also complained about the allowance awarded to the chief constable of Caernarfonshire for the upkeep of his horse, since he was earning £300 per annum.[121] Defending such payments, the chief constable explained that the system of accounting in the two counties was different, and went on to state that in the other counties of north Wales conveying prisoners to gaol, expenses incurred in the examination of weights and measures, printing of stationery and a variety of other duties came out of the county rate. In Caernarfonshire it was charged to the police rate. As if still determined to find some fault the Reverend Morgan then turned his attention to the police officers stationed in Llandudno, saying that some officers had been stationed in the town too long and should be moved. In defence of his officers the chief constable stated that in his view, 'the longer a man remained on the beat the more efficient he became and therefore should be left at his station provided he did his duty'.[122]

If, in the early years the police appeared to be constantly criticised there were occasions when they were also praised for their presence. Speaking to magistrates sitting in quarter sessions at Beaumaris in 1858, the chairman, Mr John Williams, declared, 'that if the presence of the police had the effect of lessening crime, then the county of Anglesey reaped the benefit'.[123] Such sentiments were echoed when it was reported that in Anglesey the force did an excellent job.[124] In supporting the police in

1861, Llewelyn Turner, the mayor of Caernarfon, stated that he knew of 'some men who had for years lived by thieving and sometimes by highway robbery, who now had resorted to honest modes of living, the risks of their former pursuits having become too great'.[125] If, as the mayor suggested, crime in the county was reduced by the coming of the police, it may well have accounted for a letter from the Caernarfon Union to the Secretary of State, which called for the size of the Caernarfonshire constabulary to be reduced by one third 'due to the admitted paucity of crime and the quiet disposition of the inhabitants of the county'.[126] Yet, not everyone was of the opinion that the coming of the police in north Wales was responsible for the paucity of crime. One observer, writing under the *nom-de-plume* 'Publius' was to claim that the reduction in crime had nothing whatsoever to do with police vigilance, but rather with that of a higher cause, 'The Holy Spirit and those who meet Sunday after Sunday, plus the good work of the church and Sunday schools in shaping the morals of the people'.[127]

Certainly, in attempting to assess the actual amount of crime committed in north Wales during the 1860s, one is faced with a number of difficulties and reservations. There were for example, many conflicting views on the subject. Speaking to magistrates in Flintshire in 1860, a judge declared that there were so few cases to be tried that the North Wales Circuit was a journey more for pleasure and recreation than the transacting of business.[128] Commenting on these remarks, the editor of the local newspaper believed that the paucity of crime was due in no small measure, to the imperfections and deficiency of the police who allowed 'many a thief and rogue to escape the hands of justice'.[129] That there were some inefficient police officers was illustrated in Barmouth in 1857, when a sergeant arrested a thief for stealing a pair of boots, and then allowed him to escape, still wearing the stolen footwear.[130] As David J.V. Jones, rightly points out, it is necessary to question the accuracy of crime statistics. For instance, landowners, magistrates and the police themselves, frequently declared that the number of cases brought to the higher courts bore no relation to the actual number of crimes committed daily. In Caernarfon there was a good deal of pilfering and petty theft, and on occasions people were reluctant to venture out after dark.[131] As if answering this observation, the chief constable of Caernarfonshire, speaking to magistrates at the quarter sessions, states that the small number of arrests and cases sent for trial arose from many causes but the following certainly contributed to the situation:

1. Difficulty in obtaining information of a robbery, often delayed for some weeks.
2. The unwillingness of persons to incur the expense and odium of prosecution.[132]

Finally, in assessing the amount of crime, it must be remembered that in the early years many police officers tended to turn a blind eye to some crimes. Instead of prosecuting, they handed out countless cautions and pardons to those they felt were committing offences of a petty nature. This apparent reluctance by some police officers to prosecute was probably the reason why the chief constable of Caernarfonshrie asked Inspector Jones of Bangor, why the reports of thefts made by members of the public to his officers had not been taken further.[133] It was a similar situation in Merioneth, where 'not proceeded with' was seen alongside the names of those found in a drunken state in Tywyn. In Barmouth, however, the opposite was the case. Constables David Rowlands, Enoch Roberts and Sergeant Charles Ashton, were extremely busy prosecuting all those who broke the law.[134] The apparent haphazard system of whether to prosecute, which varied from county to county, even constable to constable, ultimately led to all chief constables assuming responsibility for the prosecutions within their area, thus bringing some measure of uniformity to the legal system.[135]

If we accept that a great deal of the crime committed remained unrecorded, what then were the offences known to the police and which caused them the greatest trouble and concern when they were out on their daily patrol? From the evidence that is available every county had a large number of thieves within their borders. For example, in Caernarfonshire in 1863, there were at least eighty-two within the county, as well as an additional 114 persons who were known to be committing crime but the vital evidence on which to prosecute was missing.[136] These figures clearly indicated that the police in the county were operating some kind of early criminal intelligence system, which gathered information on those known to be actively engaged in committing crime. An offence that was frequently brought to the attention of the police was that of pick-pocketing. Although every county had its fair share of pick-pockets, there was a particularly large number, often working in groups, in towns like Caernarfon, Bangor and Llandudno.[137] Probably in an effort to stamp out the offence, an over zealous police officer wrongly arrested a man, even dragging him from his bed, in the genuine belief he was a pickpocket. This action, which was widely condemned, caused particular concern and much annoyance to the inhabitants of Conwy.[138] Prostitution at this time, though not widely prevalent in north Wales, was mainly found in ports like Caernarfon and Holyhead, and those arrested were usually still in their teens, 'with Irish, Welsh and English surnames-in-that order, and about a third of them were recent arrivals in the area'.[139]

Few murders were committed in north Wales, although one has only to examine the court records to see that a number of murderous assaults against persons did occur in the 1860s. Violent crimes against property were also frequently observed during this period. For example, eighty-two persons were brought before the assizes, mainly in the eastern counties, for acts of arson. Such crimes, were mainly committed by vagrants and unemployed labourers who claimed in their defence, that farmers and the poor-law authorities had constantly denied them food and shelter. Although judges often believed they had been unfairly treated, they nevertheless imposed long terms of imprisonment upon all those who appeared before them.[140] According to one observer, vagrants were often involved in acts of arson during the 1860s, a practice that was to continue in some areas in north Wales until the closing years of the century and was seen by many as a 'favourite method of vagrants venting their spite'.[141]

Vagrancy was certainly a problem that caused concern to the authorities and police alike throughout the whole of north Wales. In any one year, thousands passed through each county with the position in Denbighshire being particularly acute. Speaking to magistrates at the Denbighshire quarter sessions in 1862, the chief constable stated that the increase in crime was caused mainly by the large number of tramps passing through the county owing to the scarcity of work in the manufacturing districts of England.[142] That he was not exaggerating the position is illustrated by the number of vagrants passing through Denbighshire during 1861 and 1862, which came to 2,921 and 6,358 respectively.[143] An even more alarming picture was to emerge in 1868 and 1869, when the numbers increased to 11,254 and 10,336 again respectively.[144] The authorities in Caernarfonshire were also faced with a large influx of vagrants. In one night alone, in 1862, the police issued 1,413 vagrants with tickets of admission to the various workhouses, in order that they could be provided with sustenance and shelter.[145] Not that every vagrant was appreciative of the assistance given. Workhouse masters and their staff were frequently subjected to physical attack and abuse. Many vagrants would refuse to undertake any kind of work, often turning violent and wantonly destroying property such as doors and windows even bedding. One offence that many vagrants committed was that of tearing and burning of their clothes, causing as a consequence great expenditure for the authorities concerned. In fact, between June 1863 and December 1864, eighteen persons were committed for this crime at the courts in Bangor and Caernarfon.[146] It was to avoid this kind of crime that the Holywell Union requested the chief constable to have a police officer present each morning between the hours of six o'clock and ten o'clock in order to allocate vagrants their duties.[147] No doubt it was this totally unacceptable behaviour that prompted one Merioneth magistrate, Mr C.F. Thruston, to demand more stringent measures to be applied to the problem. That the magistrates in Merioneth were clearly attempting to seek a solution, was seen in 1869 when they introduced a policy of printing placards, which were positioned at the entrances to all towns and villages, clearly warning all undesirables of the type of treatment they could expect, should they decide to enter.[148] The scheme, which met with a great deal of interest and approval, was later adopted by the magistrates in Flintshire.[149]

Two other areas which created numerous difficulties for the police were drunkenness and poaching. A great deal of the early hostility experienced by the police, arose as a result of their role in enforcing the licensing and game laws. At weekends, in particular, when the numerous public houses and drinking clubs disgorged their customers in large numbers, constables would frequently find themselves being attacked. It was whilst attempting to eject a collier from the Cross Foxes public house at Pentre Broughton on the night of 11 April 1863, that Constable John Green of the Denbighshire constabulary was struck on the head and killed.[150] In a similar incident in 1867, Sergeant Thomas Mclaren and Constable John Evans of the Flintshire constabulary were savagely assaulted by two men whilst attempting to arrest a drunken man.[151] Their assailants who were later arrested were sentenced to eighteen months and twelve months respectively.[152] That the police in Flintshire had a problem with drunkenness was seen when it was reported that many a *noson lawen* developed into a weekend drinking session. Indeed, on one occasion a constable was ordered to leave a village because, according to those who told him to go, he was interfering too much with their drinking habits.[153] Quite often, as was the case in Caernarfonshire and Merioneth, magistrates under pressure from outside bodies would ask chief constables to charge everyone found drunk on the streets. In Caernarfonshire, there was already a policy of bringing before the courts all those found drunk, as between 1867-70, over 2,000 persons were charged with the offence.[154]

Poaching was a crime that many residing in rural Wales viewed as little more than a favourite pastime. Those who took a hare or a rabbit were not seen as criminals by most communities and were simply regarded as persons acting in defence of 'an aged old custom and peasant economy'.[155] However, those who were caught received little sympathy from the courts. At the inquest on a poacher shot dead in Glan Conwy in 1860, the coroner remarked that 'poachers without exception are a class, the most disreputable on the face of the earth, they are too lazy to work, too mean to honestly earn their bread'.[156] There were numerous occasions when gamekeepers and police officers were attacked when attempting to arrest those they caught poaching. A serious attack, which resulted in two gamekeepers being shot and seriously wounded, occurred on the Mostyn estate in 1869. As an inducement to capture those responsible, Lord Mostyn offered a reward of £50 which was increased when the Home Secretary offered a similar amount.[157] An earlier incident occurred in 1863, when two gamekeepers employed by Mr Brownlow Wynne confronted eight armed poachers who promptly shot the keeper's dog. Later, all eight were arrested by Superintendent Pugh and Inspector Owen.[158] Some poachers not content with taking game, would cause extensive damage to walls and buildings on the estates that they entered.[159] A controversial issue associated with poaching was the appointment of private policemen to guard the many estates in north Wales. Although such officers were paid by those employing them, they still came under the command of the chief constable whilst they were in uniform. This situation caused much concern among ratepayers, particularly when a directive from the chief constable instructed all officers to be vigilant in detecting poachers. Since, at this time, many of the estates were owned by magistrates, there was a genuine belief in some quarters, that it was local ratepayers who were shouldering the financial burden of protecting the property of the landed gentry.[160]

A matter of more concern to the police, than vagrancy and drunkenness, was the ever-present threat of civil disorder as a consequence of political and economic unrest. In 1856, there had been a very serious disturbance at the Talargoch lead mines in Flintshire, which necessitated troops being called upon to assist the police in restoring order.[161] Similar disturbances at Mold in 1863 and in the same year at Llanrhaeadr by labourers working on the mid-Wales railway line, were a clear warning to magistrates that violence was never far below the surface and was liable to erupt at any time.[162] It was the necessity to deal effectively with acts of disorder wherever they occurred that kept chief constables constantly on the alert. In Caernarfonshire, the chief constable and the magistrates did not have too long to wait, for between 1858-69, parts of the county, true to tradition, were to become centres of total opposition to the enclosure of common land. The trouble, which began with the Enclosure Act of 1858, gave some 3,500 acres to Sir Richard Bulkeley, Lord Newborough, Lord Penrhyn and several other gentlemen. Over the years it had been customary for the local inhabitants to graze their cattle on the mountain slopes, and they were determined to protect this ancient right. When the landowners attempted to build walls around their holdings they were repeatedly taken down. In many ways, the police, vastly outnumbered, appeared to be powerless, and even if their numbers had been supplemented by special constables, they still could not hope to patrol the area night and day. As the situation gradually worsened, and attitudes on both sides hardened the magistrates decided that the troubled area should be designated a new police district, a decision that was to anger many people.[163] Extra police officers were to be permanently stationed in the area and for their protection, they were to be issued with cutlasses.[164]

Throughout this period of unrest the magistrates had always been hesitant to impose any extra financial burden on those ratepayers who resided in the newly designated police district. However, the matter was to be taken entirely out of their hands, when surprisingly, General Cartwright, the government inspector, informed the magistrates that failure to do so, would see the constabulary's certificate of efficiency being withheld, thus depriving the county of the government's police grant. As an inducement to get people to inform on those committing the offences, the government offered a reward of £50 to anyone who could supply the police with information leading to an arrest. Although no arrests were made as a result of this inducement, the lawlessness which had created so much trouble for the police and magistrates, began to decrease slowly in the 1870s. However, the bitterness was to remain for some considerable time.

One perceived threat to law and order in the 1860s, was that of a Fenian attack. The chief constable of Caernarfonshire was taking no risks, and called for volunteers to act as special constables, and in Bangor alone, over eighty men were enrolled for duty.[165] A month later, a notice placed in the local newspaper by the chief constable stated that as a result of his call for volunteers, the county now had at its disposal, over 4,500 men enrolled as special constables in the event of a Fenian uprising.[166] The parliamentary elections of 1868, were also to prove a period when the conduct and efficiency of the police in every county was tested. It was during these elections that one sees for the first time in north Wales, what later became known as 'mutual aid' being fully demonstrated. In Caernarfonshire the police had become particularly stretched in attempting to keep order, and as a means of assisting them sixteen constables from Merioneth were assigned for duty in the county in order to forestall any further acts of disorder.[167] The situation in Caernarfonshire also called for a number of special constables to be enrolled during the election, and this provoked questions in the press on the expenditure involved in enrolling such large numbers of men. In reply to such questioning, the chairman of the magistrates declared 'that he would have been prepared to appoint two thousand special constables if the chief constable had requested such a number'.[168] A similar situation to that experienced in Caernarfonshire occurred later in Denbighshire during the elections of 1868, when a number of Flintshire officers were drafted into the county in order to avert serious trouble. So pleased were the authorities on the performance of both police forces that the mayor of Denbigh hosted a dinner for the officers who had assisted, and declared, 'that the chief constables of both forces and the officers under their command had worked in perfect unison and doubtless their service would be duly acknowledged at the Quarter Sessions'.[169]

Undoubtedly, one of the ugliest and bloodiest attacks on the police occurred at Mold on the 2 June 1869, when hundreds of coal-miners and their families clashed with officers of the Flintshire constabulary. Yet, in order to appreciate the position in which the police found themselves, an examination, albeit briefly, of the events that were ultimately to lead to one of the darkest days in the history of Flintshire and that of its constabulary is essential. As an industry, coal had been firmly established in north Wales since 1800 and was mainly confined to the counties of Denbighshire and Flintshire.[170] Such was its expansion that by 1860 it was estimated that over 4,000 miners were employed in Denbighshire, with a slightly lower number working in Flintshire.[171] However, despite rapid expansion, unrest and agitation which was often accompanied by violence, was rife throughout the coalfields. Low wages, coupled with high prices, and a deep distrust of management, many of whom were English and often accused of displaying anti-Welsh prejudices, simply added fuel to an already volatile situation. Strikes at Treuddyn in 1855, and the more serious disturbance at the Coed Talon Coal Company in 1863, both of which necessitated a strong police presence were clearly signalling an ever-worsening situation.[172] If further evidence of unrest was needed, it came in 1868 and 1869, when a series of wage reductions at Brymbo, Ewloe and Ruabon led several hundred angry miners to confront not only management, but the police who were present in order to keep the peace.[173] It was, however, the reduction in pay of miners at Leeswood Green colliery in May 1869 that set in motion a chain of events that were to end so catastrophically.

Incensed by what they viewed as a savage cut in wages, over 200 miners confronted the manager, one John Young, demanding that such a reduction should not be implemented. When Young refused on the grounds that it was beyond his control, a number of miners marched him to the railway station at Hope with strict orders to leave the area.[174] However, any further embarrassment and humiliation Young might have experienced, was only averted by the timely intervention of the police, who after a struggle finally managed to free him from his assailants. On laying charges later against eight colliers, who were accused by the manager of being the main instigators of the assault, the magistrates issued warrants for their arrest. One of those named, William Hughes, was soon arrested, but when he was being taken to the County Hall to appear before the magistrates, a crowd of over 1,500 miners, all heavily armed with staves and pick-handles, surrounded the police escorts and in the ensuing struggle which saw constables 'severely cudgelled', the prisoner was freed.[175] Later, when assured by a magistrate that bail would be granted, Hughes and the other seven colliers surrendered and were ordered to appear at the specially convened Mold sessions on the 2 June 1869.

On the day of the trial colliers from all the neighbouring pits assembled outside the court, having taken a day's holiday in order to show sympathy and support for the men of Leeswood Green.[176] No violence was anticipated by the miners, and on this occasion they were unarmed, many being accompanied by their wives and children. In many respects there was a carnival atmosphere with little sign of the impending confrontation. The authorities, on the other hand, were not in such a buoyant mood. Flintshire's chief constable, Peter Browne, had issued orders to the effect that the whole strength of the force should be on duty during the trial. This meant that in addition to himself, there would be three superintendents, two inspectors and thirty-three constables on duty at Mold. As a further precaution in the event of trouble, a detachment of fifty men of the 2nd Battalion of the 4th Regiment of Foot, the King's Own, from Chester, under the command of Major Paton, would also be standing by.[177] During the trial which lasted six hours, all was peaceful, until news filtered through that of the eight defendants, six had been fined, but two had been sentenced to one month's imprisonment with hard labour. The news that two of the prisoners had been sentenced to imprisonment unleashed anger amongst the assembled crowd. What had begun as a peaceful protest turned to fury and, as soon as the police and military escort came on to the streets *en route* to the railway station with their prisoners, they were immediately met with a fusillade of bricks and stones which left them exposed to a most merciless pelting.[178] As the chief constable later explained 'the stones were as thick as hail – the air was black with them, several of my own men I noticed bleeding copiously the blood streaming down their uniforms, soldiers too were in the same condition'.[179] Commenting further on the experience, the chief felt that 'life was in imminent danger at that moment'.[180] Feeling perhaps that they had completely lost control of the situation, the soldiers opened fire killing two colliers and two women and leaving several others wounded.[181] Yet despite shots being fired, the crowd continued with their attack undeterred until the train, with the prisoners on board, left the station *en route* to the gaol at Flint.

At the inquest on the deceased, which was held on 3rd and 4th of June, a verdict of 'justifiable homicide' was reached. The jury also concluded that 'the troops had shown very great forbearance during the riot'.[182] Speaking later to magistrates at the quarter sessions in July 1869, the chief constable declared that in future when dealing with rioters, 'he did not promise them the same forbearance that he had hitherto practised'.[183] Most newspapers recording the riot were fully supportive of the action taken by the authorities. One local newspaper in its editorial went so far as to say 'that the lawless tendencies of the district had received an effective check, and we hope to hear of no more lynching of colliery managers by aggrieved workmen'.[184] Yet, even with such apparent support, the whole tragic episode left a number of vital questions unanswered. The *Wrexham Advertiser*, on the one hand critical of the miners, did feel that more searching enquiries should have been made about the actions of the soldiers as the Riot Act had not been read and concluded 'it was the duty of the jury to conduct the inquest in the interest of the public and not in justification of the authorities'.[185] For the officers in the Flintshire constabulary, the confrontation had been extremely costly, eighteen police officers had been seriously injured, two of whom, Superintendent Thomas and Sergeant Dew, so severely, that they never again resumed their duties.[186] Undoubtedly, the experience in Flintshire was a salutary lesson for the rest of the forces in north Wales. Any confrontation with miners meant that the police were faced with a group that was noted for being difficult to handle. Colliers, on the whole, lived a life apart and from earliest times had developed a camaraderie and an attitude of defiance to unwelcome authority.[187] Whenever the police were involved in any kind of industrial dispute, whether it was simply keeping the peace at the time of a riot or escorting 'free labour' they stood accused of partisanship. Whatever justification might be given, the police, in the eyes of many no longer appeared to be impartial 'but were visibly the agents of the employers and their allies'.[188] Such a position, however, was not one confined to the police in north Wales; it was a situation widely experienced by most constabularies in England also during the second half of the nineteenth century.[189]

The late 1860s and early 1870s was to see several important changes and developments in the administration of the police in north Wales. In 1869, Colonel Cobbe, a former chief constable of the West Riding constabulary assumed responsibility for the inspection of the forces in north Wales, as a result of the retirement of General Cartwright.[190] During his tenure of office, Cartwright had been a most influential figure in the inspectorate. In the early years in particular, his advice had often been eagerly sought by all the chief constables. Truly a man of vision, and one who had a deep understanding of the role of the police, he had promoted a number of beneficial ideas. It was he who recognised the importance of rank, and urged the early establishment of the merit classes of constables, of scheduled pay increases, and also that each force should endeavour to possess a higher number of first class constables, 'so as not to keep a good man down too long'.[191] As for the rank of sergeant, it was his view that 'there is no rank more valuable to the wellworking of the force than this, which not only gives deserving long-service men promotion, but assists in outlying districts – remote from the superintendent – and keeps constables at such posts constantly superintended'.[192] Such observation as were particularly relevant in north Wales where so many of the police stations were situated in areas that were some distance from headquarters. There is little doubt that from the time of his appointment General Cartwright displayed a sophisticated understanding of the pressures and conflicts that weighed on a constable. Indeed, in his first report to the Home Office in September 1857, he emphasises the 'great and inevitable changes' that took place in a man's life when he became a policeman.[193] Understandably, and no doubt appropriately, when he died in 1873, he was mourned 'as the policeman's friend'.[194]

In May 1870, the chief constable of Caernarfonshire announced that he was to retire on the grounds of ill-health. Immediately this news was known, an article in the local newspaper by a writer calling himself 'Ratepayer' said that he hoped that the new chief constable would have risen from the ranks. Lord Penrhyn, speaking at the quarter sessions had other ideas, stating he had been in communication with the Inspector of Constabulary, on the desirability of merging the Caernarfonshire and Anglesey forces, under the command of one chief constable, in this case, that of Anglesey. In his opinion, it would save money and he had written to the authorities in Anglesey seeking their views on the subject. According to Lord Penrhyn, a similar arrangement had proved successful with the amalgamation of Cambridgeshire and Huntingdonshire and also in the case of Westmorland and Cumberland. However, much to the disappointment of Lord Penrhyn, such an arrangement was later to be judged as too costly if implemented.[195] When the magistrates eventually selected their new chief constable, they chose Captain Pearson, a retired army officer who resided in Caernarfon.[196] The magistrates had ignored experienced police officers within the force, such as Superintendent Cornelius Davies of Porthmadog and Superintendent John Evans of Conwy, both of whom had served with the Liverpool City police prior to joining the Caernarfonshire constabulary.[197] By 1870, the forces in north Wales had grown numerically as the following table indicates:

### Strength of Police Forces in North Wales in 1857 and 1870[198]

| Force | No. of Men in 1857 | No. of Men in 1870 | % Increase |
|---|---|---|---|
| Anglesey | 16 | 25 | 56.2 |
| Caernarfonshire | 37 | 60 | 62.1 |
| Denbighshire | 46 | 62 | 34.7 |
| Flintshire | 26 | 41 | 57.6 |
| Merioneth | 19 | 27 | 42.1 |
| Pwllheli | 1 | 1 | 0 |

In addition to the increased numbers of police officers serving in north Wales there was also at this time, a significant development in the field of criminal identification. Every force in north Wales received a directive from the Home Office which suggested that a camera should be purchased in order that prisoners in custody could be photographed, with copies and other relevant details being forwarded to the Commissioner of Police in London.[199]

Over the years, in fact ever since the passing of the County and Borough Police Act of 1856, there had been very little movement in the general structure and administration of police forces, and this allowed constabularies like those in north Wales to settle down and consolidate their respective positions. However, the situation was to change significantly in the 1870s, when a number of reforms were introduced which gave an added impetus to police legislation.[200] The first of these reforms was introduced in 1874, when in the sphere of police finance, the Exchequer increased its grant to all forces, from one-quarter to one-half in respect of the cost of pay and clothing.[201] This increase, although generally welcomed was entirely unconditional as was illustrated in a Home Office submission to Sir Richard Cross, the Home Secretary, in which it was stated that 'the very considerable addition about to be made to the contribution from Imperial funds in aid of local police expenditure, affords the government an opportunity, of which it may be well to take advantage, of endeavouring to secure for the Secretary of State a greater amount of supervision and control over the police forces of Great Britain than he now possesses'.[202] In their submission, officials were anxious to bring to the attention of the Home Secretary his very limited powers when dealing with matters that appertained to the county forces, and as for the boroughs, they went on to claim that 'he had no power whatsoever beyond that of withholding a certificate of efficiency'.[203] Such observations, which obviously called for more supervision over the police by the Home Secretary, must have alarmed many magistrates and chief constables, reinforcing in the process, their earlier fears of governmental interference in the way counties, like those in north Wales, were generally managed. That the Home Secretary was taking a greater interest in police reform was seen by the inspectorate as an encouraging sign and it felt the time was opportune to suggest several of their own proposals which they submitted to him in a report dated 1 October 1874. Here, they were extremely fortunate to find a powerful ally in the person of Sir Henry Ibbertson, Parliamentary-under-Secretary of State at the Home Office, who was shortly to become chairman of the Select Committee examining the question of police superannuation. In a letter to the Home Secretary which dealt in part with the question of police pensions, Sir Henry made it plain that 'there was a natural objection by officers who were contributing to funds which from their condition are hardly ever likely to be of benefit to them'.[204] This certainly seemed to be the bitter experience of Constable Robert Hughes, in Anglesey, when he attempted to obtain money from the superannuation fund after thirteen years service, having retired on the grounds of chronic ill-health. As he was destitute he pleaded with the magistrates for some recompense, however, the chairman Mr John Williams, although sympathetic, stated they could do little for him without the chief constable's approval. In his case the chief constable believed that his ill-health was brought about 'by his own indiscretion' and no award could be given.[205]

In London, however, the situation was somewhat different. Although officers serving in the Metropolitan Police could not expect a pension as an absolute right, they could enjoy a firm expectation that on completing their service one would be awarded and during the 1870s numerous attempts to get the provincial police a similar arrangement all ended in failure. Nevertheless, there was a clear indication at this time that the Home Office was taking a more positive interest in police affairs in general, although no one was under any illusion about the difficulties that stood in the way of any radical reform. It was clear that any progress towards police reform was being treated with extreme caution with much of it becoming piecemeal.[206] The Select Committee established in 1875 to examine once again police superannuation heard evidence from a number of sources, but its findings published in 1877 resulted in no firm conclusion on this or other questions of a vexing nature. In fact, little progress was made on the question of superannuation until the passing of the Police Act of 1890. This meant in effect, that during the intervening years superannuation not only caused endless discussion but also continuing bitterness among the rank and file serving in north Wales. Yet, despite what many officers regarded as a setback to their aspirations, the forces generally had overcome the teething troubles inherent in any new institution that concerned itself with such sensitive issues as rights, power and influence. Against all the opposition and criticism, initial difficulties and upsets, the police in north Wales were in existence, were developing rapidly and by the 1870s already an integral part of the way of life in various counties.

---

[1] T.A. Critchley, *A History of Police in England and Wales*, (London, 1967), p.116.

[2] A.J. Hinksman, *The First Hundred Years of the Warwickshire Constabulary*, (Rugby, 1957), p.6.

[3] See Appendix, ii for the rules and regulations that specifically apply to the appointment of officers in Merioneth and their respective rates of pay.

[4] Apart from the Metropolitan Police which comes under the direct authority and approval of the Home Secretary, every force in England and Wales is still subjected to an annual inspection as to their general efficiency.

[5] David Philips, *Crime and Authority in Victorian England*, (London, 1977), p.61.

[6] HO, 45/OS, 5276. That such payment should be assessed in this way can be seen in a letter to Lord Palmerston from Captain McHardy, chief constable of Essex, dated 20 February 1854.

[7] See Appendix, 3 for a brief account of the Pwllheli Borough force. There is little material available on the former Beaumaris and Denbigh forces. Also consult Martin Stallion and David S. Wall, *The British Police – Police Forces and Chief Officers 1829-2000*, (Police History Society, Bramshill, Hampshire 1999).

[8] Carolyn Steedman, *Policing the Victorian Community – The Formation of English Provincial Police Forces, 1851-1880*, (London, 1984), p.27.

[9] *CDH*, 1 March 1856.

[10] T.A. Critchley, op. cit., p.117.

[11] Ibid.

[12] Ibid.

[13] *NWC*, 1 March 1856.

[14] T.A. Critchley, op. cit., p.117.

[15] Ibid., See also Clive Emsley, *The English Police – A Political and Social History*, 2nd. edition (London, 1996), p. 22, where he states that after the French Revolution, Napoleon replaced the lieutenant general de police in Paris with what appeared to be the more sinister police system of Joseph Fouché. For a fuller account of the work of Fouché see by the same author, *Policing and its Context 1750-1870*, (London, 1983), pp.33-5.

[16] *CDH*, 16 February 1856.

[17] CQS Rolls, (Epiphany, 1857).
[18] *NWC*, 18 October 1856.
[19] D.V.J. Jones, *Crime in Nineteenth Century Wales*, (Cardiff, 1991), p.205.
[20] Ibid.
[21] Ibid., See also Hugh Owen, *History of the Anglesey Constabulary*, (Llangefni, 1952). pp.19-21, in which it is claimed that in Anglesey the superintending constable system, although given a fair trial was looked upon as a failure.
[22] Clive Emsley, *Policing and its Context 1750-1870*, (London, 1983), p.81.
[23] Ibid., p.80.
[24] Clive Emsley, *The English Police*, (London, 1991), p.54.
[25] Christopher Hibbert, *The Roots of Evil*, (Suffolk, 1963), p.150. See also W.L. Melville Lee, *A History of Police in England*, (London, 1901), pp.336-7, in which he claims that the advantages of the Act of 1856 were impossible to deny.
[26] *CDH*, 11 October, 1 November, 22 November, 6 December, 13 December, 1856 and *Chester Chronicle*, 13 December 1856. As a result of the notices placed in the newspapers quoted above the number of applications received by each county for the five vacant positions in north Wales were as follows: Caernarfonshire 112; Anglesey 21; Merioneth 104; Denbighshire 17; Flintshire 53.
[27] J.O. Jones, *History of the Caernarvonshire Constabulary 1856-1950*, (Caernarfon, 1963), p.27.
[28] T.A. Critchley, op. cit., pp.140-1.
[29] *CDH*, 6 December 1856.
[30] T.A. Critchley, op. cit., p.141.
[31] *Police Review*, 6 September 1963.
[32] *CDH*, 24 January 1857.
[33] Ibid., 21 March 1857.
[34] *CDH*, 28 February 1857. See also *Chester Courant*, 28 January 1857 in which it is reported that the writer was not quite correct, as one of the candidates, an Inspector Amos of Liverpool was fluent in the language.
[35] *CDH*, 21 March 1857. A short list which was comprised solely of police officers was completely contrary to the usual policy adopted by most county authorities at this time. The officers initially invited for interview were as follows: Superintendent Smith, Montgomeryshire; Inspector Amos, Liverpool City Police; Chief Inspector Martin, Manchester City Police; Superintendent Fitzgerald, Suffolk Constabulary; Inspector Newnham, Metropolitan Police; Inspector Moloney, Irish Constabulary; Superintendent Rattigan, Brecon and Radnor Constabulary.
[36] Ibid.
[37] FQS Rolls, (Hilary, 1857).
[38] A.G. Veysey, *Annual Report of the County Archivist*, Clwyd Record Office (Hawarden, 1975), p.23.
[39] CQS Rolls, (Hilary, 1857).
[40] J.O. Jones, op. cit., p.28.
[41] *CDH*, 7 March 1857.
[42] Ibid., 24 January 1857.
[43] George Lerry, 'The policemen of Denbighshire', *Transactions of the*

*Denbighshire Historical Society*, 2 (1953), pp.118. Here he was quoting *The Wrexhamite*, 24 October 1856.

[44] Ibid., p.119.

[45] Ibid.

[46] DQS Rolls, (Michaelmas, 1856).

[47] George Lerry, op. cit., p.121.

[48] T.A. Critchley, op. cit., p.118. There were initially two such inspectors, Major-General William Cartwright, a veteran of the Peninsular War and Waterloo, who had no previous police experience, and Lieutenant-Colonel John Woodford, who had been chief constable of Lancashire. Later, a third inspector was appointed. He was Captain Edward Willis, a former chief constable of Manchester. See also letter to Woodford, 27 August 1856, in HO, 65/5, in which the Home Secretary stresses the importance of good relations with the newly created forces. The immediate task facing the inspectorate was enormous for they had to appraise the state of efficiency of the 237 separate forces in England and Wales. Indeed, the early reports of the newly appointed inspectors of constabulary dispose of any idea that the country possessed a uniform police system in the years following the enactment of the County and Borough Police Act, 1856. Even in 1860 there were still 226 separate police forces.

[49] MQS Rolls, (Hilary, 1857).

[50] *CDH*, 14 March 1857.

[51] Hugh Owen, *History of the Anglesey Constabulary*, (Llangefni, 1952), pp.22-23. Also *CDH*, 21 February, 14 March and 30 May 1857. Also DQS Rolls (Trinity 1857).

[52] *CDH*, 21 March and 18 April 1857.

[53] Ibid., a candidate was not to exceed forty years of age and be less than 5' 7" in height. If a candidate had served in the army or navy, or in any other public employment he was expected to produce a certificate from such service showing that he left with credit.

[54] Hugh Owen, op. cit., p.22. The chief constable was also to pay his constables an extra 2s per week for lodgings. This scale of fees being the one originally applied to officers in the Hampshire Constabulary. See also *CDH*, 23 May 1857, George Lerry, op. cit., p.125. A.G. Veysey, op.cit., p.23. MQS Rolls, (Hilary, 1857).

[55] J.O. Jones, op. cit., p.31.

[56] Hugh Owen, op. cit., pp.64-77. Recorded here are the names of every member of the Anglesey constabulary from its commencement on 4 April 1857 to 30 September 1950. In the case of each member, his rank, name, place of birth, age on joining, height, stations, cause and date of leaving, superannuated, resigned and died. There are gaps in the earlier records 1857-77, the originals sadly having disappeared. See also FRO (Hawarden), F.P./29-31, for some details of the earliest officers in Flintshire.

[57] Carolyn Steedman, op. cit., p.80.

[58] V.A.C. Gatrell, 'Crime, authority and the police-man state', *The Cambridge Social History of Britain 1750-1950*, 3 (Cambridge, 1990), p.271.

[59] Carolyn Steedman, op. cit., p.81.

[60] *CDH*, 6 June 1857. The following were the officers appointed: John Jones, Pwllheli; William Hughes, Pwllheli; Thomas Turner, Nefyn; William Hughes, Llanbedrog; Richard Hughes, Llanystumdwy; Evan Roberts,

Rhydyclafdy; Owen Lloyd, Llaniestyn; with the eighth officer, Robert Jones, being domiciled in Liverpool.

[61] PP, 1867-68, xvii, Employment of Women and Children in Agriculture (First Report of Commissioners), p.307.
[62] T.A. Critchley, op. cit., p.152.
[63] *Police Service Advertiser*, 7 April 1867. In the boroughs, the watch committees were the disciplinary authorities, but they shared the power of dismissal with the justices.
[64] *Merionethshire Standard*, 24 March 1866. Explaining her reasons for leaving her husband, the woman defended her actions saying that her husband had often told her to go and on this occasion she had taken him at his word.
[65] MQS Rolls (Michaelmas, 1857).
[66] T.A. Critchley, op. cit., p.168.
[67] Ibid., pp.169-70.
[68] DQS Rolls, (Easter, 1870). It was not until the passing of the Police Superannuation Act of 1890, 53 and 54 Vic c 45, that police officers became entitled as of right to a pension after twenty-five years, or on medical grounds after fifteen years.
[69] Extracted from the reports of H.M. Inspectors of Constabulary for 1856-7. In addition the Boroughs had about 5,500 and London about 6,600 policemen in 1857.
[70] *Flintshire Constabulary Handbook*, (Holywell, 1956), p.13.
[71] Hugh Owen, op. cit., p.23.
[72] *CDH*, 27 March 1857.
[73] Ibid., 19 January 1861.
[74] MQS Rolls, (Easter, 1855).
[75] Ibid.
[76] Ibid.
[77] MQS Rolls, (Hilary, 1861).
[78] AQS Rolls, (Easter, 1858).
[79] Hugh Owen, op. cit., p.29.
[80] Ibid.
[81] Ibid.
[82] Ibid.
[83] Ibid., p.28.
[84] *Flintshire Observer*, 30 March 1860.
[85] FQS Rolls, (Michaelmas, 1865).
[86] *CDH*, 8 April 1865.
[87] Ibid., 21 March 1863.
[88] Ibid., 10 April 1858.
[89] Ibid., 16 March 1867.
[90] Ibid., 28 August 1858.
[91] Ibid., 27 April 1867.
[92] Ibid., 15 March 1862.
[93] CQS Rolls, (Easter, 1870). It has to be noted that in 1870 Pwllheli Borough was still separated from the county of Caernarfonshire for administrative purposes and a further nine years were to elapse before amalgamation eventually brought both authorities together.
[94] MQS Rolls, (Hilary, 1858).
[95] A.G. Veysey, op. cit., p.24.

[96] Ibid.
[97] Ibid.
[98] MQS Rolls, (Hilary, 1861).
[99] *CDH*, 21 November 1857.
[100] Hugh Owen, op. cit., p.26.
[101] *CDH*, 21 November 1857. Mr Richard Jones, inspector of weights and measures in Merioneth for over thirty-one years retired as a result of the chief constable assuming responsibility for these matters. See also the *North Wales Chronicle,* 17 June 1830, where it illustrates that as early as 1830 a number of traders in Anglesey were fined for using weights and measures that gave a false reading.
[102] MQS Rolls, (Hilary, 1866).
[103] MQS Rolls, (Trinity, 1869).
[104] DQS Rolls, (Michaelmas, 1868). See also *CDH*, 5 May 1849 and 26 November 1859, and DQS Rolls (Easter, 1865). It would appear that over the years that doubts had often been expressed as to the frequency Mr Denman actually visited certain parts of the county. A noted sportsman, he was sometimes accused of spending far too much of his time hunting in the Vale of Clwyd, a charge he was to strenuously refute.
[105] PP, 1852-53, xxxvi, Report of the Select Committee on Police p.60. Here he was adhering to an earlier policy as advocated by Admiral John MacHardy, chief constable of Essex.
[106] MQS Rolls, (Hilary, 1863).
[107] *Flintshire Constabulary Centenary Handbook*, p.17. The instruction book, *Rules and Regulations for the Government and Guidance of the Constabulary* was issued, but unfortunately no copy can now be found.
[108] J.O. Jones, op. cit., p.30.
[109] *CDH*, 23 October 1863.
[110] *Flintshire Observer*, 30 March 1860, also *CDH*, 26 October 1861; 4 January 1862; 24 October 1863; 1 June 1867; 24 October 1868; and the CQS Rolls (Easter, 1864).
[111] A.G. Veysey, op. cit., p.24.
[112] Ibid.
[113] *NWC*, 23 April 1870.
[114] Ibid.
[115] J.O. Jones, op. cit., p.55.
[116] Clive Emsley, *Policing and its Context* (London, 1983), pp.84-5.
[117] Ibid.
[118] *Police Service Advertiser*, 27 April 1867.
[119] David J.V. Jones, op. cit., p.215. Welsh chief constables called strongly for the Poaching Prevention and Prevention of Crimes Acts of 1862 and 1871. This legislation gave the police the right to apprehend various groups of suspected and convicted offenders who in turn, had to prove their innocence. Such police powers were unpopular and often provoked hostility.
[120] *CDH*, 22 May 1858.
[121] *CDH*, 4 January 1868.
[122] Ibid.
[123] AQS Rols, (Trinity, 1858).
[124] *CDH*, 23 October 1858.

[125] David J.V. Jones, *Crime in Nineteenth Century Wales*, (Cardiff, 1991), p.210.
[126] *CDH*, 29 May 1858.
[127] Ibid., 13 April 1861.
[128] *Flintshire Observer*, 9 January 1860. See also *CDH*, 3 August 1861, when one reads a slightly different view. Judge Baron Bramwell declared at the Flintshire assizes, that he could not congratulate the county on the state of crime, since the number of crimes committed within the county certainly exceeded anything he had witnessed in the other counties he had visited in north Wales. See also David J.V. Jones, op. cit., pp.216-18, in which he records that judges when presented with 'white gloves' at a maiden assize not only praised the honest character of the Welsh people but also expressed their thanks to the hardworking justices in quarter sessions.
[129] Ibid.
[130] *CDH*, 17 October 1857.
[131] David J.V. Jones, op. cit., p.3. See also P.P. 1862, xlv, Reports of the Inspectors of Constabulary, North Wales, p.11.
[132] *CDH*, 18 October 1862.
[133] CRO, Constabulary Records, xj/462.
[134] MRO, ZH 4/20. Sergeant Charles Ashton was also known as the 'Welsh Literary Policeman'. A prize winner at numerous *eisteddfodau*, his many works are now to be found at the National Library of Wales, Aberystwyth. See also *Police Review*, 16 February 1894, for more information on this remarkable officer. For Ashton, see in addition: *Montgomeryshire Collections*, 63 (1), 1973, pp. 47-63; *Journal of the Merioneth Historical and Record Society*, viii (i), 1977, pp. 61-70.
[135] David J.V. Jones, op. cit., p.23.
[136] Extracted from the reports of H.M. Inspectors of Constabulary, 1863-4. See also *Flintshire Observer*, 25 June 1858 in which it states that, all known information on known thieves and those wanted by the police was to be sent to every constabulary, head constable of every borough, to the keepers and governors of every prison, chief superintendents of the eight principal railway companies in England. Also to be sent to Scotland and even Ireland if it was thought appropriate.
[137] *CDH*, 18 October 1862.
[138] Ibid., 16 July 1859.
[139] David J.V. Jones, op. cit., p.196.
[140] Ibid., p.136.
[141] Clive Emsley, *Crime and Society in England 1750-1900*, (London 1987), p.81. See also C.J. Ribton-Turner, *A History of Vagrants and Vagrancy*, (London, 1887), p.313.
[142] DQS Rolls, (Hilary, 1862).
[143] *CDH*, 23 October 1869.
[144] Ibid.
[145] Ibid., 18 October 1862.
[146] David J.V. Jones. 'A dead loss to the community'. The criminal vagrant in mid-nineteenth century Wales', *Welsh History Review*, 8 (3), 1977, pp.333-4.
[147] FQS Rolls, (Michaelmas, 1868).
[148] *NWC*, 8 January 1870.
[149] Ibid.
[150] *CDH*, 1 August 1863. As a result of Constable Green's death a

subscription organised by Superintendent Bradshaw of Wrexham raised £73 for his widow. Colonel Tottenham, a magistrate, also urged that a gratuity equivalent to a year's salary should also be awarded to the family. See also *CDH*, 9 April 1864; 2 December 1865; 8 January 1875; which record the deaths whilst on duty of Constable William Jones of the Anglesey constabulary and Constables John Purcell and Thomas Owen of the Denbighshire constabulary.

[151] *CDH*, 6 June 1867.
[152] Ibid., 10 August 1867.
[153] FRO, Constabulary Records, Ps/3/9, 1865-76. Overton Divisional Letterbook.
[154] CQS Rolls, (Michaelmas, 1870).
[155] David J.V. Jones, op. cit., p.130. See also David J.V. Jones, 'The poacher: a study in Victorian crime and protest', *The Historical Journal*, xxii (4), (1979), pp.825-60.
[156] Susan C. Ellis, 'Observations of Anglesey life through the quarter sessions rolls, 1860-1869', *Transactions of the Anglesey Antiquarian Society and Field Club*, (1986), pp.132-3.
[157] FQS Rolls, (Michaelmas, 1869).
[158] *CDH*, 7 November 1863.
[159] David J.V. Jones, op. cit., p.130. In which he cites PRO, HO 45/6812. Letter from Thomas Mostyn, 31 December 1859.
[160] *CDH*, 9 August 1862.
[161] W.H. Jones, 'A strike at Talargoch lead-mines a hundred years ago', *Flintshire Historical Society Publications*, 16 (1956), p.23.
[162] *CDH*, 16 May 1863.
[163] The newly created police district included the parishes of Caerhun, Llanbedr, Llanfairfechan, Llangelynnin, Dwygyfylchi and Gyffin.
[164] CQS Rolls, (Easter, 1870).
[165] *CDH*, 18 January 1868.
[166] Ibid., 1 February 1868.
[167] J.O. Jones, op. cit., p.39.
[168] *CDH*, 16 January 1869.
[169] Ibid., 19 December 1868.
[170] Alun Burge, 'The Mold riots of 1869', *Llafur*, 3 (3), (1982), p.41.
[171] A.H. Dodd, *The Industrial Revolution in North Wales*, 3rd. edition (Cardiff, 1971), p.202. In 1861 there were seventy-eight working pits in north Wales, thirty-five were in Denbighshire, thirty-eight in Flintshire, with five in Anglesey.
[172] FRO, *The Mold Riots*, (Hawarden, 1977), p.1.
[173] *Wrexham Advertiser*, 21 March, 4 July 1867 and 4 April 1868.
[174] Alun Burge, op. cit., p.46. See also *The Times*, 4 June 1869, in which it is reported that in marching Young to the railway station, the miners felt that, far from breaking the law, they were in keeping with a longstanding and legitimate custom of the district – similarly in releasing William Hughes later they were drawing attention to what they saw as injustices and were defending their own values in attempting to gain the prisoners release. From the viewpoint of the history of the police this is the key issue – a conflict over different meanings of justice and customs that conflict with the agencies of the law.

[175] *Chester Courant*, 29 May 1869.
[176] *Wrexham Advertiser*, 5 June 1869.
[177] *Mold District Chronicle*, 5 June 1869.
[178] Alun Burge, op. cit., p.47.
[179] Ibid.
[180] Ibid.
[181] T. Herbert and G.E. Jones (eds.), *People and Protest: Wales 1815-80*, (Cardiff, 1988), p.170.
[182] Alun Burge, op. cit., p.48.
[183] FQS Rolls (Midsummer, 1869).
[184] *Wrexham Advertiser*, 5 June 1869.
[185] Ibid., 12 June 1869.
[186] FQS Rolls (Trinity, 1871), and FQS Rolls (Easter, 1873). See also FQS Rolls (Trinity, 1869), which records the following officers who were injured – Superintendents Adams, Bolton, Thomas; Inspectors Hughes and Mclaren; Sergeants Dew, Lockwood, Minshull, Ward and Constables Adams, Armer, Baxter, Denson, R. Jones, M. Jones, Knight, Mathews and Mcbride.
[187] A.H. Dodd, *Industrial Revolution in North Wales*, 2nd. edition, (Cardiff, 1951), p.399.
[188] David Taylor, *The New Police in Nineteenth Century England – Crime, Conflict and Control*, (Manchester, 1997), pp.118-119.
[189] Ibid., pp.89-127.
[190] Richard Cowley, 'Police under scrutiny – the inspectors of constabulary 1856-1990', *Journal of the Police History Society*, 11 (1996), pp.25-30.
[191] P.P. 1860, lii, Report of her Majesty's Inspectors of Constabulary, p.6.
[192] P.P. 1857-8, xlvii, Report of her Majesty's Inspectors of Constabulary, p.646.
[193] Carolyn Steedman, op. cit., p.176.
[194] *Police Guardian*, 13 June 1873. General Cartwright not only concerned himself with police administration, he was also actively engaged in promoting the welfare of officers and their families. He called for the appointment of police surgeons and generously subscribed to the Police Mutual Assurance Association, as well as to the police orphanage at Brighton which he opened. His son, who was a conservative MP for Northants, was also a vociferous parliamentary lobbyist who constantly called for the introduction of a unified system of superannuation for the police.
[195] *CDH*, 11 June 1870.
[196] CQS Rolls, (Easter, 1870).
[197] Ibid.
[198] Clive Emsley, *The English Police*, (London, 1991), pp.267-8.
[199] CQS Rolls, (Easter, 1870). See also *CDH*, 9 April 1870. The photographing of prisoners was introduced in Bristol in the 1850s and was gradually extended over the rest of the country. The use of photography in the identification of prisoners was later endorsed and recommended by the Select Committee on Gaols in 1863.
[200] T.A. Critchley, op. cit., p.127.
[201] The Police (Expenses) Act 1874. By an Act of 1890 the conditions on which a grant was payable were broadened to include management and efficiency, as well as the earlier criteria of numbers and discipline. For a

more detailed summary of the police grant see J.M. Hart, *The British Police*, (London, 1951), pp.36-8.

[202] T.A. Critchley, op. cit., p.127.

[203] Ibid.

[204] Ibid., p.128.

[205] AQS Rolls, (Easter, 1874). See also *CDH*, 18 October 1873, where the chief constable of Caernarfonshire calls for a uniform system of superannuation based on a man's length of service and not on age.

[206] T.A. Critchley, op. cit., p.129.

Chapter IV

# A Time of Consolidation, 1876-88

This period was a time of significant change in the way the counties of north Wales were policed. For instance, magistrates sitting in quarter sessions, once so anxious about any increase in expenditure were now aware that more money was required if policing was to be judged efficient. Again on the subject of expenditure, police officers were also experiencing an improvement in their conditions, even if such improvement was a slow process. For example, if there was an air of disappointment pervading the forces in north Wales as a result of the failure to settle the issue of superannuation, at least officers had the satisfaction of seeing their weekly pay increased occasionally. Not that such pay increases came easily. Sometimes, pressure by the men themselves called for a review of their pay scales. However, as early as 1871, it was the magistrates in Merioneth who asked the chief constable if he would prepare a graduated scale of pay for all members of his force up to and including the superintendent. Furthermore, in doing so, he was to take into consideration the length of a man's service, and his conduct whilst in the force.[1] But not everyone thought police officers were underpaid, as one member of a committee examining the pay of the police in Merioneth was later to explain, when he stated 'that he never saw a policeman', to which the chief constable retorted 'that it should be remembered that frequently officers were on duty all night, as more crime was committed at night than during the day'.[2] On the question of pay, there was one area that caused particular concern to many officers in north Wales, and that was the disparity between the pay scales from one county to another.[3] Indeed, so concerned were officers in Merioneth, that in 1873 they all signed a petition which they then presented to Mr Clough, the chief constable, to draw his and the magistrates attention to this anomaly.[4]

That there was continuing concern over the different rates of pay was illustrated in 1876, when the Clerk of the Peace for Merioneth was instructed by the magistrates to communicate with all the other authorities in north Wales to suggest that a committee composed of one magistrate from each county should meet in order to discuss the feasibility of a common pay structure.[5] The authorities in Caernarfonshire, however, were not too keen on such a meeting, with the chief constable claiming that the arrangement was not suitable for his force and if adopted would add a further £150 per annum to the wages bill.[6] At the meeting, which was eventually held on the 24 April 1877, at Chester, every authority apart from Caernarfonshire sent a representative, but after a great deal of discussion and the submission of various proposals, it was finally decided that since the working conditions of officers varied from county to county it was virtually impossible to agree on a uniform system of pay.[7]

If the cost of police pay was to some extent being contained then expenditure on law enforcement was rising rapidly. Every county was faced with a demand either for more police houses or stations and cells in which to hold those arrested. In 1874, land had been acquired from the Marquess of Londonderry for the erection of a police station at Corris Uchaf.[8] Two years later a site was obtained for £12 from Mr C.F. Thruston in order that a lock-up with a house attached to it could be built at Pennal.[9] Yet, despite the frequent purchasing of sites upon which police stations could be built, the chief constable of Merioneth in his annual report for 1877, brought to the attention of the magistrates his serious concern about the shortage of lock-ups and police houses in the county. It was his firm belief that should the situation be allowed to continue then the efficiency of the force would be at risk. His report then went on to stress that the only houses the constables could easily obtain were public houses and he believed it wrong to let police officers to live there.[10] Illustrating his concern even further, the chief constable went on to cite how a few years earlier a constable stationed at Corris would have had to escort an arrested wrongdoer to Aberdyfi, a distance of seventeen miles and in another county, in order to borrow a lock-up for a night.[11] In fact, on one occasion, an officer had a prisoner kept overnight in Machynlleth, only to find himself next morning presented with a bill for meals and accommodation, the cost of which came out of his own pocket.[12] In such circumstances, it is hardly surprising to find in the chief constable's report that he had great difficulty in getting officers to serve at Corris.[13]

The 1870s were to see the authorities in every county in north Wales embarking on an extensive programme in order that the severe shortage of suitable police accommodation could in part be alleviated. In Caernarfonshire, a piece of land in Llanberis was bought from Mr Assheton Smith for £60, and the county surveyor was ordered to prepare a plan for the eventual building of a police station upon the site.[14] There was also an urgent appeal by the chief constable for a lock-up at Penygroes as the amount of drunkenness was creating a number of difficulties for his officer.[15] Later at the quarter sessions held on the 5 July 1877, Mr Lloyd Edwards, a magistrate, drew attention to the dilapidated condition of the police station at Pwllheli, stating that the drains were practically non-existent, there was little plaster on the walls, and that the building generally was in need of urgent repairs if it was to be considered functional. As a first step to improving the situation the magistrates recommended that Dr Rees, the district medical officer of health, should be asked to examine the effect of bad drainage on the health of police officers and prisoners alike.[16] Stressing the importance he placed on the health of his men, the chief constable speaking to magistrates on the 11 April 1878 informed them of his concern about the houses occupied by officers at Bangor, Caernarfon and Llandudno, and asked whether there was any possibility of leasing suitable property, which in turn would greatly assist in attracting men to the force.[17]

Magistrates in Flintshire were also facing up to the task of providing, whenever possible, suitable sites on which to erect police houses. Such determination on their part did not come cheaply. At Flint, for example, it had earlier been suggested that a lock-up would cost in the region of £900 to erect. However, a revised estimate by the county surveyor gave a more realistic figure nearer £1,150.[18] There was also a call for a lock-up and a policeman's house to be built in a central position in Buckley, at a cost of no more than £300. Magistrates had a particular problem at Mostyn; there a policeman's house with three cells was to be erected at a cost not exceeding £600. When questions were asked as to the reasoning behind such a large sum as compared to the police station at Buckley, the magistrates were informed 'that since the site chosen for the new building was near the park, the Mostyn Estate trustees required that the proposed new building should look more ornamental in character than the one at Buckley'.[19] Speaking later to fellow-magistrates at the quarter sessions in 1875, Colonel Cook went on to explain that it was the Mostyn estate that demanded that the appearance of the police station should be of the highest standard, and that in effect meant that the court had little choice in the matter other than to comply to its wishes.[20]

The authorities in Anglesey were also experiencing a severe shortage of suitable accommodation for police officers and those they arrested. Colonel Thomas, the chief constable, called for better accommodation for prisoners awaiting trial at Holyhead and said also that the sergeant's house at Beaumaris was hardly fit for human habitation.[21] A further complaint about the position in Holyhead, this time voiced by the Honorable W.O. Stanley, the Lord Lieutenant of the county, claimed that the conditions under which those in custody were held were injurious to their health.[22] In 1878 a police station was built at Llangadwaladr, at a cost of £600.[23] A year later, a new police house was completed at Malltraeth and one was in the process of being built for the constable stationed at Gaerwen.[24] It was hearing that the county was short of suitable police accommodation that probably led to the London and North Western Railway Company to suggest in January 1880 that they would build a police station at Valley, which on completion, they would later lease to the authorities at a rent of £21 per annum. However, at a meeting convened in October 1880 it was revealed that a committee had purchased a site at Valley for £54 upon which a police station would be erected at a cost not exceeding £440.[25] Earlier, in 1878 the Home Office had offered to sell Beaumaris gaol to the justices for just over £1,000, but a few months later the county authorities, somewhat shrewdly, bought it for £600, the money being borrowed on the security of the police rates.[26] It was as a result of the closure of Beaumaris gaol in 1878 that prisoners found themselves being sent to prison at Caernarfon, thus allowing the old gaol to be converted eventually into a police station and lock-up.[27] One suggestion by the chief constable in 1878 was that in future all the police stations throughout Anglesey should come under the scrutiny of the county surveyor, whose task it was to inspect them in the spring of each year, and later make a report on his findings which he then had to submit to the magistrates at each Easter quarter sessions.[28] That the conditions of police stations continued to improve was seen in 1879 when in the chief constable's report he informed magistrates that, apart from Holyhead, most police accommodation was in good order although some needed the walls whitened.[29]

Between 1876-80 there were a number of significant administrative changes in the police forces of north Wales. Firstly, in the autumn of 1876 the chief constable of Anglesey, Captain David White Griffiths, announced that due to ill-health it was his intention to retire on 3 March 1877. News of his retirement was received with great sadness by the magistrates, with the chairman, Mr William Massey, stating that he was speaking for them all when he said 'he had always found the chief constable very ready under all circumstances to do whatever was required of him'.[30] Sadly, however, the chief constable did not live to see retirement and died at his residence at Beaumaris on the 24 November 1876.[31] At his funeral the following tribute was paid to him and is worth recording as it gives some insight into how much he was respected by those he had so faithfully served since assuming office in 1857: 'Rigorously as he performed the duties of his office for the checking of vagrancy and disorder, how many a poor man and woman – how many an honest, houseless wanderer through Anglesey could bear witness that he was, indeed, a Christian? Let the tears that will flow at the mention of his name suffice to attest the fact that he was generally beloved'.[32] With such eulogistic praise it is not surprising that the late chief constable was justly seen by many as being the 'father' of the Anglesey Constabulary.[33]

In the advertisement for a new chief constable no mention was made of the Welsh language, although Sir Richard Bulkeley considered it essential that the person appointed should be Welsh-speaking.[34] There was a total of thirty-seven applicants for the position including the Deputy Chief Constable, Edward Owen. However, just before the appointment he withdrew his candidature on the grounds that he favoured Captain Bulkeley Hughes for the post. This sudden withdrawal from the contest prompted Captain Bulkeley Hughes to write to the editor of the local newspaper to emphasise the fact that the Deputy Chief Constable's decision to withdraw was in no way due to any pressure from him, as he was more than willing to take his chances along with all the other candidates, whoever they were.[35] At the meeting for a new chief constable, which took place on 3 January 1877, Captain Bulkeley Hughes was chosen for the post from a short-list of three. He had formerly served as a captain with Her Majesty's 62nd Regiment, and had been

Deputy Chairman of the Anglesey quarter sessions since 1873. His salary on appointment was £250 per annum, with a further £50 being allowed for expenses.[36]

Quite unexpectedly, Captain Hughes' tenure of office was to be short, for he died suddenly on 4 July 1877 a mere six months after taking up his duties, and having had little time in which to make any significant impact on the direction of the force. This meant that once again magistrates had the task of having to appoint a new chief constable. At the quarter sessions at Beaumaris on 6 October 1877, the chairman thought a knowledge of the Welsh language should be made compulsory. Speaking in support, Mr Richard Davies agreed that the chief constable of a county where 'Welsh was spoken so generally should have a thorough knowledge of the language'.[37] Welsh was now considered essential for the post. There were twenty-three applicants, nine of whom were believed to be Welsh. Sir Richard Bulkeley Hughes MP proposed, and Dr Briscoe Owen, seconded the appointment of Colonel William Hugh Thomas, who was forty-four years of age and spoke Welsh fluently. No other candidate secured a seconder and therefore Colonel Thomas was accordingly appointed chief constable at a salary of £275 per annum. Commenting later on the appointment – Bulkeley Hughes went on to explain that he had 'watched Colonel Thomas' progress through life and a more noble, just, and efficient man he knew not'.[38] The newly appointed chief constable had a distinguished army record and for a time had been commandant of the Royal Anglesey Engineer's Militia. In addition to a great deal of experience in the army, he had also served as the chairman of the Police Committee for a number of years.[39]

Magistrates in Denbighshire were also engaged at this time in seeking a replacement for Mr Denman who announced at the quarter sessions on 26 October 1876, that he was to retire. However, such news evoked a vastly different response from that accorded to Captain Griffiths of the Anglesey force when he announced his wish to retire. Indeed, Mr Denman's decision to retire was greeted almost euphorically by several of the magistrates, with one of them, Major Cornwallis West, stating that he was more than pleased to receive the chief constable's resignation. He explained that Mr Denman's departure 'would afford an opportunity to re-organise the force which at the present time was far from efficient with the general discipline and superintendence being practically non-existent'.[40] Major Cornwallis West's view on the state of the police in Denbighshire was one that many people shared. In 1874, the chairman of the quarter sessions, Mr T. Hughes, read an extract from the *Pall Mall Gazette* which referred to the recent conviction of a policeman in Wrexham for drunkenness which stated 'the case of the inhabitants of Wrexham is deserving of commiseration. A more disagreeable and even dangerous state of affairs can hardly be conceived than a district patrolled by a number of drunken policemen whom their superior officers find it impossible to retrain'.[41] The article also stated 'even a sober burglar is a less objectionable character and less liable to injure the public than an intemperate constable'.[42] Such observations even had the chief constable and his deputy, Superintendent Bradshaw, agreeing at the same quarter sessions that drunkenness had become almost endemic in the force, and but for the fact that it was difficult to recruit suitable men, there were many within the ranks of the Denbighshire Constabulary who should be dismissed.[43] Adding to the magistrates discomfort on the state of the force was the fact that the county had recently been successfully sued by an American, a Mr D'Otis, who claimed he had been arrested and falsely accused of fraud. At the hearing, brought before Lord Coleridge at the Chester Assizes in July 1875, the jury found the case proved for the plaintiff, who was awarded damages of £550 against the authority, £50 of which had to be paid by Superintendent Bradshaw.[44] A little over a year later, in October 1876, a more disturbing situation arose for the authorities when serious rioting occurred at Hafod y Bwlch colliery. On being informed of the disorder by Inspector Wilde at Wrexham, Superintendent Bradshaw declined to act, on the grounds that he had an insufficient number of men at his disposal and, therefore, was in no position to assist. This seeming inability to act on the part of the superintendent was further compounded when he failed to telegraph the chief constable about the problems at the colliery, thus allowing Mr Denman, to remain totally ignorant of the riots for a further four days.[45] It was certainly an unsatisfactory state of affairs and clearly demonstrated to the magistrates that the Denbighshire Constabulary was in urgent need of reform and a change in its leadership. It was understandably, the fervent wish of the magistrates, that the new chief constable when appointed, would prove to be a man who would not only instil discipline, but inspire trust and respect in those under his command and perhaps, even more importantly, restore confidence in the community at large that in the Denbighshire Constabulary they had a force of which they could be justly proud.

However, before any consideration could be given to the appointment of a new chief constable, magistrates had at first to decide on the amount of pension Mr Denman should receive when he retired on 20 February 1877. Always a controversial figure, even to the end, his entitlement to a pension divided the magistrates on what some regarded as a questionable issue. During his two periods in office, Mr Denman had served as chief constable of Denbighshire for a total of twenty-nine years. When a chief constable had served for twenty years, magistrates had it within their power to grant a pension equal to two-thirds of his pay, which in this instance would have amounted to £200 per annum. Knowing this to be the position, the chairman proposed that the chief constable should receive the maximum amount and hoped there would be no objection to this arrangement. Such a hope was dashed when Mr Townshend-Mainwaring objected on the grounds that 'he did not think that Mr Denman was entitled to the maximum superannuation allowance'.[46] Despite such views, however, the chairman's motion was seconded by Sir Watkin Williams-Wynne, Bart., MP and was carried accordingly, with the result that Mr Denman was awarded the maximum pension of £200 per annum, which was to be paid quarterly out of the police rate.[47] The question then arose regarding the amount of pension that should be awarded to Superintendent Bradshaw, who was also retiring. He was sixty-seven years of age and had served the county for twenty-eight years and five months.[48] Members of the police committee recommended that he should receive £100 per annum. Here, once more, they failed to take into account the strong views of Mr Townshend-Mainwaring, who again objected, saying he had a duty to the ratepayers as Superintendent Bradshaw had brought the county into disgrace over the D'Otis affair. Furthermore, he was distinctly unhappy with the way the superintendent had dealt with the fracas at Hafod y Bwlch colliery, which had undoubtedly damaged, even further, the reputation of the force. Although several magistrates fully sympathised with his concern, they nevertheless decided that perhaps there were certain mitigating circumstances for this lapse and therefore agreed that the pension should be awarded.[49]

In the search for a new chief constable there was no shortage of candidates, with sixty-three applying for the post. A number of magistrates believed that the time was opportune to appoint a person who was thoroughly experienced in police duties. However, when the magistrates met in January 1877, they followed their previous pattern and chose Captain Augustus

William Price, of Llanrhaeadr, who immediately on his appointment announced that he was establishing his headquarters at Denbigh.[50] Whatever long-term plans Captain Price may have had for the force will never be known, because in August 1878, he suddenly and unexpectedly handed in his resignation and left Denbigh.[51] His successor was Major Thomas John Leadbetter, a native of Lanarkshire, who was appointed on 17 October 1878. Retiring from the army in 1874, he was for a time attached to the Metropolitan Police, an experience which stood him in good stead for his position as chief constable of Denbighshire. That he was obviously aware of the difficulties which had beset the force in the past was demonstrated when within a month of taking office he issued the following carefully worded general order to the force:

> Major Leadbetter, in assuming office as chief constable of Denbighshire, hopes that all ranks of the police force will give him their unstinted support in promoting a system of police management which will tend to the efficiency of the force and the suppression of crime. The Chief Constable trusts he will have no occasion to complain of negligence on the part of any member of the force, and he need scarcely point out the necessity of every man refraining from temptation to which, as a police officer, he is frequently exposed through the mistaken kindness of others, thereby endangering that freedom of action so necessary in a police constable. The Chief Constable, will at all times be glad to acknowledge and reward the activity and zeal of deserving men, but at the same time, he will have it distinctly understood that he will never pass unnoticed those who may neglect their duty or bring discredit on the Force.[52]

This general order seemed to indicate that with the coming of Major Leadbetter, a new chapter was opening in the history of the Denbighshire Constabulary.

In 1879, magistrates in Caernarfonshire were also unexpectedly seeking a replacement for their former chief constable, Captain Pearson, who had suddenly left Caernarfon without a word of explanation to anyone. Indeed, it was not until some little time had passed that it was learned that the chief constable, had at Bangor, been adjudged a bankrupt, with more than thirty creditors. Although bankruptcy did not disqualify him from holding office, he was, nevertheless, placed in an untenable position as chief constable. Much of his downfall was attributed to certain failed business ventures, as well as a fondness on occasion to follow a rather lavish lifestyle.[53] Yet, despite his failings, Captain Pearson who had taken command in 1870 had performed his duties exceedingly well. Prior to the appointment of his successor numerous letters and articles appeared in the press that related to the necessary qualities required from the new chief constable. In one report it was felt that the person appointed should be fully conversant with all aspects of police duties and 'If a Welshman possessing the requisite qualifications for the office of chief constable can be got, and if that office be in Wales, then, in all reason select him'.[54] In another hard-hitting article, a Captain Clayton was referred to as a possible candidate, who, retiring from the army on a pension, might obtain the post and 'if that was the case he would be receiving the highest salary in the force, while still an apprentice, it was a piece of absurdity'.[55] In another letter it was reported that Superintendents Cornelius Davies and Lewis Prothero from the Caernarfonshire constabulary intended to present themselves as candidates, which the writer believed was only natural if they sought promotion and were suitably qualified, adding 'they have a knowledge of the Welsh language which is desirable; they have a fine external appearance which is not to be disregarded; they are intimately acquainted with the men in the force; they possess a thorough knowledge of the routine of the work, and from what I understand their moral character is unimpeachable'.[56] Yet, despite this report, when magistrates met in April 1879, Captain James Martin Clayton, Adjutant Captain of the Caernarfonshire Militia was appointed chief constable.[57] At first, the Home Secretary declined to confirm the appointment as Captain Clayton was over forty-five years of age and, therefore, according to Home Office guidelines, not eligible to hold office. However, after consulting officers of the crown, the Home Secretary eventually sanctioned the appointment thus allowing Captain Clayton to finally take command of the Caernarfonshire force on 28 June 1879.[58]

The appointment was far from popular and led to a number of questions being asked. Firstly, there had been a demand for the person appointed to possess a thorough knowledge of the Welsh language, and although Captain Clayton could read and translate Welsh he could not speak it fluently, nor write it without consulting a dictionary.[59] Secondly, if one of the superintendents within the force had been appointed, it would have enabled the county to save money, an important consideration as far as the ratepayers were concerned.[60] Thirdly, and possibly the most damning aspect of all, was the evidence contained in a letter from the Clerk of the Peace to the Home Secretary in June 1879, which specifically referred to the candidature of the two superintendents and stated 'neither of them would have that moral power which a higher social position could command to enforce the discipline and order which are so much needed'.[61] Such thinking only served to highlight the old belief 'that authority derived, and should derive, from social rank and made the controversy over the appointment of a chief constable an event of some significance'.[62]

The first intimation the authorities in Merioneth had that they may have to seek a new chief constable came in April 1878, when Mr Clough sought leave of absence on the grounds of ill-health. This request was granted without question, and later the following year he tendered his resignation, owing, as he put it himself, to bodily infirmity. An accident with a gun some years previously had deprived him of one eye and the other was becoming impaired. His departure was widely regretted, and he was the recipient of many tributes for he had faithfully served the county for twenty-three years.[63] Moves to find a suitable successor were to result in a number of suggestions being made. One by Sir W.W. Wynne, believed it would be a good idea to join the county with that of Caernarfonshire under the command of one chief constable. This proposal, however, met with little support, with the Honourable C.H. Wynne declaring 'that Caernarfonshire was a large county and the duties of the chief constable there were very heavy'.[64] Furthermore, he was certain that in the opinion of most magistrates such an arrangement would show 'that the supervision needed to control a force like that in Merioneth would fall far short of what was required.'[65]

The post attracted a number of applicants from which a short list of five was chosen.[66] Of the five candidates, the best known were Mr Thomas Ellis of Bala, and Superintendent O. Hughes of the Merioneth Constabulary. In 1872, Mr Ellis had been appointed secretary of the Merioneth Agricultural Society and for a time had acted as chairman of the Board of Guardians in an adjoining county. He was well-respected and possessed a thorough knowledge of the Welsh language, both written and spoken. The only candidate with any police experience was Superintendent Hughes who had served in the force since its establishment in 1857. One of his supporters was to claim 'that promotion from the ranks should be encouraged by the magistrates always when practicable as it tended to the efficiency of the force'.[67] However, despite Superintendent

Hughes' vast experience, magistrates decided in April 1880, that Mr Thomas Ellis should be appointed and he was duly sworn in at Bala, before Mr E. Griffith-Jones, a justice of the peace, as the new chief constable of the county.[68] His starting salary was fixed at £250 per annum, plus a further £50 for travelling expenses, although there had been an earlier attempt to increase this amount. That the salary remained the same was something that the Board of Guardians welcomed for on 27 January 1880 they had argued that a resolution deploring any attempt to increase the wage of a chief constable should be passed unanimously. The resolution clearly demonstrated how keen the various bodies in north Wales were to keep county police expenses down to a minimum.[69]

What clearly emerges in the 1880s is the increased interest shown by certain sections of the public whenever appointments to senior police positions in north Wales were made. Undoubtedly, such interest arose, in part at least because of the emergence of the new middle class, men of substantial means, but not of the gentry. It was this class which was beginning to exert some influence over certain areas of administration. They began to serve on school boards and boards of guardians and in doing so, observed that in the sphere of policing it was the gentry, sitting as magistrates in quarter sessions who were the sole administrators. The only way open to them to criticise such a system was through the press, and they never lost an opportunity to do so, thus bringing to the attention of the general public the serious shortcomings of the magistracy. Obviously holding strong feelings about how appointments were made, and writing under the name 'Justicia', one correspondent explained 'that as an encouragement to men who had served in the police force for all their lives, a policeman should be appointed'.[70] It was in order to support his belief that he went on to say that 'as military officers they are the best men possible to arrange a campaign and lead soldiers into battle, but I know of nothing in their military career likely to qualify them for the management of a police force, excepting the strictness, promptness and the punctuality which characterises the military duties. That qualification is also a characteristic feature in the police force, and a police superintendent would be as capable, in my opinion, to stimulate the men to activity and obedience as a major exhibiting half a dozen medals on his breast'.[71]

In another article, a former police officer stated that 'when an intelligent young man joins the force, and endeavours to give satisfaction, he ought to be able to expect an adequate reward. Napoleon, I think, used to say to his military recruits, 'you have a Marshal's baton in your knapsack if you will take care of it'. But the police recruit very seldom has the chief constable's baton in his knapsack or anywhere else'.[72] In ending his article the writer asked 'why should the highest office in the force be given to a man who has no more knowledge than a shop keeper's assistant is a question difficult to answer'.[73] There were, however, still those who opposed such views, and felt that the old system of appointing persons to the highest positions should be strictly maintained. In their opinion those appointed to the office of chief constable should be men of some social standing in the community; it mattered little that the person appointed would know little if anything about police duties. They no doubt agreed with the writer who claimed that 'the arrest of thieves, and the hauling of drunkards before the magistrates was a job generally to the lower ranks of the police force, certainly not a task for the gentleman, which, apparently, a chief constable was expected to be'.[74]

However, despite the obvious unfairness in the way appointments were made, newly-appointed chief constables in the late 1870s lost little time in imposing their authority on the officers under their command. This was never more clearly demonstrated than in Merioneth, where Mr Thomas Ellis, soon displayed all the signs of being a strict disciplinarian. Shortly after taking office he issued a large number of orders to members of the force which he expected every officer to observe. One such order authorised every constable to carry a pocket dictionary so that reports were not only clearly written but spelt correctly.[75] In addition every station journal was to be kept up to date and if this was not done a fine would be imposed; if this failed then a much severer penalty would follow.[76] It was in order to ensure that weekly reports were submitted on time that a system of fines was instituted. Failure to submit a report led to a fine a 2s 6d being imposed, a second such failure brought a fine of 5s, with a third resulting in instant dismissal.[77] Typical of the many force orders issued at this time was the following:

a. Every officer to report at his station at 9 am every morning unless on duty after midnight the evening before.
b. Every officer living in a police station to be ready for duty at 9 am – his house cleaned and accoutrements

cleaned and ready for an emergency – a senior officer to report lapses to the chief constable.
c. Members of the force reported for appearing in the streets and railway stations without gloves, and on wet days without capes and gaiters – to be fined – double fines if more than one offence was committed.[78]

Officers in Anglesey were also subjected to an increasing number of force orders which many found, to say the least, irritating. In 1880, an officer was fined 2s 6d for frequently absenting himself from Divine Service. Earlier in 1878 a constable was fined 2s 6d for wearing a new greatcoat at night which was contrary to the chief constable's orders.[79] In one directive, officers were informed that when off duty they would be permitted occasionally, but very rarely, to appear in plain clothes. Even smoking whilst travelling on a bus between Beaumaris and Menai Bridge was to lead to one officer incurring a fine of 6s. Such restrictions, led many observers to believe that the chief constable was treating his men more like army recruits than police officers.[80] Indeed, in such circumstances it comes as no surprise that on occasion some officers were inclined to turn to drink in order to escape the pressures that undeniably were placed on their everyday lives.

Although officers were obviously disenchanted by the many rules and regulations they had to observe, they nevertheless continued to perform their duties in an exemplary manner. Nowhere, at this time, was this more clearly demonstrated than in Caernarfonshire during the parliamentary elections of 1880. Previous elections in the county, particularly in 1868, which a number of officers remembered only too well, had led to some riotous behaviour.[81] Learning from past experience, the authorities on this occasion, believed in being prepared, and in addition to the local constabulary had the support of sixty-two extra police officers who had been drafted in from neighbouring counties and strategically placed in areas where it was feared violence would erupt. Trouble, and criticism of the police, when it came, however, was to arise as a result of two separate incidents. The first concerned the Liberal candidate, Mr Watkin Williams, who on returning from a meeting at Bethesda accompanied by his wife, was attacked with stones, partially dragged from his carriage, and as a result sustained facial injuries. Commenting on the incident, a newspaper with obvious Tory leanings, reported that the attack was little more than an everyday occurrence committed by naughty boys who revelled in throwing stones at passing carriages.[82] When a similar attack occurred at Llandinorwic, this time on the Tory candidate, the Honourable Gordon Douglas Pennant, son of Lord Penrhyn, those responsible for the offence soon found themselves in police custody. The rapid arrest of the culprits evoked a fierce response from the *Caernarvon and Denbigh Herald* which in its editorial column strongly criticised the police and accused them of exhibiting a political bias, in that they had done little to investigate or arrest the perpetrators of the Bethesda outrage.[83]

This accusation was publicly denied by the chief constable who wholeheartedly supported his men. Writing later, in the same newspaper that had so strongly criticised members of the Caernarfonshire Constabulary, he stated that as chief constable 'he desired it to be distinctly understood that under no circumstances whatever is any member of the force to evince feelings of a political nature in connection with the election. The preservation of the peace in a wise, forbearing, patient manner, is the only duty of the Force. The excitement of the present time will demand the individual attention of all ranks'.[84] Although there was no evidence to suggest that the chief constable, or his officers had acted in any way other than impartially in carrying out their duties, the mere fact that it was the gentry sitting in quarter sessions who governed the police was enough reason for many to become suspicious, and openly question the integrity and impartiality of officers. This fact was especially true when the police dealt with issues that touched upon those with vested interests. If nothing else, at least as far as the police were concerned, the parliamentary election of 1880 had clearly revealed how closely their every action was now being monitored by the community at large.

Apart from the Tithe Wars, which will be examined in depth in a later chapter, crime in the 1880s was mainly confined to such offences as drunkenness, poaching, vagrancy and cases of a sexual nature. This was borne out, certainly in Denbighshire, when in the chief constable's report to the quarter sessions in 1881, he informed the magistrates that crime within the county was of a trivial nature.[85] In Anglesey, too, there appeared to be little crime. Speaking to magistrates at the quarter sessions in 1883, the chairman, Captain Verney R.N., congratulated the inhabitants of the county on the paucity of crime and praised the police. In his opinion 'the police force no doubt earned credit from the public for succeeding in detecting crime, but he believed that the highest ambition of the police was to succeed in preventing the commissioning of crime. That was far more important to the community than the detection of crime, of whatever description it was'.[86] A few years later, again in Anglesey, it was reported that the police around the villages of Rhydwyn and Llanfaethlu had little to do as the people were so peaceable.[87] Yet, in many ways such statements belied the true position, for the police throughout north Wales in reality, had plenty to do. As Alan Bainbridge and David J.V. Jones have pointed out on a number of occasions, whenever we examine the amount of crime committed in a particular area, we have to be extremely careful.[88] For example, we know virtually nothing about the amount of criminal activity that has remained unrecorded. The statement becomes very relevant in Wales, particularly in the north, where the forces of law and order in some areas were often viewed as being weak. Evidence to this effect is seen when one observes that in the various counties the police often adopted a different approach when dealing with certain criminal offences. In Merioneth, an examination of the Occurrence Books for the 1870s and 1880s, reveals that in Barmouth, Corwen and Tywyn, police officers favoured rebuking rather than prosecuting some of the younger members of the community, especially if drunk. There is, too, some evidence to suggest that those suspected of larceny were often not proceeded against.[89] This appeared to be the case when a twelve-year-old girl, Anne Davies, was detained for a time before being discharged, for hawking without a licence.[90]

What was a matter of growing concern for the police, throughout the counties of north Wales during the last quarter of the nineteenth century was the problem created by drunkenness. Yet, serious though the problem was, not everyone was convinced that the measures adopted by the police were stringent enough to curb excessive drinking. In Caernarfonshire, for example, it had come to the notice of the Reverend Eiddon Jones, of Llanrug, leader of the Temperance Society, that where breaches of the licensing laws had been reported to the chief constable, he had shown a marked reluctance to prosecute those responsible.[91] Therefore, in the opinion of the Society, Captain Clayton was clearly not doing enough to suppress drunkenness. Yet, on the evidence available there appeared to be no justification for the accusations levelled against the chief constable, as in the year ending 30 September 1881, 954 men and 113 women were convicted of drunkenness. A year later, and contrary to what the Reverend Jones believed, a further 799 men and 111 women were prosecuted for the same offence.[92]

Nor when the occasion arose, did the chief constable, or indeed his officers, fail in their duty to lay charges against those publicans who acted illegally. This fact was borne out in 1883, when twelve publicans were charged with offences that contravened the licensing laws.[93] It was in order to clarify the true position, especially in view of the seriousness of the accusations made against the chief constable, that the magistrates felt that it would be in everybody's interest if they instigated a public inquiry. At the hearing that followed, the chief constable was able to provide ample evidence that in a number of cases brought to his attention the grounds for prosecuting were very weak and as such, the chances of obtaining a successful conviction were slight. In fact, the chief constable was able to prove to the court that where there had been a doubt as to whether a breach of the law had been committed, he had used all his powers of discretion wisely. Although Captain Clayton must have felt at times that he and his officers were being unfairly criticised he did have support. This was seen when an article written by one using the name 'Cadwaladr' stated that although the police in Caernarfonshire were deficient in many respects, so too, were the police forces in other counties, cities and boroughs, and claimed that he was 'bold to affirm, without any fear of contradiction by facts, that the present police force in Caernarfonshire, taking it all in all, is the best that the county has seen since Robert Peel's Act came into operation'.[94]

Similar criticism at this time was also levelled at the chief constable of Merioneth. A writer in the local press stated 'that the police were extremely keen to prosecute those selling bread under weight, but no one had been brought before the magistrates for drunkenness'.[95] Continuing his observations, the writer then suggested that there was more drunkenness in the slate quarrying town of Blaenau Ffestiniog than in any other town in north Wales – a statement that must have distressed the many chapelgoers in the area who constantly advocated the virtues of temperance. Whether this letter, and others like it, spurred the police to make greater efforts is impossible to tell. What can be said about the vigilance of the police in the county, and certainly in contrast to the observations of the writer of the above letter, is that in 1880, 1881 and 1882, there had been 217, 268 and 282 prosecutions respectively against people accused of being drunk and disorderly. Surely, a clear indication that the police in Merioneth at least were not shirking their responsibilities.

Magistrates in Denbighshire were also at this time becoming alarmed by what they saw as an unacceptable level of drunkenness. Their concern was not helped either by the fact that within the county there were 431 public houses, 182 beer houses and twenty-two refreshment rooms – or one licenced house to every 165 inhabitants.[96] To determine accurately the number of offences that relate especially to drunkenness, also poses a problem, since many of the records are scanty in detail. Fortunately, some indication of the amount of drunkenness within the county can be obtained from the chief constable's annual reports for the years 1883 and 1885 which reveal that 612 and 559 persons respectively were charged with this offence.[97] In some respects adding to the difficulties faced by the police, was the passing of the Welsh Sunday Closing Act in 1881, which led to a great deal of back-door drinking, thus making it harder for the authorities to secure a successful conviction. Despite such difficulties, however, there is ample evidence to suggest that members of the Denbighshire Constabulary were constantly active in prosecuting those licensees who broke the law. It was as a direct result of police vigilance, and sometimes by information supplied anonymously by members of the public, that 131 public houses and six beer-houses were prosecuted for a variety of offences between 1882-85, which was 21.57 per cent of the total number of licenced premises within the county. Interestingly, of the number prosecuted, forty-seven were convicted of offences that blatantly contravened the Sunday Closing Act.[98] Undoubtedly, a great deal more illegal Sunday drinking did occur, but it was extremely difficult to detect, as those secretly drinking often had sentries posted outside ready to warn those inside that a visit from the police was imminent. On one occasion, the sentry outside deserted his post for a few minutes thus allowing two police officers to enter the premises where they found several people 'in the full enjoyment of the sweets of forbidden pleasure'.[99]

In Flintshire, too, the authorities were experiencing problems that arose from drunkenness. Between the years 1881-85, 318, 401, 380, 262 and 229 persons respectively were convicted of being drunk and disorderly.[100] In many respects, the authorities in the county were not too happy with the Sunday Closing Act. Mr Muspratt, the mayor of Flint Borough, was from the outset totally against the Act and went on to state that although 'an abstainer himself he had some sympathy with men wanting to drink on Sunday'.[101] A few years later, in an effort to support his earlier observations, he claimed that in 1882, thirty-four persons were prosecuted for breaching the Act and by the following year this number had risen to fifty-four, which in his view, was a clear illustration that the legislation had little effect on hardened drinkers.[102] Surprisingly, the chief constable was also opposed to the Act claiming 'the poor man should not have his mouth shut up on a Sunday if he feels disposed to drink a glass a beer'.[103] There were, obviously, a number of people, some influential, who queried the effectiveness of the Act itself, but this did not discourage officers of the Flintshire Constabulary from enforcing the law when infringement of the liquor regulations were observed. Perhaps, in his assessment of drunkenness in the county, the chairman of the quarter sessions, Mr J. Scott Bankes, captured the feelings of many when he claimed 'that although he did not believe that any effort to render people sober by an Act of parliament would be successful, he did attach importance to the fact that they may induce habits of temperance among the masses, by removing temptations to drink from their path'.[104]

Many of the most persistent offenders were the thousands of vagrants and tramps who passed through the counties of north Wales each year. Generally disliked, they were, from a policing point of view, a constant menace that posed endless problems for the authorities. At a meeting of the Board of Guardians at Holywell, Mr Thomas Jones drew attention to the difficulties 'caused by disreputable and villainous tramps passing up and down the county'.[105] An example of the type of trouble tramps created was seen at the Holywell police court in October 1883, when four tramps, William Johnson, Thomas Wilson, John Wood and Robert Lawson, were charged with burning all their clothes as well as their boots. As a result of their behaviour three of the accused were sentenced to fourteen days' imprisonment with the fourth member for seven days, all with hard labour.[106] Some idea of the enormity of the difficulties that faced the police when dealing with vagrancy, was seen in Flintshire, when in the chief constable's annual report for the year ending 30 September 1885, he informed magistrates that the problem was on the increase and during the year his officers had dealt with 3,922 applications from those seeking relief, as against a figure of 3,719 for the year ending September 1884.[107] In Caernarfonshire, this time in the chief constable's quarterly report in April 1885, he listed the number of tramps relieved in the various police districts as being: Caernarfon 154; Bangor 277; Conwy 323; Pwllheli 33 and Porthmadog 67, a total of 854, as against the corresponding quarter in 1884, when 974 had been relieved.[108]

If the pattern that emerges in the 1880s is one that points to the vagrant as being the main cause of criminal activity in the counties of north Wales, then such observations must be tempered with caution. It was true, that many had been responsible for hundreds of criminal acts, and sending those caught to prison had proved of little avail, thus creating among magistrates and police alike a feeling of exasperation, as the solution to the problem continued to evade them. Therefore, the only measure open to the authorities, and one that took up so much police time, was for officers to increase their vigilance in order that law-abiding citizens could remain unmolested. However, as the police increased their vigilance, the tramps in turn began to adopt new tactics, which resulted in them becoming even more artful in their ways. In Merioneth, one novel method of obtaining money adopted by tramps was ultimately to lead to the term 'chapel collection tramps'; the general idea being that tramps, often working in pairs would attend a chapel, join heartily in the singing, as well as listen attentively to the sermon, then at the ending of the service, would stand up and boldly ask if a collection could be made on their behalf. No doubt it was their fervent hope that few in such surroundings would refuse those they saw as less fortunate than themselves. Commenting of this ruse, a newspaper declared that if it was not stamped out very quickly, churches and chapels would be invaded by such rogues every Sunday.[109] One tramp, John Swine, was to find to his cost, that there was little compassion in the hearts of the magistrates sitting at the Aberdyfi Petty Sessions. Observed entering the village by Constable William Evans, he was seen knocking on the door of a dressmaker, where he asked for some bread, which promptly led to his arrest. On appearing before the magistrates he claimed that 'he was not asking for bread, but thread in order to mend his trousers'. The chairman, however, was not moved by such a plea and sentenced him to one month's imprisonment with hard labour.[110]

Plate 2
*A tramp circa 1860s-70s*

There were of course a number of other offences, the kind that in the main were committed most frequently by local people, and in this category was poaching. In support of this fact, one newspaper reported 'there is reason to believe that the greatest transgressions were natives, and not navvies'.[111] One area where poaching was on the increase in the late 1870s was Abergynolwyn, and when on 10 January 1878, Constable John Hughes, was savagely attacked by a gang of six poachers, some armed with spears and their faces blackened, the authorities became extremely alarmed.[112] The incident aroused a great deal of local anger, with one newspaper asking the question 'whether the attackers were Welsh or English?'[113] So incensed were the magistrates at the manner in which the officer had been assaulted that they offered a reward of £25 for any information as to the identity of the assailants.[114] That the assault on Constable Hughes was no isolated incident was seen in Caernarfonshire in 1881, when an officer was shot and seriously wounded as he got too close to a gang of poachers.[115] In 1885, in a similar incident, a member of the Flintshire Constabulary, Constable McWalters, was shot and seriously wounded in the neck by a poacher he was attempting to arrest.[116]

In addition there were other offences which entailed much work for the officers involved. Sexual offences, for example, created difficulties for the police throughout the counties of north Wales in that it was often difficult for them to obtain information that would lead to a successful conviction. Of the many offences in this category that were reported to the police, rape, indecent assault, bestiality and prostitution were the most sexually motivated, although one also has to take into consideration offences such as indecent exposure. A great deal of police time was also taken up with the issuing of Bastardy Orders, a duty most officers found difficulty in executing, since the recipients of such orders were often reluctant to accept responsibility for the claims made against them. The Tywyn Occurrence Book for the period 1881-97, reveals that twelve persons were brought before the courts, either to answer bastardy charges, or on occasion, for actually disobeying a bastardy order made against them earlier.[117] Another crime the police were anxious to stamp out was the selling of under weight bread. In Merioneth, the chief constable ordered one officer to conduct his investigations in plain clothes in order to achieve a higher conviction rate. This meant, in effect, that an officer would go from one shop to another buying threepenny loaves, having them weighed, and then issuing summonses against those who sold bread under the prescribed weight.[118]

Improved travel conditions, such as the coming of the railways caused the police to become even more vigilant. In many ways one begins to see the emergence of the travelling criminal. The ease with which many of the criminal fraternity could now travel made it possible for them to commit a crime in one town, and after a short train journey be in another, often posing as a different person and occasionally even changing their mode of dress. Another vital improvement, and one that was of benefit to the police generally was the introduction of telegraphy. This was to prove of great assistance to the constable stationed in Aberdyfi who stopped a tramp wearing a clean shirt, in the belief that it had been stolen. In order to confirm his suspicions he telegraphed the authorities in Cardiganshire to ascertain whether shirts had been stolen in the area. Back came the reply that they had 'and would he forward the suspect to them'.[119] In general, co-operation between the various forces at this time was very limited. As for scientific aids, apart from photography, they were practically non-existent. It was probably to enable police officers in Denbighshire to take a more active part in surveillance work that the police committee recommended that six more powerful telescopes should be provided at a cost not exceeding £10.[120]

A duty undertaken by officers in Flintshire, and one of national importance, was that of ensuring the safety of the Prime Minister, Mr William Ewart Gladstone, at Hawarden Castle between the years 1880-2. It was a duty that was continually surrounded by controversy, much of this being due to the extra costs incurred whilst the Prime Minister was in residence. In the correspondence between the chief constable and the Home Office it was generally agreed that one half of the expenditure should be borne by the government.[121] Later, at the quarter sessions held on 3 January 1882, the question arose again as to who should pay the costs involved; as far as the magistrates were concerned all expenditure should be paid for by the government.[122] However, not all ratepayers agreed with that suggestion; those living in Bagillt claimed that the expenditure involved should be charged to the rates. At a later meeting on 17 October 1882, the chief constable announced that four police officers would be assigned to the protection of Mr Gladstone, two of them being detectives, with half the cost being borne by the government. In a General Order dated 31 August 1882, the chief constable directed that one sergeant and two constables should always be on guard at the castle. During the day, officers were to patrol in plain clothes and at night in uniform. Officers were also to carry revolvers between the hours of 10.00 pm and 5.00 am[123]. That the Prime Minister was pleased with the way he had been protected was seen when the chief constable received a letter from Mr Gladstone early in July, which contained a cheque for £20 which was to be added to the county police superannuation fund. The letter also spoke in very glowing terms of the police in Flintshire.[124]

Pressure on the magistrates to change the old outdated system of appointing men to command the police forces in north Wales resurfaced during 1883, 1886 and 1888, when vacancies occurred in Merioneth, Caernarfonshire and Flintshire. The first occasion on which magistrates could demonstrate whether they had heeded the calls for change occurred on 7 February 1883 with the sudden death of Mr Thomas Ellis, the chief constable of Merioneth. His passing brought to the fore the question of what type of person should command the force. When a newspaper reported that one of the applicants for the vacant post was actually taking lessons for an hour a day with the chief constable, it claimed 'that this gentleman ought to be promptly disqualified, seeing that a knowledge of police duties is not deemed necessary for the police'.[125] Of the six short listed, only Superintendent Owen Hughes was a member of the force; each candidate was duly interviewed and Captain T.W. Best was chosen as the new chief constable.[126] For those in the community who wished for the appointment of a police officer it was a bitter disappointment. Later, in reporting the appointment, one newspaper was particularly sarcastic about the magistrates' choice, saying, 'Captain Best may learn Welsh and police duties from Superintendent Hughes and, when he has sucked the superintendent's brain, may discharge him without fear of censure'.[127]

The second appointment occurred in Caernarfonshire in 1886 with the death of Captain Clayton who had been in poor health for several months. There were over forty applications, many being received from Ireland. Commenting on the forthcoming appointment the Caernarfonshire Board of Guardians expressed the view that the force itself had men suitable for the office.[128] When magistrates finally met to choose their new chief constable at the quarter sessions in Caernarfon, they chose Colonel Arthur Ashley Ruck. He was a Welsh-speaker but had no knowledge of police duties, illustrating once again that magistrates, despite public opinion, continued to cling to the old habits.

The third appointment came with the retirement in 1888, of Mr Peter Browne, who had been chief constable of Flintshire for thirty-one years, and was the last of the chief constables appointed in 1857. There were thirty-six applicants for the position, six of whom were short-listed. They included Superintendent Bolton, deputy chief constable of Flintshire.[129] His police experience was to count for nothing, for when the magistrates met to appoint a successor to Mr Browne, they chose a military man, Major Tankerville Webber of the Royal Welsh Fusiliers; again a disappointment for those who had campaigned so long and vigorously for a police officer to be appointed to the highest position in the service.

Without doubt, the Local Government Act of 1888 was to prove a very important piece of legislation for the forces in north Wales. True, this Act in the very early stages was to create a good deal of confusion as to who should really control the police. Should it be the old guard representing the county gentry, or the newly-created county councils? However, throughout the counties, a compromise was reached and magistrates found themselves in a new role, becoming members of Standing Joint Committees administering the county forces in partnership with the elected county authorities. At first, not everything went smoothly and there was a certain suspicion between the two bodies, yet time was to prove a great healer and the new arrangement worked much better than anyone had ever imagined it would. With the passing of the Act, the power of the justices began to wane, and that of the local authorities to increase. There was one area in the legislation, however, where magistrates still retained their old authority. From the outset, the new Act made it clear that it did not affect the owners, duties and liabilities of the justices as conservators of the peace or of the obligation of the chief constable or other constables to obey their lawful orders. So, in times of unrest, it was still the responsibility of the justices to call upon the military if necessary and swear in additional special constables.[130] Commenting on the demise of the quarter sessions in Caernarfonshire, a writer expressed an opinion that could equally be applied to the remainder of the counties in north Wales, when he wrote 'whether for good or ill the venerable body known to the British Constitution for many a century as quarter sessions is disappearing from the scene'. The county had long come to the conclusion of the poet 'superfluous lags the veteran on the stage'. At the same time, now the quarter sessions gives what may be described in theatrical phrase as 'positively the last performance', the sternest radical amongst us may indulge in a passing regret, and may acknowledge that after all the old institution was not without some good points'.[131]

[1] *CDH*, 8 April 1871.

[2] *Cambrian News*, 3 January 1873.

[3] MQS Rolls, (Hilary, 1873). See also *Cambrian News*, 3 January 1875, which states that this differential in the rates of pay was highlighted in a newspaper article that specifically related to the position in Cardiganshire which reported, 'in these days of high wages, it is of course by no means difficult for a young man who has in him the making of an efficient officer to receive higher wages in other police forces than he can in Cardiganshire'.

[4] Ibid. Also examine *CDH*, 19 October 1872, in which the chief constable of Caernarfonshire calls upon the magistrates to consider increasing the pay of his officers, claiming that those serving in Glamorgan, Lancashire and Cheshire were all in receipt of a higher rate of pay.

[5] MQS Rolls, (Trinity, 1876).

[6] *CDH*, 21 October 1876.

[7] AQS Rolls, (Midsummer, 1877). The actual outcome of the meeting at Chester is somewhat questionable for in the MQS Rolls, (Hilary, 1878), it is stated that within a year of the meeting a uniform system of police pay was introduced throughout the counties of north Wales. An examination of the MQS Rolls, (Michaelmas, 1877), and (Hilary, 1878), also record the proposed new rates of pay for all ranks up to and including superintendent, which could only be implemented if approved by the Secretary of State. See also H.K. Birch, 'The Merioneth Police 1856-1950', MA University of Wales thesis, 1980, p.70 which also records in full a new pay structure.

[8] MQS Rolls, (Michaelmas, 1874).

[9] MQS Rolls, (Easter, 1876). In 1877 despite the shortage of accommodation the police committee was able to show that in its determination to help the constabulary it had provided houses with two cells attached at each of the following places: Corwen, Barmouth, Penrhyndeudraeth, Blaenau Ffestiniog, Maentwrog, Tywyn and Aberdyfi.

[10] *CDH*, 7 July 1877.

[11] Ibid., 11 April 1874.

[12] Ibid.

[13] Ibid.

[14] Ibid., 10 April 1875.

[15] *CDH*, 21 October 1876.

[16] CQS Rolls, (Trinity, 1877).

[17] CQS Rolls, (Easter, 1878).

[18] FQS Rolls, (Michaelmas, 1874).

[19] *CDH*, 10 July 1875.

[20] FQS Rolls, (Michaelmas, 1875).

[21] *CDH*, 5 January 1878.

[22] AQS Rolls, (Hilary, 1878). Despite the deplorable condition a site for a new police station at Holyhead was not purchased until 1891 and by April

1894 the cells and superintendent's quarters were ready for use at a cost to the county of £2,769.

[23] Hugh Owen, *The History of the Anglesey Constabulary*, (Llangefni, 1952), p.36.

[24] AQS Rolls, (Michaelmas, 1879).

[25] *CDH*, 23 October 1880.

[26] Hugh Owen, op. cit., p.36

[27] Ibid.

[28] Ibid.

[29] AQS Rolls, (Trinity, 1879). Interestingly in the chief constable's General Orders for the 16 April 1878 which dealt mainly with the issue of new clothing, officers were warned that such apparel would only be issued if those occupying police houses ensured they were kept in a neat and proper order with the walls whitewashed.

[30] *CDH*, 14 October 1876.

[31] Ibid., 2 December 1876.

[32] *NWC*, 2 December 1876.

[33] Hugh Owen, op. cit., p.31.

[34] Ibid.

[35] *CDH*, 9 December 1876.

[36] Hugh Owen, op. cit., p.32. See also, AQS Rolls, (Midsummer, 1877), which records that Superintendent Edward Owen, who had acted as chief constable during the vacancy 25 November 1876 to 2 January 1877, was granted £7.12s for the extra work involved.

[37] AQS Rolls, (Michaelmas, 1877). Also *CDH*, 27 October and 10 November 1877.

[38] *CDH*, 17 November 1877.

[39] Hugh Owen, op. cit., p.33.

[40] DQS Rolls, (Michaelmas, 1876).

[41] DQS Rolls, (Michaelmas, 1874).

[42] Ibid.

[43] Ibid.

[44] *CDH*, 24 July 1875.

[45] DQS Rolls, (Michaelmas, 1876). See also George Lerry, op. cit., p.127, where it is stated that after his retirement Superintendent Bradshaw, in conversation with Captain Griffith Boscawen, a magistrate, referred to the riot at Hafod y Bwlch and stated 'that all the policemen in Wrexham, or a great proportion of them, were given to drinking and therefore could not be relied upon in times of trouble'.

[46] *CDH*, 6 January 1877.

[47] Ibid.

[48] Ibid.

[49] Ibid.

[50] George Lerry, op. cit., p.127. Police headquarters only remained in Denbigh until the end of 1878, when it was moved to the County Buildings, Wrexham (the new name given to the old Militia Barracks), which was converted into a court house, bridewell and police headquarters for the county.

[51] *CDH*, 31 August 1878.

[52] General Order Book. 1 November 1878. See also George Lerry, op. cit., p.122. From the outset the new chief constable was fortunate to have as his chief clerk, Inspector Sheehan, an officer with exceptional ability, who had originally joined the Metropolitan Police in 1846, before being encouraged to transfer to Denbighshire in 1856 by Superintendent Bradshaw. According to those closest to him, Inspector Sheehan was said to be a 'walking compendium of police law and an expert in the compilation of Government returns'. Also see DQS Rolls (Easter, 1880).

[53] *CDH*, 14 December 1878.

[54] Ibid., 18 January 1879.

[55] Ibid., 25 January 1879.

[56] Ibid., 1 February 1879.

[57] Ibid., 12 April 1879.

[58] CQS Rolls, (Trinity, 1879).

[59] Home Office, HO 82356-20.

[60] NLW Glynllifon MSS, 1961-84. It was at this time, a government recommendation, that in the event of a vacancy occurring in the rank of superintendent such a position should not be filled. If, in Caernarfonshire one of the superintendents had become chief constable, two divisions could have been amalgamated thus reducing the total expenditure of the force by £200 per annum.

[61] GRO, CPC/CP to Home Secretary 4 June 1879.

[62] J. Owain Jones, *The History of the Caernarvonshire Constabulary 1856-1950*, (Caernarfon, 1963), p.49. See also *CDH*, 30 August 1879. The newly appointed chief constable was to find that in assuming command of the force he also became responsible for the policing of the Borough of Pwllheli which after a period of twenty-two years finally decided to amalgamate with the county of Caernarfonshire. See too, GRO, Pwllheli Minute Book, 5 August 1879, which records that the Borough council voted by eight votes to six to merge their police with that of the county and in doing so the sole Pwllheli constable became one of the last parish constables and was compensated for his loss of office with a gratuity of £30 and although stripped of all previous authority still retained his position as town crier. Also see *CDH*, 10 January 1880 which records the transfer for police purposes of Maenan parish from Denbighshire to Caernarfonshire and *CDH*, 3 July 1880, where agreement was reached at the Caernarfonshire quarter sessions for a constable to be stationed at the newly acquired areas of Llysfaen and Eirias, which formerly came under the jurisdiction of the Denbighshire constabulary.

[63] *CDH*, 10 January 1880. See also *Cambrian News*, 20 July 1877. Although

murder was rare in Merioneth, the dismembered body of a woman later identified as Sarah Hughes, was found in the River Arran outside Dolgellau. The investigation of the crime by Mr Clough eventually led to the arrest of Cadwaladr Jones, who, at the Chester Assizes, was sentenced to death and subsequently hanged by the infamous Marwood on 23 November 1877. Although the murder was in no way a *cause célèbre* Jones was the last person to be executed within the county. The gallows on which he was hanged were transferred to Carmarthen Gaol on the closing of Bodlondeb. *Llanelli and County Guardian*, 15 March 1888.

[64] *Cambrian News*, 9 January 1880.

[65] Ibid.

[66] *Cambrian News*, 9 April 1880.

[67] Ibid. The other three candidates on the short list were: Captain Adams; Major Jones and Mr E.H. Vychan Williams of Castle Deudraeth.

[68] MQS Rolls, (Hilary, 1880).

[69] Ibid., (Trinity, 1880). See also MQS Rolls, Order Book, (Trinity, 1882), where it is recorded that when at a later date an attempt was made to increase the salary to £300 per annum plus £75 for expenses, this also failed with the Home Office giving £270 per annum, plus £75 for expenses, as being a more realistic figure for such an appointment.

[70] *Cambrian News*, 16 July 1880.

[71] Ibid.

[72] Ibid., 27 February 1880.

[73] Ibid.

[74] *Cambrian News*, 5 March 1880.

[75] MCF Orders, QA/P/D/8/1, 12 May 1880.

[76] Ibid., 7 June 1880. Constables at the time were left in no doubt of orders immediately emanating from the chief constable, for such instructions were boldly written in red ink. Some interesting examples of the way in which discipline was administered towards the latter quarter of the nineteenth century are cited in *The Monmouthshire Constabulary Centenary Handbook*, (1957), pp.17-8 and Islwyn Bate, *History of the Newport Borough Police*, (1959), pp.90-1.

[77] Ibid., 19 May 1881. To a great extent a policeman's private life was restricted by the service. For example, a constable was forbidden to leave his station without the express permission of the chief constable and, even then, the purpose and place of his visit had to be recorded. Any officer in arrears with his rent or in debt to a publican was liable to instant dismissal. Such a ruling also applied to any other officer whose family incurred debts they could not pay.

[78] Ibid., 6 January 1882. See also H.K. Birch, 'The Merioneth Police 1856-1950', MA University of Wales thesis, 1980, pp.93-4.

[79] Hugh Owen, op. cit., pp.38-9. It was possible to clarify the position on dress that the chief constable in October 1879 issued the following directive. The new greatcoat (with belt) is to be worn outside, also gloves on all occasions of quarter sessions, Petty Sessions, Sundays and when otherwise

ordered. Old greatcoats (no belt) will be worn, and in very wet weather with leggings, but for patrolling duties in fine weather, capes and leggings may be worn instead of greatcoats. A fine of 1s will be inflicted for any deviation from the above.

[80] Ibid. One duty the officers in Anglesey were to be relieved of, occurred when the justices resolved that constables should no longer be allowed to take any part in finding recruits for the army and the militia. Prior to 1880 they had often been useful as unofficial recruiting officers.

[81] A.H. Dodd, *A History of Caernarvonshire*, (Wrexham, 1980), p.362. See also J.O. Jones, op. cit., pp.37-40. For an excellent account of the political scene in Wales during this period see Ryland Wallace, *'Organise! Organise! Organise!' A study of reform Agitations in Wales 1840-1886*, (Cardiff, 1991), pp.91-157.

[82] *NW Chronicle*, 20 March 1880.

[83] *CDH*, 27 March 1880.

[84] *CDH*, 3 April 1880. It was not until the passing of the Police Disabilities Removal Act in 1887 that police officers were to vote for the first time in parliamentary elections. A second such Act passed in 1893 allowed them to vote in municipal elections. See also *Hansard*, lxiii, 11 June 1914, col. 575, despite the Acts of 1887 and 1893 a number of policemen, especially those single who lived in section houses, remained unenfranchised.

[85] DQS Rolls, (Easter, 1881). See appendix v, for the victimless crimes at Petty Sessions in Wales 1881.

[86] *CDH*, 20 October 1883.

[87] AQS Rolls, (Easter, 1886).

[88] David J.V. Jones, op. cit., p.30-64, where he details the difficulties in assessing the true amount of crime committed.

[89] Corwen Occurrence Book, 10 June 1884.

[90] *Flintshire Observer*, 6 January 1882.

[91] *CDH*, 24 February 1883.

[92] CQS Rolls, (Michaelmas, 1882).

[93] Ibid. (Easter, 1883). Also see *CDH*, 22 October 1881; 7 January 1882 and 1 July 1882.

[94] *CDH*, 13 January 1883.

[95] Ibid., 12 August and 7 October 1882.

[96] DQS Rolls, (Michaelmas, 1881).

[97] *CDH*, 20 October 1883 and 27 September 1885.

[98] Ibid., 21 October 1882; 6 January and 20 October 1883; 5 January and 12 July 1884; 17 January and 24 October 1885. Also see David J.V. Jones, *Crime in Nineteenth Century Wales*, (Cardiff, 1992), p.157 and W.R. Lambert, *Drink and Sobriety in Victorian Wales 1820-1895*, (Cardiff, 1963).

[99] *Flintshire Observer*, 21 May 1885. See also *CDH*, 29 March 1885, which records that at the 'Hope and Anchor' public house in Holyhead, Ellen Jones, received a £5 fine for selling beer at an open window to a crowd of men. On this occasion the look-outs were caught napping.

[100] Ibid., 20 October 1882; 18 October 1883; 20 October 1884; 22 October 1885

and 21 October 1886.
[101] Ibid., 9 September 1881.
[102] *CDH*, 12 September 1885.
[103] A.G. Veysey, *Annual Report of the County Archivist*, Clwyd Record Office (Hawarden, 1975), p.24.
[104] *Flintshire Observer*, 3 July 1884.
[105] *Flintshire Observer*, 1 November 1883.
[106] Ibid., 22 October 1885.
[107] CQS Rolls, (Easter, 1885).
[108] *CDH*, 11 April 1885.
[109] Ibid., 1 January 1881.
[110] *CDH*, 11 June 1881.
[111] *Cambrian News*, 7 January 1881.
[112] MRO, Constabulary Records, Z/H/2/1, Journal of Constable John Hughes. Also David J.V. Jones, 'A dead loss to the community': the criminal vagrant in mid-nineteenth century Wales, *Welsh History Review*, 8 (3), 1977.
[113] *CDH*, 19 January 1878.
[114] *Cambrian News*, 22 February 1878. For a general view of poaching see J.J. Tobias, *Nineteenth Century Crime, Prevention and Treatment*, (Newton Abbot, 1972), pp.17-19.
[115] *CDH*, 8 January 1881.
[116] *Flintshire Observer*, 26 November 1885.
[117] MRO, Tywyn Occurrence Book, 1881-97.
[118] *CDH*, 12 August 1882.
[119] *Cambrian News*, 29 December 1882.
[120] *CDH*, 19 April 1884.
[121] Ibid., 22 October 1881.
[122] FQS Rolls, (Michaelmas, 1882). Later at the Easter quarter sessions, Colonel the Honourable R. Rowley, proposed that the costs involved in guarding the Prime Minister should come from the government, he then quoted that in the Metropolis, there was between 1,200 and 1,300 officers protecting ministers, but expenditure did not come out of the rates.
[123] FRO, Chief Constables General Order Book, 13 August 1882.
[124] *CDH*, 7 July 1883, also *Denbigh Free Press*, 7 July 1883.
[125] *Cambrian News*, 2 March 1883.
[126] MQS Rolls, (Easter, 1883). Others on the short list were: Lieutenant-Colonel G. Harrow Cope; Brooks S. Cunliffe; W.J. Kerr and G.A. Taylor.
[127] *Cambrian News*, 27 April 1883.
[128] *CDH*, 23 April 1886.
[129] *Flintshire Observer*, 20 September 1888. The six candidates for the position of chief constable were: Major R.T. Webber; Captain Reuben Norton; Mr James Dale Bolton, deputy chief constable of Flintshire; Superintendent Innis, Hertfordshire constabulary; Captain Edward George

Lingard, Superintendent, Cheshire Constabulary; and Captain Arrowsmith, the former chief constable of Bootle.

[130] T.A. Critchley, op. cit., p.137.

[131] *CDH*, 4 January 1889.

Chapter V

# Professionalism, Communications and Stability

The period 1889-1914 was to prove not only eventful, but important for officers serving in the various forces in north Wales. An early landmark was the passing of the Police Act of 1890.[1] With its passing, the career prospects for officers became vastly enhanced, for they were now guaranteed a pension on retirement. Prior to this time, justices lacking sound and administrative and financial advice were frequently haphazard in the exercise of their discretion as to whether to grant an officer a pension and therefore the final decision was often subject to the approval of the chief constable. Indeed, in some forces no provision at all was made for the man who retired normally, on the expiration of his service. However, under the new legislation police authorities in north Wales were allowed some flexibility in the amount of pension an officer could receive and a maximum and minimum limit was imposed. In addition, there was also laid down a minimum qualifying age before an officer became entitled to a pension, but the ordinary expectation – and in the Metropolitan Police the rule – was that a man could retire after twenty-five years service with a pension amounting to three-fifth's of his pay, regardless of his age.[2] There is little doubt that the introduction of a firm entitlement to a pension did much to curtail what previously had been a high wastage of officers who, all too frequently, left the service to find positions that offered greater prospects.

The fact that the police obtained a pension as a right was a great achievement. For this was a time when the service lacked any federation or trade union to act on its behalf. That it was eventually successful, was largely due to men of goodwill both in and out of Parliament, who recognised the importance of the police and believed that on retirement they should receive some form of remuneration. The fact that there was no formal means of making their conditions known was something that was to hamper the service over the years. However, in 1892, and with foresight, John Kempster founded a journal entitled *Police Review* which, in later years, he believed would be a vehicle in which they could air their troubles, advocate their interests, and assist better education.[3] Two years later in 1894, another organisation calling itself 'The Police and Citizens' Association' came into being with the following aims:

a. To render legal assistance in the defence or prosecution of important cases involving the rights of the police or the public.
b. To advocate a competitive system of promotion, and to discourage personal patronage.
c. To abolish the system of appointing untrained men as superior officer.[4]

Sadly, however, although the Pensions Bill was universally welcomed by the police, for many it had come too late. When Inspector Owen Jones retired from the Merioneth Constabulary in 1883, on the grounds of total infirmity, his sole reward after twenty-six years faithful service was a one-off payment of £70 from the superannuation fund.[5] As for the widow of Constable Lewis Jones, of the Caernarfonshire Constabulary stationed at Bangor, who died of typhoid fever as a result of escorting victims of disease to hospital, her regret must have been even greater, for she was granted a lump sum of £20 which was later increased to £28 at the request of the chief constable.[6]

The age at which an officer could safely retire was a matter of concern to some magistrates in north Wales. When one officer in Merioneth retired at the age of sixty-one there were members of the standing joint committee who believed he could have served for at least another four years.[7] In support of their belief, they went on to state that generals in the army went on until they were sixty-five. Answering their criticism, the chief constable reported that generals 'did not have to walk over mountains'.[8] Creating further amusement, and in agreement with the chief constable, Colonel Lloyd Evans reported 'that generals who retired at sixty-five years of age were provided with wheel chairs'.[9] However, despite criticism from some quarters, most magistrates generally agreed that an officer was justifiably entitled to a pension after years of faithful service. Speaking to the police committee in Denbighshire, one magistrate, Mr Simon Jones, although not as a rule in favour of providing pensions, felt that 'the occupation of a policeman was one of peril, and it was only right that he should be made to feel that he was cared for in his old age, and that his wife and children should not be dependent on charity'.[10] It was to enable members of the standing joint committee in Denbighshire to fully understand the position as regards police pensions, that the chief constable, Major Leadbetter, in a special report stated, 'that between 1840 and 1890 three hundred and twenty-nine men of all ranks had joined the Denbighshire constabulary. of this number, only 18 or 5.47 per cent were pensioned and their average age when superannuated was 59 years, and length of service 23.6 years'.[11]

That officers had to observe certain rules and regulations regarding the money they had paid into the superannuation fund over the years was seen in 1896, when a constable in Merioneth asked for the repayment of contributions he had made on transferring to the Liverpool City police. His request was refused with the chief constable, Major Best, making it clear in no uncertain terms that he could not recommend such payment on the grounds that the officer had left to join another force and therefore payment was discretionary.[12] Furthermore, according to the chief constable, such payment would be totally wrong when the county had gone to the trouble of training him only to see another force reap the benefit.[13] It was a selfish view but it was one that must have caused a pause for thought for those who wished to transfer to another force. It was generally the standard procedure that if an officer wished to transfer to another force he first of all had to obtain the permission of the chief constable, as failure to comply could render him open to instant dismissal.[14] In cases where an officer wished to retire, it was ordered that he must give at least three months notice and, in addition, present himself before the standing joint police committee so that a pension could be granted.[15] A typical example of the amount officers received on retirement was seen when the following retired from the Denbighshire constabulary in 1891:

|  | **Annual Pay** | **Annual Pension**[16] |
|---|---|---|
| Superintendent Thomas Hammonds | £118.12.6d | £79.1.8d |
| Inspector J. Lindsay | £100.7.6d | £68.1.4d |
| Sergeant W. Breese | £82.2.6d | £54.15.0d |
| Constable James Burgess | £73.0.0d | £48.13.4d |
| Constable John Griffiths | £73.0.0d | £48.13.4d |

There is little doubt that those in police service at this time were benefiting from the great changes that were taking place. With the passing of the Local Government Act in 1888, the strong grip of the gentry that had for so long held sway over the county forces had, if only partially, been loosened. The further Act in 1890 had given men fresh hope that at last, after a lifetime of service, a pension was to be their just reward. The earlier passing of the law that allowed policemen to vote, made them feel that they were achieving that self-respect so many felt had been denied them over the years. There was still much to be done, but all these welcome improvements were steps in the right direction as far as the officers in north Wales were concerned.

However, no matter how important and welcome the changes were, the daily routine of those serving in the counties of north Wales changed little. In addition to their normal duties of law enforcement, officers were still expected to undertake an ever increasing variety of extraneous duties, although it has to be recognised that not everyone was convinced the police were overworked. Magistrates in Denbighshire in 1891, for example, voiced their reservations and claimed that many officers had too much time on their hands and therefore 'a little harder work would do them good and make them more active'.[17] A few years later, at a meeting of magistrates, again in Denbighshire, a Mr Lumley claimed officers had so little to do they seemed for ever to be attending funerals, especially if the deceased had been a figure of importance, but strangely, if the person was unimportant then there was never a policeman to be seen.[18] However, in support of the police, Captain Best explained that if somebody important died then a large crowd would be expected to be in attendance at the funeral and it was only right for the chief constable to send officers to a large gathering. Far from satisfied with this reasoning, Mr Lumley replied 'that he hoped he would never see another policeman at a funeral again'.[19]

It was because some magistrates believed that police officers in general had little to do that there was, in the 1890s a move by the authorities to give officers additional responsibilities. Indeed, as early as 1889, at the very first meeting of the police committee in Merioneth, it was suggested their services could be used as school attendance officers and sanitary inspectors.[20] Two years later, the same committee heard a proposal 'that in the opinion of the committee it is desirable that the police should act as school attendance officers and sanitary inspectors', and called upon the chief constable to seek the views of the Home Office on such a policy being adopted.[21] In reply, the Home Office made it abundantly clear that to allow officers to perform such duties would prevent them from performing police work.[22] Furthermore, magistrates were informed in no uncertain terms that if they wished to deploy officers on such duties they should seriously consider employing more constables. In many ways the Home Office, unlike similar standing joint police committees at this time, obviously recognised and appreciated the importance of a policeman's work, a fact which many officers in north Wales took some comfort from.

However, despite the views expressed by the Home Office on officers undertaking extraneous duties, standing joint committees still continued to give officers additional work. In Denbighshire, for example, constables were expected to list and cost the number of rooms that would be available on their beats for the holding of inquests.[23] In a later order, officers were informed that where practicable no inquests should be held in public houses.[24] Another unpleasant task officers had to perform was the reporting of all infectious diseases in their area, such as scarlet fever and diphtheria, particularly if the illness occurred in a farm or shop which sold milk and butter.[25] A great deal of the work undertaken by the police during this period was concerned with the welfare of animals. One time-consuming duty was the keeping of a dog register within each police district and noting whether the owners of such animals had a licence. Some indication of the enormity of the work involved was seen in Anglesey in 1901 when a census of dogs in the county recorded a figure of 4,249.[26] In Caernarfonshire officers were faced with an even greater number of dogs within their county when the number registered was 8,680.[27] Even more responsibility would have been given to officers in the county if a suggestion by some members of the standing joint committee that they should become river watchers had been accepted in April 1894. That the idea was rejected might well have been influenced by a statement by the Reverend R.W. Griffiths who claimed 'that there was nothing more unpopular in the county, than the idea of having the police to act as river watchers'.[28]

The passing of the Dogs Act of 1906, which came into force in January 1907, increased even further the duties and responsibilities of the police. All officers were instructed to make even greater efforts to capture and detain every dog found roaming on their beats. The dogs were to be kept for a maximum period of seven days unless previously claimed. Whilst in police care the dogs were to be properly fed, with the money for food being taken from the police fund.[29] Later, in a General Order issued on 3 January 1907, it was stated that a dog had to be fed once a day at a cost of not more than 4d per head. If and when, a dog was claimed by its owner it was the duty of the police to ensure that all the costs incurred were repaid to the authority by the claimant.[30] In an order issued on 4 November 1909, which was effective from 1 January 1910, it was laid down that in future all dogs were to wear a collar bearing the name and address of the owner. The absence of such identification rendered the dog a stray and the owner, if found, to a fine not exceeding £20 (Dogs Act 1906). These were regulations made by the Merioneth County Council.[31] It was particularly due to the nuisance caused by dogs and other stray animals that the chief constable of Merioneth sought permission in 1906 to appoint as an honorary constable Inspector George Henry Eakins of the north Wales branch of the RSPCA. The chief constable stressed that such an appointment would cost the ratepayer nothing and that Inspector Eakins had a similar arrangement with the Caernarfonshire and Denbighshire police forces.[32]

The prevention of sheep-scab was also a task that was looked upon as a police responsibility and this was to prove a most tiresome duty. It was in order to facilitate the easier handling of the many thousands of sheep dipped each year that the counties of north Wales hired a large number of dipping machines.[33] By 1909 the chief constable of Merioneth was able to state, and with some pride, that under the supervision of his officers during two dipping periods, between 1 June and 30 November 1908, a total of 765,937 sheep had been dipped.[34] One newspaper writing in praise of the work done by the police described the chief constable's report as 'a credit to the county, and to the chief constable, Merioneth always comes out on top'.[35]

The question of police officers undertaking extra duties sometimes placed the chief constables of north Wales in an unenviable position. On the one hand they were answerable to police committees who strongly believed that policemen could be safely employed to carry out extra duties and, on the other, they received pleas from members of the public for the appointment of additional constables to police and protect private premises. One such request came when Mr Pritchard Morgan asked for the services of two police constables to be stationed at his gold-mine, the Gwynfynydd, which was situated at the head of the Mawddach valley.[36] In his letter he made it clear that if the authorities were unable to bear the cost he was willing to do so himself. These constables, known as private constables, were subject to the orders of the chief constable and could only be appointed with the consent of the justices of the peace. The two police officers who eventually worked for Pritchard Morgan were specially appointed by the chief constable to act as constables at his mine, in pursuance of an order made by the Merioneth courts of quarter sessions at the Hilary sessions 1888, under Statutes 3/4 Victoria, c.88, section 18.[37] The order to appoint the officers was made on the condition that the cost incurred would be borne by Morgan. The two constables, under the statutes appointing them, had all the privileges and powers of their fellow-officers in the county.[38] In Caernarfonshire, a private constable to look after and guard the Nantlle Vale Railway line was appointed as early as 1864, and in 1901 two officers were employed privately for the months of July, August and September, the cost being borne by the Llandudno council.[39] Similarly, Denbighshire had four constables and Flintshire three, who were all employed by private individuals to protect their property.[40]

However, despite some improvement in pay, the police service generally entered the twentieth century with little or no direction from the centre. It was certainly true that the Home Office had done much over the years to formulate some aspects of policing, but it still did not have any specific department to deal with police affairs. In fact, as if to show its complete lack of concern for what really went on in the various police forces, it reduced the number of its Inspectors of Constabulary from three to two in 1907.[41] In England and Wales there remained at the beginning of the century about fifty forces with a complement of fifty men or fewer in each, and these included the counties of Merioneth and Anglesey. There was little co-operation between forces, although in this respect each county in north Wales had done much to implement many of the proposals contained in the Police Act of 1890 which had called for a closer relationship between forces. There were also at this time, few common standards in pay or conditions of service, although in fairness, the police committees in north Wales had always endeavoured to ensure that as far as possible their respective wage levels were in keeping with those offered elsewhere. Unfortunately, however, this was not always possible.

As early as 1901, officers in Caernarfonshire called for their wages to be improved and submitted reasons why their pay should be more in line with those enjoyed by men serving in other forces in north Wales, making particular reference to the scale of pay in Flintshire. In their submission they gave several compelling reasons why an increase in pay was fully justified, although it was noticeable that they did not include the extra work, and at times even danger, posed by the strike during 1900-3 at the Penrhyn Quarry, which will be discussed later. In their call for a better wage scale, officers believed the following observations supported their cause:

a. That the rate of pay was lower now than it was 23 years previously, whilst the duties of the police had increased.
b. That the present rate of pay did not compare favourably with other branches of labour in the district.
c. That several neighbouring counties had either increased their rates of pay or had the matter under consideration.[42]

Their call for an improved rate of pay was answered in April 1901, when the police committee agreed that officers in Caernarfonshire should be placed on the same scale of pay as those serving in Flintshire.[43] A similar situation existed in Merioneth, where officers stressed that their wages had remained unaltered since 1878. The news that they, too, were successful came in a letter from the Home Secretary in July 1901, when he approved a new pay structure for the force.[44] Six years later, the Merioneth standing joint committee adopted a revised scale of pay for constables appointed on the strength of the force after 25 December 1907, which was later approved by the Home Secretary.[45] The improvement in the pay of officers in Caernarfonshire and Merioneth at this time may well have encouraged magistrates in Anglesey to increase the wages of their officers in 1902.[46] One of the difficulties in assessing the wages received by officers in the respective north Wales forces is that during the early years of the century they were constantly fluctuating, and it was not until 1912 that a more uniform pay structure came into being.[47] Some indication of the pay received by officers between 1900-2 is as follows:

| County | Cons(pw) | Sergs(pw) | Insps(pa) | Sup'ts(pa) |
|---|---|---|---|---|
| Anglesey | £1.4s.0d | £1.10s.6d | £90 | £115 |
| Caernarfonshire | £1.4s.0d | £1.11s.6d | £95 | £135 |
| Denbighshire | £1.4s.0d | £1.11s.6d | £95 | £135 |
| Flintshire | £1.4s.0d | £1.11s.6d | £95 | £135 |
| Merioneth | £1.4s.0d | £1.11s.6d | £100 | £135 |

However, despite some slight variation in the scales of pay for those serving in north Wales, members of the various police committees could still feel justly proud of the achievements. Apart from the annual reports of the Inspectors of Constabulary, which in the main contained very little information on forces outside London, there were few sources from which members of the standing joint committees could obtain information. This, in effect, meant that the forces in north Wales had frequently to operate in the dark, relying to a large extent on the principle of trial and error. Therefore, any failure by members of the respective standing joint committees to be fully conversant with such matters as pay and conditions of service, in no way reflected upon their abilities as administrators. Whenever any information was received, members always acted promptly. As far as they were concerned, any communication which contained information that offered guidance was always welcome, as it allowed them to understand and appreciate more readily the conditions under which officers in the counties worked. When statistical information was presented to members of the Merioneth police committee in 1901, it was natural that they would be appreciative, for it afforded them the opportunity of examining in detail vital figures that related not only to their own county but to neighbouring counties as well. Among the many details contained in the document were figures which enabled members to make certain comparisons.[48] For example, Merioneth had the smallest force in north Wales (thirty-five in strength) compared with Caernarfonshire (eighty-three) and Denbighshire (eighty-two), yet the average acreage per constable was 12,223 as against Caernarfonshire's 4,342 and Denbighshire's 5,288. Flintshire, with an establishment of fifty-eight officers achieved 2,815 acres per man. Provided with such information magistrates in Merioneth were able to see that constables in the force far outstripped their colleagues in the other three counties in the arduous business of 'foot slogging'. This type of information became more readily available as the years went by, and eventually magistrates dealt with police management in a more professional way.

Yet, despite the improvements introduced during the 1890s and the early years of the twentieth century, life for officers in north Wales was generally still hard. There was little sign of officers having a day off and as one editorial explained 'very little is being done in Wales about one day's rest in seven for policemen. There is strong objection to paying increased rates in order to merely save the souls of policemen'.[49] The conditions under which many policemen lived and worked appeared, in so many instances, to be getting no better. For example, most police stations remained cheerless places, and if a police officer desired a gas supply, standing joint committees made it plain that no way were they prepared to pay for such a luxury.[50] Also the restrictions on an officer's private life were getting no easier. For instance, many officers were to find that after working hard for a year, the time in which they could take their annual leave was somewhat limited. In an order issued by the chief constable of Merioneth, officers were informed that in future only in very exceptional circumstances could leave be granted during the Easter and Whitsun weeks; this order also applied to all bank holidays.[51] A year later, even more stringent measures were introduced when officers were informed that on no account could leave be taken during July and August.[52]

Whatever the feelings of the men might have been regarding such regulations and restrictions, they continued to carry out their duties, taking leave on those occasions the authorities considered were appropriate. Such restrictions, however, were not the only cause of concern for police officers at this time. Their duties and responsibilities were also increasing, placing an even greater strain on the men themselves. The Children's Act of 1908 which related specifically to juvenile smoking, called for the police to be ever watchful in detecting and prosecuting those shopkeepers who persistently violated the Act by selling cigarettes or cigarette papers to those under sixteen years of age. The law on this issue was quite clear and constables in north Wales were urged to seize and confiscate from those caught smoking under age either in the street, or other public place, all cigarettes in their possession.[53] The passing of the Shop Act of 1912 was also another example of the growing tendency to place on the shoulders of the police even more responsibility. The Act clearly laid down that it was the duty of every police officer in charge of a district to visit all the shops on his beat and inform the owners of the requirements under the new Act. Owners were also to be informed that the enforcement of the new regulations was a commitment which the police intended to apply vigorously.[54]

Rigorously enforcing the law was not the only duty officers had to undertake. They were also expected to read as much as possible as this would not only improve their knowledge but also their spelling. In Denbighshire, for example, the chief constable issued instructions to all his senior officers that whenever possible they were to question constables on various aspects of the law and their daily work.[55] Later in 1903, officers in the force were compelled to sit examinations, and in the chief constable's view, those who failed badly should seriously consider resigning.[56] Instructing officers to become proficient in first aid was also looked upon as being an essential part of police training. Speaking to members of the Denbighshire standing joint committee the chief constable was able to report that the force had a close working relationship with the St John's Ambulance Brigade and two-thirds of the men were now qualified in first aid.[57] A similar situation existed in Flintshire where the chief constable was able to confirm that ambulance classes were being held in every police division in the county.[58] In Anglesey the chief constable was able to report in 1901 that officers had been attending first aid classes at Menai Bridge and Holyhead and twenty-one members of the force had qualified.[59]

Although classes in first aid were extremely valuable, attending lectures in their own time, in addition to their other many and varying duties, meant in effect that officers were finding that they had very little time to relax and be with their families. There was no doubt that by 1910 the work of the police in north Wales was becoming increasingly complex and in no way were their duties and responsibilities diminishing. Long hours of work, year in and year out, naturally took its toll and, as a consequence, the health of many police officers deteriorated. It was the fear of sickness and the financial distress it created, that led many of them to remain on duty long after they should have reported sick, for it has to be remembered that until the passing of the National Insurance Act in 1911, there were no means available for a police officer, or indeed any other employed person, to receive medical treatment as a right. Therefore, the chief constables in north Wales in 1913 called upon their officers to register with a local doctor so that in the event of illness they would receive proper medical attention. The Act of 1911 was hailed by the police as a piece of progressive legislation. The Act was a great advancement on the time when such medical attention would have had to be paid for out of the superannuation fund, and even then, only at the discretion of the magistrates and chief constable. Under the new Act each officer paid 9s per annum, which was the inclusive fee for all medical attention and medicine necessary during illness.[60]

A further and much welcomed benefit for the police came when Winston Churchill, on assuming office as Home Secretary in February 1910, ensured that the Police Force's (Weekly Rest Day) Act was piloted safely through Parliament.[61] Its passing was the culmination of what had been a long drawn out debate.[62] In Merioneth, magistrates meeting in Bala on 15 October 1912, decided to adopt the Act and make it operational in the county as from 1 November 1912.[63] This decision was welcomed by officers in the county for the Act itself did not become compulsory until after 26 July 1914. In granting a day off, however, the chief constable made it clear that he still expected members of the force to attend a place of worship on a Sunday and this practice 'was not to be curtailed because of the additional boon of the weekly rest day'.[64]

The implementation of the Act meant that a scheme had been formulated for the forces in north Wales which allowed every officer below the rank of superintendent fifty-two days off every year and this was to include fourteen days annual holiday. This was a tremendous step forward; at last those who could afford it would be able to enjoy a holiday with their families. As one report stated, the new Act 'allowed the children of a police officer to at least see their father once a week'.[65] Undoubtedly, the passing of the Act was an important milestone for the police. As one chief constable observed 'the additional relaxation from duty should have the effect of infusing new life and energy into the police, and if that end is attained, not only would members of the police force benefit but so too would the inhabitants of the counties they served'.[66]

If at this time mutual aid was recognised as being advantageous, then so too was the use of a bicycle for police purposes. It was, therefore, in order to assist officers to apprehend more criminals, many of whom now possessed bicycles, that the standing joint committee in Merioneth in 1896 agreed that a mileage allowance of one penny a mile should be awarded to constables using bicycles in the course of their daily duties. Although to ensure that no undue use of a bicycle was made, it was stressed that no more than 4s should be allowed for any one day.[67] The standing joint committee also informed officers that bicycles could only be used for certain purposes and gave examples which included, 'only to be used in hot pursuit of a criminal, or when rapid travel will ensure an arrest, and in an emergency, such as circulating urgent news, when other forms of communication such as trains and telegraph were unavailable'.[68] All expenses had to be carefully scrutinised by a senior officer and if a cycle was damaged while being used for police purposes it was no way the responsibility of the county.[69] The mileage allowance at this time must have appeared particularly attractive to constables who previously had to walk everywhere, for the boot allowance amounted to only 1d a day. However, by 1900 it had become obvious to members of the standing joint committee that some police officers were using their bicycles too much, and as a deterrent, many mileage claims were refused.[70] In Caernarfonshire bicycles were used for the first time in 1897. At first, only sergeants who possessed bicycles were allowed to use them, and those that did so were allowed 7s 6d a quarter for maintenance. Believing that the force would achieve even greater efficiency if bicycles were more widely used, the chief constable, Colonel Ruck, reporting to his police committee in November 1897, informed members that already twenty-five counties had purchased a limited number of bicycles, and seventeen granted allowances to officers using their own machines.[71] That his call for the greater use of bicycles was heeded, was seen later when ten machines were purchased from the Swift Cycle Company at a cost of £101.5s.0d.[72] In Flintshire, too, the authorities were beginning to recognise the importance of bicycles, and on the recommendation of the chief constable, agreed that eight constables should be allowed 7s 6d a quarter towards the cost and maintenance of their machines.[73]

If bicycles were seen as a blessing by the police, there were others who looked upon them as a curse and a dangerous innovation. At a meeting of the Flintshire standing joint committee in May 1895, Mr W. Wynne asked the chief constable as to what action the police were taking against those riding bicycles in a reckless fashion, particularly in Rhyl. Retorting angrily at the suggestion that those riding bicycles were dangerous individuals, Mr G.A. Parry, asked why those using bicycles 'should be treated as outlaws and if he had to carry a brass plate and a number on his back he would give up cycling'.[74] That some cyclists were riding too fast at times was seen in 1899, when officers in Merioneth were asked to place on the charge sheets 'that the person was riding at such a pace as to endanger life'.[75] It was in order to enable officers to arrest those speeding that the chief constable of Denbighshire requested that a bicycle should be purchased for headquarters at a cost not exceeding £12.[76] That Mr G.A. Parry, had the safety of the public in mind was seen at the quarterly meeting of the Flintshire police committee when he stated 'that all vehicles including bicycles, should be compelled to display lights from one hour after sunset, until one hour before sunrise.[77]

The 1890s was also a time when telephones were installed in the various police stations of north Wales. Yet, the erection of telegraph poles, certainly on a Sunday, was distasteful to some magistrates. At a meeting of the police committee in Caernarfon in July 1891, Mr R.O. Jones wanted to know whether the police had the power to prohibit such work on the Sabbath day. In his opinion, such a desecration was very obnoxious in a quiet county, and he asked what action could be taken to prohibit it. In reply the Lord Lieutenant, Mr J.E. Greaves, said that in such matters the 'police had no power whatsoever to prevent people from working on a Sunday'.[78] It was the hesitancy of some police authorities that prompted the National Telephone Company to urge magistrates to consider taking advantage of the facilities now open to them.[79] The magistrates in Denbighshire had seen the importance of the telephone to the police and had authorised the placing of one in the county building at Wrexham as early as 1893.[80] In Caernarfonshire there was not quite the same enthusiasm to install telephones and as a means of encouragement the National Telephone Company offered to connect the police stations at Llandudno, Conwy, Bangor, Caernarfon and Penygroes for an annual fee of £40. As an added inducement, the magistrates were informed that the stations at Caernarfon and Penygroes would have free communication with each other, with a similar arrangement becoming operational between Conwy and Llandudno. If at some future date other police stations within the county wished to be linked by telephone, then the standard charge of 3d for every twenty-five miles would have to be levied in accordance with the post office tariff.[81]

Although Colonel Ruck, the chief constable, saw certain advantages in the installation of telephones, he expressed certain reservations, mainly on the grounds of cost, wondering whether such expenditure was justified. In his opinion, the question of telephones was an issue best left to the magistrates. On discussing the matter at some length magistrates concluded that the police should 'take advantage of new discoveries and that a telephone would enable the chief constable to keep in touch with officers in other parts of the county and beyond'.[82] The telephone company's response was swift, for within six months of the meeting telephones were in daily use at the police stations at Llandudno, Conwy, Caernarfon, Bangor and Penygroes.[83]

In fact, nowhere was this recognition of the importance of professionalism more clearly demonstrated than during the years 1907-12 when the command of four forces in north Wales changed. Although here one must go back to 1894, when an event of great importance, and one that to some degree changed the course of police history in north Wales, occurred in Anglesey. The occasion, which must have given much encouragement to so many offices in the counties, occurred when the chief constable of the county, Lieutenant-Colonel William Hugh Thomas, retired on the grounds of ill-health and was succeeded in office by Inspector Lewis Prothero of the Caernarfonshire Constabulary.[84] In making the new appointment magistrates had departed from their usual custom of appointing an individual from outside the police service to the most senior position. In fact, the appointment of Inspector Prothero was historic for he was the first professional policeman in north Wales to be appointed to the highest position in the service.[85] Chosen from a short list of three he had an excellent and long police record having joined the Caernarfonshire force on 28 September 1862.[86] The appointment was a popular one, and no magistrate was more pleased than the Reverend S. A. Frasier, who had long campaigned for a man with police experience to be appointed to the highest position because he claimed 'it would entice intelligent young men to join the force in the firm hope they too would eventually rise to responsible positions'.[87] He went on to state 'that if an outsider to the service was appointed they would stand no chance in the future against a Bombay captain or Bengal major'.[88] The new chief constable received a salary of £250 per annum plus a travelling allowance of £25.[89]

It was the meagre travelling allowance awarded by the magistrates in Anglesey that led to a special meeting of the police committee being convened in August 1894, on receipt of a letter from the Home Secretary. In it he expressed grave reservations about the amount, stating that if such a small sum was awarded, then the chief constable would be unable, as was his duty, to visit the fifteen stations within the county. In response to this criticism, the magistrates, many of whom were angered by the interference and the tone of the letter, felt that the chief constable's salary alone was sufficient for his needs. There was even a call by several of the magistrates at the meeting that further expense could be saved if the county force amalgamated with that of Caernarfonshire.[90] At a later meeting it was decided that the committee should raise the amount for travelling to £50.[91]

Although the appointment of Inspector Prothero in 1894 was seen as successful, when Major Best announced his retirement in April 1907 many magistrates in Merioneth expressed their concern that the person appointed to succeed him might well be someone from outside the police service. Some support for this feeling of uncertainty was highlighted in a local newspaper when its editorial column took up a familiar theme stating 'the last chief constable of Merioneth was a Major. The next may be a Colonel, or a General, or an Admiral, but my hope is that he will be a policeman. I am not a candidate'.[92] However, despite such concern, the person favoured for the position was the deputy chief constable, Superintendent Thomas Jones, who had the confidence of the police committee. In his favour, too, was the fact that he had the full support of the retiring chief constable, Major Best, who in a testimonial supporting his application remarked, 'what little good I may have done for the force I could not have done without him'.[93]

The post was advertised in the *Cambrian News* on 10 May 1907, with a similar advertisement appearing in the *Caernarvon and Denbigh Herald*. When it was suggested that an advertisement should be placed in the *Police Review* it met with little support and, therefore, was not adopted. All candidates were asked to submit twenty-four copies of their application, and twenty-four copies of no fewer than three recent testimonials. It was also stated that although a knowledge of Welsh was desirable, it was not essential.[94] Over forty applications were received for the post, from which a short list of seven was drawn up.[95] After each candidate had been interviewed a shorter list of four was chosen which included Deputy Chief Constable Thomas Jones, Major C.J. Lloyd Carson, Detective Sergeant J.A. Prothero and Captain C.R.C. Hill. Following further discussion on the merits and experience of the four candidates, it was decided that the new chief constable should be Superintendent Thomas Jones. His salary was fixed at £250 per annum, and in addition he was to receive a further £50 for expenses.[96] The appointment was widely welcomed and from one source came the comment 'no appointment is more popular than that of Superintendent Thomas Jones'.[97]

Sadly the new chief constable's term in office was to be short, for he died suddenly at his home in Dolgellau on 2 March 1911.[98] His passing inevitably meant that once again the county had to appoint a new chief constable. Any doubts that may have been expressed about the late chief constable Thomas Jones, had long since been dispelled. Indeed, his success in office had firmly set the seal on future appointments, and there were few who doubted that his successor would be anything else but a police officer. The vacant post attracted ten applicants and it is interesting to note that there was still a tendency for those outside the service to apply for the vacant position. In this instance, three of the applicants were former army officers.[99] From the number applying, the police committee drew up a short list of five which included the following: Deputy Chief Constable David Thomas Morgans, Inspector Stephen Owen, Detective

Inspector R.D. Roberts, Superintendent W.R. Williams and Superintendent Richard Jones.

From the outset it was clear that Superintendent Richard Jones was by far the most impressive candidate, not only in his bearing, but in the manner in which he answered the many searching questions that were put to him. In fact, the committee was so impressed that when it came to the vote it was found that he had the support of every member, and – therefore – was unanimously elected the new chief constable. The salary for the post was £250 per annum,[100] although this was raised in 1912 to £300 per annum with an additional allowance of £50 being added for expenses.[101] It was also confirmed that Superintendent David T. Morgans should continue to act as the deputy chief constable of the county.[102]

In Flintshire, the sudden death of the chief constable, Major R.T. Webber in 1909 stunned the county. He had been in command of the force for twenty-one years. The post which was seen by many as being an attractive one attracted a total of thirty-seven applicants including a number of former army officers as well as a baronet.[103] After conducting a number of interviews the police committee eventually chose Superintendent John Ivor Davies, the deputy chief constable, to be the new head of the Flintshire constabulary. He was forty-three years of age and a native of Llanbryn-Mair, Montgomeryshire, and had begun his career as a school-teacher before leaving the profession to join the Flintshire force as a constable on 1 June 1888.[104]

The year 1911 was to witness the retirement of Major T.J. Leadbetter, the chief constable of Denbighshire, who had faithfully served the county for a period of thirty-three years. His career had been long and distinguished and on his retirement he was the most senior chief constable in the whole of the United Kingdom. In their search for a successor, the Lord Lieutenant of the county made it clear that he personally favoured a military man to be the new chief constable. However, many members of the police committee felt they had to move with the times, and believed an experienced police officer should be appointed. That their views prevailed, was demonstrated when the committee unanimously appointed Superintendent Edward Jones, the deputy chief constable. A native of Llanarmon, and at fifty-five years of age, he had joined the Denbighshire Constabulary at Ruthin in 1874.[105]

In 1912 magistrates in Caernarfonshire were also seeking a replacement for Colonel Ruck, the chief constable, who was retiring after twenty-six years, having been appointed to the force on 6 May 1888. Many tributes were paid to him, for during his time in office he had overcome many difficulties, especially those that were concerned with industrial unrest. In appointing his successor, Superintendent John Griffiths, members of the Caernarfonshire standing joint committee, like their counterparts in the other north Wales counties, were also adopting the same approach, for he was the first chief constable of the county to have risen from the ranks. A native of Llanwrin, Montgomeryshire, he had enrolled in the force in 1886 and had been rapidly promoted becoming a Superintendent in 1903. Over the years he had become noted for the way he presented evidence in court, and it was said 'that he was a capable cross-examiner in English and Welsh'.[106] With the appointment of Superintendent Griffiths, every force in north Wales was for the first time in over seventy years now firmly in the hands of professional policemen, something ambitious police officers everywhere must have welcomed.

However, what has constantly to be borne in mind when examining the late nineteenth and early twentieth century, is that policing was still, as it had been for over sixty years in north Wales, very much a local function and there was little call for any dramatic changes to be made. Nevertheless, changes occurred, and in some ways quite dramatically, not as might be imagined as a result of some important governmental decision, but as the result of the advent of the motor car. The car brought to those who could afford one, confrontation for the first time with the policeman as a figure of authority.[107] Cars first appeared on the English roads in the 1890s but being so few, they posed little problem to the police. Even when the law was broken, the police often turned a blind eye, preferring to put off as long as possible, the evil day when conflict would arise between the authorities and the motoring public.

At first, the speed limit of a steam propelled vehicle on an open road, preceded by a man on foot, was limited to four miles per hour. Later this limit was raised to twelve, then fourteen, until in 1903 it was fixed at twenty miles per hour.[108] From a policing point of view, the new limit was realistic enough to be enforceable, but the motorist viewed such restrictions as irksome and consequently a challenge for many to break the law. In north Wales, the advent of the motor car, at least in the early days, caused little if any trouble, but later as the number of vehicles increased, the picture of once peaceful and contented counties soon changed, with the sound of the cart and wheels being replaced by that of the throb of engines.

One of the earliest references to cars in north Wales appeared in the editorial column of the *Cambrian News* in 1903. The article, which praised the police on their ability to gauge with some accuracy the speed of cars, also congratulated the magistrates for sending drivers considered to be driving at a reckless pace, to prison. Furthermore, the article stated 'heavy fines are not intolerable, but a month or two in gaol cools the heart of the most ardent. The cyclist did not give the pedestrian much chance, but the racing motor car gives him none at all'.[109] Indeed, so alarmed were members of the town council in Beaumaris that they wrote to the chief constable informing him that it was their intention to place, in various parts of the borough, notices which called upon motorists to drive slowly.[110] Llangollen councillors were also anxious about motorists driving too fast and in a letter to their chief constable they claimed 'that during the holiday period in particular the inhabitants of the town were at the mercy of scorching motorists and cyclists'.[111]

Inevitably, the coming of the motor car soon created administrative problems for the authorities. Therefore, in order to place the licensing of vehicles on a sound footing, it was agreed by magistrates in Merioneth that the deputy chief constable, Superintendent Thomas Jones, be given the duty of registering all cars and cycles, and in addition, grant licences to drivers under the Motor Car Act of 1903. It was also the responsibility of the superintendent to be in charge of all the necessary forms and returns.[112] The duty was unpaid, although it was later resolved by the standing joint committee that Superintendent Jones be paid a percentage of 2s in the pound on all sums received by him.[113]

The speed of vehicles, which was causing great concern to the authorities in England, soon brought complaints to the notice of the police in north Wales.[114] As the traffic increased, numerous complaints were received from the public regarding the speed at which vehicles travelled when passing through villages, and the complete disregard some drivers had for human life when going around corners.[115] Denbighshire, for example, was noted for the large number of motorists who drove through the county at excessive speeds.[116] It was to stamp out this practice, that the chief constable, Major Leadbetter, informed officers that they were to stop all motorists who they believed were behaving in a manner likely to endanger life, and order them to produce their driving licences. However, it was probably to ensure that the Denbighshire force would not be accused of harassing every motorist that he laid down certain guidelines that called upon his officers to behave at all times respectfully towards those they suspected of committing an offence. Recognising too, even at this early stage, that the speeding motorist may well have committed a more serious crime elsewhere, prompted the chief constable to impress upon his officers the importance of making a mental note of the drivers attire, whether they appeared furtive or rough, and whether they seemed unduly aggressive on being questioned.[117]

To answer many of the concerns that were expressed at this time about the dangerous behaviour of some motorists, a report dated 12 October 1908 described the outcome of a meeting held earlier in London, between members of the Royal Automobile Club, chairmen of standing joint committees and a number of chief constables from England and Wales.[118] The main discussion centred on the various ways and means of controlling inconsiderate drivers. Several proposals emanated from the Royal Automobile Club, including one that suggested that its experts should assist the police in cases where drivers had been prosecuted for a traffic offence. This idea, however, found little favour among the chief constables present, with the spokesman, Colonel Ward of Kent, stating that in no way was it desirable to make use of experts, and in any case the police were equal in ability to assess cases concerned with dangerous driving.[119] Another proposal, again from the Royal Automobile Club, believed that it alone should be the sole body to issue licences and be the complete judge of a person's ability to drive a motor car. Like the previous suggestion, this idea drew a swift response and one of general disapproval from the chief constables. The meeting, although seen as useful, terminated without any definite decisions being made and in view of the differences that arose, may well explain the attitude later shown by those representing the motoring public and the police.[120]

Speed was the crucial issue in the frequent disputes that arose in the early years of motoring. The magazine *Autocar* published a number of articles that dealt specifically with police speed traps. It was noticeable that the counties of Surrey and Merioneth were marked in black, which denoted areas to avoid, for according to the editor 'persecution of the motorist had reached such a pitch that it was advisable for all to keep out of them'.[121] It was true that as early as 1901, a leading newspaper had as its headlines 'Surrey police make war on automobiles'.[122] In Merioneth there was no similar state of war between the police and the motorist although it is recognised that the number of vehicles passing through were fewer than in Surrey. *Autocar* made a point of giving details of speed traps which readers should be made aware of in Merioneth. Special attention was to be paid by drivers when approaching the head of Bala Lake, for it was reported that police officers were often observed crouching behind a white wall. At Dolgellau, motorists were warned to keep a sharp eye for a man dressed in old clothes who could turn out to be a policeman and was often seen lounging by the bridge as one entered the town.[123] Mention was also made in the magazine of a letter written by a Barmouth butcher to a correspondent stating: 'I hope you won't let the ignorant Welsh policeman deter you from coming to Barmouth. They are taking all sorts of liberties with the rights of the people at present, owing, I suppose, to their compatriot Lloyd George being at the head of affairs'.[124]

Despite what many believed, not everyone was of the opinion that the police were out to prosecute every motorist on even the most trivial offence and support for officers came from a writer in a local newspaper who declared 'that the police allowed up to five miles an hour over and above the permitted speed limit, and were only anxious to deter those taking dangerous and undue risks on the roads'.[125] It was to examine, and if possible reduce, the number of road accidents, some of which had proved fatal, that the chief constable of Denbighshire attended a meeting convened this time by the Automobile Association in July 1909. After a lengthy discussion, the findings that eventually emerged clearly indicated, that apart from excessive speed the following were the main contributing factors in most of the accidents that occurred:

a. Cutting corners on the wrong side of the road.
b. Driving in the middle and wrong side of the road.
c. Entering main roads from by-roads at excessive speed.
d. Crossing from nearside to offside of the road without warning.[126]

Clearly, such findings were a cause for general concern and in the circumstances, the magistrates in north Wales called upon the police to be extra vigilant in order to deter the motorists behaving in a manner likely to endanger life.

In a report to the police committee in July 1909 the chief constable claimed that there had been more prosecutions for motoring offences during the quarter than anywhere else in Wales proving that the police in Caernarfonshire were vigilant.[127] According to the report, the number prosecuted in 1908 was thirty-one, with the next highest prosecutions occurring in

Carmarthenshire which had twenty-one offences recorded. Asked by a member of the police committee whether the figure beat that of Merioneth, the chief constable replied 'we beat them hollow and without laying speed traps'.[128] Most offences in Caernarfonshire were confined to the area around Conwy and Llandudno. However, despite the number prosecuted in Caernarfonshire, there appears little evidence to suggest that the police in north Wales were in any way exceeding their powers.

There had been a great deal of hysteria expressed when speed traps were first introduced into the counties. In the early years, the *Autocar* and later the magazine *Field* did little to allay the fears of many motorists, especially when the latter publication stated north Wales was fast becoming a speed-limit-ridden country.[129] That genuine fears existed was borne out when a gentleman from Birkenhead, Alfred Montgomery, wrote to the chief constable of Caernarfonshire, asking for his views on motorists. In his letter he stated that he was visiting north Wales, in particular the counties of Caernarfonshire, Denbighshire and Anglesey, but he was specifically avoiding Merioneth, another illustration that the county was an area to avoid.[130]

The emergence of the motor car and its impact on society added new dimensions to the duties and difficulties of the police in north Wales. They now not only had the task of ensuring public compliance with the increasing number of regulations, but the whole area of possible conflict with the public and the press was increased with the creation of many traffic offences.[131] The situation called for great understanding, and to their credit, officers tackled the novel range of duties and problems with the same spirit that had stood them in such stead in so many difficult situations in the past.

Therefore, what we see at the end of the Edwardian era, is the emergence of a police service that is already adopting some of the features and characteristics that we associate with today's modern police. We see a police service continually adjusting to new needs and shouldering ever increasing duties. There is to be discerned, a broader and certainly more progressive approach to the whole range of police work. In the various rules and regulations there was an increasing emphasis on the importance of training police officers based on the best experienced practice. There was some awareness of the desirability of crime prevention and some insistence on the responsibility of the police to assist the general public whenever possible. This is a far cry from the concept of a body of uniformed officers dedicated only to the apprehension of wrong-doers.

In the early years there was perhaps, the unjust impression that the police might be considered as another means of maintaining the interests of rank and privilege, but by the first decade of the twentieth century such protection was for all the population irrespective of class – indeed, such a policy seemed to pervade all police thinking and activity at this time. Furthermore, this outlook was even more symbolised by the democratic appointment of professional policemen to the senior ranks in the police. Also, of great significance, and a pleasing factor as far as the Home Office was concerned, was the emergence of inter-force co-operation, a development which, though not foreseen at this time, was to prove invaluable practice for the changes to be instigated by the circumstances of the forthcoming world war.

---

[1] Clive Emsley, *The English Police – A Political and Social History*, 2nd. edition (London, 1991), p.204. See appendix v, for a copy of the Police Act of 1890.

[2] T.A. Critchley, *A History of Police in England and Wales*, (London, 1987), pp.169-71. See also J. Owain Jones, *The History of the Caernarvonshire Constabulary 1856-1950*, p.31, where as late as 1889 the standing joint police committee was to decide on whether a sergeant with twenty-two years service was to receive a pension of 14s or 18s a week.

[3] PP, Vol. IX (1908). Report of the Select Committee on the Police Force's Weekly Rest Day and Minutes of Evidence. To Kempster must go much of the credit for the fact that during 1906 and 1907 the Order Paper of the House of Commons contained repeated questions urging the need for policemen to be allowed one day's leave in seven, a campaign which eventually led to the appointment of a select committee on the matter in 1908, and the passing of the Police Force's (Weekly Rest Day) Act, two years later.

[4] *CDH*, 21 September 1894. The offices of the above association were located at 18 Catherine Street, London. See also MQS Rolls, (Trinity, 1884) – whereby such an association might well have assisted Sergeant Thomas Roberts, who found himself facing an action for false imprisonment brought against him by a Mr Octavius Carter.

[5] MQS Rolls, (Michaelmas, 1883).

[6] CQS Rolls, (Michaelmas, 1882). See also *CDH*, 7 April 1883. An allowance of £10 was made towards the cost of providing medical aid for police officers and their families whilst in hospital at Bangor suffering from typhoid fever. Another officer, Constable Samuel Jones, stationed at Caernarfon was also to succumb to the disease.

[7] *Cambrian News*, 3 July 1893.

[8] Ibid.

[9] Ibid.

[10] *CDH*, 12 December 1890. Also *Flintshire Observer*, 25 December 1890. When the Flintshire standing joint police committee met in December 1890 it was agreed by all members that on completion of twenty-five years service a full pension should be awarded and that the age limit for those retiring should be fifty-five. The committee also agreed that there should be a fixed age placed on those joining the service. It was at this meeting that the chief constable reported that he encountered great difficulty in recruiting suitable men to the force as the area was a recognised recruitment centre for the forces of Liverpool, Manchester and other large towns.

[11] G. Lerry, 'The Policemen of Denbighshire', *Transactions of the Denbighshire Historical Society*, 2 (1953), p.137.

[12] *Cambrian News*, 3 July 1896.

[13] Ibid.

[14] MCF Orders, QA/P/D/8/1, 19 February 1885.

[15] Ibid.

[16] DSJ Committee, 23 July 1891.

[17] DSJ Committee, 23 April 1891. See also *Flintshire Observer*, 5 February 1891, which shows that magistrates in Flintshire were also concerned about police wasting time, when it was reported that a number of constables were being used as beaters at the various shooting parties held in the county.

[18] DSJ Committee, 17 January 1895.

[19] Ibid.

[20] *CDH*, 28 June 1884. See also ASJ Committee, 3 October 1889, where officers were also expected to act as inspectors of explosives.

[21] MQS Rolls, (Michaelmas, 1891).

[22] Ibid. See Home Office letter 20 August 1891, also ASJ Committee, 24 July 1891. Hugh Owen, op. cit., p.35 and *CDH*, 30 October 1891.

[23] DRO, Chief Constable's Papers 1878-1922 DPD/2/1, 26 July 1890.

[24] Ibid., 16 January 1907.

[25] Ibid., 10 December 1894.

[26] ASJ Committee, 18 July 1901. See also FRO, Flintshire Constabulary General Orders 1903-1921, F/P/2/9, 15 December 1909, which relates to stray dogs, and DRO, Chief Constable's Papers, 1878-1922, DPD/2/1/, 19 October 1907, on the practice and cost of disposing of an unclaimed stray dog.

[27] CSJ Committee, 20 October and 22 July 1896.

[28] Ibid., 25 April 1894. See also *CDH*, 21 October 1898, where at a meeting of the MSJ Committee, members appeared to question the validity of employing policemen as relieving officers, saying that if officers were not paid for the duty they should resign.

[29] MQS Rolls, (Hilary, 1907).

[30] MCF Orders, QA/P/D/8/1, 3 January 1907. Also FRO Flintshire Chief Constable's Order Book 1877-1902 FP/2/8, 7 January 1907.

[31] Ibid., 4 November 1909.

[32] MQS Rolls, (Trinity, 1906).

[33] MCF Orders, QA/P/D/8/1, 25 July 1907. In Merioneth dipping machines were placed at strategic centres like Bala, Corwen, Llanuwchllyn, Dolgellau, Llwyngwril and Trawsfynydd.

[34] MQS Rolls, (Hilary, 1909).

[35] *Cambrian News*, 15 April 1910.

[36] MQS Rolls, (Hilary, 1888). See appendix vi, for an extract of a letter from Mr Pritchard Morgan requesting that two officers should be stationed at his gold-mine at Gwynfynydd.

[37] Ibid. See also H.K. Birch, op. cit., pp.128-9, also *CDH*, January 1890.

[38] H. J. Owen, *The Treasures of the Mawddach*, (1950), p.67. Interestingly, one of the constables appointed was ex-Sergeant Cheake, formerly of the Surrey Constabulary, who asked, as a part of his condition of service that his annual holiday should coincide with Epsom week, where he carried out special racecourse duties, including the supervision of the Derby.

[39] CSJ Committee, 18 July 1900. The chief constable reported to the police committee that he had great difficulty in recruiting men to serve during the summer months at Llandudno and had resorted to employing two former, and now retired officers, of the Liverpool City Force. Also see CSJ committee, 22 July 1901, when it was decided to grant the request of the Llandudno Commissioners for a policeman to be stationed in the town to look after the bathing machines, the promenade and enforce the Bye-Laws.

[40] MQS Rolls, (Trinity, 1901).

[41] T.A. Critchley, op. cit., p.176.

[42] CSJ Committee, 23 January 1901.

[43] CSJ Committee, 17 April 1901. It was also agreed by the committee that such increases should be retrospective for all ranks and that they should become operative as from the commencement of the financial year, namely 31 March 1901.

[44] *Cambrian News*, 5 July 1901, where it is also reported that Major Best, the chief constable, was given approval by his police committee to place a constable or sergeant on a higher scale of pay irrespective of length of service, for meritorious conduct. It was at this meeting that the chief constable was able to report with pride that every member of the force could read and write in Welsh. See also Hugh Owen, op. cit., p.41, where it states that in January 1901, the chief constable, Lewis Prothero, was allowed to promote deserving constables in each class, before they had served the regulation number of years. At the same time his salary was raised from £250 to £275 a year, as he had now served six years.

[45] MQS Rolls, (Hilary, 1908). Under the revised pay scales, constables who enrolled in the force were to serve ten years, where previously they only had to serve eight years before reaching their maximum pay as a constable of £1.10s.0d per week.

[46] Hugh Owen, op. cit., pp.41-2.

[47] ARO Statement of pay of Police in North Wales Counties, Chief Constables Office, Llangefni, 1 April 1912. See also Appendix vii.

[48] MQS Rolls, (Trinity, 1901). In addition to listing the numbers of officers serving in the respective counties, the documents also contained information on the number of public houses and off-licences in each force area. Caernarfonshire had 408; Denbighshire 591; Flintshire 571 and Merioneth 187. See also North Wales Police, op. cit., letter dated 25 April 1911, which lists the strength of the forces in north Wales in 1910: Anglesey 32; Caernarfonshire 88; Denbighshire 91; Flintshire 60; Merioneth 34.

[49] *Cambrian News*, 10 June 1910.

[50] MCF Orders, QA/P/D/8/1, 13 July 1907.

[51] MCF Orders, QA/P/D/8/1, 10 June 1905.

[52] MCF Orders, QA/P/D/8/1, 22 September 1906. See also read DRO, Chief Constable's Papers, 1878-1922, DPD/2/1/, 25 April 1912, where the chief constable of Denbighshire warns officers that there were restrictions on the times annual leave couldbe taken. See also H.K. Birch, op. cit., p.152, for further details of how the chief constable of Merioneth issued an order in September 1906, which forbade all officers, irrespective of rank, of holding any office in a church or a chapel, and the serious repercussions that followed that decision.

[53] MCF Orders, QA/P/D/8/1, 11 July 1914.

[54] MCF Orders, QA/P/D/8/1, 7 November 1912.

[55] DRO, Chief Constable's Papers 1878-1922, DPD/2/1/, 30 November 1891 and 4 March 1897 and 20 January 1898.

[56] Ibid., 1 January 1903.

[57] *Police Review*, 30 January 1893.

[58] Ibid., 12 June 1893 also FSJ Committee, 18 May 1893 and 14 May 1896.

[59] *CDH*, 26 July 1901. See also DRO, Chief Constable's Papers 1878-1922, DPD/2/1/, 23 February 1909, which records first aid training in Denbighshire.

[60] MCF Orders, QA/P/D/8/1, 10 February 1913.

[61] Christopher Pulling, *Mr Punch and the Police*, (London, 1964), p.158.

[62] T. A. Critchley, op. cit., pp.171-5.

[63] MCF Orders, QA/P/8/1, 18 October 1912. See also DRO, Chief Constable's Papers 1878-1922, DPD/2/1/, 21 March 1913.

[64] Ibid., see also DRO, Chief Constable's Papers 1878-1922, DPD/2/1/, 17 February 1896, where officers in Denbighshire were always expected to attend a place of worship when their duties permitted, also 28 August 1893, where in another order the chief constable insisted the importance of always saluting magistrates, all senior officers including officers in the armed forces in uniform, or if known to the police officer whilst in plain clothes. In an order issued by the chief constable of Merioneth in 1911 saluting had also to be extended to aldermen and county councillors. On a personal note I can remember in the 1930s as a small boy in Caernarfon always seeing officers saluting not only the chief constable but also members of his family whenever they appeared in the street.

[65] PP, (1908), Vol. ix, Qn., 2012.

[66] MCF Orders, QA/P/D/8/1, 18 October 1912.
[67] MCF Orders, QA/P/D/8/1, 2 November 1896.
[68] Ibid.
[69] Ibid.
[70] MCF Orders, QA/P/D/8/1, 28 June 1900.
[71] *Police Review*, 5 November 1897 and *CDH*, 23 July 1897.
[72] CSJ Committee, 18 April 1900 and 17 January 1900.
[73] *Police Review*, 11 March 1897. See also Hugh Owen, *History of the Anglesey Constabulary*, (Llangefni, 1952), p.42, whereby a grant of £18 was made in July 1909, to be divided amongst those police officers who used bicycles, for the repair and maintenance of their machines.
[74] *Flintshire Observer*, 23 May 1895.
[75] MCF Orders, QA/P/D/8/1, 4 July 1899.
[76] *CDH*, 9 April 1887.
[77] FSJ Committee, 22 August 1895.
[78] *CDH*, 22 July 1891. See also *Flintshire Observer*, 24 May 1894, where railway companies were requested to stop organising Sunday excursions into the towns of north Wales, which brought in their wake rowdy and unruly day trippers to places like Llandudno and Llangollen. See also David J.V. Jones, *Crime in Nineteenth Century Wales*, (Cardiff, 1992), p.212.
[79] CSJ Committee, 23 October 1895.
[80] DSJ Committee, 19 October 1893.
[81] CSJ Committee, 17 January 1900.
[82] Ibid.
[83] CSJ Committee, 18 July 1900. See also *Flintshire Observer*, 1 March 1900, where in response to a question in the House of Commons by Mr J. Herbert Lewis, MP, he was informed that telephone exchanges had been opened in five places in Flintshire – Buckley, Connah's Quay, Holywell, Mold and Rhyl and that a further exchange would soon be opened in Flint.
[84] *Police Review*, 10 August 1894.
[85] Hugh Owen, op. cit., p.40.
[86] Ibid. See also ASJ Committee, 18 July 1894, which in addition to Inspector Prothero lists the following for the position of chief constable: Superintendent R.D. Davies, Holyhead; Inspectors J. Harris, Caernarfon; T.D. Morgans, Ffestiniog; J. Jones, Menai Bridge; Sergeants R. Jones, Metropolitan Police; G. Jones, Llangefni; Thomas Jones, Beaumaris; Constables James Lewis, Cardiganshire Constabulary; Joseph Lewis, Swansea; and Captain Owen Pierce, Llanfair PG.
[87] ASJ Committee, 20 June 1894.
[88] Ibid.
[89] Ibid. For an excellent account detailing the office of chief constable read Robert Reiner, *Chief Constables*, (Oxford, 1991), and Arthur Brown, *Police Governance in England and Wales*, (London, 1998).

[90] ASJ Committee, 15 August 1894.

[91] ASJ Committee, 12 September 1894, and 22 July 1896. See also Hugh Owen, op. cit., p.41. In January 1901, the chief constable's salary was raised to £275 per annum.

[92] *Cambrian News*, 26 April 1907.

[93] Ibid., 7 June 1907.

[94] *CDH*, 10 May 1907.

[95] *Cambrian News*, 7 June 1907. The seven officers on the short list were as follows; Inspector J. Davies, Cardiff City Police; Captain C.R.C. Hill, Dwyran, Anglesey; Deputy Chief Constable Thomas Jones, Merioneth Constabulary; Major L. W. Jones, Penarth, Glamorganshire; Major C.J. Lloyd-Carson, Dyffryn; Detective Sergeant J.A. Prothero, Metropolitan Police; Detective Sergeant R.D. Roberts, Swansea Borough Police.

[96] MQS Rolls, (Trinity, 1907).

[97] *Cambrian News*, 2 August 1907. His appointment was a personal success for two of the candidates for the vacant position, Detective Sergeant Roberts, Swansea, and Detective Sergeant Prothero were later to achieve great distinction in the service. Detective Sergeant Roberts, was to become the chief constable of Swansea in 1921, and Detective Sergeant Prothero, who was the son of the chief constable of Anglesey, went on to become a senior officer at New Scotland Yard and on his retirement in 1934, was to take a keen interest in local government becoming the mayor of Beaumaris in 1943. See Walter William Hunt, *To Guard My People – A History of the Swansea Police*, (Swansea, 1957) and *CDH*, 5 March 1943.

[98] *CDH*, 3 March 1911. It is of great interest to note that on his gravestone in the churchyard at Llanelltyd, his full service history is engraved.

[99] *Cambrian News*, 28 April 1911. The full list contains the names of the following applicants: Superintendent J. Griffiths, Caernarfonshire Constabulary; Superintendent S. L. Guest, Caernarfonshire; Major C.I. Hope-Johnstone, RA, Liverpool; Superintendent Richard Jones, Cardiganshire Constabulary; Lieutenant-Colonel L.W. Jones, Penarth, Glamorgan; Lieutenant E. Tudor Jones, RWF, Dublin; Deputy Chief Constable David Thomas Morgans, Merioneth Constabulary; Inspector Steven Owen, Merioneth Constabulary; Detective Inspector R.D. Roberts, Swansea Borough Police; and Superintendent W.R. Williams, Deputy Chief Constable, Montgomeryshie Constabulary.

[100] MQS Rolls, (Easter, 1911).

[101] *Cambrian News*, 25 October 1912.

[102] MCF Orders, QA/P/D/8/1, 8 May 1911.

[103] *CDH*, 9 July 1909.

[104] Ibid.

[105] G. Lerry, op. cit., pp.142-3. See also appendix viii, for Major Leadbetter's letter of farewell to members of his force.

[106] J. Owain Jones, op. cit., p.67. See also *CDH*, 19 April 1912.

[107] A.J. Durrant, *A Hundred Years of the Surrey Constabulary*, (Guildford, 1950), p.31.

[108] T.A. Critchley, op. cit., p.177. Also *CDH*, 18 September 1903. That cars were still a comparatively rare sight, was seen when the Marquis of Anglesey created much interest and excitement, when he brought to the streets of Llandudno his powerful Pullman motor car with a 40mph engine.

[109] *Cambrian News*, 12 June 1903.

[110] ASJ Committee, 16 July 1903.

[111] *CDH*, 17 July 1903.

[112] MQS Rolls, (Hilary, 1904).

[113] MSJ Committee, 5 January 1904. See also H.K. Birch, 'The Merioneth Police 1856-1950', MA University of Wales thesis, 1980, pp.137-40, and Christopher Pulling, *Mr Punch and the Police*, (London, 1964), p.188.

[114] A.G. Hailstone, *One Hundred Years of Law Enforcement in Buckinghamshire* (1956).

[115] MCF Orders, QA/P/D/8/1, 7 October 1907.

[116] DRO, Chief Constable's Papers, 1878-1922, DPD/2/1, 20 May 1903 and 4 August 1907.

[117] Ibid., 25 May 1905. Also examine David J.V. Jones, *Crime and Policing in the Twentieth Century – The South Wales Experience*, (Cardiff, 1996), p.289. Where he explains that in one way or another, the motor car has been the greatest influence on the changing character of twentieth century crime. See also MCF Orders, QA/P/D/8/1, 19 January 1909, in which it is recorded that some car drivers were reported for driving dangerously at night displaying poor, and in some instances no lights. However, in the Motor Vehicle Act 1907, which was specifically passed to deal with practice, it became law for a vehicle to display lights between one hour after sunset and one hour before sunrise. In addition, any car displaying a rear light had to have it showing red.

[118] MQS Rolls, (Michaelmas, 1908).

[119] Ibid.

[120] Ibid.

[121] *Cambrian News*, 16 July 1909. See also ARO, Chief Constable's General Order Book 1911-18, 6 May 1908.

[122] *Daily Mail*, 11 July 1901. For an account of the early relationship between the motorist and the police read David Keir and Bryan Morgan, *The Golden Milestone – 50 years of the Automobile Association*, (London, 1955).

[123] *Cambrian News*, 16 July 1909.

[124] Ibid.

[125] Ibid., 23 July 1909.

[126] DRO Chief Constable's Papers 1878-1922. D/P/D/2/1, 22 July 1909. See also the *Daily Mail*, 11 February 1998, where in an article on early motoring it is recorded that the first driver to be killed was Henry Lindfield, who lost control of his Imperial electric carriage on a steep hill in south London, on 12 February 1898. The first person to be killed by a motor car was Bridget Driscoll of Croydon who was knocked down and fatally injured at Crystal Palace in 1897. See also T.A. Critchley, op. cit., p.177, where he states that

when the Automobile Association was formed in 1905 its main function was to protect motorists, with the result that police officers were soon prosecuting road patrols who dared to warn drivers of possible speed traps, thus obstructing the police in the execution of their duties.

[127] CSJ Committee, 28 July 1909.

[128] Ibid.

[129] *CDH*, 21 April 1911.

[130] Ibid., 20 August 1909.

[131] MCF Orders, QA/P/D/8/1, 30 March 1909. Officials in Merioneth were fully aware that as the number of vehicles on the road increased each year, legislation to control them was inevitable. For example, in a Bye-law passed on 6 November 1907, the police county surveyors and the inspectors of weights and measures had the authority to weigh all vehicles which, in their opinion, carried loads above the permitted weight. See also MCF Orders, QA/P/D/8/1, 21 October 1909, where in addition to the above legislation, the attention of all road users was drawn to section 73 of the Highway Act of 1835, which was still operative. It stated that owners of carts were compelled to place their name and place of work on the side of their vehicles, and they were also reminded that failure to keep to the left or nearside of the road would be looked upon as a traffic offence and therefore punishable. See also Anglesey Chief Constable's General Order Book 1911-18, November 1908.

## Chapter VI

# Social Conflict and Mutual Aid, 1886-1911

No history of policing in north Wales would be entirely complete without reference to three particular events that perhaps, above all others, illustrated the tremendous difficulties and pressures which at times were exerted upon chief constables. These raised the question of the relationship between the police and the community when they were sometimes led to request assistance from neighbouring county forces and on occasion: even the military during periods of unrest. The events were the Tithe War, particularly for the years 1886-88, the Penrhyn Quarry Strike at Bethesda 1900-03, the Royal Visits in 1889 and 1894 and the Investiture of the Prince of Wales at Caernarfon in 1911.

However, before the role of the police during these troublesome years can be properly assessed, it has to be appreciated that crime, admittedly not of a serious nature drunkenness, disorderly behaviour and the frequency of assaults – were all matters that continued to cause great concern to the authorities in the various counties of north Wales.[1] Therefore, we must understand that the frequent requests to chief constables for a police presence during times of unrest, in no way, according to the magistrates, exonerated officers from returning to their normal beats, frequently tired and hungry and immediately continuing with their daily and often difficult duties. Bearing these factors in mind we cannot but conclude that the 'Welsh policeman's position during times of trouble was not a happy one'.[2] Indeed, commenting on this period Donald Richter is correct when he explains that whereas most historians writing on the Tithe Wars have tended to focus their attention on the political and ecclesiastical aspects of the agitation, few have actually written on the crucial part played by the police during these turbulent years.[3] Although, fortunately, there were no fatalities during the agitation, the amount of violence and disorder displayed was likened by one historian, to that seen earlier in the century during the Rebecca Riots.[4]

**The Tithe War (1886-88):**
Several factors led to the outbreak of open conflict. Firstly, the growing resistance to tithe paying was really only one manifestation of Welsh dissent which had been steadily gaining strength throughout the seventeenth and eighteenth centuries, but was only taken seriously following the Methodist Movement of the early nineteenth century when the Calvinistic Methodists broke away from the Anglican Church in Wales in 1811. In fact, so rapidly were events moving that by the 1850s it was calculated that Welsh nonconformism accounted for approximately three quarters of the worshipping population.[5] Coinciding with this increase in nonconformity was the emergence of a favourable press led by such charismatic stalwarts as Thomas Gee, a Methodist lay preacher and publisher who through his weekly newspaper *Baner ac Amserau Cymru* was to make Denbigh 'a central theatre of radicalism and militant nonconformity in north Wales'.[6]

Another potent factor in the armoury of those opposed to paying the tithe was the important land question. The anglicization of the Welsh landlords which could be traced back to late medieval times meant that the ownership of land tended to stay through the centuries in the hands of an English-speaking Anglican class. Therefore, even though the Anglican community was losing its appeal in the nineteenth century, it was still the Church that retained the loyalty of the governing class. This was certainly a fact that Mr Gladstone recognised when he stated that whilst the Welsh were 'a nation of nonconformists, all the social and political advantages of state recognition, all the religious and to a large extent many of the educational endowments which the piety and foresight of our ancestors devoted to the good of all their fellow countrymen, are retained as the exclusive privileges of the Establishment – the church of the wealthy and largely alien minority'.[7] Thus with such views prevailing, the Welsh tenant farmer found himself alienated from his landlord, religiously, economically and linguistically.

In the continuing and often passionate attack on what the tenant farmers saw as a privileged class and a Church that was alien, no single factor proved more provocative than the collection of the tithe rent. Opposition to its payment was not new, for there is ample evidence that as early as the 1830s the Welsh radical press was constantly critical of the system.[8] Originally, the tithe was a tax paid in kind and was considered a cumbersome procedure, alleviated somewhat by the Tithe Commutation Act of 1836 which converted the obligation into a monetary payment, styled a rent charge.[9] The amount of tithe-rent to be paid was calculated annually by the Ecclesiastical Tithe Commissioners according to a formula based on the prices of wheat, barley and oats over a seven-year period.[10] Although such payment was always made reluctantly by the tenant farmers it became a sheer impossibility when the agricultural depression of the late 1870s and early 1880s made a 'nuisance and irritant into an actual economic hardship'.[11] In such circumstances, therefore, tenant farmers were left with only one option and that was the non-payment of a tithe.[12] This left the Church with only one legal recourse under the Commutation Act, which was a process termed a distraint, a costly and time-consuming procedure that ultimately led to the employment of auctioneers and bailiffs in an attempt to secure payment.[13] The battle lines were now drawn and as Kenneth O. Morgan observes 'the Welsh tithe war had begun'.[14] No county in north Wales was to escape the wrath of those who refused to pay the tithe rent. Prior to 1885 there were only scattered instances of distress sales and at first they posed no threat to the forces of law and order. However, the mood of many tenant farmers was soon to change and the anti-tithe campaign exploded into active militancy. It was true, in some instances, that local clergy did agree to reduce the amount of tithe due to them, sometimes by as much as 25 per cent. Yet, there were others who refused all requests to compromise and this only served to ignite even more agitation.[15]

In December 1887 the *Caernarvon and Denbigh Herald* reported that the tithe war had reached Anglesey, and that the Reverend Skinner Jones, vicar of Bodffordd, Hen Eglwys, had refused to lower the tithe by 10 per cent. Faced with this refusal and rightly fearing it would lead to further trouble, the chief constable, Colonel Thomas, had a large number of special constables sworn in.[16] Like the neighbouring counties in north Wales, Anglesey was experiencing a depression in agriculture, and this led to tenant farmers making a stand against what they considered an unjust system; in short they were no longer willing to contribute what little money they possessed in paying a tithe rent.[17] Reporting on the unsettled state of affairs a newspaper claimed that in Anglesey the police, who were expecting trouble, 'were making desperate efforts to appear formidable and awe inspiring'.[18] It was certainly the case that in order to bolster the strength of the force, four special constables were sworn in at Llangefni, and later, before two magistrates, Captain Evans and Major Lloyd, a further seventeen were enrolled. As a further precaution the regular force at Llangefni was also increased by the addition of officers drafted in from other parts of the island.

Knowing of this show of strength by the police the farming community repeatedly stressed that in no way was it their intention to become violent. In support of this claim one farmer went so far as to state 'the police can come and visit Heneglwys if they like, it will doubtless be a pleasant excursion for them. They will not have any duties to perform whilst amongst us'.[19] Such restraint on the part of farmers, however, was not what Mr Peterson, a solicitor for the Tithe Defence Association experienced when he attempted to obtain tithe payments in February 1888. Although escorted by a number of men armed with cutlasses he met with stiff opposition and farmers they wished to visit had locked and barred their gates. On complaining to the chief constable he was informed that on future visits he would be assisted by a large number of officers who would quell any disturbance that might arise.[20] True to his word the chief constable then issued the following General Order from his office in Beaumaris on 6 March 1888:

### General Order

A list of farms in the Order in which the sales will take place is this day forwarded for the guidance and information of the superintendent and inspector and on the day and hour to be hereafter named. The superintendent will be at the farm first mentioned with a large force of police. He will take care to have free ingress to the farm, a wide space kept clear for Mr Peterson when he arrives, and he is held personally responsible that such is done. He will also take care that during the day the Mob never gets within 20 yards of Mr Peterson at any one farm. All stone throwing to be instantly checked and persons arrested if necessary. The inspector will be mostly with the chief constable to carry his orders, etc.[21]

In issuing the above order the chief constable also informed his officers that his instructions were to be strictly adhered to as there was no room for complacency and laziness.[22]

The disturbances in Anglesey were also causing concern to Mr Thomas Lewis MP, who in the House of Commons, asked the Home Secretary whether an application had been made for the assistance of the military in the county, and if so, by whom, and on what grounds. Since a report he had received from the chief constable had stated there was no need for military intervention, he wondered whether anything had happened to necessitate such assistance. He also wished to know that if an application was made for military intervention would it be readily granted. In his reply, the Home Secretary stated that the court of quarter sessions had sanctioned the application after full inquiry, on the grounds that resistance was expected. The county police force was inadequate and there was some difficulty in obtaining assistance from neighbouring counties. He was sorry that the assistance of the military should have been necessary, but since the application had obtained the approval of the magistrates he expected the military authorities would grant it.[23]

In Merioneth, the involvement of constables in the collection of tithes was a duty not welcomed by the officers themselves. Serving in a community which was largely nonconformist, many officers probably found their duties at times somewhat unpalatable, but although their integrity was often put to the test, they stood firm and did what was required from them. In many ways they were helped by the fact that they did not have to face the widespread disruption experienced by the authorities in other counties, a circumstance for which they were, no doubt, extremely grateful. In the chief constable's report for 1888, Major Best reported that forty-one farms in the Tywyn area alone had been called upon for the non-payment of tithes.[24] Fortunately for all concerned, and especially thanks to Inspector R.W. Hughes for his tact and judgement, there were no serious incidents to report. Several farms in the Corwen area had also refused to pay and Major Best had been forced to send constables to act as escorts for the bailiffs, although apart from two farms near the Denbighshire border, all paid without a serious incident arising.[25] Recognising the dilemma some officers found themselves in, as one newspaper in their defence stated, 'they must obey orders, however distasteful those orders may be, and it is to be hoped that the people, however deeply irritated, will not in any way act against the police'.[26] The Home Office too, at this time, recognised the problem of tithes in Wales and in a letter dated 29 December 1887 addressed to the chairman of the Merioneth quarter sessions, it drew attention to the disturbances and the difficulties faced by the police in the collection of tithes. The letter wanted to know how many chief constables expected trouble, and whether, in the event of it arising, arrangements could be made by the county forces to render mutual assistance when required.[27] In this respect Merioneth was known for its helpfulness at all times to neighbouring forces when assistance was asked for, as in the case when the authorities in Caernarfonshire requested help during the general election of 1868.[28]

The fact that tenant farmers in Merioneth had not been more militant in their approach to the payment of tithes is a little surprising considering the years of unrest that had existed within the county. It may well be that the election in 1886 of Thomas Edward Ellis, the son of a tenant on the Rhiwlas estate, as MP for Merioneth and a champion of the peasantry had helped to cool tempers.[29] Certainly, his great victory, achieved at the expense of an opponent who belonged to the landed class, was evidence in itself of the mood of the people. In recognising these facts, however, it must not be forgotten that officers in the Merioneth Constabulary, in what appears to have been a 'softly, softly' approach in the collection of the tithe, deserve a great deal of credit for what now appears to have been a fine example of diplomacy and tact when faced with a difficult and unpleasant duty.

If the collection of the tithe in Merioneth had posed no problems for the police, then the same could not be said for the officers in Flintshire and Denbighshire who experienced tremendous difficulties during the Tithe War. In Flintshire, many tenant farmers, angry at having to pay the tithe met at the Bluebell Assembly Rooms in Holywell. They were particularly angered by the actions of the duke of Westminster, Lord Mostyn and the earl of Denbigh, who they accused of charging excessive rents which many considered 'nothing more than downright robbery'.[30] News of the meeting spread quickly and a further meeting of disgruntled farmers took place, this time at the Alexander Hotel, Rhyl, during the first week in January 1886.[31]

In August, 1886, the Reverend Evan Evans of Llanarmon, Denbighshire, in an attempt to defuse what he believed was an unacceptable challenge to the authority of the Church, initiated distraint proceedings against two of his leading defaulters, who, in turn, were warned that their goods would be distrained if they did not comply with the order to pay the tithe.[32] However, on the day of sale a crowd of anti-tithe campaigners intercepted the distraint party and successfully prevented the sale.[33] At Llandegla, the attitude of the rector was so uncompromising that unrest in the area began to gather momentum. Three bailiffs from Chester were refused entry into a number of farms and met so much opposition that they had to flee for their lives to Llandegla where they were housed for the night. Not that their stay in the village was comfortable, for during their time there they were refused all food and drink and eventually had to seek refuge in the Wynnstay Arms at Ruthin. According to one eye witness, the rector was a 'Tory and like other Tory parsons, was true to the instincts of his creed-bigotted'.[34]

There was little doubt that the tithe agitation was spreading very quickly and those who refused to pay were ably supported by Thomas Gee's *Baner* which constantly encouraged the anti-tithe cause.[35] It was this encouragement by men like Gee that led to questions being asked of the Home Secretary in the House of Commons. In reply, he stated that in a recent communication from the chief constable of Denbighshire, Major Leadbetter, he had been informed that 'opposition to the collection of tithes was of an organised nature'.[36] Therefore, it comes as no surprise in view of the concern being expressed by the authorities, that we see the police being increasingly involved in tithe disturbances. It was due to what he believed was a deteriorating situation, that the chief constable of Denbighshire had the following notice circulated throughout the districts where agitation was at its highest and which reads as follows:

> Whereas large and riotous assemblies of persons having recently taken place within the Petty Sessional Division of Rhuthun, notice is hereby given, that at a meeting of the justices for the above petty sessional division, held this day, directions were given that proceedings should be taken against all persons who riotously assemble with the object of preventing the law being carried out, by shouting, gesticulating, or other acts tending to intimidate and that such offences are punishable by indictment at Quarter Sessions, and persons convicted thereof render themselves liable to be imprisoned and kept to hard labour for a term not exceeding two years.[37]

It was as a result of this notice that a correspondent in a local newspaper observed 'that to imprison a man who ventures to gesticulate is rather severe'.[38] Despite such observations, it was certainly true that by the end of 1886 hardly a distraint sale could be effected without the protection of the police.

Like most county police forces, those of Denbighshire and Flintshire were mainly trained for normal police duties and, therefore, were unprepared to deal with what amounted to a widespread and concerted campaign of crowd obstructionism.[39] Fortunately, for all concerned, both chief constables were men of long experience. Major Leadbetter of Denbighshire had served in the army and had been chief constable since 1878. Mr Peter Browne, chief constable of Flintshire, had been in command of the county for some thirty years. Major Leadbetter believed that in any future confrontation a large number of police officers would be required, and to this end, he did not hesitate to acquire officers from neighbouring counties especially Flintshire. An early indication that he was prepared to show strength was seen at Llanarmon in September 1886 when he led a force of eighty-one officers drawn from four counties, a process that he would constantly adopt whenever trouble was envisaged at a tithe distraint.[40]

An early test for the police in Flintshire came in December 1886 when the Ecclesiastical Commissioners gave notice they were going to sell some of the goods belonging to farmers at Whitford.[41] The task of handling the distraint sales was placed in the hands of Mr Charles Stephens, professional Chancery Lane distraining agent, and fearing a hostile reception he called for police protection from the outset.[42] That his early fears were justified was seen when he and his escort met nothing but hostility from the moment they entered the village. In fact, the mood of the inhabitants was such, that not a village in the county would supply the party with food and drink.[43] During the interval between seizure and auction at Whitford, Mr Browne, with a view to cooling tempers, consulted with local farmers as to how many officers they thought should be present at future distraint sales, and was informed that eighty officers should be an adequate number to control events. However, when the distraint sales took place they were conducted during a severe snowstorm which supplied the protestors with an endless store of missiles. Recalling the incident later, Mr John Bolton, deputy chief constable of the county, and with a certain amount of humour, described how he and the auctioneer were pelted with snowballs and rotten eggs, although he had to admit that at one stage in the proceedings a hole had been made in the ice covering a pond and it had been the intention of some of those present to throw him and the auctioneer into it.[44] Whether such violent action would have been taken against the deputy chief constable is a matter of conjecture. What can be said, however, is that towards the end of 1886 a dangerous viciousness crept into the conflict and there was a definite hardening of attitudes. For example, in a letter to the editor of the *Caernarvon and Denbigh Herald*, the Reverend William Venables, vicar of Colwyn Bay, stated that he had received a letter on 12 November from an anonymous writer and written in Welsh, calling for a reduction of 25 per cent in the amount of tithe paid in the parish adding that failure to comply would lead 'to him, his house, and all he possessed being blown up'.[45]

Although throughout 1887 various parts of north Wales experienced disturbances, two of the most serious occurred in Denbighshire, at Llangwm on 25 and 27 May 1887, and at Mochdre on 15 June, when the Ecclesiastical Commissioners attempted to seize the cattle of some recalcitrant farmers.[46] At Llangwm, the anti-tithers, who, determined that no tithe sale would be held, not only attacked the auctioneer but also several members of his police escort who found themselves powerless to act against such overwhelming odds.[47] Although officers had been assaulted and the distraint sales severely disrupted, they were perhaps a little more fortunate than the six bailiffs especially brought in from Chester a week earlier who were not only attacked but also robbed and only saved from further embarrassment by the arrival of the police.[48] The first intimation that the chief constable of Denbighshire would seek the assistance of the military was seen at Bodfari on 11 June 1887 when, accompanied by seventy-two soldiers and fifty constables, Major Leadbetter attended a tithe distraint. Immediately on their arrival they encountered stiff opposition and in the ensuing skirmish, the auctioneer, two bailiffs and four police officers, including the chief constable himself were injured.[49]

One of the ugliest confrontations of the whole tithe war occurred at Mochdre, a small village not far from Colwyn Bay, on 16 June 1887. A little earlier in the month the auctioneer, Mr Stephens, had seized animals to the value of £40 from five farms in the area, and in order to ensure that the distraint sales could be successfully completed it was deemed necessary to supply adequate protection. In fact, some of the largest protective forces ever used for distraint protection arrived at Mochdre in the afternoon. It included seventy-six soldiers of the XXII Cheshire Regiment under the command of Major Hare and Lieutenant Tucker, seventy-six police officers under the command of the chief constables of Denbighshire and Flintshire, Superintendents Bolton, Mold, and Hughes, Holywell. Mr Stephens the auctioneer, several court bailiffs and a Denbigh magistrate.[50] Obviously anticipating trouble they were not to be disappointed, for on their arrival they were faced by a crowd that was estimated to be in the region of 1,500, all very angry and armed with stout staves. Having failed to reach an agreement with the owner of Mynydd Farm, and sensing the assembled crowd was now becoming even more restive and hostile the chief constable thought it was time to return to a more strategic position. It was then that the attack began; stones were hurled and staves were used to batter the police, who in turn used their truncheons to beat off their attackers. Although the attack lasted but a few minutes it was severe enough to account for eighty-four of those present being injured, thirty-four of whom were police officers. At one stage so serious was the confrontation that the magistrate was forced to read the Riot Act.[51]

Not surprisingly, in view of the disturbance at Mochdre and the widespread sympathy for the anti-tithers, questions were bound to be raised both in and out of parliament about the conduct of the police.[52] Those injured, loudly proclaimed their injuries and the unfairness of the entire distraint process, to a very sympathetic audience. One of those present at Mochdre stated, 'he only went to the village to shout encouragement as a bit of fun and accused the police of treating the people as wild beasts – who only thought of killing them'.[53] Another critic, a Mr Sweatenham, of Stokes Farm, Caergwrle, who had frequently complained about the amount of tithe he had to pay, went on to explain 'that he thought it would be best for him if he met the police in the market town to take no notice of them, if he met them at fairs, that he would not speak to them, and if he met them in the country lanes, that he looked to the opposite side of the road. That was what he should do, they could judge for themselves whether they would follow his example'.[54] The police found a staunch ally in the Home Secretary, who in the Commons claimed 'that persons who accompanied a riot during an attack on the police must not complain if they suffered injury in the course of the collision'.[55] In an attempt to appease those who attacked the police however, the Home Secretary did agree to set up a Department Committee, under the chairmanship of Mr John Bridge, a Metropolitan Police magistrate. Taking evidence from a number of witnesses, including police officers, the Committee's report 'fully exonerated both county authorities and individual police constables'.[56] The Committee also, and no doubt wisely, avoided inflaming the situation even further by not condemning too harshly those who supported anti-tithe sentiments. However, despite its mild tone, the Bridge Committee report was to lead to no immediate alleviation of anti-tithe disturbances.[57]

The continuing attendance of police officers at the sales in addition to their normal duties placed a great strain not only on police resources but on the constables as well. The police presence was also proving extremely costly, as when constables were loaned by other counties they had to be paid for.[58] It was the additional expenditure incurred that eventually led Major Leadbetter to ask magistrates whether the county treasurer could advance money from time to time in connection with the collection of tithes – 'for his officers were out day after day and had to pay their own expenses. Such payment, he considered, was particularly hard on a man with a family who often had to wait a month or more before he could obtain his money'.[59] It was as a result of escalating costs that various self-policing ideas were suggested from time to time. One such scheme was called 'moral suasion' and was introduced quite successfully in Montgomeryshire by the chief constable, Major Godfrey. In effect it was a gentleman's agreement with members of the anti-tithe league that allowed them vigorously to protest but without a police presence, thus placing the onus for keeping the peace on the league itself. With the exception of a few instances the idea worked well in Montgomeryshire and Caernarfonshire. There is, however, little evidence to suggest the idea received support in Denbighshire or Flintshire, although Major Leadbetter did claim that at one stage he had offered a similar arrangement.[60]

Early in 1888, and possibly encouraged by the findings of the Bridge Report, the Ecclesiastical Commissioners and the Clergy Defence Association embarked on a concerted effort to recover unpaid tithes. In Flintshire, for example, there were a number of tithe sales in areas around Whitford and Holywell, scenes of earlier confrontations. This time the crowds were urged by Howell Gee to show constraint and not mar the anti-tithe movement by acts of violence. The authorities, however, taking no chances, still required the presence of over fifty mounted Hussars from Manchester under the command of Captain C. Williams and an equal number of constables, some seconded from Denbighshire and Caernarfonshrie, in order successfully to complete the tithe sales.[61] Querying the cost of employing the military, one magistrate, Mr Edward Williams, who believed the measure unnecessary, thought the police would have been quite safe at tithe sales 'if only they acted with discretion and coolness'.[62] In Denbighshire, the Church, following Flintshire's example, began distraint proceedings against 615 farmers throughout the Vale of Clwyd. During the early stages Major Leadbetter attempted to attend sales without a military escort. In fact, a total of over seven hundred police officers, including many borrowed from other counties were used throughout the county on fifty-four separate occasions.[63]

The desire on the part of the chief constable to minimise

expenditure resulted in approaching riots in several instance, as a consequence of inadequate police supervision. This was certainly the case at Llannefydd on 10 May 1888, when on two separate occasions Mr Stephens, the auctioneer, with an escort of fourteen constables, failed to conduct a number of tithe sales. Determined that the law would be obeyed, Major Leadbetter, this time with thirty-two police officers returned to Llannefydd on 17 May, and immediately on their arrival a fierce fight broke out. So serious was the confrontation that over twenty people were injured, several seriously. According to one newspaper 'men were knocked down often without the slightest provocation, and blood was streaming everywhere, it was a sickening sight'.[64] Even more lurid was the account in the *Wrexham Advertiser*, where it was reported that in some of the farmhouses where the injured had been taken 'the floors were more like a slaughter house, blood mingled with hair formed a carpet'.[65] On 18 May, the day following the disturbance at Llannefydd, the chief constable, obviously wishing to avoid further conflict, decided that in the interest of law and order, and to save further bloodshed he would seek military assistance. In his request to the magistrates he explained why such assistance was deemed vital, stating that the strain on a small force like Denbighshire was excessive, and very unfair to the ratepayers of the county, where many places were denuded of their constables during times of unrest.[66] As a result of his request, which was readily granted by the magistrates, a further 223 farms were later visited around the areas of Llannefydd and Mochdre without any further breaches of the peace.[67]

As a consequence of the disturbance at Llannefydd the Denbighshire standing joint committee held an inquiry into the conduct of the police. The chief constable's evidence to the quarter sessions fully justified the actions taken by the police, stating that 'the mob instigated and provoked confrontation'.[68] Writing a little earlier to the editor of the *Caernarvon and Denbigh Herald* he not only defended the role of the police throughout a most difficult period in the force's history, but went even further and explained how the officers themselves felt about the whole affair, stating 'I can assure you this tithe work is most irksome and annoying to all ranks, and had they any choice in the matter would rather be employed in their usual criminal work, than being brought into contact with the agricultural classes whose friends they are, and I hope will remain'.[69]

When magistrates met on 4 July 1888 to discuss the findings of the Inquiry on the events at Llannefydd they concluded 'that the chief constable and his force had acted with great discretion and that the magistrates were fully justified in their decision to call out the military in aid of the civil power for the maintenance of law and order in the county'.[70] However, the Liberal element in the Commons led by men like Tom Ellis thought otherwise, and protested strongly about the use of the military. Osborne Morgan even accused Major Leadbetter of being 'like many military men, more remarkable for zeal than for discretion'.[71] Such opinions as those expressed by Ellis and Morgan made little impact on the views of the Home Secretary, who strongly supported the role of the Denbighshire Constabulary and declared that 'far from exceeding their duty, they have behaved with great moderation under very trying and difficult circumstances'.[72] Although disorders tended to persist at times in places like Whitford, Mold, St Asaph, Pwllheli and in parts of Anglesey, they never reached the intensity of violence that was seen at Llangwm, Mochdre and Llannefydd and by 1889 there was a marked relaxation of tithe tension.[73] By this time, too, many people had also become simply bored with constant confrontation and even in anti-tithe circles there were calls by moderate voices for a more silent protest.[74] Therefore, with such a dramatic change in attitude on the part of those who had previously resorted to violence, it comes as no surprise that the Tithe Wars in north Wales, which had flared up so quickly in 1886, were ultimately to disappear from the scene as a result of the Tithe Rent Charge Act of 1891 which effectively solved the problem.

For the police in north Wales the ending of the Tithe War was seen as a blessing. Their position throughout the campaign was certainly not a happy one. The earlier sentiments of Major Leadbetter on the feelings of his men, were echoed by Mr Peter Browne, of Flintshire, who told magistrates 'that no duty has been so painful to us, as the police of this county, as that which has fallen upon us in connection with these tithe sales'.[75] It is somewhat surprising that despite all the disturbances and the involvement of so many police officers there were so few arrests and convictions. At the request of the Home Office, the twelve counties in Wales were asked in 1890 to submit a report on the numbers arrested and convicted as a result of the troubles since 1886. Five counties in north Wales showed no arrests, apart from the thirty-one Llangwm 'Tithe Martyrs', of whom only eight appeared at the Assizes, Denbighshire showed only two arrests and Flintshire one.[76] There were no imprisonments, and the heaviest fine imposed was £5. Such apparent judicial leniency, as

Richter rightly points out, does tend to give additional credence to the view that the local Welsh authorities, faced with the enforcement of unpopular laws, sought to maintain public order as much by persuasion as by police coercion.[77] Credit for so few arrests must also go to the police, for despite the many pressures exerted upon them they displayed a high degree of professionalism and restraint. They had risen to the challenge, and were, without exception, a credit to the various forces in which they served.

### The Penrhyn Quarry Strike (1900-03):
One of the longest lasting disputes in the industrial history of Britain occurred at the small slate quarrying village of Bethesda in Caernarfonshire at the beginning of the twentieth century. The Great Strike at the Penrhyn quarry began in November 1900 and did not come to an end until November 1903. The dispute arose 'from the special nature of the quarryman's craft, from the particular ethos of the quarrying communities and from the way in which the second Lord Penrhyn (1836-1907), interpreted his rights as an employer'.[78] From the beginning of the dispute Lord Penrhyn failed miserably to understand his workforce. The workers, in most instances, were monoglot Welsh, fervent chapelgoers and increasingly radical. Lord Penrhyn, for his part, was arrogantly English, ardently Anglican and perhaps above all an unyielding Tory. It was generally accepted that the Penrhyn family with their schools and hospital were paternalistic employers, but at a price, for in return they demanded complete obedience and submissiveness.[79]

The strike was not unexpected because, for some considerable time, the relationship between management and the workforce had gradually been deteriorating due to the management's determination to abolish the traditional way of working. With the quality of the rock face being so variable, the traditional way of working was through what was known as the 'bargain'. This method was, in effect, an agreement between a group of quarrymen and the management. In a sense, this 'bargain' system allowed the quarrymen to regard themselves more as contractors than employees. However, the management in each of the main quarries sought change, which if allowed would have undermined the autonomy the workers enjoyed through the 'bargain' system.[80] It was certainly a method of work that found little favour with Mr E.A. Young, an accountant from London, who had been appointed manager of the Penrhyn quarry in 1885, and who, on assuming office, declared that the 'bargain' system should be abolished. Fearing the worst, and wishing to retain the traditional way of working, as well as seeking a wage increase (5s a day had been suggested). The quarrymen felt that trade unionism within the quarry should be strengthened. Such suggestions as a wage rise and an increase in trade unionism was something neither Penrhyn nor Young could accept and they responded by dismissing all members of the quarrymen's committee in September 1896. It was as a direct consequence of their actions that the Penrhyn quarry closed and work there did not resume until August 1897.[81]

When a dispute over the 'bargain' surfaced again in 1900 men felt that the time had come to stand firm and on 22 November, the 'Great Strike' began. (Although an indication that there would be trouble had arisen a little earlier, at the end of October, when a group of very angry quarrymen violently assaulted some officials and drove them out of the quarry.[82]) Fully aware that industrial disputes and intimidation elsewhere had often led to serious rioting, Colonel Ruck, the chief constable, asked the magistrates to call for military assistance. The magistrates granted his request and on 4 November, a detachment of the Cheshire Regiment arrived at Bangor, and were later joined by 180 soldiers from Preston under the command of Captain Thorold.[83] Leaving nothing to chance, the chief constable also arranged for a number of officers from Anglesey, Flintshire and Merioneth to be present, bringing the total number of police on duty in Bethesda to 120.[84] Many questions were later asked about the very large numbers of police officers and troops that had been deployed in Bethesda, where fortunately on this occasion there was no further trouble. Members of the standing joint police committee were also critical, believing the chief constable had overreacted to the situation and would not endorse his actions. Nevertheless, despite their reservations, members were ready to concede 'that the chief constable acted throughout with the best intentions'.[85]

Magistrates sought clarification on the procedure to be followed by the chief constable in times of civil unrest in April 1901, when at a meeting of the police committee, Mr C.H. Darbyshire, called attention to a minute passed at a previous meeting which was recorded as follows: 'that the chief constable should consult a committee of five members, who were also members of the police committee, when he considered the situation so serious that the police force of the county needed to be strengthened by the addition of a large number of officers from other counties, or if the disturbance was such that military aid was required'.[86] It was also stressed that in no way was it the intention of the committee to tie the chief constable's hands. Where the assistance of a few extra constables was required, perhaps on a special occasion, then the consent of the chairman of the police committee would suffice.[87] Fortunately for all concerned, the early months of 1901 were relatively peaceful. However, the situation was about to change, for on 10 May 1901, Lord Penrhyn, who had reopened the quarry, informed Colonel Ruck that officials and others who wished to return to work were likely to face 'interference and violence; from the strikers and therefore he was seeking police protection for them.[88] Fortunately there was no trouble, apart from a few women banging tins, and those returning were able to enter the quarry unmolested. Their police escort was also kept to a minimum and consisted of a sergeant and two constables.

By June some 600 men had offered themselves for employment at the quarry. Not all were former employees; many had been brought into the district by Lord Penrhyn's agents in the hope that they might break the strike. Others were recruited from the surrounding districts, with little or no experience of working in a quarry. Some of those returning were strikers who chose to give up the fight, thus breaching the unity of the men. Those returning to the quarry, especially the men who broke ranks were to find their lives particularly unbearable. Subjected to continual harassment they were hooted and jeered at whenever they or their families appeared in the streets. The day after the reopening of the quarry a demonstration of 3,000 people ended with twenty people being summonsed for threatening behaviour. In fact, demonstrations and processions marching around Bethesda and the neighbouring villages became a regular feature of the strike.[89] On passing the homes of blacklegs, processions would often stop to hoot, shout abuse and often to break windows. There were numerous arrests for obstruction and abusive language.[90] Reporting on the situation to the police committee, Colonel Ruck stated he had received information from Sergeant Owen in Bethesda, who claimed, he could 'no longer control the unruly elements in the town'.[91] Although sympathetic, the committee turned down the suggestion that troops should be deployed in Bethesda, but did agree that more police were needed in the area and a force of between fifty and sixty officers were drafted into the town.[92]

At a special meeting of the standing joint committee on 15 August the chief constable declared that the position in Bethesda was rapidly worsening. Hostility towards his men was now a daily occurrence and this would mean officers being stationed in the area for some considerable time. Disturbances had occurred on 6, 13, 20 and 27 July. Stones, some heavy, were being thrown at workmen and their families. Two of his officers had been injured and several others assaulted whilst attempting to protect workmen going to the quarry. As a result of the report the committee resolved to recommend to the magistrates in Bangor that they enrol no fewer than a hundred constables. It was also agreed that if the situation got even worse the chief constable should seek assistance from the neighbouring counties for additional officers.[93] The situation did worsen a few days later when fighting broke out between the police and striking miners. Responding to the situation the authorities sent for the military and a detachment of 200 soldiers, including thirty dragoons, were ordered to take up duty at Bethesda.[94] At any one time during the summer of 1901, the number of police officers stationed at Bethesda varied between 25 and 50 per cent of the total county force and incurred a cost of £1,300.[95]

The large number of police officers on duty in Bethesda caused many people to complain. Letters in the press frequently drew attention to the fact that whilst Bethesda seemed inundated with police officers, other parts of the county never saw a policeman. According to one correspondent, Porthmadog, Tremadog and Cricieth had been without police protection for days, and at a time when the area was full of visitors. A similar situation was also reported by those living in Pwllheli and Nefyn.[96] Yet, even with such a large number of officers in attendance the chief constable and the authorities were still of the opinion that many more were needed in Bethesda if the situation was to be contained. Seeking more assistance, Colonel Ruck wrote to the Head Constable of Liverpool stating that as many officers as possible sent under the mutual aid scheme, 'should be able to speak Welsh as he was reliably informed that the Liverpool force had within its ranks a considerable number of Welsh speakers'.[97] His request for assistance from Liverpool was granted when eighteen constables and two sergeants from the force arrived in the county.[98]

Although the situation in Bethesda remained generally tense throughout the summer of 1901, the police faced no major confrontation. Indeed, confident that perhaps the worst was over, magistrates decided that eight of the police officers stationed in the town could be released to continue with their normal duties. Similarly, they decided that officers from Liverpool, who were stationed at Bangor and elsewhere in the county, could also return home.[99] However, at a meeting of the police committee in November, the chief constable still concerned at the amount of vandalism that was being committed, particularly against property of those who had returned to work, reported that he was compelled to retain twenty-one officers in the town.[100] As Christmas approached, Lord Penrhyn informed Colonel Ruck that extra protection was needed for his workers, particularly since it was estimated that at least 2,000 men would be returning to the district from south Wales for Christmas. The chief constable responded by saying that he had doubled the number of officers serving in Bethesda and if need be, magistrates would allow him to secure additional officers from the neighbouring counties.[101] In an attempt to avoid conflict he also informed Lord Penrhyn that it would assist the situation if he advised his workers to keep away from the main streets of the town particularly on a Saturday and, above all, to avoid any form of provocation.[102]

Christmas in Bethesda passed off relatively peacefully and even at the mass meeting attended by 1,800 people a few days later there was little trouble, but, in a sense, it was the calm before the storm, for on 31 December the situation changed dramatically and the town that Ben Tillet had called 'crimeless Bethesda' erupted into violence. The windows of the Victoria Hotel and the Waterloo Inn were shattered, for they were places that served drink to 'traitors'. Numerous houses were attacked and extensively damaged. According to the *Caernarvon and Denbigh Herald*, the violence continued more or less unabated throughout New Year's Day.[103] The scale of the disturbance created alarm amongst the magistrates who, after listening to the views of Colonel Ruck, lost little time in signing an order which called upon the military to assist. Answering the call on 2 January 1902, a hundred men of the Staffordshire Regiment and forty soldiers from the Regiment of Hussars arrived in the town. Workers returning home from the quarry were particularly vulnerable to attack and were constantly stoned. In fact, some quarrymen fearing for their lives had to leap into the River Ogwen to escape their attackers.[104]

Colonel Ruck believed that the rioters intended to frighten the working quarrymen by breaking as many windows as possible before they themselves returned to south Wales after their Christmas holiday. He also explained to those critical of the police for making so few arrests that it was difficult to know where the strikers would hit next, so the police were continually at a disadvantage. Nevertheless, some of those causing damage were arrested. As a result of the disturbance on New Year's Day, David Thomas was fined 20s with costs, for incitement to disorderly behaviour and Owen Owen was fined 5s with costs for throwing stones.[105] A little earlier, Elizabeth Griffiths was fined 5s with costs, for using indecent and abusive language towards a policeman who was escorting a workman home from the quarry.[106] The *Cambrian News* 'blamed the rioting on the men's leaders who had deliberately obscured and misrepresented the whole situation'.[107]

When the standing joint committee met on 24 January 1902, there was a call by some members for Bethesda to become a new police district.[108] This may well have resulted from an earlier letter received by Mr Kneeshaw, a magistrate, from the Home Secretary which stated, that he strongly deprecated a policy whereby a county force relied on the military for the maintenance of law and order. Fortunately, for a short time at least, the situation quietened down with the result that a number of police officers were withdrawn from Bethesda.[109] As Easter approached, fears were expressed that the rioting seen at Christmas would be repeated, so as a precaution, Colonel Ruck arranged for a force of eighty-five officers, twenty-five of whom were mounted, to be drafted into Bethesda.[110] However, to the relief of all concerned, fewer of the strikers who had left the area returned for Easter, so the holiday passed off with very little trouble. It was more or less the same situation at Whitsun. Many strikers were expected to return home, but in reality, only about 300 actually arrived; so as at Easter, the holiday period proved uneventful.[111]

In many ways the quietness of the holiday periods was extremely deceptive for there were still numerous instances of workers being attacked and their homes vandalised. There was serious trouble in Bangor in September and the police from Lancashire arrested a number of people including David Jones, who was fined £2.10s for assaulting a striker.[112] Workers on their way home were still hooted, branded as traitors and assaulted. Passions continued to run high and anger burned deep in the hearts of many, especially when they saw their neighbours and former friends desert the cause and return to the quarry. The once peaceful and solid community became divided against itself.[113] Suspicion and bitterness was everywhere and was even beginning to seep into family life. Former loyalties were constantly being eroded and swept aside. Even the chapels, around which the community had grown, were split – to the outside observer it was a very tragic scene.

It was in order to ascertain the attitudes of the people and indeed the police, that at the end of January 1903, a committee set up by the standing joint police committee undertook an investigation into the state of affairs in Bethesda. The committee also examined in some depth the prosecutions undertaken by the police and the additional police expenditure incurred in the district.[114] The committee met for the first time in Caernarfon on 6 November 1902 and held a further seven meetings, including one in Bethesda itself. During the course of their investigation they took evidence from twenty-six police officers, and fifty-five witnesses representing strikers. One of the first to present evidence was Colonel Ruck who testified that quarry officials had reported 852 incidents to him between 2 June 1901 and 24 December 1902. The committee also heard evidence from people living in Bethesda itself, most of which related to the alleged need for a large additional police force. Those who signed the majority report freely admitted that before the investigation they had no conception of the strife and bitterness engendered by the dispute. Such an admission was, in itself, an indictment of the way the dispute had been perceived by those in authority.

In their findings the committee reporting the majority view made the following observations:

a. They paid tribute to the ministers of religion and other leading members in the community who had consistently called for calm and encouraged respect for the law.
b. The report was far less favourable about the part played by quarry management and declared 'the method by which the complaints of the men at work were conveyed to the police by the quarry officials was calculated to do mischief, to increase tension and deepen the ill-feeling already existing between the parties to the dispute.'[115]
c. The report was also highly critical of the way the police had presented their evidence, especially in relation to complaints about unnecessary violence. Their conduct on escort duty was also questionable, for it was claimed, that police employed to escort working quarrymen had failed to show due consideration for the feelings of the former employees and as such, had caused a natural feeling of resentment among ex-quarrymen thus leading to frequent breaches of the peace. The committee also recommended that the number of police officers stationed in Bethesda should be reduced, as the presence of a large force had the effect of irritating people.

d. The number of convictions obtained was 57½ per cent of arrests, which was considerably lower than the normal ratio: thirteen of the 125 prosecutions had been withdrawn and of the remaining defendants seventy-one had been convicted, thirty-nine had been discharged and two had absconded.[116]

e. On the question of expenditure of £4,418.11s.11d for extra police and other assistance, the report claimed that the charges made by other police authorities were exorbitant and better arrangements should be made if assistance was required in the future.[117]

The minority report was drafted by Mr Issard Davies and approved by Captain Stewart. It contained the following observations:

a. Whilst strikers had given evidence the working quarrymen had not, because the latter, through their manager, made a condition that the evidence of the former should be placed at their disposal – the committee deeply regretted what they termed 'the fatuous attitude of the manager on this point'.

b. The report stated that acts of real violence were now more rare and most of the quarrymen had dispensed with police protection – although the committee did concede that there had been riots of a very serious nature at which some feared for their lives.

c. It completely rejected the suggestion that the police had acted in a partisan or vindictive spirit and observed that when an angry and excitable crowd advocated violence, the strike leaders had protested only by pointing out the legal limits of intimidation.

d. Like the majority report, it too, condemned the way in which complaints had been brought before the police, but it noted that the chief constable had taken action on only six of the 852 reports, and this indicated no vindictiveness on the part of the police.

e. Both the majority and minority reports agreed that police expenditure was excessive and acknowledged the 'firmness and courtesy of Colonel Ruck'.[118]

On 23 January 1903 the *Daily News* noted that the majority report had confirmed its allegations against the police, but argued that the minority report was the more important because while exonerating the police it condemned the 'exaggeration and malice' with which complaints against the old workmen had been conveyed to them. However, the standing joint committee adopted the majority report by fourteen votes to seven.[119] The chairman, Mr Menzies, expressed surpise that there had not been far more disturbance, and that the reports represented 'the honest opinion of those who wrote them and which contained evidence which admittedly was conflicting.[120]

The strike itself ended in November 1903. Undoubtedly, the community had become totally exhausted after such a long and bitter struggle. The effect on a family existing on 10s a week strike pay had, for many, become unbearable and what is more, as the chances of a settlement receded, men became frustrated and even frightened and the will to continue the fight collapsed. As for Lord Penrhyn, his hollow victory was to cost him dearly, for the slate industry never recovered from the damaging effects of a dispute that had lasted three years.

Finally, what was the real position of the police? So often over the years they had been charged with a lack of impartiality, with acts of cruelty, tactlessness, abuse of power and with providing false evidence. Yet, even the report which listed some of the failings of the police, had to concede that there was little in the way of evidence to support such charges and that many were of an assumptive and inferential nature. On the whole the report stated that perhaps with one or two exceptions, officers in the Caernarfonshire Constabulary had performed their duties well during what had been a trying time and were a credit to the county in which they served.[121]

Undoubtedly of great assistance to overworked officers, particularly at times of civil unrest, had been the introduction of the mutual aid scheme. The scheme, which was part of the Police Act of 1890, clearly stipulated that there should be standing agreements between forces, like those in north Wales, that would allow them to assist each other in times of difficulty. Yet, as late as 1908 fewer than sixty forces out of a total of nearly 200 had entered into such an agreement.[122] In fact, mutual aid agreements did not become general until 1925, following a recommendation by the Desborough Committee.[123] It was in 1908 that a select parliamentary committee discussed the use of the military in times of disturbance and reported that troops had been called upon to aid the police on twenty-four occasions during the previous thirty-nine years, on two of which, the order to fire had been given.[124] The committee deplored the use of the military and recommended that the Home Secretary should have the authority to requisition up to 10 per cent of any county force and direct them to any area threatened by disorder. Although this recommendation was not accepted, two years later on the appointment of a new Home Secretary, Winston Churchill was given a similar demonstration of the way the old principle of local responsibility for law enforcement could be subordinated to the overriding authority of the crown by a strong and determined Home Secretary.[125] One of the earliest forces to recognise the importance of mutual aid was Merioneth, which immediately called for talks between the neighbouring counties of north Wales as well as Cheshire, including the city of Chester, whereupon it was agreed that in future, should mutual assistance be required, they would readily respond to any request. An early illustration of mutual assistance was demonstrated in 1893 when the deputy chief constable of Flintshire, Superintendent Bolton, called upon officers from the Cheshire constabulary to assist his men during an industrial dispute at the Leeswood and Coed Talon collieries.[126] A further illustration was seen in 1898 when the chief constable of Merioneth was authorised by the police committee to secure the services of three detectives for duty at the National Eisteddfod held at Blaenau Ffestiniog.[127]

**Royal Visits**
Visits of royalty to the counties of north Wales were also occasions that called for the implementation of the mutual aid scheme. Queen Victoria's visits to Flintshire in 1889 and 1894 called for a large number of officers to be on duty including five who were mounted.[128] Similarly, when the proposed visit of the Prince and Princess of Wales to Caernarfonshire on 10 July 1894 was discussed by magistrates, they were informed by the chief constable, Colonel Ruck, that at least 250 officers would be needed if the crowds were to be adequately controlled and security assured.[129] Of this number, fifty would be on duty in Bangor, where the royal couple were expected to arrive, with a similar number on duty at the pavilion field in Caernarfon. The chief constable also explained that up to a further 200 officers would be required on the streets of the town as it was expected that on the day of the visit up to 40,000 people would flock into Caernarfon.[130] In answer to further questions about police numbers the chief constable stated that at least 150 officers, including six who were mounted constables, would be provided by the Liverpool city force, at an estimated cost of £500 – this was an excellent example of the mutual aid scheme in practice.[131]

Occasionally, mutual aid created problems and this was certainly the case for the Caernarfonshire Constabulary who, in

1911, was mainly responsible for the general arrangements, including that of security, during the time of the Investiture of the Prince of Wales at Caernarfon. The request for a large number of police officers to be present came from the chief constable, Colonel Ruck, who wanted to ensure that the police were fully prepared to deal with any eventuality. In all, just over 1,200 police officers were sent to Caernarfon, with 200 of them being drawn from Welsh forces.[132] Of the remainder, 1001 men were drafted to the town by the Metropolitan Police.[133] Furthermore, the chief constables of Flintshire and Glamorgan reported that they were unable to send officers to the Investiture as a consequence of industrial unrest within their force area.[134] Some indication of the effect the secondment of officers had, particularly on the smaller forces, was seen in Merioneth where fifteen officers were supplied, practically half the strength of the force, which inevitably meant that those who remained in the county were expected to undertake extra duties.[135]

Officers on duty in Caernarfon were not necessarily more fortunate than those who remained at home. Indeed, many found their time at the Investiture an unpleasant experience. In a report submitted to the Merioneth police committee, Inspector Stephen Owen, stated that the men under his command complained bitterly about the accommodation provided for them in Caernarfon, explaining that the beds and toilets were in a filthy condition.[136] Nor was the Inspector's complaint an isolated one; officers from many forces voiced their anger at what they believed had been a lack of proper organisation by the Caernarfonshire Constabulary.[137] No force was more critical of conditions than the Metropolitan Police. They not only complained about poor accommodation, but reported that the food provided was badly cooked and the men often found their clothing covered with cockroaches.[138] In fact, it was later reported by officials at Scotland Yard that the men were so disgusted with their conditions that many simply walked out of their lodgings and slept on the beach.[139] However, such criticism and behaviour by the Metropolitan Police did little to impress one Caernarfonshire officer who claimed 'that they were inveterate grumblers'.[140]

At a meeting of the Caernafonshire standing joint committee in September 1911, members examined in some depth many of the complaints submitted to them by the various forces who had been billeted in the town during the Investiture and came to the following conclusions:

a. That despite numerous complaints the accommodation provided for officers had on the whole been more than satisfactory.
b. As to the arrangements for catering; complaints about the quantity and quality of the food provided were, in the main, greatly exaggerated. They did concede, however, there was a possibility on the warmest day of the hottest summer, that some of the meat might well have become tainted.
c. They were all of the opinion that much unpleasantness might have been avoided if better organisation had existed and better order maintained in the attendance and conduct of the men at their meals.[141]

It was at this meeting that members notified the county council that the sum of £2,000 was required in order to defray the expenditure incurred in bringing extra police officers into the county during the Investiture.[142] Of the eleven Welsh forces at the Investiture, six made no charge for their services. The total expenditure for the remaining five forces, which included Anglesey, Carmarthenshire, Monmouthshire, Merthyr Tydfil and Denbighshire amounted to £185.5s.3s.[143] As to the cost of the four English forces, which included officers from London, Liverpool, Manchester and Birmingham, only the amount claimed by the Metropolitan Police, which was by far the largest contingent, is recorded, and amounted to £341.10s.1d.[144] Although the arrangements at the Investiture had been strongly criticised, members of the Caernarfonshire standing joint committee considered the event an outstanding success, with the police generally performing their duties in an exemplary manner, which they believed was a tribute not only to the men themselves, but also to the forces they served. It was this willingness to assist neighbouring forces in times of need that probably explains why the chief constable of Denbighshire requested aid from Merioneth on the occasion of the strike at Brynkinallt colliery in 1912. That the request was readily granted is seen in an extract from the chief constable's report dated 4 April 1912, in which he states that because of a request from the authorities in Denbighshire, two sergeants and thirteen constables had been sent to quell a disturbance in the area.[145] The need to counter the threat of more industrial action probably accounted for the Home Office circular which was issued to all chief constables in August 1911. Its contents made it clear that whenever possible during a trade dispute, it was the duty of the police to ensure no worker was intimidated and made to strike against his will.[146] Mention was also made later of the position when a rail dispute arose. Although railway companies employed their own peace-keeping officers, they could in the event of a strike call upon the services of the local constabulary.[147]

---

[1] David J.V. Jones, *Crime in Nineteenth Century Wales* (Cardiff, 1992), p.89, where he states the Methodist revival and the work of others attempting reform, had greatly increased the public awareness of the problem of drunkenness.

[2] Donald Richter, 'The Welsh Police, the Home Office, and the Welsh Tithe War of 1886-91', *The Welsh History Review* 1984-85, Vol. 12, p.69. In assessing the role of the police at this time it should not be forgotten that the service generally was experiencing a number of novel benefits, such as the emergence of faster transport, an increase in the use of photography and telegraphic communications, as well as the introduction of fingerprinting which came into use in 1901 with the opening of the fingerprint bureau at New Scotland Yard under the supervision of Sir Edward Henry. See Fred Cherrill, *Cherrill of the Yard* (London, undated), pp.28-44, where he acknowledges the father of fingerprinting as being Sir William James Herschel (1833-1917). For a more detailed account, see Eugene Block, *Fingerprinting* (London, 1969), pp.1-14, and George Dilnot, *Scotland Yard* (London, 1926), pp.281-89.

[3] Ibid., p.50. See also W.C. Maddox, *A History of the Montgomeryshire Constabulary 1840-1948* (Carmarthen, 1982), pp.16-17.

[4] David Williams, *A History of Modern Wales* (London, 1951), p.264, where he claims 'The "tithe war" was the Rebecca Riots of north Wales'.

[5] Donald Richter, op. cit., p.50. Although unevenly distributed Wales was now dominated religiously by Baptists, Unitarians, Wesleyans, Independents and the largest body the Calvinistic Methodists – or Methodists as they were styled in Wales. It was during this period that one sees a gradual increase in the building of chapels.

[6] Donald Richter, op. cit., p.52. It was estimated that by the 1870s so extensive was nonconformity that it accounted for ten weekly newspapers, sixteen monthlies and two quarterly publications. See also E.D. Jones, 'The Methodist Revival', *Wales Through the Ages*, Vol. 2, edited by A.J. Roderick (Carmarthenshire, 1960), pp.101-9.

[7] *CDH*, 6 February 1886. It is also important to remember that if one takes all these factors into account, Welsh nonconformity was to find a readily acceptable institutional base in the Welsh Liberal Party. See also Donald Richter, op. cit., p.51, where he claims that the earlier Liberal gains in the great election of 1868 in Wales must have given Welsh tenant farmers much encouragement in that they began to believe that the days of Tory landlordism was coming to an end.

[8] David Williams, op. cit., pp.250-1.

[9] Donald Richter, op. cit., p.54.

[10] Ibid., see also David Williams, op. cit., p.50, where he also lists the payment of a tithe on cattle, sheep, wool, poultry, milk and cheese, and the personal tithes on wages and in the profits of trade and industry.

[11] Ibid., p.55.

[12] Ibid.

[13] See J. P. D. Dunabin, *Rural Discontent in Nineteenth Century Britain*, (London, 1974), pp. 212-13, where he describes the complex procedure in attempting distraint more fully.

[14] Kenneth O. Morgan, *Wales in British Politics 1868-1922*, (Cardiff, 1991), p.84.

[15] Donald Richter, op. cit., p.56. See also W.C. Maddox, op. cit., pp.16-17, where he cites the militant mood of farmers in Meifod, Montgomeryshire, where on 27 May 1887, the chief constable, Mr J. Danily, accompanied by a force of 130 men, which included detachments of officers from Caernarfonshire, Flintshire and Shropshire, failed in their attempt to ensure that the district sales could be safely conducted and were forced to withdraw from the scene. Reporting the incident later, the agent for Christ Church College, stated that had they stayed, they would have faced a running fight all along the eight mile stretch of road to Welshpool. Fortunately for the authorities these disturbances resulted in the Archdeacon of Montgomery announcing to the satisfaction of all, that having regard to the state of agriculture the tithes would be reduced by 10 per cent. The farmers agreed with the decision and the troubles ended. See also *Flintshire Observer*, 26 May 1887 and 2 June 1887; also *CDH*, 19 October, 30 November and 14 December 1888.

[16] *CDH*, 2 December 1887.

[17] See Merfyn Jones, 'Class and society in nineteenth century Gwynedd', in *People and a Proletariat – Essays on the History of Wales 1780-1980*, ed., by David Smith (London, 1980), p.207, in which he states that a significant proportion of the people in Gwynedd were involved in agriculture, an agriculture moreover which was characterised by the most brutal poverty as families endeavoured to make a living from ever hostile heath and hills. See also *CDH*, 20 February and 13 March 1886, which cite that due to the high rate of unemployment children in Caernarfon received what became known as 'halfpenny dinners' on four days of the week.

[18] *CDH*, 9 December 1887.

[19] Ibid.

[20] Ibid., 24 February 1888. See also ASJ Committee, 19 October 1886, where Mr Peterson, aware that trouble might well confront him when visiting Anglesey requested military assistance.

[21] Hugh Owen, *History of the Anglesey Constabulary*, (Llangefni, 1952), p.34.

[22] Ibid, op. cit., p.35. Also *CDH*, 2 March 1888, which recorded that Mr Peterson was accorded an escort of fifty constables on his next visit to Anglesey.

[23] *CDH*, 27 April 1888, where it is reported that where military assistance

was requested the costs involved would be borne by the War Office.
[24] *CDH*, 6 July 1888.
[25] MQS Rolls, (Michaelmas, 1890).
[26] *Cambrian News*, 3 June 1887.
[27] MQS Rolls, (Hilary, 1888).
[28] J. Owen Jones, *The History of the Caernarvonshire Constabulary 1856-1950*, (Caernarfon, 1963), p.39. At election time in 1868, Caernarfonshire was experiencing a great deal of trouble and sixteen constables were sent to the county from Merioneth to forestall further disorder.
[29] David Williams, op. cit., pp.264-65.
[30] *CDH*, 2 January 1886.
[31] Ibid., 9 January 1886. For details of further meetings see *CDH*, 30 January, 13 February and 4 June 1886 and *Flintshire Observer*, 6 January and 17 February 1887.
[32] Ibid., 27 August 1886.
[33] Donald Richter, op. cit., p.57. On this occasion there were no police officers present, but later, with a police escort, distraint proceedings were successful against those who had defaulted.
[34] *CDH*, 27 August 1886.
[35] Donald Richter, op. cit., p.56. It was at this time that we see the young David Lloyd George attending dozens of meetings in Caernarfonshire and speaking out against a tithe system which he considered unjust.
[36] *CDH*, 27 August 1886.
[37] Ibid., 24 September 1886.
[38] Ibid.
[39] Donald Richter, op. cit., p.58.
[40] *The Denbigh Free Press*, 11 September 1886, where the figure of ninety constables was reported. In his later testimony to the Bridge Commission hearing, Major Leadbetter recollected that there were only eighty-one officers in attendance. See also *CDH*, 27 August 1886.
[41] *CDH*, 3 December 1886.
[42] Donald Richter, op. cit., p.58. It was estimated that he had an escort of seventy constables.
[43] Ibid. See also *CDH*, 24 December 1886 when it is reported that earlier efforts to conduct distraint sales in Whitford had failed and on one occasion bailiffs were escorted to Mostyn station by an angry mob and told never to return. See also *Flintshire Observer*, 16 December 1886.
[44] *CDH*, 24 December 1886. In addition to Mr Bolton, the deputy chief constable, other officers present were Superintendent Hughes, Holywell, Inspectors Minshull, Connah's Quay and Maclaren, Rhyl. Police from Denbighshire were under the command of Inspector Lindsay and the officers from Caernarfonshire under Sergeant Roberts – total number of officers present was eighty.
[45] *CDH*, 3 December 1886. The Reverend Williams was also keen to point

out how 'Irish notions have been imported into, and have apparently taken root in hitherto peaceful and law abiding Wales'. Here he was undoubtedly making a pointed reference to the powerful speeches by the Irishman, Michael Davitt, who wished to broaden the agitation. See also Kenneth O. Morgan, op. cit., pp.54, 78, 84 and 212.

[46] Kenneth O. Morgan, op. cit., p.85.

[47] Donald Richter, op. cit., p.59. Later, thirty-one of those involved in the disturbance were charged with riot and assault, although only eight were ever brought to trial (and those were merely bound over to the amount of £20 each). On the same day as the Llangwm disturbance, an angry crowd at Rhyl, not only prevented a distraint sale, but forced the auctioneer to promise he would never again conduct a tithe sale.

[48] *Flintshire Observer*, 19 May 1887.

[49] Ibid., 16 June 1887. Although none of the military personnel present were used, they were frequently taunted and accused of only carrying guns for show, and it was only after one of the soldiers produced cartridges from his pouch that the taunts ceased. See also *The Tithe War*, a Clwyd Record Office Publication, (Hawarden, 1975), p.3.

[50] *Flintshire Observer*, 23 June 1887.

[51] Donald Richter, op. cit., p.62. Surprisingly, although it was a very hot day the police were still wearing their winter clothing which must have made their position even more uncomfortable.

[52] Ibid. Also *CDH*, 24 September 1886, which records a meeting in Manchester at the Liberal Club of Welsh residents who wished to help their fellow-countrymen in the tithe struggle.

[53] Ibid.

[54] *Flintshire Observer*, 7 July 1887.

[55] Donald Richter, op. cit., p.62.

[56] Ibid.

[57] Ibid., p.63. See also *CDH*, 21 October 1887, where at the Flintshire quarter sessions, held at Mold on 17 October, the chief constable defends the honour and integrity of his men, also *CDH*, 25 November 1887 and 23 December 1887.

[58] Ibid.

[59] DQS Rolls, (Easter, 1888). After some discussion it was claimed by the chairman, Captain Griffiths, Boscawen, that such an order to release money had been given some months ago.

[60] Donald Richter, op. cit., p.63.

[61] *CDH*, 20 January 1888.

[62] Ibid., 10 February 1888.

[63] George Lerry, op. cit., 'The policemen of Denbighshire', *Transactions of the Denbighshire Historical Society*, 2 (1953), pp. 131-3.

[64] *CDH*, 8 June 1888.

[65] *Wrexham Advertiser*, 19 May 1888.

[66] George Lerry, op cit., pp. 132-3. As a consequence of this request a troop

[66] of nine Lancers arrived at Denbigh on 23 May under the command of Major Gough and Lieutenant Colvin. See also CRO, *The Tithe War*, op. cit., p.7.
[67] Ibid., p.133. The tithe sales within the county were successfully completed by 22 June 1888. See also *CDH*, 1 June 1888.
[68] Donald Richter, op. cit., p.64, also *CDH*, 22 June 1888.
[69] *CDH*, 11 May 1888.
[70] George Lerry, op. cit., p.133 and *CDH*, 6 July 1888.
[71] Donald Richter, op. cit., p.65. See also David J.V. Jones, op. cit., p.98 where he records that during the tithe riots the Welsh press asked the question 'whether too much, and insensitive policing had been the catalyst which had turned a quiet people into a furious mob'.
[72] Ibid.
[73] Ibid., p.66. See also *CDH*, 15 June; 29 June; 13 July; 28 September and 21 December 1888, also for the position in Montgomeryshire the *Flintshire Observer*, 26 June and 17 July 1890.
[74] Donald Richter, op. cit., p.66.
[75] PP, Vol. xxxviii (1887), *Report of an Inquiry as to Disturbances Connected with the Levying of Tithe Rent Charge in Wales*, Q 1061; Q 3343.
[76] Donald Richter, op. cit., p.71. At the Denbighshire Assizes held at Ruthin on 27 February 1888 – the eight accused who all pleaded guilty were: William Williams, 38 a farmer; Thomas Thomas, 28 a grocer; Edward G. Roberts, 23 local Wesleyan minister; John Lloyd, 36 farmer; James Metcalfe, 21 draper's assistant; John Jones, 48 farmer; David Jones, 27 farmer; and Edward Davies, 51 farmer.
[77] Ibid.
[78] John Davies, *A History of Wales*, (London, 1994), p.485.
[79] Ibid., p.486.
[80] Ibid. 'Bargains' were parts of the rock face to which the quarrymen were allocated. Their wages were dependent on the quality of the slate in a particular bargain. Men could be victimised by being given bargains of inferior slate to work – if one annoyed a particular officer, it could tend to men being removed completely from the rock face and allocated a less important task. See also J. Owain Jones, op. cit., p.59.
[81] Ibid. It was this desire on the part of management to abolish the 'bargain' system that ultimately led to the lock-outs at Dinorwig in 1885-86 and Llechwedd in 1893. Also read Ivor Wynne Jones, *The Llechwedd Strike of 1893*, (Blaenau Ffestiniog), 1993.
[82] J. Owain Jones, op. cit., pp.59-60. Throughout the strike Lord Penrhyn was continually praised by those who opposed trade unionism, whilst trade unionists on the other hand collected thousands of pounds to assist the strikers.
[83] *CDH*, 9 November 1900. The troops were quartered in the Garth Board school and the arrangements for their stay was organised by two police officers.
[84] J. Owain Jones, op. cit., p.60. See also J. Roose Williams, 'Quarryman's

Champion', *Transactions of the Caernarvonshire Historical Society*, Vol. 29, (1968), p.117, where Colonel Ruck is told at the beginning of the strike 'to make arrangements for a three year struggle'.

[85] *CDH*, 9 and 16 November 1900, where in the editorial column it points out some of the difficulties that chief constables experienced in times of unrest.

[86] *CDH*, 19 April 1901.

[87] Ibid.

[88] Jean Lindsay, *The Great Strike – A History of the Penrhyn Quarry Dispute 1900-1903*, (Newton Abbot, 1987), p.130. At a mass meeting in Bethesda reported by the *Manchester Guardian* on 28 May, Colonel Ruck's promise of police protection was greeted with a 'tremendous outburst of hooting and laughter'.

[89] Jane Morgan, *Conflict and Order – The Police and Labour Disputes in England and Wales 1900-1939*, (Oxford, 1987), p.150. See also *CDH*, 12 July 1901.

[90] Ibid.

[91] Jane Lindsay, op. cit., p.133.

[92] Ibid.

[93] CSJ Committee, 15 August 1901. See also *CDH*, 31 August 1901, where it is reported that at a meeting between magistrates in Bangor and Colonel Ruck, no order for the swearing in of special constables was made.

[94] Jane Morgan, op. cit., p.150. Read *CDH*, 13 December 1901, where the Home Secretary sanctions the temporary appointment of twenty officers to the regular force. As a result of this agreement the chief constable asks the county council to vote for £194 for their maintenance until the end of January 1902.

[95] R. Merfyn Jones, *The North Wales Quarrymen 1874-1922*, (Cardiff, 1982), p.245. Prior to the dispute, Bethesda was a peaceful town policed by one sergeant and four constables.

[96] *CDH*, 5 July 1901.

[97] R. Merfyn Jones, op. cit., p.245.

[98] *CDH*, 30 August 1901. Most of the officers sent to assist were Welsh speakers – an important fact in a community like Bethesda.

[99] *Liverpool Daily Post*, 26 September 1901.

[100] Jane Lindsey, op. cit., p.157.

[101] Ibid., p.159.

[102] Ibid., p.160.

[103] *CDH*, 3 January 1902.

[104] *The Times*, 3 January 1902.

[105] *Liverpool Daily Post*, 8 January 1902.

[106] Ibid., 4 December 1901.

[107] *Cambrian News*, 20 January 1902.

[108] CSJ Committee, 24 January 1902. See also *CDH*, 24 January and 11 April 1902.

[109] *Liverpool Daily Post*, 4 February 1902, and Jane Lindsay, op. cit., p.167.

[110] *CDH*, 28 March 1902. The officers were quartered in a disused cafe in the High Street in Bethesda, and included officers from Liverpool, Stockport and Bath, although it is questionable whether officers from the latter force were actually in attendance.

[111] *Liverpool Daily Post*, 20 May 1902.

[112] *Manchester Guardian*, 15 and 24 September 1902.

[113] J. Owain Jones, op. cit., p.60.

[114] Jane Lindsay, op. cit., p.197. Members of the committee consisted of Chairman Mr J.R. Pritchard; Captain N.P. Stewart; Mr D.P. Williams; Mr J.A. Picton; Mr Jones Morris; Mr J. Issard Davies and Mr E.R. Davies.

[115] Ibid., op cit., p.198.

[116] Ibid., p.199. See also for a fuller account R. Merfyn Jones, op. cit., p.243.

[117] Ibid. See also CSJ Committee, 17 April 1902, where the cost of employing constables from several forces is listed. One magistrate at the meeting stated that 29s a day for a man and his horse was too much – another magistrate disagreed stating, it was the cost of the man that was too much – not the horse. See also, R. Merfyn Jones, op. cit., p.245, where he lists the forces that supplied officers to Caernarfonshire in 1902.

[118] CSJ Committee, Minutes of Evidence and Report of the Sub-Committee Appointed to Enquire into Matters at Bethesda, 1903.

[119] *The Times*, 13 February 1903.

[120] *CDH*, 13 February 1903.

[121] CSJ Committee, Report of 1903, op. cit.

[122] T.A. Critchley, op. cit., p.179.

[123] Ibid.

[124] Parliamentary Papers, 1908, Vol. ix.

[125] T.A. Critchley, op. cit., p.129. For a brief account of the part played by Winston Churchill during the Tonypandy riots of 1910, read pp.179-81. Soldiers were also called in to aid the police in Liverpool on the 13 August 1911, following large-scale rioting on Merseyside, when men of the Royal Warwickshire Regiment helped to restore order. Soldiers were again used in Liverpool in 1919, during the occasion of the second police strike.

[126] *Flintshire Observer*, 21 September 1893.

[127] MSJ Committee, 28 June 1898.

[128] *Flintshire Constabulary Centenary Handbook* (1956), p.27. Queen Victoria also visited the Royal National Eisteddfod at Rhyl in 1892.

[129] CSJ Committee, 25 April 1894.

[130] *CDH*, 15 June 1894.

[131] CSJ Committee, 25 April 1894. At this meeting the chief constable informed magistrates that when Queen Victoria visited Wrexham in 1888, there were at least 300 officers on duty. See also George Lerry, 'The policemen of Denbighshire', *Transactions of the Denbighshire Historical Society*, 2 (1953), p.139, where it is reported that for his service and

organisation during the visit to Wrexham, the chief constable, Major Leadbetter, was presented with a silver cup by members of the Denbighshire standing joint committee, as a mark of their appreciation.

[132] CSJ Committee, 19 September 1911. The number of officers seconded from each Welsh force was as follows; Pembrokeshire 15; Cardiganshire 7; Newport 9; Carmarthen 22; Swansea 19; Cardiff 49; Monmouth 28; Merthyr Tydfil 8; Merioneth 15; Denbighshire 31. These figures exclude officers from Caernarfonshire and Anglesey who were only present for the day.

[133] *CDH*, 30 June 1911.

[134] North Wales Police: Letters dated 29 April 1911 and 24 June 1911 that relate to the Investiture of the Prince of Wales in 1911, currently in the possession of the force at Colwyn Bay will be deposited at the Gwynedd Record Office, Caernarfon with copies on completion of this work placed at the National Library of Wales, Aberystwyth. See also *CDH*, 21 April 1911. At the meeting of the standing joint committee in Caernarfon the chief constable informed members that he had sent forty-one officers under the command of a superintendent to south Wales during the strike by miners at Tonypandy at the request of the chief constable of Glamorgan.

[135] *Cambrian News*, 20 October 1911.

[136] North Wales Police, op. cit., letter dated 5 August 1911.

[137] Ibid., op. cit., letters dated 3, 4, 5, 8, 11 and 12 August 1911, which related to numerous complaints about food and accommodation by members of the Merthyr Tydfil, Swansea, Newport, Cardiff, Carmarthen and Pembrokeshire forces.

[138] Ibid., op. cit., letter dated 17 July 1911.

[139] *CDH*, 21 July 1911.

[140] Ibid.

[141] CSJ Committee, 21 September 1911.

[142] Ibid. See also North Wales Police, op. cit., letter dated 9 May 1911, which highlights how some of the expenditure was incurred. The letter from Richard Jones, furnishers of Caernarfon, shows that the cost for the hire for four days of 1,000 mattresses, blankets and pillows, amounted to £225.

[143] CSJ Committee, 19 September 1911.

[144] Ibid. See also MSJ Committee, 2 January 1912 which records that every officer from Merioneth who was in attendance during the Investiture should receive 5s towards the cost of providing food. See also North Wales Police, op cit., letter dated 2 August 1911, where the chief constable of Caernarfonshire received a letter from the Home Office which requested him to forward the names of all the officers on duty at the Investiture who had served for ten years. Interestingly, officers from Cardiganshire were not to be included and no explanation for the omission is given.

[145] MQS Rolls, (Easter, 1912). Recognition for the Merioneth constabulary came in October 1912, when twenty-five members were presented with the Coronation Medal. The number of medals presented represented a larger proportion than that received by any other force in Wales. See also *Cambrian News*, 18 October 1912.

[146] MCF Orders, QA/P/D/8/1, 22 August 1911.
[147] Ibid., 14 February 1912.

## Chapter VII

# The First World War, 1914-18

The difficulties and strains imposed by the advent of the First World War affected the development of the police in England and Wales in several ways. For example, as Clive Emsley explains 'they contributed to the unrest which resulted in the police strikes in 1918 and 1919'.[1] It was also a time when further encroachments by central government upon the way police committees conducted their affairs can be discerned.[2] What is also significant at this time, is the fears generated by the Russian Revolution, for it raised political surveillance by the police to a level 'unknown at least since the struggle against Revolutionary and Napoleonic France'.[3] At the outbreak of hostilities it was estimated that the number of police officers serving in England and Wales amounted to approximately 53,000 men, the majority of whom were of military age. Indeed, a large number of men had already seen service in the armed forces during the Boer War and were already reservists; this was certainly the case for many of the officers serving in the county forces in north Wales.[4]

In the wake of the outbreak of war in August 1914, a whole series of emergency measures that the police were expected to rigidly enforce were implemented. However, the police in north Wales, as elsewhere, were not entirely unprepared to meet the demands made upon them. As early as 1911 mobilization posters had been sent to every police station to await distribution when the appropriate time arose.[5] As if to demonstrate that the police in Merioneth were prepared for any eventuality, the chief constable, Mr Richard Jones, acting on a Home Office circular, reported with pride to his police committee in September 1914 that he had already secured the names of 325 men who were willing, if necessary, to act as special constables.[6] A similar situation existed in Anglesey where there was no shortage of volunteers.[7] In Caernarfonshire, too, over 300 special constables had been enrolled by October 1914.[8]

One of the first measures to be introduced by the chief constables was the cancellation of the weekly rest day and annual leave, although the right of a day off was partially restored later. The general mobilization notices held at police stations were immediately distributed and a call was made for every reservist and territorial to report for duty. It was also a duty of the police, to inform where possible, all who had deserted from the army or navy before the outbreak of war, that a free pardon was offered if they surrendered themselves before 4 September 1914.[9] A duty which the police considered of vital importance was the internal security of the counties in which they served. In fact, one of the first priorities of the police in north Wales in 1914 was to ensure that no vital information was leaked to the enemy. In many ways, officers began to undertake those duties which in later years were looked upon as being within the realms of the special branch. One area of great concern to the authorities was the possibility of information being passed to the enemy via wireless transmission, and to prevent such an act, an order from the Postmaster General requested the closure of all transmitting installations within each county area, whether licensed for private or experimental purposes.[10] Even the keeping of pigeons which could be used for carrying messages, required special permission from the chief constable,[11] although the government itself did use carrier pigeons for certain purposes. The public were warned that on no account were they to interfere in any way with pigeons whilst in flight.[12] Another area of concern for the authorities, and which called upon the police to be extra vigilant, was the danger posed by enemy shipping, which it was feared might slip silently at night into the many inlets dotted around the coastline in north Wales. Places like Aberdyfi, Barmouth, Mochras and Porthmadog were viewed as being particularly vulnerable to raids by enemy vessels and the police, in close co-operation with customs officers, paid special attention to these and other ports.[13] This duty was considered so important that in order to ensure that proper security was maintained, officers were requested to appoint some responsible person or persons in each village where an alien was known to reside, so that any suspicious movement could be notified immediately to the authorities. Obviously, there was always a danger that communication with the enemy could be achieved by flashing lights to a vessel out at sea, or to an aircraft circling overhead.[14]

The motor car was seen as a vehicle that could prove very advantageous to an enemy residing in north Wales. It was for this reason that an order issued by His Majesty's Council on 5 August 1914 stated that the police were to seize every motor vehicle owned by a German.[15] Furthermore, before a German could own a vehicle in the future, permission had first of all to be obtained from the chief constable. All garages had to be visited by the police who informed the owners that it was their responsibility to see that no vehicle was loaned to an alien.[16] As a further precautionary measure, Merioneth's chief constable also ordered his officers to stop and question all car drivers using vehicles not carrying the county registration plates.[17]

A great deal of police time was devoted to checking all German and Austrian men between seventeen and forty-two years of age resident within their particular beats. Those who fell into this category were considered as being of military age and, therefore, were liable to be interned. If, however, a German or Austrian could be vouched for as to his or her personal character, by a British citizen, no internment would be made. What made the task of police officers more difficult when dealing with aliens was that a number of them had changed their name at the beginning of the war. This situation was somewhat eased when an order issued by the police in October 1914, instructed those who had changed their name to revert to the one they had formerly used, and warning that failure on their part to do so could lead to proceedings being taken against them.[18]

As a result of the emergency, standing orders such as those that related to sheep scab inspection and sheep dipping had to be suspended, but the danger of the disease reappearing led to the suspension being lifted in April, 1915.[19] The early months of the war were also a time when members of the various standing joint committees in north Wales expressed their concern at what they believed was an alarming rate in expenditure. For example, they were of the opinion that too much stationery was being used and called for drastic cuts to be made. Here, however, there was an apparent failure by some committee members to fully appreciate that in order to undertake their many administrative duties efficiently, some increase in paperwork was not only necessary but vital.

The fact that some standing orders had been suspended, in no way lightened the workload of officers in north Wales. Indeed, as each month of the war progressed even more duties were imposed upon them. For instance, there was a daily flow of new regulations which officers not only had to assimilate, but on occasion, even distribute. One such duty came in an order from the General Officer, Western Command, Chester, to officers in Merioneth, which informed them that not only was his car bearing the headplate 'G.O.C.' never to be stopped when passing through the county, but that he was also to be given priority at all times over all other road users.[20] Another order, which again referred to military vehicles stated that it was the duty of officers to ascertain that the headlights displayed were of the correct colours – upper half deep blue, lower half deep orange. For many officers, such an order seemed trivial and unimportant and it was the kind of order that the police found tiresome and even frustrating.[21]

Undoubtedly, the extra work created by so many additional duties placed a great strain on the police. Being, generally, small forces responsible for policing very wide areas meant that any change in the administrative pattern automatically created problems. In this respect, it was fortunate that the chief constables had at their disposal a large reserve of manpower in those who had volunteered to act as special constables. The value of these volunteers was soon appreciated.[22] One of the first villages in north Wales to benefit and make use of the extra arm of the law was Aberdyfi, where thirteen men had enrolled.[23] That great use would be made of special constables became evident during the first few months of the war, when a call was made for all Welsh police forces to release more officers to serve in the army. As a way of recruiting more police, an officer from the Welsh Guards was appointed specifically to recruit as many police officers as possible.[24] Flintshire's chief constable actively encouraged as many of his officers as possible to join the colours.[25] In fact, recruitment in Flintshire had always been good and by the summer of 1915 seven officers were already serving in the army.[26] One of the first officers to join the Welsh Guards in June 1915 was Constable William Pritchard of the Merioneth Constabulary.[27] Two other officers, Sergeant D.R. Davies stationed at Dolgellau and Constable Mayberry Morgan stationed at Maentwrog had been seconded to the military authorities in October 1914 as drill instructors to train newly enrolled recruits at Wrexham barracks, as both officers had previous army experience.[28]

It was the fact that these officers had merely been seconded to the army rather than actually joining up, that led the chief constable of Montgomeryshire, Mr William James Holland, to write in May 1915 that the Merioneth Constabulary was the only force with not one officer in the army. Obviously, quick to rebuke such a remark, the *Cambrian News* denied this was the case and insisted that 'Merioneth was more likely to lead the way than follow others'.[29] Whatever doubts there may have been regarding the patriotism of members of the force, they were soon banished, for within a matter of weeks several officers had left to join various army units.[30]

Throughout 1915, Lord Derby's recruiting scheme placed considerable pressure on police forces to release more men for the services. Indeed, the shortage of men had reached such a state that a Home Office directive allowed police officers who volunteered, to choose which regiment they wished to serve in. In a further communication from the Home Office in November 1915, a call was again made to release more men, and to facilitate such releases it was decreed that the less essential police work could be dispensed with.[31] In a communication from the chief constable of Anglesey, it was suggested that every member of the force, even when considered indispensable, should be, nevertheless, passed into the army reserve.[32] So serious had the manpower situation become, that by October 1915, a plea was made to all chief constables and postmasters asking them to act as recruiting officers during the crisis, the idea being that every police officer and postmaster should be supplied with leaflets showing the conditions of service and qualifications required by those wishing to serve in the army. Furthermore, the police and postal authorities were expected to issue railway warrants to those enlisting.[33] As a further inducement for the police themselves to enlist, an order issued in June 1915 gave the rates of pay a married officer could expect on enlistment. It was laid down that in addition to his army pay an officer would also receive payment from police funds so no loss of income would be incurred. Single men were to receive 8s a week for their legal dependants (both allowances being the maximum under the Police Emergency Pension Act 1915).[34]

As the war progressed, the number of those either wounded or killed rose steadily with battles like the Somme, Verdun and Passchendael inflicting great carnage. The drain on manpower was such that the war cabinet, meeting in May 1917, agreed that further demands would have to be made on the police forces of England and Wales. It was as a direct result of this decision that the chief constable of Merioneth received orders compelling him to release one further officer for military duties. This order superseded that issued in December 1915, which had left it entirely to the discretion of each chief constable whether or not an officer could be spared.[35] As forces throughout north Wales became more and more depleted, the officers remaining had to work additional hours in order to carry out their everyday duties. In many instances the strain on officers' family life at times almost reached breaking point. Long hours away from home on the never-ending enforcement of regulations placed them in an intolerable position. Yet, officers may well have smiled in Merioneth when a notice from the chief constable's office made the suggestion that if any member of the force had time on his hands he might consider helping the local farmer. The notice did, however, inform officers that on no account were they to place themselves at the farmer's beck and call.[36] One duty connected with farming which the police were expected to undertake was the distribution and collection of census forms relating to the number of animals and implements on each farm.[37]

There were also a variety of other duties that officers in north Wales had to undertake. In Flintshire, a new munitions factory had been established at Queensferry and several members of the force under the command of the deputy chief constable, Superintendent Robert Yarnill Davies, were seconded in 1917 to take charge of security at the site.[38] In Merioneth, officers found themselves guarding the water supply at Llyn Tecwyn in order to ensure that there was no tampering with the water supply by the enemy.[39] Police officers were also on duty at the prisoner of war camp at Fron-goch near Bala, and on more than one occasion police officers were vigilant in capturing German prisoners of war who had escaped from their place of confinement.[40] Sergeant J.M. Jones, nicknamed 'Royal' by his friends, because he had acted as bodyguard to Queen Victoria when she visited Llandderfel in 1889, secured the arrest of two German officers. Both men, Lieutenant Von Sanders Leben and Ober Lieutenant Andler, had escaped from Dyffryn Aled, Llansannan, on 4 April 1915, and had managed to remain free until recaptured a week later on 11 April near Harlech.[41]

It was in order to partially compensate officers for the many hardships created by war conditions that the various standing joint committees in north Wales introduced war bonus payments in 1915. In Anglesey, the standing joint committee granted a war bonus of 2s a week to all married men in the force, to be paid from 1 July 1915, and to be continued for the duration of the war. This was followed in January 1917 by a further war bonus of 3s a week to married men and an extra 1s a week to single men. In August 1918 it was decided to pay a war bonus of 12s a week to men of all ranks, with an additional 1s.6d weekly in respect of each child.[42] On some occasions, officers not only received extra money but found themselves contributing as well. In Denbighshire the chief constable hoped that men would make a small contribution to the Prince of Wales fund in order to help those in distress as a consequence of the war.[43] In Merioneth, a sum of £14.0s.6d was forwarded to the Prince of Wales fund and in addition to this sum a further £5.5s.0d was contributed from the force testimonial fund.[44]

Although the payment of a war bonus helped, it did little to alleviate the many pressures officers had to endure. Many extra duties had still to be undertaken, despite the fact that most forces were now under strength. The war had brought into north Wales many thousands of soldiers under training. This fact alone, created for the police an additional burden as they were the body responsible for billeting them. It was the responsibility of the police to see there was no overcrowding, that soldiers were not housed too long on licensed premises or that they slept two in a bed.[45] In Anglesey, strict guidelines were laid down which officers had to adhere to when seeking accommodation. For example, the following houses or premises were not to be used for billeting without the full consent of the occupants:[46]

a. houses in which only women and children resided;
b. houses of military and naval officers who were absent on duty;
c. houses which were occupied by female religious communities;
d. all bank premises.

Another duty allocated to the police was to accompany buyers who travelled through the various counties in order to acquire horses for the cavalry. Indeed, at one period during the war the idea had been mooted that there should be a Welsh cavalry regiment.[47] Officers in Anglesey were ordered by the chief constable that if members of the military while seeking horses for the cavalry failed to get petrol for their vehicles, it was the duty of the police to seize whatever amount they required.[48]

What was of immense assistance to officers and, in so many instances, must have saved them untold hours in time, was the use of the telephone. In an order issued by the Postmaster General in December 1914, officers were allowed to use the telephone for local calls without pre-payment in certain circumstances. This was a privilege that constantly helped constables in their everyday administrative duties.[49] However, in an order issued by Mr Richard Jones, chief constable of Merioneth, on 24 July 1915, it was made plain that on no account must the telephone be used for either a local or trunk call unless it was absolutely necessary, and even then, pre-payment had to be made.[50] There was some consolation for officers when an order issued later stated that they could communicate with the military authorities by telegram without pre-payment being necessary.[51]

Despite their many commitments officers also found themselves enforcing laws that came under the category of the Defence of the Realm. They became responsible for seeing that food prices did not increase beyond those authorised by the Food Controller. Even the price of milk was, to some extent, under the jurisdiction of the police, and officers were continually expected to check with shopkeepers that prices remained steady. A crime viewed as serious during the war was damage to allotments. The growing of food for home consumption was seen as important in the battle for survival and the police were urged to take swift action against those caught trespassing.[52]

As a result of enemy action at sea, bodies were periodically washed ashore along the coastline of north Wales. Instructions as to the procedure to be followed when such circumstances arose were issued to all police stations in 1917. Officers were expected to describe the body in some detail, giving height and approximate age as well as any distinguishing marks that might assist in identification. In Merioneth, such information was sent to the coastguard at Pwllheli. A report issued in 1917, stated that twenty-two inquests had been held on bodies washed ashore between Harlech and Llwyngwril. It was also reported that due to investigations carried out by the police several bodies had eventually been identified.[53] The Home Office also set rules that had to be followed in the event of aircraft wreckage being found. On no account was wreckage to be moved without first being examined by an expert and it was the first duty of the police to inform the authorities of the aircraft's location, giving such details as the type of aircraft and whether prior to crashing it had released any bombs.[54]

In absorbing so many notices and regulations, officers found their time for normal duties severely curtailed. Therefore, it was somewhat fortuitous that during the war years the rate of crime in the counties did not markedly change. There were, however, some observations made on drunkenness which, in the early years of the war, were to prove interesting. In Holyhead, for example, it was noticeable that since the Intoxicating Liquor Restriction Act of 1914 was put in force there had been a marked improvement in public order in the town.[55] Later, the Inspector at

Llangefni reported that although drunkenness had decreased among men it was noticeable that the drinking habits of women, such as the wives and dependants of soldiers, was on the increase. It was the Inspector's view that this was due, in part, to women receiving a more regular income than they did before the war.[56] Commenting in 1916 on the general decrease in crime, the *Justice of the Peace* believed there were several factors that contributed to this situation. For instance, many of those who had formerly committed offences were now serving in the forces and some were proving good soldiers or sailors. The booming wartime economy had done much to relieve poverty and want and as a consequence there was less inclination to steal.[57] There was, too, another factor, Sir Leonard Dunning, one of His Majesty's Inspectors of Constabulary, stated in his report for 1915, 'if the police are reduced in number, or are withdrawn from ordinary to special duties, offences escape notice, and prosecutions drop as surely as they would in the case of an actual decrease of offence'.[58]

As the war drew to a close in 1918, a change occurred in the type of duties undertaken by the police. In many ways they began to adopt a role that in later years became associated with those involved in social work. Over the years they had become an integral part of the community and the First World War had brought them that much closer to the people they served. When the war finally ended, the terror it had created began to be fully realised. Hundreds of thousands had been maimed and killed and the counties of north Wales did not escape unscathed. Every county suffered greatly since every town and village had made sacrifices. Far too often, it had been the unwelcome duty of constables to be the bearers of bad news. In many instances, too, it had been the police who consoled the bereaved, thus bringing themselves that much nearer to the people. It was this closeness to the people that probably prompted the standing joint committee in Merioneth in 1917, to believe that the police were by far the most appropriate body to compile a list of all those who had fallen in the war. They were also to ascertain the rank and unit of the deceased, so that after the cessation of hostilities a roll of honour could be placed in the county hall at Dolgellau.[59] In February 1918 the police were also asked to compile a register of all ex-servicemen who had lost limbs in the war.[60] At a meeting held on 17 February 1918, a similar request was made for the police to make a register of all those who were blind.[61] When the war came to an end in November 1918, members from the respective forces in north Wales who had been on active service were released from their military duties and in the fullness of time returned home. Sadly, however, fourteen officers were never to return.[62] During the period of hostilities a number of police officers from north Wales had also served with great distinction.[63] The officers who had remained on duty in north Wales throughout the war could also feel justly proud, for they had all performed their many and often difficult duties with a high degree of professionalism, at times under trying conditions which the state of war inevitably creates.[64]

The First World War undoubtedly added to the stature of the north Wales forces. The early years of the twentieth century had not always been smooth, and therefore, the police had suffered the trials and tribulations of any organisation that was in the process of expanding. Yet, despite difficulties, the police seemed to have achieved an independence within and under the law, which helped dispel the suspicion that had lurked in the minds of many, that the police had simply been established to act as a tool for the authorities. True, there was still much to be done in the sphere of pay, conditions of service, and professional training, but, the experience of the past, such as the employment of professional policemen to the highest positions, was now helping forces like those in north Wales, to emerge better equipped to play an even more important role in the post-war world.[65]

---

[1] Clive Emsley, The English Police – *A Political and Social History*, 2nd. edition (London, 1991) p.121.

[2] Ibid.

[3] Ibid.

[4] *CDH*, 25 January 1901. *Police Review*, December 1899; 18 October 1901 and 17 October 1902. It was estimated that by the end of 1915 about one man in five from the provincial forces had joined the colours. The exodus of men from the Metropolitan Police to the military was even greater, with just over a quarter of the men being recruited.

[5] MCF Orders, QA/P/D/8/1, 17 February 1914.

[6] *Cambrian News*, 11 September 1914.

[7] ARO, Chief Constable's General Order Book, 1911-18, WH/1/62, 23 August 1914. At the Holyhead police station an order was placed for twenty-three special sergeant's armlets with red stripes, 220 special constables armlets, 260 staves and sixty badges; at Llangefni police station orders were placed for 160 staves, ten sergeants red armlets, 100 special constables armlets and forty special constable's badges. See also *Police Review*, 30 July 1915 – where it is reported that in Flintshire special

constables were to be enrolled in order to replace officers who had joined the services. Also consult Hermann Mannheim, *War and Crime*, (London, 1941), p.97, where it is claimed that the loss of so many trained policemen may have been somewhat repaired by the establishment of the special constabulary.

[8] J. Owain Jones, *The History of the Caernarvonshire Constabulary, 1856-1950*, (Caernarfon, 1963), p.67.

[9] MCF Orders, QA/P/D/8/1, 21 August 1914.

[10] Ibid., 9 August 1914.

[11] Ibid., 8 December 1914.

[12] ARO, Chief Constable's General Order Book, 1911-18, WH/1/62, 30 November 1914.

[13] MCF Orders, QA/P/D/8/1, 5 August 1914. See also Anglesey Chief Constable's General Order Book, op. cit., 12 January 1915.

[14] MCF Orders, QA/P/D/8/1, 13 August 1914, also Home Office Letters to Chief Constable of Anglesey 1913-19, WH/73, 15 September 1915.

[15] Ibid.

[16] DRO, Chief Constable's Papers 1878-1922, DPD/2/1, 13 August 1914.

[17] MCF, Orders, QA/P/D/8/1, 6 August 1914.

[18] ARO, Home Office Letters to Chief Constable of Anglesey 1913-19, WH/73, to December 1914.

[19] MCF, Orders, QA/P/D/8/1, 13 April 1915.

[20] Ibid., 7 September 1914.

[21] Ibid., 12 June 1915.

[22] For an interesting account of the special constabulary see Ronald Seth, *The Specials – The story of the Special Constabulary*, (London, 1961).

[23] *Cambrian News*, 27 August 1915. Those who had volunteered were as follows: Marmaduke Lewis JP, J. M. Howell JP, E.L. Rowlands JP, E.B. Proctor JP, D.L. Howell JP, Hilton Kershaw, Douglas Hewett, R. Griffiths, D. Glover, Edward Jones, W.H. Hickman, J. Lumley and E.H. Hughes.

[24] MCF Orders, QA/P/D/8/1, 19 April 1915. Those recruited were assured that their posts would be kept open and their army service would count for pensionable purposes. See also ASJ Committee, 16 September 1914.

[25] *Police Review*, 21 May 1915.

[26] Ibid., see *Police Review* 11 December 1914, where it is reported that Constable Albert Jones who was twenty-four years of age, a reservist with the Grenadier Guards was killed at the battle of Ypres.

[27] MCF Orders, QA/P/D/8/1, 12 June 1915. Sadly, he was killed on 16 September 1916. During his service in France he frequently sent letters to his chief constable which described his meetings with men from the county who, like him, were serving in the various battle zones.

[28] MQS Rolls, (Michaelmas, 1914). Sergeant Davies had served in the army during the Egyptian campaign of 1884-85, and Constable Morgan had been called up as a reservist during the South African War. See also *Police Review*, 31 July 1914 and 27 October 1916.

[29] *Cambrian News*, 4 June 1915.

[30] MCF Orders, QA/P/D/8/1, 18 November 1915. In June 1915 Constable A.H. Williams joined the Royal Welsh Fusiliers and Constables William Dresser Williams and George Morgan, the Royal Field Artillery. Later, in October, Constable James G. Davies joined the Pembrokeshire Yeomanry and in November Constables Oliver Cromwell Davies, Morgan Davies and Griffith Williams, all joined the Royal Garrison Artillery.

[31] Ibid., 1 November 1915.

[32] ARO, Chief Constable's General Order Book, 1911-18, WH/1/62, 9 December 1915.

[33] MCF Orders, QA/P/D/8/1. 29 October 1915.

[34] Ibid., 29 June 1915.

[35] Ibid., 23 May 1917.

[36] Ibid., 10 September 1917. Also see ARO, Chief Constable's General Order Book 1911-18, WH/1/62, 3 July 1918 where a similar suggestion is made to officers in Anglesey.

[37] ARO, Chief Constable's General Order Book 1911-18, WH/1/62, 16 April 1917. Some indication of the enormity of the task of taking a census of animals was seen in the correspondence of the chief constable of Anglesey, Mr Lewis Prothero, 1915-18, WH/1/67 when, in a letter dated 10 October 1918 from Sergeant H. Williams, he requests 2,000 census forms for the Holyhead division. See also Hugh Owen, *History of the Anglesey Constabulary*, (Llangefni, 1952), p.46, which records that in 1918 the police had supervised the dipping of 49,599 sheep and delivered and collected 2,274 census of horses forms, and in doing so, had travelled 1,164 miles.

[38] *Flintshire Constabulary Handbook* (1956), p.29. Mr Yarnell Davies received special mention in 1920 for his work at the factory and was awarded the MBE, and later, in 1937 was a recipient of the OBE. In 1927 he was also invested with the Kings Police Medal, having, as the citation read 'rendered exemplary service, distinguished by special merit and ability'. At a recent Sotheby sale at Billingshurst on 24 March 1995, at the request and on behalf of the North Wales Police, I purchased all these medals, and today they can be seen on display in the Senior Officers Dining-room at the headquarters of the Force in Colwyn Bay.

[39] MSJ Committee, 29 June 1915.

[40] MCF Orders, QA/P/D/8/1, 16 March 1915.

[41] MRO. From information obtained from the back of a group photograph. Also MCF Orders, QA/P/D/8/4, 3 May 1918, which records how Constable Davies, stationed at Harlech, arrested another German Officer, Lieutenant Koch, after he had made an unsuccessful bid for freedom.

[42] Hugh Owen, op. cit., p.43. Also ARO, Chief Constable's General Order Book, 1911-18, WH/1/62, 10 December 1917. Similar war bonuses were received by officers in the other forces in north Wales. See MCF Orders, QA/P/D/8/1,
5 January 1916. *Police Review*, 28 April 1916 and 30 March 1917.

[43] DRO, Chief Constable's Papers 1817-1922, DPD/2/1, 10 September 1914.

[44] MCF Orders, QA/P/D/8/1, 7 September 1914.
[45] Ibid., 18 December 1914.
[46] ARO, Chief Constable's General Order Book, 1911-18, WH/1/62, 24 September 1914.
[47] MCF Orders, QA/P/D/8/1, 5 August 1914.
[48] ARO, Chief Constable's General Order Book 1911-18, WH/1/62, 7 August 1914.
[49] Ibid., 17 December 1914.
[50] MCF Orders, QA/P/D/8/1, 24 July 1915.
[51] Ibid., 15 August 1915.
[52] Ibid., 9 June 1917.
[53] MQS Rolls. (Hilary, 1918).
[54] DRO, Chief Constable's Papers 1878-1922, DPD/2/1, 23 February 1915. Also Home Office Letters to Chief Constable of Anglesey 1913-19, WH/1/73, which also relates to the procedure to be followed in the event of an aeroplane or airship crashing.
[55] ARO, Correspondence of the Chief Constable of Anglesey 1915-18, WH/1/67, 20 March 1915.
[56] Ibid., 7 December 1915.
[57] *Justice of the Peace*, lxxx, 18 March 1916, pp.133-4, also Hermann Mannheim, op. cit., p.94, which records offences which did increase steadily, bigamy, the stealing of fruit and plants and, of course, offences against naval and military laws. See also John Brophy, *The Five Years*, (London, 1936), pp.224-6, which gives the total enlistments from all sources up to 11 November 1918, as: England 4,006,158 and Wales 272,924.
[58] Clive Emsley, op. cit., p.123 and the *Report of His Majesty's Inspectors of Constabulary 1915*, p.5.
[59] MCF Orders, QA/P/D/8/1, 3 January 1917.
[60] ARO, Chief Constable's General Order Book, 1911-18, WH/1/62, 4 February 1918.
[61] MCF Orders, QA/P/D/8/4, 17 April 1918.
[62] See J. Owain Jones, op. cit., p.95. *Flintshire Constabulary Handbook*, op. cit., p.33, and H.K. Birch, 'The Merioneth Police 1856-1950', MA University of Wales thesis, 1980, p.200. The officers killed in the respective forces in north Wales were as follows: *Caernarfonshire* (7): T.C. Orris; R. Morris; J.L. Thomas; R.O. Roberts; R. Jones; D.L. Jones; S. Evans. *Merioneth* (1): William Pritchard. *Flintshire* (4): Albert Jones; John G. Jones; Robert John Hughes; Harold William Davies. *Denbighshire* (2): Reginald Prince; John Henry Williams. No officers were lost by the Anglesey Constabulary.
[63] *Cambrian News*, 24 April 1915. *Flintshire Constabulary Handbook*, op. cit., p.34. Hugh Owen, op. cit., p.46. Constable Oliver Cromwell Davies of the Merioneth Constabulary gained the Croix de Guerre at Passchendaele, the Belgian Military Medal at Arras and the Meritorious Service Medal at St Quentin. In Flintshire, one officer Constable David Hewitt was awarded the Distinguished Conduct Medal and Constable Albert Griffiths the Military

Medal, with a further two officers Constable Edward George Hughes and William John Parry, being mentioned in Despatches. In Anglesey, Constable Owen Jones was also mentioned in Despatches.

[64] Hugh Owen, op. cit., pp.46-7, which records that in October 1918, the Chief Constable of Anglesey, Mr Lewis Porthero, retired after completing fifty-seven years in the police and was succeeded by his son, Superintendent Robert Humphrey Prothero. One of the first duties of the newly appointed chief constable was to transfer his office and police headquarters from Menai Bridge to Holyhead. Also see the *Flintshire Centenary Handbook*, op. cit., p.29, which reports the death on 26 January 1918, whilst still in office, of the Chief Constable, Mr John Ivor Davies, who was succeeded on 6 February 1918 by Superintendent and Deputy Chief Constable, Robert Yarnell Davies.

[65] G.W. Reynolds and A. Judge, *The Night the Police went on Strike*, (1968), p.18.

## Chapter VIII

# The Inter-War Years, 1918-39

The ending of the war saw police officers everywhere engaged in a battle of another kind. During the war years the living standards of the police had deteriorated, a fact highlighted by ex-Inspector John Syme, formally of the Metropolitan Police.[1] His actions in addressing large public meetings focussed attention on the plight of policemen and their families. Certainly, the police at this time were very resentful that they never had the 'opportunity to confer'. With the ending of the war the police generally also had another grievance, that concerning pay. They found that those who had worked in factories making munitions were much better off, and that even with the additional war bonus they still lagged behind other workers. Many officers returning to duty after serving in the forces were disillusioned, with the result that morale was low. As one writer observed 'temptations held out by bribes of food and money must have been irresistible'.[2] There was no doubt that the situation was tense, and bitterness and militancy lay beneath the surface.

By May 1919, protest marches were being organised and officers, especially in London, openly displayed hostility towards the government. Earlier, in March 1919, faced with a worsening situation, the government set up a committee under the chairmanship of Lord Desborough to examine the pay and conditions of the police. Working speedily, the committee produced a list of major recommendations in May 1919. It advocated a higher rate of pay and, more importantly, urged that it should be standardised. There was also a recommendation that machinery should be established for the police and police authorities were to make representations when necessary to the Home Secretary. The Home Secretary promised to accept the

Desborough Committee's findings and agreed that the pay of the police would be substantially increased. On 26 May 1919, legislation was introduced to prohibit police officers from belonging to a trade union and a little later, it was announced in the House of Commons that any officer who went on strike would be dismissed.[3]

This measure somewhat dampened the enthusiasm of those who belonged to the newly formed Police Union. However, the Bill to improve conditions, which was introduced into the House of Commons on 8 July 1919, did provide for the establishment of a Police Federation and create a Police Council as a consultative body.[4] The Bill stipulated clearly that in no circumstances could a police officer belong to a union. On hearing of this, leaders of the Police Union called a strike, but by then passions had cooled and many police officers were willing to accept the new deal. The promise of a pay rise and the formation of a Police Federation had made them close ranks. Striking was not for them and they displayed their loyalty to the police service and the government by standing firm. There were others, however, who remained militant and as a result 2,364 men decided to strike. The forces worst affected were the Metropolitan Police and Liverpool, where 1,056 and 954 officers respectively decided to strike. Support for the strike, but to a far lesser degree, also came from police officers serving in the City of London, Birmingham, Birkenhead, Bootle and Wallasey forces.[5] In Liverpool, there was severe rioting and steel helmeted troops and even tanks were sent to Merseyside where there were bayonet charges and some bloodshed.[6] Every officer who had gone on strike was ultimately dismissed from the service and never reinstated, despite the fact that many representations on their behalf were made. The dismissal of so many officers obviously weakened the forces in which they served.

The passing of the Police Act 1919 put into effect the main recommendations of the Desborough Committee. It provided the police service with a united system that was centrally controlled. The Act forbade policemen to join a union and any attempt to make a police officer strike was made a criminal offence. There was, however, one exception to the union rule. If an officer was a member of a trade union before joining the police he could, provided his chief constable agreed, continue to be a member in order to receive the union benefits to which he was entitled.[7] With the establishment of the Police Federation, there came into being a representative body for all police officers up to and including the rank of chief inspector. Its neutrality was guaranteed by the prohibiting of association with any person or organisation outside the police service on the grounds that, 'the responsibilities of the police to the community require that they shall at all times be manifestly free from any partisan bias or sectional interest'.[8] The Home Secretary was given the power to regulate all police pay and conditions of service and the Police Council was established as a consultative and advisory body, before which, any proposals and regulations were to be laid.[9] Finally, and perhaps for the smaller forces such as those serving north Wales a most important stipulation, was the fact that in view of the increase in pay and pension arrangements which fell on public funds half the cost of the police (and not as formerly, only half the cost of the men's pay and clothing) would be borne by the Exchequer. As a result of this change, the cost of the police in England and Wales rose from £6,900,000 in 1914 to £19,912,000 in 1922.[10]

For officers serving in north Wales the regulations proposed by the Police Act were especially welcome. They were looked upon as being necessary measures that would give the service the degree of professionalism it had so sorely lacked previously. Undoubtedly, the police strike had to some extent tarnished, if only briefly, the image of the police, so the hope was that the changes to be implemented would help imbue officers with fresh hope for the future. There was never any mention of the police in north Wales taking strike action during this troublesome period: to a man they remained loyal. In fact, the county authorities in north Wales achieved some measure of agreement on standardised pay without resorting to strike action. At a meeting held at the Queen's Hotel, Chester, on 9 July 1915 representatives of the police authorities in north Wales had agreed to a uniform pay structure for their officers. This agreement was carried a stage further when the standing joint committee in Merioneth announced that the new rates would take effect as from 1 January 1919.[11] In recognising these improvements the chief constable reminded his men that the standing joint committee had always taken a great deal of interest in the welfare of officers and that in return they 'should carry out their duties in the best possible manner, with energy, zeal and fidelity'.[12] A further and long awaited improvement in the conditions of the police came on 23 November 1918 with the passing of the Police Widows Pension Act. Under the Act the widows of constables and sergeants would receive a pension of £26 per annum, with the widows of inspectors receiving £32 per annum. For widows of officers who had held senior rank, a pension of £40 per annum was payable.[13] Although the pension was small, it did at least offer a degree of security to the wife of a police officer.

As a result of a letter from the Home Office about pay, the police authorities in north Wales convened a meeting in Rhyl on 20 May 1919 to which the four police authorities, of Caernarfonshire, Anglesey, Denbighshire and Flintshire sent representatives to the meeting. Merioneth declined the invitation to attend, possibly in the belief that the imminence of the Desborough Report made such attendance unnecessary. Although the conference was not able to reflect the views of all the police authorities in north Wales, it was agreed that the following resolutions on pay be communicated to the Desborough Committee which was to meet on 28 May 1919 in the House of Lords:[14]

> That owing to the diversity of conditions in the areas of Police authorities, the Conference is of the opinion that it is not practicable to adopt a flat rate which would be satisfactory for the whole country, but it approves of a flat rate in grouped areas which are similar in character.

Two of the earliest forces in north Wales to adopt the recommendations of the Desborough Committee on pay were Anglesey and Merioneth where on appointment, officers received the following new rates:

> Constables £3-10s-0d pw rising by ten annual increments of 2s pw to £4-10-0d.
> Sergeants £5-0s-0d pw on promotion or appointment rising by five annual increments of 2s 6d to £5-12s-6d pw.
> Inspectors on appointment £310 pa rising by four annual increments of £10 to £350 per annum.
> Superintendents on appointment £370 pa rising by four increments of £15 every two years to £430 pa.
> Chief Constable on appointment £510 pa rising by four increments of £35 every two years to £650 pa.[15]

The uniformity in pay would obviously eradicate many of the anomalies that had existed for so long in the pay structure of forces in England and Wales. For instance, when the Cardiganshire police authority asked that a comparison be made between the pay received by the chief constable, which was £400 per annum, and the wages payable to the chief officers in the counties of Breconshire and Merioneth, the result clearly showed a considerable disparity, for they received £650 and £450 respectively. On learning of this difference, the Reverend David Griffiths of the Cardiganshire police committee called for the position to be remedied.[16]

The improvement in pay was only one of several new measures to be introduced at this time. In many ways, the years 1919-20 were particularly significant for officers in north Wales, for not only did they witness the introduction of new pay scales, but they also saw a change in the system of management. When the Police Federation came into existence in the autumn of 1919, its purpose was defined as 'enabling members of the police forces in England and Wales to consider and bring to the notice of police authorities and the Secretary of State all matters affecting their welfare and efficiency other than questions of discipline and promotion affecting individuals'. In Anglesey, the chief constable told members of the force that he would like them to set up a body to represent sergeants and constables in matters that concerned conditions of service and general welfare.[17] In a General Order dated 1 May 1919 a similar request was made by the chief constable to members of the Merioneth force, but here three ranks were to be represented, those of constable, sergeant and inspector, on what were to be known as branch boards. Members of such boards were also expected to elect annually, a delegate who would represent the force at the central conference. Branch boards when formed were also permitted to submit evidence not only to the chief constable and the police authority but, if necessary, directly to the Secretary of State. Instructions were also issued to forces in north Wales on the procedure to be followed when holding elections for places on branch boards. Reference was made to the Ballot Act of 1872 which required secrecy when voting and this provision was to be strictly adhered to.[18]

Further history was made when the Police Council met for the first time on 6 July 1920. In attendance were all those concerned with the policing of England and Wales, the Home Office, local authorities and police officers of all ranks. Taking the chair, Mr Edward Shortt, Home Secretary, informed delegates of the significance and importance of the occasion.[19] In Sir Arthur Dixon's words, the Council was 'an invaluable medium, not only for getting things settled relatively quickly, smoothly and expeditiously, but also for giving the Police Federation a chance to find their feet as a consultative body and for easing both them and the police authorities into a co-operative attitude of mind'.[20] For four days the delegates discussed at length a number of police problems which led to regulations being drafted which came into effect on 1 October 1920. The new regulations, which affected officers in north Wales, established universal standards for most of the conditions of service. A standard code of discipline had to be laid down and a certain procedure established for the hearing of disciplinary offences. An officer's right to appeal against a decision was not established until 1927. There were certain restrictions on a policeman's private life which also had to be agreed upon. In the Police Council's examination of the service, the problems discussed were wide-ranging and concerned such matters as education and the minimum height of a candidate before he could be accepted into the force. It was also agreed by members that the efficiency and authorised strength of a force should always be subject to the approval of the Home Secretary. Indeed, the Police Council's recommendations in 1920, was to result in regulations being put into practice that were to last in some instances for the better part of half a century.[21]

The Desborough Report had recommended that an officer in each force should be appointed to supervise educational classes and instruct probationers. In Anglesey, doubtless anxious to comply with this recommendation, the chief constable appointed Sergeant John Fair to be the officer responsible for all force training.[22] The importance of education was also high on the agenda of Mr Richard Jones, chief constable of Merioneth. In a General Order issued in July 1919, he ordered all probationary constables to submit to him each week one or two pages of foolscap upon which they had written a composition so that judgement could be passed on their ability to communicate.[23] That the chief constable did not see education as being only important to probationers was witnessed on 14 October 1920 when in a General Order he stated that in future all advancement to the ranks of sergeant and inspector would be made by selection from among those officers who had passed the police promotion examinations.[24] It was to prepare candidates for the promotion examinations that the chief constable decided to issue periodically exercises in arithmetic, police law and general knowledge, and officers who wished to study privately could submit their answers along with their weekly reports. Many officers were also to benefit from the help they received from correspondence courses, notably the Bennett College in Sheffield and the institution established by Thomas Walton, also of Sheffield. These two colleges developed courses specifically for policemen and frequently advertised the subjects that could be studied in the *Police Review*, particularly during the inter-war years.[25] In a further effort to improve the educational standards of officers, the chief constable encouraged members of the force to read good daily newspapers whenever possible. It was this belief in the importance of reading that led him on 14 May 1924 to issue an order encouraging officers to speak more English rather than Welsh. He was of the opinion that if officers spoke to each other in English on matters concerning police duties, a marked improvement in their written work would follow.[26] In fact, so keen were some officers to improve their standard of education that they frequently entered competitions which appeared weekly in police newspapers. In January 1929, Constable Jesse Roberts won a consolation prize of books in a competition organised by the *Police Chronicle* and Constable Howell Jones, son of the chief constable, gained a prize of £2 in a similar competition run by Bennett College in co-operation with the *Police Review*.[27]

The early 1920s were difficult years economically and it was felt there had to be substantial cuts in police expenditure. The amended police regulations issued on 24 March 1922, set out in some detail what these cuts would mean for forces like those in north Wales. The Home Office suggested there should be a reduction of 5 per cent in the establishment of all police forces in England and Wales.[28] One of the first forces in north Wales to comply with this decision was Anglesey and as a direct consequence the chief constable, Mr Prothero, effected some very stringent economies.[29] For example, the cuts in expenditure meant there was little, if any, money available for new building projects and equipment. The allowances received by officers on such items as rent, refreshments and footwear were also reduced as a result of these economies.[30] In Denbighshire, the chief constable, Mr George Guest, issued an order in April 1922, 'that no refreshment allowance should be paid save in very exceptional circumstances'.[31] On the whole, the police committees in north Wales had little to worry about as far as expenditure was concerned. As early as 1919, the chief constable of Merioneth had shown a keenness to save the county any unnecessary expenditure. He frequently informed his officers that the inhabitants of the county must never be allowed to gain the impression that the police earned their money easily. In fact, his keenness was such that when the standing joint committee considered installing a telephone system in 1919 so that the police stations at Bala, Barmouth, Corwen and Tywyn could be connected, he asked members to reconsider their decision because of the possible expenditure involved.[32] Even before the government's call for a decrease in expenditure on such items as food, the chief constable had discontinued the refreshment allowance of £2 a quarter which was payable to the superintendent and two inspectors.[33] However, despite efforts to economise by the forces in England and Wales, police expenditure was still rising at an alarming rate. In 1923, a Home Office official commenting on this fact stated that government subsidies to the police between 1914-22 had practically quadrupled.[34]

When examining crime during the 1920s one is immediately faced with a serious problem because so many valuable and essential records had been destroyed. However, some indication that crime, particularly that which remained undetected, was causing concern was seen in a General Order issued by the chief constable of Denbighshire in March 1924, when, not only, did he express worry about unsolved cases but urged his officers to make an even more determined effort to apprehend those responsible.[35] Later, in a General Order issued in July 1927 the chief constable claimed 'that no efficient constable should ever allow any undetected crime committed on his beat to be absent from his thoughts and should always keep himself well-versed with all the undetected offences committed in other parts of the district'.[36] In Merioneth, it was not the amount of crime that was causing concern but the manner in which certain offences were being committed, for, in several instances, crimes where explosives had been used were reported. Obviously, the war had taught many the technique of handling explosive materials and now, that knowledge was being used in the furtherance of crime.[37] Some indication of the crimes known to the police in Caernarfonshire during the years 1920-30 and the number that remained unsolved might well be a sign that the chief constable of Denbighshire was probably not alone in expressing concern about the detection rate.

Table 6.1 Crimes known to the Police in Caernarfonshire 1920-30,[38]

| Year | Number of Crimes | Number Unsolved | Failure Rate (%) |
| --- | --- | --- | --- |
| 1920 | 265 | 82 | 30.94 |
| 1921 | 315 | 104 | 33.00 |
| 1922 | 250 | 81 | 32.40 |
| 1923 | 251 | 46 | 18.32 |
| 1924 | 236 | 70 | 29.66 |
| 1925 | 250 | 55 | 22.00 |
| 1926 | 341 | 92 | 26.97 |
| 1927 | 320 | 79 | 24.68 |

| | | | |
|---|---|---|---|
| 1928 | 250 | 70 | 28.00 |
| 1929 | 278 | 79 | 28.41 |
| 1930 | 318 | 78 | 24.52 |

Although crime in the counties of north Wales was generally not considered as serious throughout the 1920s, there was sadly one exception, and that occurred in Anglesey on 21 November 1924, when Constable Robert Pritchard, stationed at Gwalchmai, was shot by John Davies, a tenant farmer at Cemaes farm. The incident arose as a result of a dispute over unpaid rent and when called to the farm by the auctioneer, the officer was shot by Davies and succumbed to his injuries the following day at Bangor.[39] At a special meeting of the standing joint committee on 4 December 1924, it was resolved that his widow should receive an annual pension of £86-3s-0d and that an allowance of £16-0s-0d per annum be paid to each of his children until they reached the age of sixteen.[40]

It is difficult to assess the public regard for the police after the troubles and tensions of 1919, and the changes, both social and economic, that followed the ending of the First World War. However, no history of the police in the 1920s would be complete if the General Strike of 1926 were not discussed. The strike, which lasted nine days from 3 to 12 May paralysed much of the country's activities and as a consequence brought organised labour as near as it ever came to achieving a revolution.[41] The 1926 strike not only allowed the police to demonstrate the way in which Desborough had healed past wounds, but it also provided the service with valuable experience in dealing with a major emergency, a factor that was to prove so vital thirteen years later at the outbreak of war. On the whole, the strike had little effect on the rural areas where many farmers openly expressed their contempt at the miner's stand.[42] In the north-east, with its 17,829 miners there was considerable support for their cause especially among railwaymen.[43] Railworkers were also supportive of the miners in Anglesey and this led ultimately to the closure of the port of Holyhead because they withheld their labour.[44] In Caernarfon, there was great enthusiasm for the miners from the printers in the town although the strike itself passed off without incident in the county.[45]

Although all the forces in north Wales were on emergency alert, no force was probably more active than that of Denbighshire where the chief constable issued at least eleven General Orders during the nine days, all of which referred to the emergency and the measures which he expected his officers to carry out.[46] In

Flintshire, as a result of the strike motor cycle patrols were introduced when a number of constables performed duty on their private machines and were paid a mileage allowance for their use.[47] Undoubtedly, without the presence of the police on the streets, serious trouble might have erupted. When the General Strike ended, *The Times* initiated a fund as an expression of gratitude by the nation, 'for the large measure of peace and safety' it had enjoyed during the troubled days.[48] The public was generous and nearly £250,000 was raised, this sum later becoming the foundation for the National Police Fund. Ironically, the strike, which was so catastrophic, did much during this period to enhance the reputation of the police. It was during this turbulence that links were forged with the public, which, over the years, became even stronger and the police service had just cause at this time to feel proud of its achievements.

A question that continually came to the fore during the 1920s was that associated with the amalgamation of small forces. There was certainly a view circulating among some north Wales authorities at this time that considerable economies could be achieved by amalgamating forces. In 1922, one newspaper quoting figures of the respective strengths of forces in north and mid-Wales suggested that such an idea was feasible.[49] In April 1923 the *Caernarvon and Denbigh Herald* adopting a similar theme, made comparisons with forces in England. It pointed to Cumberland and Westmorland, both of which had separate forces and standing joint committees, but were under the command of one chief constable. To add weight to this argument, the paper listed the number of officers serving in several of the Welsh forces. Merioneth had a complement of twenty-five constables, Montgomeryshire thirty-eight, Radnorshire twenty-two and Anglesey forty-one.[50] In Merioneth, there were some responsible figures in the community who felt that the police in the county had very little work to do. When the county education committee discussed truancy among schoolchildren, one member, Mr E.P. Jones of Carrog, stated that the chief constable should be asked to curb this tendency. Explaining his belief he went on to state 'the police had plenty of time, they were now only watching farmers dipping their sheep'.[51]

In 1925, officials in Merioneth received a letter from the authorities in Montgomeryshire, asking whether they would be interested in a joint force under one chief constable.[52] The suggestion came to nothing although in 1931 the proposal was put forward for consideration once more. Indeed, at a meeting held in July 1931, the authorities of Cardiganshire,

Montgomeryshire, Merioneth and Radnorshire, met to examine the possibility of appointing one chief constable for several small counties.[53] This was an idea that found favour in some quarters, for in 1929, a Mr C. de Courcy Parry, referring especially to Welsh forces said 'my impression of many of the Welsh counties with small forces is that some chief constables have very little work to do. I am sure that amalgamation of many of these counties into groups of two, or even three under one chief constable would tend considerably towards economy and efficiency'.[54] This idea eventually came into being in the 1940s when various Welsh forces were amalgamated. However in 1929, such proposals were looked upon as being a little premature and, therefore, were shelved until a more opportune time.

It was certainly the case that the police in north Wales entered the 1930s with a feeling of confidence. Indeed, ever since the early 1920s there had been plenty of evidence that the standards of the police in the various counties was growing. One newspaper reported as early as 1921, 'that nobody has the right to look down on a policeman, according to the qualifications he is expected to possess'.[55] Three years later, in April 1924, Mr Richard Jones, chief constable of Merioneth delivered a lecture to the members of the Salem Chapel, Dolgellau, which enumerated these qualifications. He recalled the time when anyone joining the police was viewed with as much disdain as the public hangman. Explaining further, he said, 'nowadays, thanks to educational facilities, police recruits in addition to possessing good health and fine physique, must have excellent characters and superior intelligence. Each officer must be able to differentiate between larceny and false pretences, pick-pocketing and profiteering. In short, a policeman must be a walking encyclopaedia to cope with the various regulations he has to comply with'.[56] The educational facilities he referred to were, of course, those that came into being under the 1920 Police Act.

The importance of the recommendations contained in the Desborough Report have already been stressed, but its passing certainly opened up a new era in the police service, for its main recommendations had not only by the early 1930s become permanent, but deep-rooted, and as such, an integral part of policing. There were now standard conditions of service, uniformity in pay, and national representation boards for all ranks. Chief constables met frequently so that there was an exchange of views and a gathering of ideas, such meetings proving beneficial to the service as a whole. The influence of the Home Office, gradual at first, had within a decade of Desborough become a permanent feature of central control.

There were also other great changes in the inter-war years, for example, in the field of crime detection and investigation. Wireless communication was fast becoming an essential police aid. The increase in usage of the telephone allowed forces such as those in rural areas to be in frequent contact with each other on matters of mutual importance. With such advancement there was a general pooling of knowledge, and the experience gained by one force could prove to be of great benefit to another. Several of the counties in north Wales were now becoming mechanised, with horse-drawn vehicles and bicycles becoming things of the past.[57] In regions such as north Wales, what in the early years had been regarded as parish pump policing was no longer adequate and change was becoming a necessity. Whereas previously crime was largely committed by local men and women, it was increasingly being carried out by outsiders who were moving into every locality. Yet, despite the changes, few officers wanted to see more alterations made. Over the years the police had largely gained many of the advantages of an integral nationwide system without sacrificing the local ties that to most people were considered so important.

However, despite the improvement there were some difficult days ahead for the police. The pay cuts of 1922 were repeated, and for similar reasons, in 1931. A General Order issued on 24 September announced that the government had ordered drastic cuts in police pay. Constables were to have 4s 3d per week deducted, sergeants 5s 6d, inspectors 6s 9d, and superintendents £21-10s-0d per annum, which was in effect 5 per cent of pay. The chief constable was to have £30 per annum deducted, which again was equal to 5 per cent of pay. All deductions were to take effect from the first pay-day in October.[58]

These cuts were not welcomed by the police, who looked upon them as a return to a lower standard of living. Sensing bitterness, the Police Federation called a meeting in London. Many resolutions were passed and none was more pointed in its condemnation than the following which stated, 'that the members of the service, as a whole, consider they have been singled out for the quite unnecessary and drastic treatment, without an adequate enquiry having been made into the justification, or otherwise of such recommendations, and presumably without any thought for any hardship that might be, and in fact has been inflicted'.[59] Later, at an emergency meeting held at the Royal Albert Hall in December 1931, which occurred with the full sanction of the Home Secretary, the police made an impassioned plea for the position to be reconsidered. However, faced with a grave financial crisis the government stood firm. An even greater blow for the police came in November 1932 when the 5 per cent cut was doubled.[60] This increase only gave rise to even more discontent within the service, which only ended with the restoration of full pay in July 1935.[61]

If pay was uppermost in the minds of most police officers in north Wales then their concern over the motor car came a close second. Without doubt, the motor car became a serious problem for officers everywhere in the 1920s and 1930s. The number of vehicles on the roads was increasing so quickly that it was inevitable that sooner or later they would prove a serious problem in north Wales. In Merioneth, officers were constantly receiving complaints from the public about the behaviour of some motorists in the county. Dolgellau residents were angered by what they saw as inconsiderate drivers who parked for hours at a time along the streets and causing serious congestion.[62] One newspaper reporting on the situation said that, on the whole, ordinary motorists were not too bad, but the conduct of charabanc drivers was unbearable.[63] There was even a suggestion at a meeting of the police committee in Denbighshire that a plain clothes officer should travel on some of the buses in order to ascertain what actually was going on.[64] Not everyone was happy with the police spending so much of their time checking the conduct of motorists. In Flintshire, one magistrate, Mr J.P. Jones of Holywell, suggested that rather than the police spending time on traffic regulations the work could be undertaken by ex-servicemen.[65] A little earlier, a newspaper commenting on the conduct of some motorists went so far as to accuse them of using the King's highway as their own personal property and therefore 'drive in a manner which pales Prussian arrogance into insignificance'.[66]

It was in order to ascertain the number of vehicles passing through the towns in Merioneth that a census was taken of all motor traffic passing through certain towns between 3pm and 8pm on 30 May 1925. From the evidence collected, the following figures throw some light on the volume of traffic during what was regarded as a busy peak period, as 30 May was Whit Sunday.

Census of Through Traffic Taken 30 May 1925, from 3pm-8pm

|  | Motor Cars | Other Vehicles[67] |
| --- | --- | --- |
| Barmouth south end entrance | 357 | 156 |
| Barmouth north end entrance | 294 | 212 |
| Corwen | 628 | 239 |
| Penrhyndeudraeth | 243 | 117 |

According to witnesses, even these figures would have shown a marked increase if a further census had been held on the Sunday or Monday.

It was to ease the situation in Merioneth that the Home Office suggested in 1930 that the police committee should consider purchasing a motor car.[68] However, this was viewed by committee members as completely unnecessary, as road traffic could equally well be supervised by police officers using their own vehicles providing they were in receipt of a mileage allowance.[69] A similar arrangement had been operating successfully in Anglesey since 1 January 1926.[70] In Denbighshire also, a mileage allowance was made in May 1927 to officers who used their own motor cycles for police patrol work.[71] As each year passed, officers were finding that they were using their vehicles much more frequently in the course of their work. In Merioneth, the chief constable's report dated 29 March 1935 stated that the mileage allowance for officers using their vehicles should be 4d a mile. The same report also listed the transport owned by officers in the county, which, in the event of an emergency, could be used for patrol purposes – in all there were fourteen cars, seven motor cycles and six bicycles.[72]

By 1936 it was becoming obvious to all concerned that official police patrol cars were necessary if the various road traffic acts in operation were to be fully observed. In fact, only two counties in Wales, Montgomeryshire and Merioneth, were without official police vehicles at this time. Anglesey possessed one motor car, Cardiganshire and Radnorshire two motor cars each, Denbighshire had three motor cars and three motor cycles. Caernarfonshire had four vehicles. Flintshire, with six patrol cars, was the county with the highest number of police vehicles in north Wales.[73] Two years later, in 1938, Merioneth found that it was the only Welsh county not in possession of a police vehicle. Even Radnorshire, the smallest county, had by this time three patrol cars. Faced with the inevitable, the standing joint committee in Merioneth agreed it had to move with the times and decided that arrangements should be made to acquire a car for the year beginning 1 April 1939. Such a purchase was long overdue and the *Police Review* was prompted to comment saying 'at last the Merioneth standing joint committee has decided to acquire a car'.[74] The acquisition marked an important date in the history of the north Wales police, for after nearly a century of policing every force could now finally claim to be mechanised.

The absence of serious crime in north Wales did not mean that officers were unprepared. Indeed, as early as 1921, their attention was drawn to two recently published booklets on criminal investigation. The booklets, *Modus Operandi in Criminal Investigation* and *Detection and Work of Investigation* were written by General Atcherley, the Inspector of Constabulary. From time to time officers were also issued with instructions which had to be followed when investigating a crime. However, it was not until later that any real thought was given to the study of criminal investigation and detection. In 1925 the Inspector of Constabulary had suggested that all officers in charge of a division, section or sub-section should be acquainted with the following if their district was to be classified as efficient.[75] Officers in north Wales were expected to be fully conversant with all aspects of crime and criminal investigation procedures and in addition possess knowledge about the use that could be made of photography in the detection of crime. Familiarisation with court work and the type of offenders appearing before the courts was also considered an area police officers would do well to study if they wished to become more proficient. The Police Council, with all its administrative machinery, was the body responsible for the eventual changes that occurred in criminal investigation. The regular meetings between police forces, police authorities and the Home Office all assisted in breaking down the age-long barriers of suspicion. There was a greater mutual understanding which, in turn, paved the way for technical developments in the field of criminal investigation and detection. Although forces had previously co-operated with each other, there was little evidence that in doing so, they had pooled their knowledge and experience.

It was in order to improve the method of detection that the Home Secretary set up a committee in 1933 to inquire into all aspects of detective work. The committee spent nearly five years on this special piece of research and at the end produced a 500 page report.[76] Evidence was obtained from forces throughout the United Kingdom, with additional information being obtained from countries such as Canada and the United States of America. The police also became aware of the importance of harnessing the work of the scientist to other aspects of police work. With the assistance of Captain Athelstan Popkess, chief constable of

Nottingham, who established a primitive scientific laboratory within his own force and Mr C.T. Symons, a former government chemist in Ceylon, there came into being seven forensic science laboratories to serve forces in their respective areas.[77] A laboratory to serve Wales was opened in Cardiff in 1938.

Following the recommendations of the committee set up to examine detective training, a standard syllabus of instruction for prospective detectives was introduced. Specialised courses in detective training, lasting eight weeks were started at Wakefield and Hendon in 1936.[78] During the weeks and months that followed the introduction of detective training courses, many officers from north Wales were to attend such centres. In fact, some officers had already attended courses on crime detection as early as 1928, when two officers from Denbighshire received instruction at the headquarters of the West Riding Constabulary.[79] As a further incentive for officers to become crime conscious, orders that had originally emanated from the Home Office called upon them to be much more observant. In August 1936 the chief constable of Merioneth ordered his men to read the *Police Gazette* daily. They were told in particular to check those persons on the 'wanted list' and note the numbers of 'stolen cars'. As a way of ensuring that the *Gazette* was read, senior officers would often question constables on the information it contained.

In addition to the improvements in the field of detection, advancement was also made in the training of newly-appointed officers, although even in the 1930s the initial training given to recruits was far from satisfactory. The Desborough committee had recommended that every force should have a training officer, but small forces such as those in north Wales were unable to appoint an officer for this particular duty. In such circumstances it was left to each force to make arrangements as best they could for the training of their own officers. A number of the larger forces did maintain their own training schools, but they varied in size and many of the facilities offered were mediocre. Nevertheless, in north Wales, forces were able to take advantage of the opportunities offered them and officers found themselves undergoing their basic course of instruction at the police training school in Cardiff.[80] The type of training probationers received was indicated in a report issued on the 30 June 1931, which stated that officers were examined as to their proficiency in the following subjects: foot drill, fire drill, swimming and life saving, first aid to the injured, examinational subjects, and police law and practice.[81]

A subject that was constantly raised during the 1920s and

1930s was the appointment of women police officers. Reports from America claimed they did excellent work and August Vollmer, chief of police at Berkeley, California, expressed the opinion 'That policewomen of the future would be the most potent agent for crime prevention'.[82] In north Wales, the Association for Aiding Friendless Girls asked the police authorities to give urgent consideration to their appointment. However, in Merioneth, the chief constable maintained, 'that in his opinion women police are not a necessity at the present time'.[83] In fairness, it was the kind of reply most chief constables at the time would have given. Yet, this outright rejection was completely at odds with three Committees of Inquiry which, during a twenty-year period, had all with varying degrees of emphasis believed in the value of women officers. Nevertheless, opposition to the employment of women officers was deeply entrenched in the minds of police committee members who regarded the appointment of policewomen as an extravagant luxury.[84] It was not until the outbreak of the Second World War that the true value of policewomen was finally appreciated.

Although, as previously stated, serious crime was minimal in north Wales there was one ugly incident in Denbighshire in 1935 when members of the county force attended a disturbance at the Bersham Colliery near Wrexham. The dispute arose as a result of a change in the terms of employment at the colliery and efforts to settle the strike amicably by the Welsh Miners' Federation had failed. Knowing of this failure the owners of the colliery took a course of action that infuriated the workforce by bringing in miners from another colliery which they owned. Crowds assembled at the gates of the colliery and as the buses bringing in miners from outside appeared, stones and bricks were thrown which resulted in a police officer, Constable William Jones, and a bus driver being injured. Fearing further trouble police reinforcements were summoned to the area and during the scuffles that followed the police drew their truncheons. As a result of the confrontation, between twenty and twenty-five civilians and several police officers were injured. A consequence of this was to bring them into conflict with a group of workers who, understandably, were bitter at the conduct of the colliery owner in seeking outside labour.[85]

The 20 July 1935 was to prove a most historic day in the calendar of the police service, for an inspection by His Majesty King George V, took place in Hyde Park. The number of police officers who took part in the parade amounted to 3,445 and this figure included a contingent from the Royal Ulster Constabulary.

North Wales was well represented with officers from each county being detailed to attend.[86] It was at this time that a number of officers in north Wales became recipients of the King's Jubilee Medal.[87] Two years later, in 1937, a number of other officers were to receive the King's Coronation Medal.[88]

In many ways, this was a period when officers in north Wales could feel justly proud of their achievements. Yet, in 1937 there occurred an incident in Merioneth that marred the whole period. The incident not only soured men's minds but created within the force an atmosphere of friction and suspicion. The first indication that all was not well came in a General Order dated 3 April 1937, which stated that a charge had been made against Constable William Evans, stationed at Dyffryn Ardudwy, which claimed he had committed a serious breach of confidence. He was accused of attending an unauthorised meeting held at midnight in the Blaenau Ffestiniog division. The meeting had been secretly called to discuss the recent election results to the branch board, which apparently were being questioned. When summoned before the chief constable, Constable Evans pleaded for leniency, a plea that was accepted by Mr Richard Jones. On fixing the penalty at £1, the chief constable said that 'by constant good conduct in the future and strict attention to his duties, this serious lapse – prompted by others – will soon become an event of the past, and need not be a bar to progress and advancement'.[89]

That Constable Evans had not been alone was clearly evident because twelve other officers were charged with the same disciplinary offence. The actual charge read 'they attended a secret meeting without the knowledge of their superior Deputy Chief Constable, John Francis Evans. Such meetings constitute a gross breach of discipline and shows great disrespect for their superintendent, without any other allusion'.[90] The eventual outcome was that every member attending the meeting admitted doing so and apologised in writing, with some even adding verbally to their written protestations. In acknowledging their apologies, Mr Jones said, 'I am glad to state that in consequence of the admission of every officer, I feel justified in dealing with the offence in a very much more lenient manner than I would have otherwise have done'.[91] He then fined five officers, all first class constables, £1 each, stating they ought to have shown an example to the younger men. The remaining officers, all with under ten years service escaped fines but were severely reprimanded.

Later, on addressing all those who had taken part in the meeting, the chief constable reminded them of the following: 'In future remember one and all, that we are members of an honourable profession – the British Constabulary. Do everything within your power to rid yourselves of any underhanded sentiments, and forget not the adage: "Do unto others as you would like others do unto you" '.[92] The scars this incident left were deep and in May 1937, when a request was made for the chief constable to act as presiding-officer-at-count for constables nominated to serve on the branch board, a duty he had often undertaken, and on occasion at some inconvenience to himself, he refused, saying, 'that some members of the force doubted the last election results as not fully representing the wishes of the electorate'.[93] There had been some serious allegations made that the votes cast in the last election had been tampered with. This allegation, naturally, was a source of embarrassment to the chief constable, who on that occasion had acted as the presiding officer. That he felt deeply about the whole affair was evident when he further remarked, 'the controversy is revolting to me, and it may, at some future time, disgust the authors of it'.[94] It was for these reasons that the chief constable declined to act as the presiding officer. His decision led to other members of the branch board resigning over the issue. The final curtain to this most unfortunate affair occurred some months later in September 1937, when Sergeant Morgan Davies admitted he knew of the unauthorised meeting. For his failure to inform Superintendent Evans he was fined £3, which was deducted from his pay in accordance with Article 24 of the Police Regulations.[95]

It was the war clouds gathering over Europe and the preparations being made at home, that to some extent helped direct minds away from more localised issues. Certainly, the doubts and suspicions cast were never erased but, at least, they receded somewhat into the background amidst the external duties and training that accompanied preparations for war. In north Wales, the police were made aware of the possibility of war as early as 1934 when an order issued by the Home Office called upon officers to take a census of all horses within their area.[96] A further indication that the government was preparing for an emergency came two years later in 1936 when orders were issued that army recruiting posters were to be displayed outside every police station. Should a person volunteer and be accepted as a result of the posters, a sum of 4s upwards would be donated to the Police Benevolent Fund.[97]

[1] T.A. Critchley, *A History of Police in England and Wales*, (1967), pp.184-5.

[2] Ibid., p.188, also George Lerry, 'The Policemen of Denbighshire', *Transactions of the Denbighshire Historical Society*, 2 (1953), p.143. Where the Chief Constable of Denbighshire, Mr Edward Jones, informs his officers that if they strike they will be dismissed from the force, also ARO, Home Office Letters to Chief Constables of Anglesey 1913-19, op. cit., 29 May 1919.

[3] See *Police Review*, 31 May 1918, which calls for reforms such as the right to some form of representation for police officers.

[4] *The Times*, 4 August 1919, also T.A. Critchley, op. cit., pp.188-9, which lists in addition to the number on strike in the Metropolitan Police and Liverpool the following: City of London fifty-seven officers on strike; Birmingham 119; Birkenhead 114; Bootle sixty-three and Wallasey one.

[5] Ibid., p.189.

[6] MCF Orders, QA/P/D/8/4, 11 August 1919.

[7] Home Office Memorandum of Evidence to the Oaksey Committee (1949). See also H.K. Birch op. cit., pp.204-7.

[8] T.A. Critchley, op. cit., p.188.

[9] *CDH*, 15 June 1923, (quoting Mr A.L. Dixon, Home Office, giving evidence before the Royal Commission on Local Government).

[10] MCF Orders, QA/P/D/8/4, 1 January 1919. (See Appendix, ix.)

[11] Ibid.

[12] Ibid.

[13] MQS Rolls, (Trinity, 1919). (See Appendix, x.)

[14] Hugh Owen, op. cit., pp.48-9 and MQS Rolls (Trinity, 1919). In Anglesey the chief constable's travelling allowances were also increased as well as the bicycle and car allowances to members of the force.

[15] *Cambrian News*, 9 May 1919.

[16] T.A. Critchley, op. cit., p.194.

[17] Hugh Owen, op. cit., p.48. See also ASJ Committee, 23 May 1919, where officers on the newly formed branch board lost little time in submitting a whole list of recommendations which they would like to see introduced into the force. The board believed that all officers with ten years service and over should be provided with a house free of charge. It was also suggested that the wives of officers should receive 2s.6d for each case when called upon to attend to a female prisoner. That the allowance for those using bicycles should be increased from 1d to 3d per mile. Also Denbighshire Chief Constable's Order Book 1921-29, 1 September 1921.

[18] MCF Orders, QA/P/D/8/4, 21 October 1919. The first officers to be appointed to the branch board in Merioneth were: Constables J.J. Griffiths, Llandrillo; Evan Davies, Ffestiniog; John Jones, Harlech; Josiah Jones, Corris and D.L. Davies, Bala. The first formal meeting of the newly formed branch board took place at the police station, Barmouth on Friday, 24 October 1919. Later, on 17 November 1919, Inspector Ben Evans attended the first Police Federation Central Council at the Central Buildings, Westminster.

[19] T.A. Critchley, op. cit., p.196.

[20] Sir Arthur Dixon, *The Home Office and the Police between the Two World Wars*, (unpublished 1966), p.22.

[21] T.A. Critchley, op. cit., p.197.

[22] Hugh Owen, op. cit., p.48. See ASJ Committee, 20 October 1921, where the chief constable informs the committee that Sergeant John Fair would revert to street duty and would be replaced by Constable Hope who is an experienced clerk and more suitable for the position. In 1923, Sergeant John Fair was appointed to the rank of superintendent and deputy chief constable.

[23] MCF Orders, QA/P/D/8/4, 16 July 1919.

[24] Ibid., 14 October 1920. Also Denbighshire Chief Constable's General Order Book 1921-29, 23 April 1924.

[25] Clive Emsley, op. cit., p.207. Also MCF Orders, QA/P/D/8/4, 5 July 1923. Changes were introduced in April 1923 in the length of service a man had to do before sitting the promotion examinations. Constables could, if they wished, sit the sergeants examination on completing five years service. Further changes occurred in July 1923 when the length of service before one could sit an examination was lowered to four years.

[26] MCF Orders, QA/P/D/8/4, 14 May 1924.

[27] Ibid., January 1929. Also Denbighshire Chief Constable's General Order Book 1921-29, 7 November 1928.

[28] Hugh Owen, op. cit., p.49.

[29] Ibid.

[30] *Cambrian News*, 7 April 1922.

[31] Denbighshire Chief Constable's General Order Book, 1921-29, 19 April 1922. The chief constable, Mr George Guest, was appointed to office in May 1921, in succession to Mr Edward Jones who retired after forty-seven years in the Denbighshire Constabulary. It should be noted that Denbighshire's General Order Books for the period 1921-50 are currently in the possession of the North Wales Police at Colwyn Bay.

[32] MQS Rolls, (Trinity, 1919).

[33] MCF Orders, QA/P/D/8/4, 21 October 1920 and *Cambrian News*, 19 October 1922 and 6 April 1923.

[34] *CDH*, 15 June 1923.

[35] Denbighshire Chief Constable's General Order Book 1921-29, 20 March 1924.

[36] Ibid.

[37] MCF Orders, QA/P/D/8/1, 6 August 1915.

[38] CSJ Committee Reports, 1920-30. See also J. Owain Jones, op. cit., p.69. Where it is reported that the chief constable of Caernarfonshire, Mr John Griffiths, died and was replaced by Superintendent Edward Williams, a native of Bethesda who had joined the force in 1895.

[39] *Liverpool Daily Post*, 9 February 1985. John Davies who was sixty-two years of age was later committed for trial at Beaumaris Assizes in 1925 and sentenced to seven years penal servitude. On the 8 February 1985 a plaque

commemorating Constable Pritchard was unveiled in the presence of his family at the headquarters of the North Wales Police at Colwyn Bay. Also Hugh Owen, op. cit., p.49.

[40] ASJ Committee, 4 December 1924.

[41] T.A. Critchley, op. cit., pp.198-9.

[42] John Davies, *A History of Wales*, (London, 1993), p.554.

[43] Ibid.

[44] Ibid.

[45] Ibid. See also J. Owain Jones, op. cit., p.70.

[46] Denbighshire Chief Constable's General Order Book 1921-29, 3 May 1926, also 17 January 1927.

[47] *Flintshire Constabulary Handbook*, op. cit., p.35.

[48] T.A. Critchley, op. cit., p.199.

[49] *Liverpool Daily Post*, 13 July 1922. See also Critchley, op. cit., pp.240-1. The amalgamation of small forces continued to be advocated throughout the inter-war period by both the Home Office and the Inspectors of Constabulary, but to little effect.

[50] *CDH*, 13 April 1923, also DSJ Committee, 12 July 1922.

[51] *Liverpool Daily Post*, 14 September 1923. See MCF Orders, QA/P/D/8/4, 30 October 1922. In January 1922, the chief constable informed officers that sheep scab was prevalent in the county, which resulted in the police supervising the double dipping of 400,000 sheep, a very tiresome duty.

[52] MSJ Committee, 30 July 1925.

[53] *Cambrian News*, 17 July 1931.

[54] *CDH*, 22 February 1929.

[55] MRO, Chief Constable's Papers, M/1/201. Newspaper cutting, *The Star*, 10 September 1921.

[56] MRO, Chief Constable's Papers, M/1/201. Newspaper cutting, *Liverpool Courier*, undated.

[57] Denbighshire Chief Constable's General Order Book, 1921-29, 10 May 1927, also J. Owain Jones, op. cit., p.72, and *Flintshire Constabulary Centenary Handbook*, op. cit., p.38, which records that in 1925 four 10 hp cars were purchased and in 1936 each vehicle was equipped to receive wireless messages.

[58] MCF Orders, QA/P/D/8/5, 24 September 1931.

[59] Ibid., 18 November 1931.

[60] Denbighshire Chief Constable's General Order Book, 1930-42, 14 November 1932.

[61] MCF Orders. QA1P/D/8/5, 3 July 1935.

[62] *CDH*, 23 September 1921.

[63] *Flintshire Observer*, 19 April 1923 and 6 September 1923, which records that within recent weeks twelve motorists were fined for speeding – one for driving a charabanc at a speed exceeding 8 miles per hour, five for driving cars at over 20 miles per hour, two for not being in possession of a licence, one for dangerous driving and three for riding motor cycles at over 20 miles

per hour. They were convicted as a result of a speed trap on the road between Denbigh and Ruthin.

[64] DSJ Committee, 13 April 1923 and 9 July 1924.

[65] FSJ Committee, 6 September 1922.

[66] *Cambrian News*, 19 August 1921.

[67] MQS Rolls, (Trinity, 1925), See also H.K. Birch, op. cit., pp.238-9. In addition to the police there were also, at this time, other bodies that were concerned about the amount of traffic. The West Merioneth Presbytery, for example, condemned the railway companies for running train services on a Sunday. However, it was the chief constable's belief that to curtail rail services would only add to further chaos on the roads.

[68] *Cambrian News*, 3 April 1931.

[69] Ibid.

[70] Hugh Owen, op. cit., p.51.

[71] Denbighshire Chief Constable's General Order Book, 1921-29, 10 May 1927.

[72] MQS Rolls, (Easter, 1935).

[73] MQS Rolls, (Michaelmas, 1936).

[74] *Police Review*, 9 December 1938.

[75] MCF Orders, 24 August 1925.

[76] T.A. Critchley, op. cit., p.210.

[77] Ibid., p.213.

[78] Ibid., p.214.

[79] Denbighshire Chief Constable's General Order Book 1921-29, 22 November 1928, and MCF Orders, QA/P/D/8/5, 15 May 1957, also Clive Emsley, op. cit., p.161.

[80] MCF Orders, QA/P/D/8/5, 1931. See also Denbighshire Chief Constable's General Order Book 1930-42, 20 January 1931, and 12 June 1934.

[81] MQS Rolls, (Trinity, 1931), also J. Owain Jones op. cit., p.75.

[82] *Cambrian News*, 1 December 1922.

[83] *County Times*, 5 January 1929.

[84] T.A. Critchley, op. cit., pp.215-18. In the inter-war years any suggestion that policewomen should be appointed to the service was met by apathy and prejudice. In 1919 there were approximately 150 policewomen in the service and during the course of the next twenty years this figure had only risen to 230.

[85] George Lerry, op. cit., pp.144-5, also DSJ Committee, 12 April 1935.

[86] DSJ Committee, 12 April 1935, MCF Orders, QA/P/D/8/5, 3 July. Denbighshire Chief Constable's General Order Book, 1929-42, 6 July 1935. Within six months of this notable occasion the King passed away and as a mark of respect all ranks in the police were to wear a black armband on their left sleeve for a period of six months.

[87] *Hugh Owen*, op. cit., p.51, also Denbighshire Chief Constable's General Order Book 1929-42, 5 June 1935, and George Lerry, op. cit., p.144.

[88] Denbighshire Chief Constable's General Order Book, 1929-42, 23 September 1937, and MCF Orders, QA/P/D/8/5, 6 July 1937.

[89] MCF Orders, QA/P/D/8/5, 3 April 1937.

[90] Ibid., 13 April. The accused officers were Constables R.D. Roberts, David Thomas, Jesse Roberts, Gwilym Davies, W.A. Rowley, E.D. Jones, B.D. Evans, A.I. Pugh. Also charged were two probationer constables, H.C. Jones and P.K. Gilmore. Some of the details concerning the incident were conveyed on tape to me when I visited the late Constable Jesse Roberts at his home in Llwyngwril a few years ago. He also gave me some of the correspondence that passed between the officers involved and representatives of the Police Federation in England and Wales which on completion of this work will be deposited at the Meirionnydd Record Office, Dolgellau.

[91] MCF Orders, QA/P/D/8/5, 13 April 1937.

[92] Ibid. It is interesting to note that in an order dated 26 April 1937, one officer, Constable B.D. Evans, who had attended the meeting, requested a transfer to another force, due to the county being unsuitable for his wife's health. The request was readily granted.

[93] MCF Orders, QA/P/D/8/5, 3 May 1937.

[94] Ibid.

[95] Ibid., 6 September 1937. The officers who resigned from the branch board as a mark of protest were Constables I.H. Morris, W.I.G. Lewis, L. Davies and D.C. Davies.

[96] Denbighshire Chief Constable's General Order Book, 1929-42, 1 May 1934 and MCF Orders, QA/P/D/8/5, 1 May 1934. This order issued by the Home Office originally emanated from the Secretary of State for War.

[97] MCF Orders, QA/P/D/8/5, 28 July 1936.

## Chapter IX

# The Second World War, 1939-45

From the mid 1930s officers in north Wales were detailed to attend anti-gas training courses so that should an emergency arise they would be fully trained.[1] On completion of the courses they were then expected to deal efficiently with such subjects of warfare as the detection of poison gas, the treatment of casualties, rescue work, decontamination of material, fire fighting drill and the general protection of the public during an air raid. The officer appointed to take charge of anti-gas training for the north Wales forces was Sergeant D.N. Hughes of the Caernarfonshire Constabulary.[2] As a further precautionary measure all police stations were issued with a booklet which gave precise details of the action to be taken in the event of an air raid. Initially, chief constables were to be vested with the overall responsibility for supervising the air-raid precautions within their respective areas.[3] In effect, this meant that it became the responsibility of the police in each county to ensure that members of the public were issued and correctly fitted with gas masks.[4] Such additional work meant that sooner or later there would be a need for extra police officers, and to meet such an eventuality steps were taken in 1938 to secure the names of the men who would be prepared to act as special constables in a crisis.[5] That the authorities in taking such precautions were right to do so, came when their worst fears became reality on 3 September 1939 when the Prime Minister, Mr Neville Chamberlain, informed the country that a state of war existed between Great Britain and Germany.

The police authorities in north Wales were certainly not alone in their belief that extra officers would be required in the event of war. Indeed, an increase in manpower was seen as vital by the government if police everywhere were to enforce the large number of restrictions that inevitably would be imposed. Legislation which called for this increase eventually resulted in the total establishment being increased by about 50 per cent.[6] Such expansion and the subsequent contraction, brought about as pressure on the police eased, was controlled from the beginning to end by the government. The reasons why the government thought it was essential to increase the strength of the police were manifold. For instance, it was widely expected that the country would be subjected to heavy aerial attacks, followed by fires and, in some cases, looting. It was believed that this possibility, if not tightly controlled by a strong police force, could lead to an inevitable breakdown in the general morale of the people. Because of their importance to the security of the nation, about 3,000 police officers with reservist obligations and a further 6,000 under the age of twenty-five in England and Wales who were liable to be conscripted, had their call-up deferred. Therefore, the strength of the police in 1939 stood at approximately 60,000 men.[7]

However, despite the number of officers, forces were not complacent. It was realised that arrangements for the future manning of the service had to be put into operation. At this time there were four main sources from which the service could obtain extra manpower. Firstly there was the First Police Reserve, which consisted mainly of ex-policemen and numbered about 10,000 men, more than double the figure available in 1914. The second source was the Special Constabulary, which had an establishment of about 130,000 men. In addition, a Police War Reserve, consisting of men over the age of thirty who were recruited for the duration of the war, was also formed.[8] The fourth and final source, and one constantly neglected over the years, was the recruitment of women police officers. This led to the formation of the Women's Auxiliary Police Corps, which consisted of women between the ages of eighteen and fifty-five. At first, these women performed a restricted range of police work such as the driving and maintenance of transport, as well as some clerical, radio and telephone duties.[9]

When war broke out and the expected air attacks on the scales visualised earlier did not occur, the War Office had to review the position of the police in England and Wales. For example, within three months of the outbreak of war, the reservists who had earlier had their call-up deferred were joining the colours, thus reducing the number of regular police officers to around 57,000 men.[10] Added to this figure, however, were the additional auxiliaries who numbered a further 35,000 full-time men made up as follows: First Police Reserve, 7,000; paid special constables, 3,000; Police War Reserve, 24,600. Therefore, the total strength of the police force during the early months of the war consisted of approximately of 90,000 men, to which must be added a number of policemen and members of the Women's Auxiliary Police Corps. There were also thousands of part-time special constables, who, according to one Inspector of Constabulary, 'find it easier to strengthen the watch by night rather than carry out the watch by day'.[11] As the war progressed, however, the call by the armed services for additional manpower became even greater and led the War Cabinet to tap police resources. This in turn, had the effect by 1944 of seeing the total establishment of the regular police being reduced in size to a figure similar to that seen in 1939. An example which illustrates the varying composition of the police during the war years is seen in the following table:

Table 6.2 Police Personnel 1940-1945[12]

| Year | Regular Police | Police War Reserve & Full Time Specials | First Police Reserve | Police-women | Total |
| --- | --- | --- | --- | --- | --- |
| 1940 | 57,012 | 25,220* | 5,725 | 282 | 88,239 |
| 1941 | 55,868 | 29,719 | 6,782 | 325 | 92,694 |
| 1942 | 49,735 | 27,706 | 5,374 | 340 | 83,155 |
| 1943 | 44,430 | 25,350 | 4,655 | 346 | 74,781 |
| 1944 | 43,026 | 17,527 | 2,568 | 385 | 63,506 |
| 1945 | 46,623 | 12,951 | 1,646 | 418** | 61,638 |

* In June 1940, 2,611 of these were full-time special constables, all but 242 of them in London. Their number fell sharply as the war progressed.
** In addition, there were in September 1945 over 3,000 whole time unattested members of the Women's Auxiliary Police Corps, together with 342 attested members.

The outbreak of war saw little immediate change in the duties undertaken by officers in north Wales. As in peacetime, their primary function was the prevention and detection of crime and the maintenance of public order. Crime in the counties in 1939 posed no serious threat and many who had previously caused trouble were now serving in the armed forces and so relieved the police of their presence. Traffic was certainly less as petrol rationing restricted the use of vehicles. However, if police officers were relieved of some problems they found themselves taking on new ones. For example, they had a number of war time regulations to enforce and this was never easy in north Wales where so many of the communities were small and widely scattered. Officers also found themselves working closely with the various civil defence organisations.[13] In addition, at the outbreak of the war in September 1939 the police undertook the new task of training the many auxiliaries.[14]

Police officers in north Wales were soon ordered to familiarise themselves with the far-ranging code of new offences and numerous restrictions embodied in the Defence Regulations. For example, all places of entertainment were ordered to be closed.[15] In an order issued on 4 September 1939 officers were informed of the regulations to be imposed on all aliens.[16] The Aliens Order gave the police the power to detain, or impose restrictions on any person, with a view to preventing acts damaging to the public safety or the defence of the realm. Under the Act, the police took into custody enemy aliens and others who the authorities considered it advisable to intern. Others found their movements severely restricted, and in many instances even possessions were confiscated. Articles such as cameras, maps, fieldglasses, radios and cars were looked upon as being extremely useful in the hands of an enemy agent. Even flying carrier pigeons was considered an offence for which a person could be prosecuted.[17] In some respects the police adopted the role of being a kind of intelligence agency during the war, feeding back to regional headquarters all information they considered might prove valuable to the authorities in London. Such information included the state of public order and the morale of the civilian population, the extent to which refugees were evacuating heavily bombed cities, or the effect of enemy propaganda on members of the public[18]

On 20 July 1940 it was reported that reliable information had been received from military intelligence about the possible landing in Britain of twenty-eight German agents. Since the north Wales coastline, particularly around Anglesey, was seen by the authorities as being suitable for such landings, steps were taken to ensure that no enemy agent could pose as a police officer, and special identity cards with the holder's photograph were issued to officers.[19] As an additional precaution, the chief constable of Merioneth appointed Detective Sergeant H.O. Jones to be responsible for the investigation of all 'fifth column' activities within the county.[20] A little earlier, a similar arrangement had been made in Anglesey when in 1940 the chief constable appointed a detective sergeant to investigate all information that might relate to subversive activity in the county.[21]

With the Welsh coastline being so vulnerable to a possible

landing by enemy agents, there was, at all times, the closest cooperation between the police in north Wales and the coastguards and local defence volunteer units which later became known as the Home Guard. Each morning police officers in charge of stations had to telephone their divisional officer to report the number of persons who had volunteered for such duties.[22] Early in the war the police were issued with rifles and revolvers and later they were reinforced by members of the Home Guard who also carried arms. As a further defence measure, a list of persons such as farmers, who were willing to supply arms such as shotguns and ammunition to the Home Guard was compiled by the police in the event of an invasion taking place.[23] Officers in north Wales were also issued periodically with a number of Home Office leaflets which gave them advice on a number of things that they might encounter in their daily work. Guidance was given on the procedure to be followed on the discovery of an enemy transmitter or an unexploded bomb in an area frequented by members of the general public.

Police in north Wales as elsewhere were prepared for the eventuality of an invasion by the enemy in a directive issued to all ranks on 15 June 1942. In it they were informed that while they were not to make independent attacks on the enemy, as such action might result in impeding British military forces,

> they should hinder and frustrate the enemy by every means which ingenuity can devise and common sense suggest and if the help of the police is asked for by the military authorities, as it may well be, it is their duty to answer wholeheartedly any call, however exacting which may be made upon them. In this matter, by reason of their training as policemen and the confidence which the general public repose in them, the police are specially qualified to provide an example and leadership to the general body of private citizens.[24]

As a further measure to stem any advance by enemy forces landing in Britain, the police were ordered to remove all road signs in June 1940. This order was to remain operative until July 1944 when most restrictions of this kind were lifted.[25]

A duty, and one that had to be rigidly enforced, was that which called for the black out regulations to be observed. This could on occasion cause problems as was the experience of Constable Jesse Roberts stationed at Pennal. One of his nightly duties was to ensure that before going on duty his police station and place of residence were completely blacked out. Where there was difficulty was that the village was divided into what became known as the 'black-outs and dim-outs'. Half the village came under the jurisdiction of the Tywyn Urban District Council, a scheduled controlled coastal area, which had to be completely blacked out, while the other half of Pennal came under the Machynlleth Rural District Council, a non-scheduled area enjoying dim-out concessions and as such, not totally blacked out.[26] That the police had sweeping powers was seen at the Rhyl Petty Sessions in 1940, when a man charged with infringing the black out regulations complained bitterly about the actions of a police officer who had forced his way into his house. Replying to the complaint, Superintendent A.E. Lindsay, spoke about the special powers conferred on the police in such matters and said that 'a police constable has a right to enter any premises where a light is showing during the black-out – he is also empowered to use force if necessary'.[27]

The early months of the war saw the Home Office exerting some pressure on forces to recruit women to the services. Indeed, in July 1939 the *Picture Post* devoted six of its pages to pictures on the 'Life of a Policewoman', which might also have been termed 'The Recruitment and Training of the Metropolitan Police Women', for it was nothing less than an advertisement.[28] In north Wales such pleas by the Home Office found little support in Merioneth where the chief constable, Mr Richard Jones, 'could personally see no justification whatsoever for their employment'.[29] Even when the subject was raised again in July 1942, one member of the police committee Mr D. Rowland Williams 'failed to see what the need was to appoint women police in an agricultural county like Merioneth. He had been a magistrate for twenty years and never recollected any woman offender being brought before the Bala bench'.[30] There was little enthusiasm in Anglesey to appoint policewomen, although it was agreed that three should be appointed in December 1940, and in 1942 a further three were enrolled.[31] However, despite employing policewomen, the chief constable appeared unimpressed with the innovation and in speaking to his police committee claimed 'that he did not think women were effective as police officers except in those instances when female prisoners needed to be escorted to prison'.[32] Although there is little information on the position in Flintshire it is known that during the war six members of the Women's Auxiliary Police Corps were appointed and assigned various duties in the county.[33]

Denbighshire was much more favourable to the appointment of women police. In September 1941, the chief constable, Mr George Guest, claimed that: 'In view of the importance in the national interest of making the fullest possible use of female labour in the present circumstances he would be prepared to favourably consider applications'.[34] He also stated that if there were wives of constables who had experience in clerical duties they might like to consider applying for such posts.[35] There was no shortage of candidates and within a short time of the posts being advertised there were at least five auxiliary policewomen on duty in the county.[36]

Opposition to the appointment of women police officers in Caernarfonshire was particularly strong. At a meeting of the police committee in January 1940, one member agreeing with the chief constable stated 'there was no need for the help of women in the county to keep the peace'.[37] In September 1940 at a meeting of the Llŷn and Eifionydd Temperance Association, the Reverend G.R. Roberts proposed that the police committee gave serious consideration to the appointment of female officers as there was growing concern about the drinking habits of young women.[38] This proposal was criticised by a correspondent in a local newspaper who claimed, 'that it is with some feeling of horror that we read so frequently of an agitation which gives voice in Caernarfonshire for the appointment of women police and when we read that the Presbyteries and similar bodies give support to the proposal we begin to wonder – in place of women police would it not be appropriate to form a Spiritual Patrol made up of the many ministers who thrive in the county'.[39] However, by November 1941, perhaps as a result of calls for women to be appointed, the chief constable sought permission to employ four female officers for clerical duties, to be stationed at Caernarfon, Bangor and Llandudno.[40] Later, at a meeting of the police committee, Mrs Marks, who had been a keen advocate of the appointment of female officers, asked the chief constable whether the newly-appointed were doing a good job and in reply he said 'they were doing very well, they were well worth the money'.[41] When members of the police committee met in 1944 they were informed that the Home Office had approved the appointment of a further six officers, and that they would be paid for by the Home Office. Welcoming the decision the chief constable hoped they would be Welsh-speakers. Surprisingly, there was only one candidate and she later withdrew her application. Speaking about the situation, Mr Isaac Jones said 'the county had never asked for women police officers, and if we eventually get them I am afraid it will not be a new world', but Mrs Marks in reply said 'not a new world perhaps but a better one'.[42]

Forces in north Wales were much better equipped in 1939 to

meet an emergency than they would have been a few years earlier. For example, in December 1939 the chief constable of Merioneth was able to inform his police committee that every police station in the county, apart from Abergynolwyn, was now linked by telephone.[43] A little earlier, as a result of a directive from the Home Office, a wireless receiver had been bought and placed at headquarters, thus allowing all messages of national importance to be taken down and, if necessary allow immediate police action to be taken.[44] As for transport at this time, the car purchased in April 1939 had by March 1940 patrolled 21,000 miles and was in need of an overhaul. In order that the county would not be deprived of transport a further car was delivered on 31 May 1940.[45] In Anglesey, a Vauxhall 14 hp car and a motor cycle for despatch purposes were purchased in July 1941.[46] When the Caernarfonshire Police Committee met in February 1940, questions were raised about the mileage of each of the four police cars. On hearing that the mileage was considered high the committee ordered as a matter of urgency, that they should all be replaced by 24 March 1940.[47] As a further move to improve police mobility, officers were informed in September 1939 that if they were the owners of cars they could, if used for police purposes, obtain petrol coupons.[48] The police in north Wales also had the duty of warning all those who possessed cars to completely immobilise them in the event of a German agent landing by parachute.[49]

In 1940, a further measure to increase police efficiency was introduced with the implementation of the Regional Police Reinforcement and Mutual Aid Scheme.[50] The object of the scheme was to ensure that one force would render aid to another in the event of an emergency, such as a county suffering continued air attack resulting in heavy damage and numerous casualties. Under the scheme, forces in the region were arranged in groups and each group had a centre. The forces in north Wales constituted a group area and the centre chosen was the county police headquarters at Wrexham. Since forces with establishments of fewer than fifty officers were not scheduled to supply aid under the scheme, only three of the counties qualified to provide reinforcements. Caernarfonshire and Denbighshire supplied two units and Flintshire one. Although Merioneth and Anglesey were not included in the scheme, the chief constables were still expected on request to supply officers when the need arose.[51]

Early in 1941 there was a proposal that officers serving in the quieter areas of the county might like to volunteer and exchange duties with policemen who needed rest after being subjected to air attacks in heavily bombed areas like London, Liverpool and Birmingham.[52] Although there is little evidence to suggest that many officers in north Wales moved for a time to the larger cities, the chief constable of Caernarfonshire did receive a letter of thanks in 1941 from the chief constable of Swansea for the exchange of officers.[53] Officers in north Wales probably felt that they, too, had been subjected to difficulties of another kind. In small forces officers at times did the work of two men. No doubt recognising such hardship, the chief constable of Flintshire, Mr Yarnell Davies, in a New Year's message to all county chief constables said: 'All ranks of the police service, regular and auxiliary have valiantly discharged the many and onerous duties imposed upon them, and I know they will continue to do so whatever the cost. The cost has already been heavy, many colleagues have made the supreme sacrifice, whilst others have suffered grievous injury, all in the discharge of a policeman's duty.[54] A year later, following a long illness, Mr Davies passed away whilst still in office. He had completed over thirty-eight year's service and had served with great distinction. His successor was Mr Albert Edwin Lindsay, the deputy chief constable, who was appointed to office on 1 March 1942.[55]

Throughout the early years of the war, officers in north Wales were working very long hours, often under very difficult conditions and undoubtedly the health of many must have suffered as a consequence. Some officers who were eligible to retire were prevented from doing so by the Police and Firemen's (War Reserve) Act of 1939. This particular Act suspended the right of an officer to retire except on medical grounds, or where the consent of the chief constable had been previously obtained.[56] It was generally hoped that the retention of such men would in some ways offset the reduction in strength as police officers were called up for military duties. The strain on the older members of the police must have been considerable especially when added to this was the cancellation of the weekly rest day. Therefore, officers were advised to take a few hours off each week when possible.[57] Yet, despite the fact that men were denied both a day off and most of their annual leave, the chief constable of Merioneth still expected officers to attend a place of worship on a Sunday.[58]

It was because of the extra responsibilities now being shouldered by the police in north Wales that the Home Office approved increases in the strength of some forces. In Merioneth, the chief constable appointed two extra sergeants, and in February 1941 increased the strength of the police war reserve.[59]

Similarly in Caernarfonshire more men were recruited for the police war reserve.[60] Such increases were to prove essential in July 1942, when it was announced that all officers under the age of twenty-five were eligible for service with the armed forces. Later, on 31 March 1943, it was confirmed that the government intended calling on police authorities throughout the country to release more men. This resulted in the Ministry of Labour and National Service calling for the release of three members of the police war reserve in Merioneth.[61] In the House of Commons, the Home Secretary, Mr Herbert Morrison, stated that the total strength of the police force had to be reduced and claimed 'that this is a risk justified at the present stage of the war, and that we can rely on the loyal co-operation of the whole service to secure that the reduction shall result in the least possible diminution of efficiency'.[62] However, even before officers were ordered to join the colours, many in north Wales had already volunteered to do so, preferring to enter a branch of the armed services which particularly appealed to them.[63]

An area of increased expenditure during the war was the provision of hundreds of extra uniforms for the additional officers now enrolled in the county forces in north Wales. In Caernarfonshire alone, there were 660 special constables, and uniforms were considered essential for those in the police war reserve although such provision would qualify for a Home Office grant.[64] Meeting in September 1941 the police committee did agree to obtain clothing for 208 special constables at a cost of £697.14s.6d. This was the lowest tender, and in the event of the supplier being unable to deliver, members agreed to accept the next lowest tender which was £746.4s.0d.[65] In Denbighshire, the number of special constables totalled 590, of whom sixty were willing to serve outside the county if called upon to do so; the problem here was that they would have to be provided with uniforms, and the cost to the authority was estimated at being £2,000.[66] In Flintshire, the number of special constables available for duty numbered some 400 and they, too, had to be provided with clothing.[67] The position in Merioneth was that 270 persons between the ages of thirty-five and sixty had volunteered to act as special constables by January 1941.[68] Not all special constables wore uniforms although speaking to members of the police committee in Bala in April 1944, the chief constable stated that sixty had been provided with an uniform and were also entitled to a boot allowance of 1s a week. This was later increased to 2s a week and extended to all members of the Merioneth Constabulary.[69]

Police pay and conditions of service changed considerably during the war and these changes were reinforced in developments during the immediate post-war period.[70] In July 1940 the rent allowance for married constables in Merioneth was raised to 15s a week.[71] Officers residing in police stations also had their coal allowance increased to 2s a week as a result of having to burn fires night and day, for it has to be remembered that during the war police stations everywhere were open night and day and were used not only by regular police officers but became, in many instances, administrative centres for the special constabulary and civil defence organisations.[72] Further increases in pay came in an order dated 3 March 1942 which raised the wage of those serving in the police war reserve from 70s to 74s a week, the increase taking effect from 2 March 1942. In 1944 the pay of those serving in this branch of the service was again raised, this time to 80s.6d a week. In addition to this increase, an extra allowance for each year of service was granted. A member of the police war reserve with one year's service received an additional 4s a week, with two years 8s and with three years 12s.[73] An order issued in April 1945 decreed that the pay and allowances received by members of the police war reserve should be assimilated with those enjoyed by regular constables with the same period of service. Members of the police war reserve also became eligible for pensions under the Police Pensions Act if they were injured whilst on duty. It was also decided that in future they would be referred to as temporary constables.[74]

Further improvements in police pay for constables and sergeants were introduced in 1945. The starting wage for men under the age of twenty-three was 88s a week and 90s for those above this age. This was then followed by ten annual increments of 3s until a maximum wage of £5.17s.0d a week was reached. A further sum of 3s a week could be awarded to a constable at the end of seventeen years service at the discretion of the chief constable with a further 3s being awarded on completion of twenty-two years in the force. Newly promoted sergeants started at £6.8s.0d a week to rise by five annual increments of 3s, until a maximum pay of £7.3s.0d was attained. The introduction of these new pay rates automatically led to the war supplementary payments being phased out.[75] A new pay structure for those holding senior ranks was introduced on 16 January 1946, with the raised scales being as follows; an inspector received £410 per annum rising by four annual increments of £10 to a maximum of £450; a superintendent received £500, rising by four annual increments of £15 to a maximum of £560, with the chief constable receiving £610 per annum, rising by four annual increments, £50 to a maximum of £810.[76]

Although recorded crime in the counties of north Wales during the Second World War was minimal, it was nevertheless somewhat surprising, since there were thousands of service men and women of all nationalities stationed in the area.[77] There were a number of cases of petty pilfering and many of those who failed to observe certain wartime restrictions were prosecuted. Much concern was also expressed about the number of crimes committed by the younger elements of the community.[78] At a meeting of the police committee in Caernarfonshire in November 1940, one member complained about the amount of crime committed by juveniles and was informed by the chief constable 'that frequently such offences were committed by evacuees'.[79] Some concern was also voiced about teenage drinking, especially among young women, and it was hoped that the situation would not be allowed to worsen.[80] When a number of religious denominations in Merioneth became alarmed at what they believed was a rise in teenage drinking, the chief constable, Mr Richard Jones, anxious to allay such anxiety, stated 'that while he agreed with them that more young people were frequenting licensed premises he believed they were there more for a sit down and company than for drinking'.[81] This was a tolerant and liberal view, but his observations were no doubt soundly based on what he knew to be the truth, for the incidence of drunkenness recorded in the county was very small.

As the war in Europe drew to a close in April 1945 all officers in north Wales were informed that leave on Victory Day, and possibly the following day, would be cancelled.[82] When Victory in Europe and Japan was finally accomplished some wartime conditions of service were lifted. For example, a Home Office circular informed all members of the Police War Reserve that they were now free to return to civilian life.[83] Members of the special constabulary were also allowed to tender their resignation without first of all seeking the permission of the chief constable.[84] The months that followed the cessation of hostilities saw many officers in north Wales who had been serving with the armed services resuming duty with their respective county forces.[85] Throughout the war years all members of the police in north Wales had performed their duties in an exemplary manner and chief constables were often the recipients of letters expressing appreciation of the work done by officers.[86] One must also remember acts of bravery, as when two Caernarfonshire officers, Constables William John Jones and Robert Elwyn Williams, were attacked by an armed soldier who they later disarmed. For their bravery they were each awarded the King's Police Medal.[87]

Reporting on the work of the police generally the Inspectors of Constabulary in the report for 1945 stated 'the public's appreciation of the police has never been greater and the confidence that is placed in the police has never been higher, and the relationship between the public and the police service was never better'.[88] Without a doubt all members of the police service – men and women, regulars and auxiliaries, part-time and full-time alike could feel justly proud. However, this devotion to duty in time of war was not without cost; 278 members of the police service were killed as a result of enemy action while on duty with their own forces, and 1,275 police officers serving with H.M. forces were killed and of this number at least three were from north Wales.[89] Despite such endeavour and sacrifice, the years that immediately followed the ending of the war were to become somewhat soured by a number of disappointments. True, relations with the public had never been better but as T.A. Critchley observes 'such intimacy was in any case bound to cloy, a crescendo of high endeavour had to fall away in the humdrum of peace'.[90]

---

[1] Hugh Owen, op. cit., p.51, and Denbighshire Chief Constable's General Order Book, 1929-42, 24 February 1937.

[2] MQS Rolls, (Michaelmas, 1936).

[3] Roy Ingleton, *The Gentlemen at War – Policing Britain 1939-1945*, (Maidstone, 1994), p.17, and MCF Orders, QA/P/D/8/5, 28 September 1938.

[4] MCF Orders, QA/P/D/8/5, 28 September 1938.

[5] Ibid.

[6] T.A. Critchley, op. cit., p.223.

[7] Ibid., p.224.

[8] Ibid. The First Police War Reserve to be set up was in the Metropolitan Police in May 1938. It was followed soon afterwards by similar organisations in the City of London and in a number of county and borough forces. The Reserve was finally disbanded on 31 December 1948.

[9] Ibid., pp.224-5. See also *CDH*, 5 May 1939, which records that Mr Edward Williams, chief constable of Caernarfonshire retires after forty-four years police service. His successor was Superintendent Thomas John Pritchard who had joined the Caernarfonshire Constabulary in 1905 and became deputy chief constable in May 1928.

[10] Denbighshire Chief Constable's General Order Book 1929-42, 12 February 1940.

[11] T.A. Critchley, op. cit., pp.225-6.

[12] Ibid. Extracted from the Report of His Majesty's Inspector of Constabulary for 1940-45.

[13] Roy Ingleton, op. cit., pp.16-25. Also *CDH*, 17 March 1939, where the chief constable of Anglesey seeks permission to appoint a constable clerk to deal with the measures considered necessary in the event of an air raid, and *Flintshire Observer*, 6 April 1939, where the Home Office offers Caernarfonshire 20,000 sandbags to protect the police stations in the county. One magistrate, Mr R.T. Jones, failed to see the necessity for such an offer in an area allocated to receive evacuated children. The chief constable believed that the enemy might concentrate attacks on such an area in order to destroy morale.

[14] T.A. Critchley, op. cit., p.232.

[15] MCF Orders, QA/P/D/8/5, 3 September 1939. Also MCF Orders, QA/P/D/8/6, 11 March 1944 and 16 August 1944 where further restrictions were imposed which prohibited people from travelling to Ireland were promulgated. This measure was to prevent leakage of information to the enemy regarding preparations for allied landings in Europe. An order dated 13 March 1944 allowed travel to Ireland only to those going there on business of the highest national importance, or on compassionate grounds. Later, in August 1944, some of the regulatoins were lifted, for instance, those with wives and families in Ireland were allowed to visit them.

[16] Ibid., 4 September 1939.

[17] T.A. Critchley, op. cit., p.232.

[18] Ibid., p.233. See MCF Orders. QA/P/D/8/6, 6 July 1940 and 26 March 1942. According to information compiled by the police in Merioneth there were, in July 1940, seventy-seven aliens registered in the county, by March 1942 this number had risen to 138. No information has come to light to account for the rise in the space of less than two years.

[19] MCF Orders. QA/P/D/8/6, 31 July 1940.

[20] Ibid., 25 January 1941.

[21] Hugh Owen, op. cit., p.51 and *CDH*, 12 July 1940 where it is reported that two officers in Caernarfonshire were appointed detectives for special duties, they were constables Owen Pritchard (Caernarfon) and Llewellyn Roberts (Conwy), and *Flintshire Observer*, 1 August 1940, where Flintshire also appointed two officers, Sergeant Idwal Jones (Buckley), and William Victor Cook for special detective duties and Denbighshire Chief Constable's Order Book, 1929-42, 12 February 1940, and 6 August 1940 where four officers, Detective Sergeants Owen Jones and John E. Pugh, along with Constables Glyndwr E. Jones and H.D. Richards were appointed for special war duties.

[22] MCF Orders. QA/P/D/8/6, 16 May 1940.

[23] Ibid., 18 May 1940.

[24] Ibid., 15 June 1942.

[25] Ibid., 19 June 1940.

[26] *Cambrian News*, 22 September 1944 and *CDH*, 20 April 1945, which report that the Home Secretary, Mr Herbert Morrison, announces that full street lighting is to be restored on 15 July 1945.

[27] *Flintshire Observer*, 15 August 1940.

[28] Joan Lock, *The British Policewoman*, (London, 1979).

[29] MRO, Chief Constable's Papers, M/1/201, undated newspaper cutting and Joan Lock, op. cit., p.176, where in Cardiganshire the chief constable thought differently and employed policewomen making the county at the time the only authority in Wales to do so. In employing one policewoman, a sergeant, the chief constable was fortunate for she spoke German and, therefore, was extremely useful in the control and search for enemy aliens. Not that Merioneth was alone in its opposition. There had been opposition in Cornwall when a similar decision was taken against the advice of the Federation of Women's Institutes and the National Union of Teachers who called for the services of women police officers.

[30] *Cambrian News*, 10 July 1942. Not that all members shared this view, Dr J. Pugh Jones was strongly in favour of having women police, particularly in Barmouth. When voting took place on the matter, four voted for the appointment and seven against.

[31] Hugh Owen, op. cit., pp.51-2. All members of the Women's Auxiliary Police Corps automatically left the service on 31 March 1946.

[32] ASJ Committee, 11 May 1944.

[33] *Flintshire Constabulary Centenary Handbook*, op. cit., p.39, and *Flintshire Observer*, 21 September 1944 and 4 October 1945, also FSJ Committee, 31 October 1945, which records the appointment of Miss Elizabeth Emily Jones of Denbigh as a member of the Women's Auxiliary Police Corps and posted to Rhyl.

[34] Denbighshire Chief Constable's General Order Book, 1929-42, 23 September 1941.

[35] Ibid.

[36] Ibid., 10 and 17 December 1941; 5 March, 25 August, and 9 September 1942. *Flintshire Observer*, 15 January 1942 and 13 January 1944. The first female officers appointed were: Gertrude Davies, Dorothy E. Roberts, Olive Jones, Florence M. Shipley and Phyllis Badwick. On 25 August 1942 Olive Jones resigned and was replaced by Joan Chapman on 9 September 1942. In February 1944 Glenys Jones was appointed and was stationed at headquarters.

[37] *CDH*, 19 January 1940 and 20 September 1940. The North Wales Association for the care of Friendless Girls and Women urged every county in Wales to appoint women police officers.

[38] Ibid., 15 November 1940.

[39] Ibid., 29 November 1940; 21 February and 9 May 1941.

[40] Ibid., 28 November 1941. They were to be on probation and their employment could be terminated at short notice. Their pay was to be

£2.7s.0d a week and they were to be between twenty-one and fifty years of age. Also *CDH*, 16 January 1942. The four appointed were: Miss H.B. Owen; Miss Ivy M. Roberts; Miss Mair Evans and Miss M. Wright.

[41] CSJ Committee, 13 February 1942.

[42] *CDH*, 1 December 1944.

[43] MQS Rolls, (Hilary, 1940).

[44] MQS Rolls, (Michaelmas, 1939) also *Flintshire Constabulary Centenary Handbook*, op. cit., p.39.

[45] MQS Rolls, (Trinity, 1940).

[46] Hugh Owen, op. cit., p.52. See *Flintshire Observer*, 24 December 1941, where the police committee in Flintshire agreed to purchase six second-hand motor-cycles.

[47] CSJ Committee, 22 February 1940. The mileage of each car was as follows: car 1 – 51,000 miles; car 2 – 36,000; car 3 – 45,300; car 4 – 34,206.

[48] MCF Orders, QA/P/D/8/5, 15 September 1939.

[49] Ibid., 22 May 1940.

[50] Denbighshire Chief Constable's General Order Book, 1929-42, 16 May 1940.

[51] MCF Orders, QA/P/D/8/6, 13 April 1940.

[52] Ibid., 25 April 1941, also *Flintshire Observer*, 2 November 1944, which records that between June 1940 and January 1942, 400 high explosives and 4,500 incendiaries were dropped in Flintshire resulting in five people being killed and forty injured.

[53] CSJ Committee, 25 July 1941.

[54] *Flintshire Observer*, 16 January 1941, also *Cambrian News*, 4 October 1940, and Hugh Owen, op. cit., p.52, and *CDH*, 5 September 1941. One officer who made the supreme sacrifice was Constable George Arthur of the Anglesey Constabulary who died on 28 August 1941 whilst making a very gallant effort, with others, to rescue the crew of a British bomber which crashed into the sea off Rhosneigr. He had been a member of the force for ten years. Read *CDH*, 23 January 1942, Constable Arthur was awarded the Bronze Medal by the Royal National Lifeboat Institution. Also Hugh Owen, op. cit., p.51. One unpleasant duty performed by Anglesey officers during the early part of the war was the removal of bodies and their identification from the submarine *Thetis* which sank in Liverpool Bay just prior to the outbreak of war.

[55] *Flintshire Constabulary Centenary Handbook*, op. cit., p.30, and *Flintshire Observer*, 5 February 1942.

[56] T.A. Critchley, op. cit., p.225, also H.K. Birch, op. cit., pp.272-3.

[57] MCF Orders, QA/P/D/6/6, 12 June and 7 August 1940. Also Denbighshire Chief Constable's General Order Book, 1929-42, 20 March 1940, where the chief constable was willing to consider applications which would allow an officer to take a little leave.

[58] MCF Orders, QA/P/D/8/6, 27 February 1941. It was also ordered that

such church attendance should be recorded in their journals and weekly reports.

[59] Ibid., 20 February 1941.

[60] CSJ Committee, 25 September 1940, and Hugh Owen, op. cit., p.52.

[61] MSJ Committee, 31 March 1943. Also Denbighshire Chief Constable's Order Book 1942-50, 13 October 1943, which records seven officers being released to join the armed forces.

[62] *CDH*, 19 February 1943.

[63] MCF Orders, QA/P/D/8/6, 25 January and 31 August 1942. See also H.K. Birch, op. cit., p.277 for the names of several officers in the Merioneth Constabulary who joined the forces, also *Flintshire Observer*, 30 November 1939; 17 December 1942 and 16 September 1943.

[64] *Flintshire Observer*, 6 April 1939.

[65] Ibid., 2 October 1941.

[66] Ibid., 10 July 1941.

[67] Ibid., 21 May 1940.

[68] MQS Rolls, (Hilary, 1940).

[69] MCF Orders, QA/P/D/8/6, 12 April 1944. Read Hugh Owen, op. cit., p.52, for the provision of uniforms in Anglesey. Also MCF Orders, QA/P/D/8/6, 16 March 1944, where in accordance with Home Office instructions, war service chevrons were issued to all full time members of the police service, as well as those serving with the special constabulary. The period covered for the wearing of such chevrons was from 3 September 1939 until 31 January 1944. In the chief constable of Flintshire's report dated 5 September 1945, members of the police committee were informed in a letter from the Home Office, that the payment of 1s a week boot allowance to part-time special constables should now be restricted to those who performed on average four or more hours a week, such allowances to operate from 1 July 1945.

[70] Denbighshire Chief Constable's General Order Book 1929-42, 21 September 1940.

[71] MCF Orders, QA.P.D.8.6, 20 July 1940.

[72] Ibid., 1 October 1941.

[73] Ibid., 11 September 1944.

[74] Ibid., 18 April 1945.

[75] Ibid., and *CDH*, 6 April 1945.

[76] Ibid., 16 January 1946. Important to remember that in north Wales some chief constables were on higher rates of pay than others as much depended on the size of the force and area policed.

[77] One of the great difficulties facing the researcher during the Second World War when attempting to record accurate crime figures is seen in Denbighshire Chief Constable's General Order Book, 1929-42, 21 November 1941, which records that due to a national shortage of waste paper, files and occurrence books which related to crimes between 1931-41 should be destroyed. This fact probably accounts why so much valuable material that

relates specifically to north Wales is no longer extant.

[78] Ibid., 22 July 1943, and *CDH*, 31 July 1942. It was to combat the possibility of an increase in juvenile delinquency that counties like Merioneth established youth committees in 1943 which worked closely with the police on current problems.

[79] CSJ Committee, 22 November 1940; 25 July 1941; 26 February 1942; 20 November 1942 and 5 May 1944. Also, *CDH*, 31 July 1942; 19 February 1944 and 16 February 1945.

[80] *CDH*, 15 November 1940 and 18 February 1944, and CSJ Committee, 20 November 1944.

[81] *County Times*, 10 September 1943.

[82] MCF Orders, QA/P/D/8/6, 18 April; 14 May; 4 July and 18 August 1945. With the war in Europe at an end all ranks were awarded an additional three days leave which was later increased to five when victory over Japan was finally achieved in August 1945. To mark the ending of six years of war a Victory Parade was held in London to which every force in the United Kingdom sent a representative. Only four county chief constables were invited to the celebrations, one of whom was Mr Richard Jones, chief constable of Merioneth.

[83] MCF Orders, QA/P/D/8/6, 13 August 1945 and Denbighshire Chief Constable's General Order Book 1942-50, 26 February 1949, which records that the Police War Reserve was finally disbanded on 31 December 1948.

[84] *CDH*, 3 August 1945. It was to mark their appreciation of the work undertaken by members of the special constabulary that the Caernarfonshire standing joint police committee sent a letter of thanks to every officer.

[85] FSJ Committee, 5 September, 31 October 1945; 6 February 1946 and *Flintshire Constabulary Centenary Handbook*, op. cit., p.38, which reports that the last officer to return to duty after service with the armed forces resumed duty on 20 June 1947. Also Denbighshire Chief Constable's General Order Book, 4 March and 11 June 1946 and *CDH*, 25 August 1945 and 25 January 1946.

[86] Merioneth Chief Constable's Papers, M/1/201, undated letter from Merioneth War Agricultural Committee which expressed appreciation of the work undertaken by Detective Inspector Howell O. Jones. Also *Flintshire Constabulary Handbook*, op. cit., p.30, where Superintendent John Ffenlli Roberts was awarded the MBE, for his valuable services during the war.

[87] *Flintshire Observer*, 6 January 1944 and *CDH*, 7 January 1944.

[88] Report of His Majesty's Inspectors of Constabulary 1940-45.

[89] J. Owain Jones, op. cit., p.95, and *Flintshire Constabulary Centenary Handbook*, op. cit., p.38. Caernarfonshire lost two officers, Constables E.M. Owen and T. Williams and Flintshire one, Constable James Lewis Evans. All officers in Merioneth and Anglesey returned safely – the position in Denbighshire is not known but to date there is no information that any officer was killed whilst serving with the armed forces. See also, *CDH*, 25 August 1944 and 2 March 1945, which records the death whilst serving with the armed forces of Lieutenant T.H. Lloyd Jones RNVR, who served

with the special constabulary in Caernarfon before joining the navy, and Meirion Evans, a boy clerk in the chief constable's office at Caernarfon who was killed in Normandy.

[90] T.A. Critchley, op. cit., p.237.

Chapter X

# Amalgamations and the Gwynedd Constabulary, 1945-74

With the ending of hostilities in 1945 the police authorities in north Wales, as elsewhere, began to consider what they believed would be their role in the post-war world. What was absolutely clear to all, was the fact that the police service which had undergone many changes during the war years would never be quite the same again. For example, the amalgamations which had been enforced on a number of forces during the war, particularly in Kent, were retained.[1] In other areas where amalgamations had also been imposed, forces were allowed to return to their pre-war position, but this proved to be only temporary, for during the next two decades, they, too, eventually found themselves reluctantly accepting that amalgamation was very much a part of the Home Office post-war policing strategy.

Indeed, the seeds for reforming the police had been quietly sown during the war. As T.A. Critchley acknowledges, as early as 1944, 'there was a readiness, hitherto rare in the police service, to challenge the accepted order of things'.[2] In that year the Home Secretary set up a committee which consisted of chief constables and representatives of the Home Office. They were asked to examine both immediate post-war problems and what the future policy on policing should be. The committee's terms of reference were extremely wide. For example, they were asked to consider the role of policewomen within the service and whether there should be a national police college. Members of the committee were also asked to look at the way police forces were organised, the distribution of senior ranks in a force, the arrangements available for training recruits and promoting men to supervisory rank, communications systems, police buildings and welfare.[3]

Within three years of the establishment of the often overworked committee, four reports were published. The first of these was of tremendous importance to the future of the service, for it concentrated on the higher training of police officers and its main consideration was the establishment of a police college. So important was the recommendation in the eyes of the Home Office that it was put immediately into effect.[4] The first police college was opened in 1948 and was housed in temporary accommodation at Ryton-on-Dunsmore, near Coventry, but in 1961 it moved to its present headquarters at Bramshill House, near Hartley Wintney in Hampshire.[5] A White Paper issued in 1947 sets out the basic purposes of the college, 'which is that of helping appointing authorities to choose their senior officers from men who joined the service as constables, and have merited promotion by reason of their personal qualities, technical qualifications, experience of police service, and aptitude for leadership'.[6] In addition to the establishment of the police college the committee was also responsible for the setting up of a number of district training centres. The centre for Wales, to which male recruits were sent for their initial training, was the Glamorgan County Police Training School at Bridgend. Female recruits attended a similar centre at Bruche near Warrington. In the late 1940s and early 1950s officers in Flintshire also attended courses on law and general subjects at the Flintshire Technical College.[7]

In its second report the committee dealt mainly with the general organisation of the service but went to great lengths to point out 'that the committee had no sweeping reforms or radical alterations in the present organisation to suggest'.[8] The report also placed great emphasis on the difficulties facing the police and whether such long established practices as the traditional beat system was still appropriate in the post-war world. In its assessment of the future role of policewomen in the service the committee was unanimous in declaring that it believed it would be one of great importance. The third report dealt mainly with areas that covered police buildings and accommodation as well as the general welfare of officers.[9] In its fourth and final report, issued in 1947, the committee was quite specific in its recommendations. It centred on the responsibilities of those holding senior ranks, as well as setting out the type of organisation, work, and conditions of service that should be accorded to members of the Special Constabulary. Obviously, such recommendations could not be implemented overnight, but as this history of the police in north Wales continues to unfold, it will be clearly seen that all eventually came to fruition.[10]

One of the immediate tasks facing chief constables in north Wales in 1945 was that of securing the release of officers who were still serving in the various branches of the armed forces. Here, to some extent, their position was helped by a decision taken earlier by the War Cabinet which urged that, when possible, every effort should be made to release all officers who were not urgently required for military duties.[11] Most police officers readily accepted the opportunity to leave their units and return to their former occupation. Some, however, chose to remain, for many had reached high rank and therefore the very thought of returning to the humdrum 'life of a constable was not always appealing'.[12] However, by the end of 1945 and the early months of 1946, most officers from north Wales had returned to their respective forces. Many of those who returned had served for the whole duration of the war in the armed services and it was for this reason, that in Anglesey, the chief constable fearing that some of them might well have lost their appetite for police work, sent eleven of them to undertake refresher courses at the Glamorgan Police Training School, near Cardiff.[13] A similar situation in Flintshire saw the chief constable, Mr Lindsay, also ordering a number of recently released officers to attend refresher courses which were provided by the chief constable of Lancashire at his headquarters near Preston.[14]

Yet, despite the welcome return of officers to their respective forces, chief constables in north Wales were all bemoaning the fact that they were still faced with a chronic shortage of suitable recruits to the service. Commenting on this shortage in January 1946, Mr Richard Jones, chief constable of Merioneth, announced that his force was numerically well below its authorised strength and called for urgent action in order to remedy what he viewed as a deteriorating situation. Meanwhile, in order to alleviate the difficulty, he urged his officers to undertake additional duties until such time as the position improved.[15] It was a similar position in Anglesey and in his annual report for 1945 the chief constable, in agreement with his police committee, sought the approval of the Home Office to increase the strength of the force from forty-four to fifty-four officers.[16] In Flintshire, the chief constable not only faced a shortage of recruits, but in order to maintain efficiency, had to resort to offering short-term engagements of not less than three or not more than six months to members of the Auxiliary branches.[17] In his report to the police committee in July 1947, the recently appointed chief constable of Denbighshire, Mr Phillip Tomkins, who had succeeded Mr

Thomas Guest, on his retirement, went on to explain what the consequences of a shortage of recruits meant to the county generally and stated that 'there was no doubt that the country districts were robbed of policemen to towns like Denbigh and Ruthin on market days – and some parts of Wrexham never saw a policeman'.[18] Speaking to the same committee a year later, the chief constable declared that the Denbighshire Constabulary had always prided itself on only accepting into the force those who had reached a high standard of education. However, since there was now a dire shortage of suitable men applying for entry such former standards might well have to be lowered in the future.[19]

Caernarfonshire's problems at this time were twofold, for not only were they seriously undermanned and short of suitable recruits, but the authority had also lost its chief constable with the passing of Mr T.J. Pritchard, who had been in command of the force since 1939. There were nineteen applicants for the vacant post, nine of whom were officers serving within Wales, including the Acting Chief Constable of Caernarfonshire, Griffith William Roberts.[20] After lengthy deliberation the police committee eventually chose a short-list of four which included the following: Major Robert Hughes, BEM, Inspector, Liverpool City Police; Detective Inspector Evan William Jones, Special Branch, Metropolitan Police; Mr William Rees, Chief Constable of Leamington Spa and Lieutenant Colonel William Jones Williams, Chief Inspector, Birmingham City Police. After interviewing each candidate a ballot was taken which resulted in the latter named officer being appointed as the new chief constable of Caernarfonshire at a salary of £775 per annum to rise by biennial increments of £50 to a maximum of £975 per annum.[21]

There is little doubt that an important factor in deterring many from joining the police, in the years following the ending of the Second World War, was the poor rate of pay. When, in 1919, the Desborough Committee recommended the raising of police pay, it had the immediate effect of bringing many years of stability to the service. Between the wars, the pay of the police was on average, according to official reports, about 55 per cent higher than that earned by workers engaged in industry.[22] It also has to be recognised that police officers at this time also benefited from paid holidays, a good pension, and 'immunity from the risk of unemployment – itself a prized asset in the 1930s'.[23] Therefore, it comes as no surprise that during this period, the police were able to attract to the service a large number of suitable recruits.[24] This apparent glowing position was to change dramatically with the commencement of war in 1939. Those working in factories, with their high wages and the increases in the cost of living, began to outstrip the value of supplementary war bonuses granted to the police to such an alarming degree that by 1945 police officers and those engaged in industry were more or less on a par as regards pay. The 55 per cent lead they once enjoyed had more or less disappeared. Such a loss bred discontent in the police service generally and in order to appease officers, new scales were introduced in April 1945.

However, not even the new pay structure could soften the resentment felt by policemen over their eroded position. Recruitment in north Wales was falling fast and every force found the inadequacy of pay to be a primary cause. In London, for instance it was particularly serious, with the Metropolitan Police in 1946 having fewer officers than it had in 1901, a position that caused much disquiet in official quarters.[25] Alarmed by being confronted with such a situation, the Government introduced a further increase in 1946, on the strict understanding that pay would remain unchanged until 1 January 1950, with the whole range of conditions of service being referred to an independent review body before the end of 1949. By 1948, however, the position had worsened to such a degree that the Government, now even more alarmed, decided to advance by a year the appointment of the review body and in May 1948 a committee was set up under the chairmanship of Lord Oaksey.[26] Its remit was 'to consider in the light of the need for recruitment and retention of an adequate number of suitable men and women for the police forces in England, Wales and Scotland and to report on pay, emoluments, allowances, pensions, promotions, methods of representation and negotiation and other conditions of service'.[27] The committee presented two reports in April and November 1949.[28] The first report dealt with police pay, pensions and numerous other factors that related to conditions of service. In its second report the committee concerned itself with a wide range of issues including the appointment, training and promotion of police officers, their discipline, housing and amenities and the important establishment of negotiating machinery.[29] Certainly, from the recommendations of this committee stemmed many improvements in a policeman's conditions of service, but unfortunately pay could not be said to be one of them. The Police Federation had hoped that an increase in the region of between $33^1/_3$ and 54 per cent would be awarded. Much then was the disappointment felt by officers in north Wales, when they were informed that the committee only recommended an increase of some 15 per cent for the constable on his maximum. In awarding the increase the Oaksey Committee, like Desborough before it, acknowledged the excellent work performed by policemen, but were forced to recognise the recently published Government White Paper on Personal Incomes, Costs and Prices, which stated 'each claim for an increase in wages and salaries must be considered on its national merits'.[30]

When the new pay scales were introduced in Merioneth, in July 1949, a constable on appointment earned £330 per annum, rising by annual increments of £10 to a maximum of £400; sergeants on promotion received £445 per annum, rising by four annual increments of £10 to a maximum of £485; inspectors on promotion £550 per annum, rising by three annual increments of £15 to a maximum of £575. In addition to the above scales, constables were also awarded an increment of £10 per annum on completion of fifteen years and twenty-two years respectively.[31] In awarding these increases, the Oaksey Committee firmly believed it would lead to a long period of stability. Such hopes, however, were soon to be dashed. The real economics of the day was still doing its corrosive work and within a matter of two years of the Oaksey recommendations, a second independent review gave the police a further rise of some 20 per cent over and above the award of 1949.[32] Such an increase also raised the pay of the police above 'its seemingly tireless competitor – average industrial earnings'.[33] Even this increase failed to stem the mounting anger felt by the police and in 1954 further negotiations were conducted by a newly created body, the Police Council for Great Britain, which had been formed on the earlier recommendations of the Oaksey Committee. As a result of the Police Council's findings, a further increase of 9 per cent, was awarded, but it was the last of its kind, for on no fewer than three further occasions between 1945-60, when the Royal Commission on the police was introduced, the two sides of the Police Council found their positions so wide apart, that agreement of any kind was virtually impossible and arbitration appeared the only answer to the problem.[34] Such a stalemate did little to lighten the disappointment or diffuse the anger felt by the officers serving throughout north Wales.

If police pay, the shortage of suitable recruits and conditions of service generally were sources of anxiety for members of the standing joint committees in north Wales, they were soon to be faced with an additional problem which called for the amalgamation of the smaller forces. Wide as its review was, the committee, set up in 1944, had not been asked to examine one of the most controversial aspects of the police service, which was the future of the smaller police forces. The amalgamation of small forces was not something new. For example, the Police Act of 1856 had begun the process of encouraging the amalgamation of small forces. The 226 forces in existence in 1856 had been reduced to 183 by the Second World War as a result of this and later legislative inducement.[35] Events leading to more amalgamation were to move on apace, when in 1945 following the General Election, Mr Chuter Eade, replaced Mr Herbert Morrison as Home Secretary. Within a few months of taking office he introduced a Bill into Parliament which called for the abolition of all non-county borough forces.[36] The Bill was also explicit when it stated that the Home Secretary had the power to amalgamate any other force where to do so would be in the interest of efficiency. Before any amalgamation became operative, there would be a local inquiry and the Order making the scheme would be subject to parliamentary approval. A provision in the Bill, which was important for several of the counties of north Wales, was the fact that all obstacles, that impeded in any way two county forces or two county borough forces from merging, would be removed.

The Bill introduced by the Home Secretary, became the Police Act of 1946 and from the outset was viewed as controversial. There were many who accused the Home Secretary of seeking powers, that in time would allow him to establish regional police forces by joining the remaining separate forces together. Many members of standing joint committees saw such a move as being only a short step away from nationalising the police. It was certainly true that the passing of the Police Act on 15 April 1946 was to have a profound effect on the police in north Wales. Its passing was to signal the end of small forces which, in so many instances had outlived their usefulness. The proposal to merge the counties of Anglesey, Caernarfonshire and Merioneth was not entirely unexpected. An article in the *Police Review*, December 1947, had hinted that forces like Cardiganshire and Merioneth would sooner or later have to face up to such a proposal. The article also claimed among other things, that neither county had the population nor the police establishment to justify a separate existence.[37] The first intimation of the Home Secretary's intentions to merge Anglesey, Caernarfonshire and Merioneth, came in a letter dated 23 July 1948, in which members of the respective standing joint committees were informed that he had under review the deposition of the police forces in north Wales. In his letter, the Home Secretary called upon the clerks of the standing joint committees of the counties concerned to ascertain whether members had examined the possibility of a voluntary amalgamation scheme, in particular one that would combine the police forces in Anglesey, Caernarfonshire and Merioneth.[38]

Following the receipt of this letter, representatives of the standing joint committees met in Caernarfon on 17 December 1948 and again on 2 January 1949, both under the chairmanship of Sir W.B.H. Hughes-Hunter, Bart.[39] After discussing, at some length, the possibility of voluntary amalgamation, the joint committees passed the following resolution:

> That having considered the provisions of the Police Act 1946 and the terms of the Home office letter of 23 July 1948, the conference recommends that the Standing Joint Committees of Anglesey, Caernarfonshire and Merioneth express agreements in principle to a voluntary amalgamation scheme combining the Police Forces of the three counties subsequent to agreement being reached between the three authorities upon the question of representation of the counties on the proposed Combined Authority, the basis of financial contribution and other matters for inclusion in the scheme.[40]

The standing joint committees at this time had many other things to occupy their minds, in Merioneth for instance, it was the question of appointing policewomen, there was no disguising the fact that uppermost in the minds of members and the officers themselves was the forthcoming amalgamations.[41] Frequent meetings between representatives of the forces to be merged led members to be confronted daily with endless paperwork. It was understandable that the thought of the impending amalgamation should awaken in officers a certain degree of uncertainty, because for many, service with their particular force had been a whole way of life and it was natural they were apprehensive. Probably the words of the writer commenting on the post-war amalgamations in general mirrored the feelings of officers in the counties when he wrote: 'they were still alive enough with old tradition, and many recent brave memories of war and peace, to cause real pangs at the parting'.[42] What may have served well as a palliative to the dread of coming change was the success experienced earlier when three other Welsh forces. Montgomeryshire, Breconshire and Radnorshire amalgamated in 1948 to form the Mid-Wales Constabulary.[43] With this in mind, officers may well have felt, that given time the same success could be repeated and with the eventual outcome proving most beneficial.

In accepting the situation, officers felt that the stage was set for the final scene. There was to be a complete break with the past, which many felt was a step into the unknown. However, despite the many misgivings officers had about the merging of the counties, there was a combined determination to help their respective standing committees to make the amalgamation proposals a success. Many viewed the changes as a challenge, and they had never shirked their duty previously. Indeed, many saw the changes as the beginning of what could well result in a new and exciting chapter in the history of policing generally. In many ways such a hopeful outlook augured well for the future. The early months of 1950 saw the arrangements for the proposed amalgamation of the forces of Anglesey, Caernarfonshire and Merioneth nearing completion. In so many instances the whole exercise had gone smoothly with the respective authorities conducting their affairs in a most cordial manner. It was the fervent hope that this same harmony would continue, that led Colonel Wynne Finch, the retiring chairman of the Caernarfonshire standing joint committee, to claim 'that when eventually the three counties amalgamated, the people concerned would give the same support to the new body'.[44]

The only issue, on which there had been a difference of opinion, was that which concerned the financial contributions to be made by each county. In order to settle the matter amicably, it was jointly agreed that the whole question should be referred to the Home Secretary, and as a consequence all would abide by his decision. It was also agreed that, assuming the financial aspects of the merger could be satisfactorily settled, the Amalgamation Scheme should become operative as from 1 April 1950.[45] In his reply the Home Secretary, in a letter dated 12 August 1949, stated 'that the most equitable methods of apportioning the net cost of the proposed combined police authority between the constituent councils would be on the basis of combined rateable value, and weighted population and the Secretary accordingly favours the compromise suggested by the standing joint committee in Anglesey'.[46] It was as a result of this decision that at a later meeting it was decided that the proposed amalgamation should be deferred until 1 October 1950. This delay then allowed the counties a further six months in which to complete the necessary transfer of their powers to the new constabulary.[47]

Having agreed on the date for amalgamation, it was decided that the new force should be known as the Gwynedd Police Authority. Members of the three authorities also agreed, that Lieutenant Colonel William Jones Williams, chief constable of Caernarfonshire should be the first chief constable of the new constabulary. There was much discussion on the composition of the new authority but it was decided that it should consist of twenty-two members: six from Anglesey, six from Merioneth and ten from Caernarfonshire.[48] In each case half the membership was to consist of justices of the peace, with the remaining half being members of their respective county councils. Finance too, was high on the agenda, and it was passed that the contribution made by each authority should be based on 50 per cent of the rateable value and 50 per cent weighted population.[49]

Sadly, amidst all these successful arrangements, the county of Anglesey was to lose its chief constable with the sudden death on 12 December 1949 of Mr Robert Humphrey Prothero.[50] He had been in command of the force since 1919 and, during the time of the proposed amalgamations, had done much to make the transfer to Gwynedd a success. For the months that remained prior to the force becoming part of the new Gwynedd Constabulary, Superintendent Gilbert William Brown, the deputy chief constable was appointed acting chief constable of Anglesey.[51] It was in order to further facilitate the passing of the final draft of the Amalgamation Order, that Mr Richard Jones, chief constable of Merioneth, announced in April 1950 that it was his intention to retire. His retirement was to break a link with the police service that had lasted some sixty years and one which started in Cardiganshire in 1891. It was, to say the least, a truly remarkable record and one that few will ever equal.[52] Indeed, his service as chief constable was only surpassed in Wales by that of Mr Edmund Gwynne, who had commanded the Breconshire Constabulary for forty-nine years.[53] That Flintshire and Denbighshire had not been part of the Home Office's amalgamation scheme must have been welcomed by the respective standing joint committees, but any satisfaction they may have experienced, was eventually to prove short-lived, for within a matter of twenty years their forces, too, would lose their individual identity.

The amalgamations in 1950 brought to an end what had been for the three counties concerned a long and proud history and one that had lasted the better part of a century. Over these years, officers had surmounted numerous obstacles and had carried out their many and varied duties with a dignity that only comes with the pride that men have in the things they cherish. It was somewhat comforting when it was stressed at the time that the merging of small forces, like Anglesey, Caernarfonshire and Merioneth, was in no way indicative of past inefficiency on the part of any of them. The changes that came stemmed from a wide variety of factors, some social, some economic. Many of the factors were present before the advent of the Second World War, while others surfaced during the war itself. Early recognition of these changes was in part the result of the keenness of the Home Secretary, Mr Herbert Morrison, himself the son of a former policeman, who in 1943 placed before Parliament a series of regulations made under the Emergency Power (Defence) Act, which enabled him, if he so desired to join two or more areas together.[54] The mergers which had occurred during the war, led some chief constables to believe that such measures would in time lead to a greater degree of efficiency and deployment of manpower. Certainly, in north Wales, there were officers, especially the younger members, who, in many instances, said that the amalgamations had opened up new and exciting possibilities, with perhaps a greater opportunity to advance in the service. Indeed, this thinking on their part, was to be echoed by Lord Harlech, who commenting on the amalgamation of the three counties stated 'that he could not help thinking that in the interest of young men there might be a wider career open to them, especially to those with zeal and ability to gain promotion'.[55]

The decade that followed the merging of the three counties saw many changes in the way and manner north Wales was policed. For example, where formerly there had been five county forces there were now only three: Gwynedd,* Flintshire and Denbighshire, and many officers viewed the situation as a challenge. Of immediate concern to the authorities was the rise in crime and with records either lost, or in many instances deliberately destroyed, often at the instigation of chief constables, it becomes difficult to truly assess the true scale of the increase,** but there appears to have been very little serious crime. Where statistical evidence does survive, there were between 1950-60, three cases of murder and thirty cases of rape in Gwynedd,[56] and four cases of murder and six of rape in Flintshire.[57] The most common offences in both counties during this period, were simple and minor larcenies and shopbreaking. What tends to create a further problem, when attempting to ascertain the actual number of offences that had been committed, is the fact that there is little uniformity in the way chief constables present their annual statistical data. All is not lost, however, for a far more revealing picture on the state of crime, and often its causation, can sometimes be obtained from the views of the chief constables themselves, when addressing their respective police committees.

Addressing the police committee of Caernarfonshire in

December 1947, the chief constable, Lieutenant Colonel William Jones Williams, made what could only be described as a veiled criticism of the magistrates when he declared that 'when the police after a laborious investigation have succeeded in prosecuting the criminal to conviction the responsibility for administering such punishment as will impress upon the offender the futility of continuing with his activities against the community rests with our Courts of Justice. There is a danger that many new offenders embark upon their first efforts in crime knowing that persons convicted of criminal offences often escape punishment on the first and even the second occasion'.[58] Obviously, times were changing and Caernarfonshire's chief constable's criticism was an early indication that chief constables no long felt they had to be subservient to the whims and wishes of their respective police authorities and began stating their beliefs with conviction.

If the upsurge in crime was the number one concern of the authorities in the 1950s and 1960s, then the growth in road traffic with its inevitable number of fatalities came a very close second. Even before the advent of the Second World War it was estimated there were more than 21,000 licenced private cars on the roads of north Wales.[59] During the war itself there was some respite but afterwards, the increased affordability of motor cars and the end of petrol rationing, called for a new and more effective way of policing the highways. Some idea of the scale and magnitude of the accidents in just one county, that of Gwynedd, shows the annual figures including fatalities for the period 1950-65, viz.:

**Table 9.1 Road Accidents including Fatalities 1950-65,**

|      | No. of Accidents | Injured | Fatalities |
|------|------------------|---------|------------|
| 1950 | 414              | 162     | 4          |
| 1951 | 1895             | 711     | 24         |
| 1952 | 1779             | 705     | 24         |
| 1953 | 1961             | 800     | 16         |
| 1954 | 2057             | 816     | 24         |
| 1955 | 2371             | 1043    | 24         |
| 1956 | 2295             | 1044    | 15         |
| 1957 | 2138             | 994     | 22         |
| 1958 | 2397             | 1122    | 25         |
| 1959 | 2468             | 1160    | 19         |
| 1960 | 2828             | 1311    | 31         |
| 1961 | 2758             | 1258    | 25         |
| 1962 | 3036             | 1379    | 33         |

| 1963 |       | 2943   | 1362   | 25  |
| 1964 |       | 3430   | 1611   | 28  |
| 1965 |       | 3501   | 1760   | 25  |
|      | Total | 41,957 | 17,238 | 364 |

Of the 41,957 accidents recorded, 21,256 occurred in towns and 20,701 in the country.[60]

Concerned about the number of road accidents, some of which had proved fatal, the Home Office launched a campaign to educate the general public on the importance of road safety. In north Wales, forces were urged by the Government to increase the number of police patrol vehicles in each area. When in the 1930s police patrol cars were generally introduced, the Home Office had allocated a certain number of vehicles to each force. Anglesey for instance was allocated two cars, whilst Caernarfonshire and Merioneth were allowed to possess four cars each. However, when these counties amalgamated in 1950, there were only seven cars available for operational duties and the chief constable requested his police committee to purchase three more. In addition, an order was also placed for four new motor cycles so as to further advance police mobility.[61] A further purchase, this time for five Vauxhall Velox patrol cars, was made in August 1952.[62] To increase efficiency even further, it was also agreed that all ten police vehicles should in future be equipped with wireless, and to assist in the transmitting of messages a radio mast was erected at Llanddona at a cost of £1,937.12s.9d.[63] Later, a Home Office directive issued in 1965 ordered that all police cars should be equipped with a two-tone siren for use in an emergency.[64]

The authorities in Denbighshire also introduced a policy which they believed would improve road safety. At a meeting of the standing joint committee in 1951, a question was raised as to whether patrol cars in the county should display police signs and one member, Mr W.S. Woods, believed that to do so would act as a deterrent to speeding motorists. It was not, however, an idea that found much favour with Mr Philip Tomkins, the chief constable, who believed it would be 'a retrograde step to identify any police car'.[65] A change in this opinion, if only of a little, occurred in 1953 when the standing joint committee decided that purely as an experiment, police cars in the Wrexham division would display police markings.[66] In 1956, in an effort to increase the number of patrol cars in the county, the chief constable requested the police committee to purchase at the earliest opportunity, one van and nine motor cycles. To reinforce the need for such vehicles, the chief constable informed members that one of his officers had a beat of twenty-one square miles and was also expected to cover some forty miles of hilly country on a pedal cycle.[67] The question of whether police vehicles should display identification markings was to rise again at a meeting of the standing joint committee in July 1957. This time the question was put to the newly appointed chief constable, Mr Arthur Morgan Rees, who had succeeded Mr Tomkins earlier in the year.[68] In reply Mr Rees stated that all police vehicles within the county would display markings in the future.[69] He was also of the opinion that police efficiency would be vastly improved if all police cars were equipped with a camera for use when in attendance at a scene of an accident.[70] Another improvement and one the chief constable considered vital, was the immediate installation of wireless equipment for the force area. Although the idea had first been suggested in February 1955, no action had been taken and two and a half years were to elapse, before the subject was raised again in November 1957. On this occasion and at the insistence of Mr Rees, the standing joint committee agreed that three transmitting stations should be erected, at an estimated cost of £20,000 thus bringing Denbighshire into line with the other county forces in north Wales.[71]

In Flintshire, six police patrol vehicles had been fully operational on the roads of the county since the traffic department was established in 1950.[72] Later in 1956, police mobility was further increased when five motor cycle patrols were added to the strength of the traffic division.[73] Periodically the chief constable, in his reports to members of the standing joint committee, would detail the factors that were mainly responsible for most road accidents. They were: (a) errors of judgement as to the clearance between vehicles, (b) overtaking improperly, (c) skidding and swerving, (d) turning right without due care and attention, (c) travelling at excessive speed.[74] The authorities were also aware at this time, that if road safety was to be strictly observed then it was essential that a police telephone network was urgently required. Arrangements, therefore, were put in place to install in all eight police patrol cars, the necessary wireless equipment that would allow officers to send and receive messages. As a further aid to wireless transmission an order was also made for a mast 120 feet high to be erected on the top of Halkyn mountain.[75] To their credit, the police in Flintshire did not simply confine their concern about road safety to the roads in the county. Often the force adopted particular schools in the county to which officers were sent to speak and show slides to the pupils on a number of issues including road safety.[76] Indeed on average over some forty schools a month were visited by police officers in an attempt to teach the dangers continually posed by vehicular traffic.[77]

As a further measure to improve road safety, officers in every county in north Wales had for some time been allowed to use their own cars, motor cycles or bicycles for which they were paid certain allowances.[78] However, not all officers who wished in the past to use their own cars for police purposes were looked upon favourably by their chief constable. Such was the experience of Inspector W.D. Williams, of the former Merioneth Constabulary, when he offered to save the county money by purchasing a car which would only be used for police duties. The offer, which he made directly to the chairman of the standing joint committee, was referred to the chief constable, Mr Richard Jones. In his reply to Inspector Williams, the chief constable firmly rebuked him, 'stating he had departed from normal procedure in applying direct to the police authority, therefore his offer was refused'.[79]

Of immense concern to police authorities everywhere during the 1950s and 1960s, and particularly to the respective county treasurers, was the rapid escalation in the cost of policing. In north Wales due to the destroying of so many records, once again one is left with a somewhat incomplete picture. However, some indication of the rising costs can be obtained from the position in Gwynedd where fortunately one is able to examine in some detail material that has somehow survived the passage of time. The amalgamations in 1950, although very much a success had not been accomplished cheaply. One of the immediate effects was that the new force area was to be divided into four divisions, namely Caernarfonshire, Anglesey, Conwy and Merioneth.[80] Such a large force area called for a new administrative centre and plans for a modern police headquarters situated in Caernarfon were approved by the Caernarfonshire standing joint committee as early as February 1950.[81] A number of possible sites were inspected, and eventually a decision was taken to purchase three fields at Maes Incla, Caernarfon, for £350 plus legal fees, with half the cost being borne by the Home Office.[82] In a letter from the Home Office in 1949 it was suggested that a new headquarters could be built at a cost of £20,000, although it was not expected that work could start immediately on such a project.[83] Tenders for the work were then called for and the lowest received was from Messrs. G. and J.P. Gregory, Caernarfon, quoting a figure of £38,062.162.7d. On hearing this figure, one member of the police committee, Mr S.V. Beer, asked about the original figure which had been quoted as £20,000. In reply, the clerk, Mr Gwilym T. Jones, stated that a revised figure of £30,000 had been put to the Home Office and the sum of £38,062 was only a little above this.[84] In fact, when the new headquarters were eventually completed the total sum for the work amounted to £40,942.11s.7d.[85] The new headquarters were officially opened in March 1953, by the Home Secretary, Sir David Maxwell Fyfe. He declared that it was the first new police headquarters in England and Wales to be opened since the war, although a number of others were in the process of being built.[86] A few years later it was proposed that a new divisional police headquarters should be built at Conwy. Although negotiations with the borough's officials went on for many months, it was eventually decided by the Gwynedd Police Authority, that the proposal should be withdrawn. Instead, it was generally agreed that an extension to the existing police building in Llandudno would answer the same purpose.[87] An extension could be built at a cost of £14,000, which would be approximately half of what it would have cost to build a completely new building in Conwy.[88]

It was not just police buildings that were proving expensive. The erection of houses for officers and their families were even more expensive. No longer were officers willing to accept poor accommodation or be separated from their families. This situation it seems had certainly been the experience of some police officers in England, who, during the war had married, and on returning to their respective forces found that there was no suitable housing for them, and therefore were separated from their wives and children once again.[89] In north Wales, the authorities, in fairness to them, had heeded a report from the Home Office in 1944, which urged them to ensure that as far as possible there was sufficient suitable accommodation for all police officers.[90] It was with this in mind, that the chief constable submitted to his police committee a list of housing requirements. He stated that now counties had amalgamated there was a need for the authority to adopt a completely new housing programme.[91] In his submission, he called for the erection of seventy-seven police houses, at an estimated cost of £5,000 each.[92] There were also a further large number of houses and police stations in urgent need of renovation.[93] Neither did the cost of erecting houses or police stations end there. One has to take into consideration such items of expenditure as rents, rates, insurances, lighting, cleaning, architectural services, legal charges, officers travelling allowances, clothing, telephone charges and printing etc. – the list is endless.[94] The amalgamations also created an additional cost since many officers were now being transferred to other areas. Expenditure of removing furniture and adapting curtains and carpets in the new accommodation meant that officers would have to be recompensed by a grant.[95] Some indication of the rise in the annual cost of policing the Gwynedd area is seen in the following figures: the cost in 1954 was £259,635, by 1958 this had risen to £331,230 and by 1964 it had reached £536,290.[96]

Training was proving equally expensive. No longer, as in the past, could certain training be undertaken at a local level. Sophisticated techniques and methods of training and management were now taught at a number of established specialised centres, which were usually attached to the larger forces. As the police service entered the second half of the twentieth century, there was a requirement that men who were destined for higher rank should be provided with the necessary opportunities for study and experience on a scale much broader than their daily work allowed. The need was clearly underlined by the fact, that a large number of police officers worked alone and the opportunities for exercising such skills as supervision and ability to command were severely restricted. Unlike in the past, it was becoming widely recognised that the senior posts in the service had to be occupied by men who had risen from the ranks.[97] However, without the proper training and guidance, the chances of obtaining such men from within the service was somewhat bleak. Therefore, throughout the 1950s and 1960s there was a constant stream of officers from north Wales attending a wide variety of courses, some of which lasted a few weeks and others several months. A number were chosen to attend specialist courses which prepared them for higher command at the police college at Ryton-on-Dunsmore.[98]

Detective training at this time was considered particularly important. Therefore, when regional crime squads were introduced in the mid 1960s, many officers in north Wales who had attended courses in the past, were already trained and experienced in this sphere.[99] The plan envisaged for north Wales was that there should be two regional offices, one at Prestatyn, the other at Wrexham. These centres were to be manned by officers from Gwynedd, one would be based at Prestatyn, two at Wrexham, with a fourth being seconded to work in Liverpool.[100] Concerned as they were about crime, the police generally were no less anxious about the situation on the roads. They were becoming more congested and the numbers of those injured or killed were also rising at an alarming rate. In many ways, the solution to these problems was beyond the resources of the police – some improvement could be made by building better roads and street lighting, more vehicle safety checks and seeing that speed limits were strictly observed. It was to ensure road safety and the expertise to travel at high speeds, often in pursuit of those who had committed serious crime, that officers, in order to improve their driving skills, were sent on advanced driving courses.[101] Others again undertook numerous refresher courses in order to ensure their earlier ability to deal with particular emergencies was not lost. All this training was expensive and another reason why expenditure on the police was escalating, and why, understandably, the authorities in north Wales as elsewhere were concerned.

The early 1960s was a time of uncertainty for the police service and for the organs of local and central government, which administered it. This situation, in part at least, led in 1960 to a Royal Commission on the police being established, with terms of reference 'sufficiently wide-ranging to require it to examine afresh the fundamental principles on which the service had always relied'.[102] The Commission had a difficult task and was ordered to inquire into a number of important issues. It was asked to examine, for example, the relationship between the police and the public it served, also it was to inquire into the manner in which complaints against the service were dealt with. What made the Commission's task even more difficult, was that, for some time, there had been so much disquiet about policing. The announcement that there was to be a Royal Commission was favourably received. What may have prompted even further the call for a Commission, was the fact that in the late 1950s, as Robert Reiner explains, 'a series of *causes célèbre*' involving the chief constables of Cardiganshire, Brighton and Worcester, who not only received a great deal of media coverage, but focussed attention on the question of accountability.[103] This question of accountability had been highlighted in 1959, when a dispute arose between the chief constable of Nottingham, Captain Atheleston Popkess, and members of his Watch Committee.[104] It arose as a consequence of the chief constable investigating, what he believed had been certain irregularities by members of the council. On refusing to divulge to the Watch Committee, the findings of this investigation he was immediately suspended. The Home Secretary, however, intervened and the committee had little alternative but to reinstate him.[105] The dispute was to focus attention on the lack of clarity about the respective roles of a Chief Constable, a Watch Committee and a Home Secretary.

The Commission took two years to complete its inquiries and in May 1962 presented its final report.[106] Amongst its many proposals, the Home Secretary was granted new powers which called on chief constables to submit reports and when found inefficient, they could be compelled to retire. His power to approve or disapprove the appointment of a chief constable (available in the counties since 1839 and in the boroughs since 1920), should also be extended to the deputy and assistant chief constables. He was also granted additional powers to make compulsory, co-operation between forces on such matters as the setting up of crime and traffic squads.[107]

What was of great significance for north Wales, was the proposal that a fresh assault should be made on the smaller police forces. According to the Commission, the Home Secretary's power to compel the amalgamation of police areas, should not be stifled by the limit of 100,000 population, imposed by the Police Act of 1946. In fact, it was considered that forces with fewer than 200 officers suffered much hardship and that the retention of a force with fewer than 350 men could only be justified in exceptional circumstances. It was the Commission's belief, that the optimum size of a force was upwards of 500 officers. A further improvement in achieving some uniformity within the service was in the Commission's view, the appointment of a chief inspector of constabulary who would assume overall responsibility for strategic planning.[108] To assist him in this work it was suggested that a number of inspectors should be appointed, one for each of the eight police areas, into which England and Wales had been divided.[109] Setting out the functions of future police authorities the Commission recommended that they should be restricted to the following: to provide pay, equip and house the police; to give advice and guidance to the chief constable about local problems; to appoint, discipline and remove senior officers – subject to the Home Secretary's overriding authority and to foster good relations with the public. As a direct result of these recommendations, the idea of local control was set aside, 'in a way that would have been totally incomprehensible to most nineteen watch committees'.[110]

In May 1963, the report of the Commission, which had been conducted under the chairmanship of Sir Henry Willink, QC, was debated in the House of Commons.[111] By this time, a chief inspector of constabulary had been appointed and the inspectorate had been increased to seven. In addition to this, a Police Research and Planning Board had been set up in the Home Office, which it was envisaged would give top priority to the fight against serious crime. On informing the House of these achievements, the Home Secretary, Mr Henry Brooke, stated there would be a stronger initiative from the Home Office in the future. He also believed that the time was also approaching when the number of police forces would have to be reduced, especially in view of the Local Government Commission which was examining county boundaries.[112] In November 1963 some eighteen months after the Royal Commission Report, the Government introduced its Police Bill. It contained few surprises and it was clear that the local authority associations had achieved little success in their campaign to persuade the Government to abandon some of the Commission's more radical proposals. The Bill was eventually given an unopposed second reading and passed, with little opposition, through the House of Lords receiving Royal Assent in June 1964.[113] Two years later in May 1966, Mr Roy Jenkins, the Home Secretary in Harold Wilson's Government, began to use his powers to amalgamate the 'smaller forces quite vigorously'.[114] He announced that it was his intention to reduce the 'number of provincial police forces from 117 to forty-nine, and despite many protests, the proposed amalgamations were largely achieved by the end of the decade'.[115] In fact, the Local Government Act of 1972, reduced the number of provincial forces yet again.

For the authorities in Flintshire and Denbighshire, news that they would inevitably be forced to amalgamate with the neighbouring Gwynedd Constabulary, was viewed with a certain amount of trepidation. As county forces, they had between them served their respective communities for a total of 238 years. Yet, like their fellow officers, some seventeen years earlier in 1950, they accepted the change knowing that they would continue to serve diligently as they had always done. At a meeting held in Llandudno in October 1966 between the authorities of Gwynedd, Flintshire and Denbighshire, the arrangements for the forthcoming amalgamations were discussed at some length. Of immediate concern to all was where the new headquarters for the enlarged force should be sited. It was clear that the Gwynedd Headquarters in Caernarfon would no longer be a suitable location for the extended force area.[116] Most members believed that new headquarters should be built in the Llandudno or Colwyn Bay area. This idea was strongly supported by the officials from Denbighshire, but Flintshire members acted more cautiously believing any decision should be deferred. When discussing the membership of the new police authority it was agreed that it should consist of thirty members with Anglesey having three members, Merioneth three, Caernarfonshire six and

Flintshire and Denbighshire having nine each. Members also accepted that the chief constable of the new authority should be Lieutenant Colonel William Jones Williams, the then head of the Gwynedd force.[117] The new authority was to be known as the Gwynedd Police Authority and the appointed day for the amalgamation with Gwynedd would be 1 October 1967 and, if that were not feasible, 1 April 1968.

Having accepted that amalgamation was inevitable, officials had to consider the question of filling the senior positions in the new Gwynedd Constabulary. Mr Walter Stansfield, MC, chief constable of Denbighshire was appointed to the position of deputy chief constable of the force, with Mr Akins of Flintshire occupying the position of assistant chief constable .[118] It was estimated that when the force became fully operational on 1 October 1967, it would have an establishment of about 1,036 officers.[119] In a letter to the police committee in Gwynedd in August 1967, Mr Atkins informed members that he would sooner resign than become the assistant chief constable.[120] Later however, on the appointment of Mr Stansfield to the position of chief constable of Derby County and Borough Force, Mr Atkins was offered the post of deputy chief constable and was given to the end of the year to decide his future position.[121] Mr Atkins was not tempted by the position of deputy chief constable and eventually tendered his resignation to the Gwynedd Police Authority.[122] When the position was subsequently advertised there were eleven applicants and from a shortlist of five, Chief Superintendent P.A. Myers of the West Mercia Constabulary was appointed on 25 March 1968.[123] The position of assistant chief constable had been advertised a little earlier and there were seven applicants from which four were called for interview.[124] The successful candidate was Chief Superintendent John St David Jones, of the Gwynedd Constabulary.[125]

The siting of a new police headquarters was top of the agenda when the Gwynedd Police Authority met in May 1967 and it was considered essential that the following criteria had always to be borne in mind before a final decision on its location was reached.[126] For instance, the patent advantage of siting headquarters within a reasonable distance of centres where there was a large population and usually a high incidence of crime. Good road, rail and air communications were also considered a very important factor. It was also thought technically desirable to select a site which could provide satisfactory radio communication with all parts of the combined police area as well as with forces in adjoining areas. Another important consideration was that headquarters with an estimated staff of at least fifty officers would require housing accommodation within a reasonable distance from the place of work.[127] The headquarters itself would have to provide certain essential requirements. It would have to be large enough to accommodate in time, between 110 and 120 police officers, as well as civilian personnel. Provision would have to be made for large parking areas and motor maintenance workshops, control rooms, administrative offices and storerooms as well as welfare amenities. Looking to the future, the authorities were of the opinion that the site chosen must have sufficient land around it to cater for future expansion. It was to their credit, that members of the police committee were attempting to achieve the very best for the force, and this augured well for the future policing of north Wales.

The first real test, of the new Gwynedd Constabulary's ability to deal with a major event came in July 1969, with the Investiture of the Prince of Wales at Caernarfon Castle. The whole event had to be meticulously organised and called for the most detailed planning by senior members of the force. Certainly, the demands on the force during the period before the investiture as well as on the day itself were to prove exacting. However, assisted by officers from other forces, all demands were met with credit and this was emphasised by the many tributes the force received about the way in which it had performed its varied duties. Congratulatory letters were received from Her Majesty the Queen, the Prince of Wales, the Duke of Norfolk and the chairman and clerk of the Gwynedd Police Authority.[128] For his services at the investiture the chief constable, Lt Colonel William Jones Williams, was later knighted. The Assistant Chief Constable, Mr John St David Jones also became the recipient of the Queen's Police Medal for Distinguished Service.[129]

In his last report before retirement, Sir William Jones Williams, gave detail of the proposed new police buildings which had received the approval of the Secretary of State. They were: new headquarters at Colwyn Bay and a divisional headquarters at Wrexham. It was also the intention of the authority to erect two sub-divisional stations, one at Rhyl and the other at Holyhead. Sir William also gave details of the number of indictable offences in 1969 which amounted to 776, a decrease of thirteen on the figure in 1968.[130] In reporting the number of motoring offences he stated that a total of 22,954 involving 17,782 persons of whom 3,229 were cautioned and 14,553 prosecuted. In his first report to members of the police committee, Mr Phillip Myers, who had succeeded Sir William on 1 October 1970 stated that he found the force had settled well after amalgamation and was fully prepared to meet the challenge of the seventies.[131] He believed that one of the most important innovations during the year had been the employment of civilians, which released policemen from posts that did not require police expertise. The chief constable also expressed his concern about the number of outbreaks of gang hooliganism in resorts like Abersoch and Rhyl. It was found that most offenders possessed cars or motor cycles and drove, especially at weekends, from the Midlands or Lancashire.[132] In his report, Mr Myers was very supportive of the Special Constabulary and he believed they provided invaluable support for their regular colleagues.[133] The strength of the Special Constabulary on 31 December 1972 was 655 which included ten women.[134]

On the 9 October 1973 the new Police Headquarters at Colwyn Bay was officially opened by the Home Secretary, Mr Robert Carr.[135] A year later, the chief constable was able to report that there had been a period of consolidation in the headquarters' operations room, during which time various improvements and modifications to equipment and organisation had been carried out. He believed that the concept of a central control room had been fully justified, and during 1974, 17,840 emergency calls had been received, 379 of these resulting in an arrest.[136] What was of importance during 1974, was that the Gwynedd Police Authority ceased to exist, at least in name. It was replaced on 1 April 1974 by the North Wales Police Authority.[137] As we approach the last quarter of the twentieth century, we will examine the many changes that have occurred during this exciting period in the history of the police in north Wales.

---

[1] M.B. Taylor and V.L. Wilkinson, *Badges of Office, 1829-1989*, (Oxford, 1989), p.35. In 1943 the following nine borough forces were merged with the Kent County Constabulary – Canterbury, Dover, Folkestone, Gravesend, Maidstone, Margate, Ramsgate, Rochester and Tunbridge Wells. See also Anon, *Kent Police Centenary*, (Kent, 1957), pp.114-26.

[2] T.A. Critchley, *A History of Police in England and Wales*, (London, 1956), p.239.

[3] Ibid. Also *Flintshire Constabulary Handbook*, (Holywell, 1956), pp.39-40. For an excellent account of police training generally see John Coatman, *Police*, (London, 1959), pp.137-51.

[4] *Flintshire Constabulary Centenary Handbook*, op. cit., p.40.

[5] J.R. Martin and Gail Wilson, *The Police a Study in Manpower*, (London, 1969), p.100. Also James Cramer, *The World's Police*, (London, 1964) p.37 and Sir Harold Scott, *Scotland Yard*, (London, 1955), pp.44-55.

[6] Cmd. 7070 of 1947.

[7] *Flintshire Constabulary Centenary Handbook*, op. cit., pp.39-40.

[8] T.A. Critchley, op. cit., p.239.

[9] Ibid.

[10] Ibid.

[11] Roy Ingleton, *The Gentlemen at War – Policing Britain 1939-45*, p.373. During the period 1944-45, it was estimated that some 15,000 police officers were serving in the armed forces. Some 9,000 were in the army with the remainder either in the Royal Navy or the Royal Air Force. See also Home Office Circular 189/1945. (Release of policemen from the armed forces), and F.S.J. Committee, 31 October 1945 and 6 February and 4 September 1946 and Denbighshire Chief Constable's General Order Book, 1942-50, 11 July 1946. Also C.S.J. Committee, 15 February 1946.

[12] Roy Ingleton, op. cit., p.375.

[13] Hugh Owen, *History of the Anglesey Constabulary* (Llangefni, 1952), p.54.

[14] FSJ Committee, 5 September 1945.

[15] MCF Orders, QA/P/D/8/6, 16 January 1946.

[16] Hugh Owen, op. cit., p.54.

[17] FSJ Committee, 6 February 1946. Short-term engagements were therefore offered to, and accepted by, three members of the First Police Reserve, eleven members of the Police War Reserve and five members of the Women's Police Auxiliary Police Corps. By such means the strength of the Flintshire Constabulary on 1 February 1946 was maintained at 111. This figure included ninety-seven Regular Police officers, three members of the First Police Reserve and eleven members of the Police War Reserve. On 20 May 1947, Mr Lindsay, chief constable of Flintshire passed away and on 1 December 1947 he was succeeded by the deputy chief constable, Mr John Ffenlli Roberts; there were nine applicants for the vacant post. See also *Police Review*, 30 May and 28 November 1947.

[18] *Police Review*, 18 July 1947 and 10 April 1946. Also see George G. Lerry, 'The Policemen of Denbighshire', *Transactions of the Denbighshire Historical Society*, 2 (1953), pp.144-5.

[19] *Police Review*, 30 July 1948.

[20] CSJ Committee, 11 January 1946.

[21] CSJ Committee, 15 February 1946 and 11 January 1946. At the time of his appointment Lieutenant Colonel William Jones Williams, B.Sc., LL.B., was seconded from Birmingham City Police and was Deputy Senior Military Government Public Safety Officer, Westphalia, Germany. It is interesting to note that such military titles as lieutenant colonel, major, captain or lieutenant were bestowed on police officers, like the recently appointed chief constable of Caernarfonshire, who for a time had been seconded from their respective forces to serve as Public Safety Officers in Europe. Apart

from the four officers shortlisted the following fifteen were applicants for the vacant position: Superintendent A. Cartwright BA, Indian Police; Chief Constable William Vincent Doolen, Neath Borough Police; Superintendent Owen Goodwin Eames, Caernarfonshire Constabulary; Inspector Edward Hamer Hirst, Stockport County Police; Superintendent Louis Jones, Denbighshire Constabulary; Superintendent Robert John Jones, Pembrokeshire Constabulary; Detective Inspector Thomas Rees Jones, Metropolitan Police; Superintendent David Edgar Morgan, Swansea Borough Police; Inspector Arthur Morgan Rees, Metropolitan Police; Acting Chief Constable William Griffith Roberts, Caernarfonshire Constabulary; Inspector Hywel Thomas, Denbighshire Constabulary; Inspector William Prosser Thomas, Hampshire Constabulary; Major C.F. Walker, Edinburgh City Police; Inspector Thomas John Williams, Caernarfonshire Constabulary and Detective Sergeant Kenneth George Williams, Cardiganshire Constabulary.

[22] Interim Report on the Royal Commission on Police (November 1960). Cmd. 1,222 para.21. * In looking at police pay between 1919-39 we must take into account the fact that the economic crisis in 1922 and 1931 compelled the Government to erode the Desborough scales. In 1922 pay was reduced by 2½ per cent, a reduction which in 1926 was converted into a contribution towards pensions. The cuts in 1931, part of the country's general economy measures, were from 5 to 10 per cent, with a reduction in pay for newly enrolled officers – the former lasted until 1935, the latter until 1945. Nevertheless, despite such reductions, police pay still remained throughout the inter-war period relatively high in relation to average incomes and the cost of living.

[23] T.A. Critchley, op. cit., p.249.

[24] Ibid., also Interim Report of the Royal Commission on the Police, op. cit., para.22. Here it is stated that Lord Trenchard, Commissioner of the Metropolitan Police, had not been too impressed by the quality of the recruits – at all events up to 1931.

[25] Ibid., pp.249-50.

[26] J.P. Martin and Gail Wilson, op. cit., pp.66, 75, 89, 91 and 97.

[27] T.A. Critchley, op. cit., p.250.

[28] Cmd. 7674 and 7831.

[29] T.A. Critchley, op. cit., p.250 and Arthur Brown, *Police Governance in England and Wales*, (London, 1998), pp.169-70. * The Police Act of 1919 required that a member of the police force must pass a qualifying examination before becoming eligible for promotion from constable to sergeant and from sergeant to inspector. Examinatons were conducted locally and the standard, to say the least, varied widely. The Desborough Committee and the Police Post War Committee had recommended the introduction of a centralised promotion system and the Oaksey Committee concurred, it was however not until 1958 that a start was made by arranging for the examination to be conducted by the Civil Service Commission on behalf of a Police Promotion Board composed of representations of the service associations, the police authorities and educational experts.

[30] Cmd, 7321 (January 1948).

[31] MCF Orders, QA/P/D/8/6, 19 July 1949.

[32] Conducted in 1951 by Sir Malcolm Trustram Eve and two assessors.

[33] T.A. Critchley, op.cit., p.251.

[34] Ibid.

[35] Robert Reiner, *The Politics of the Police* 2nd. ed. (London, 1992), p.272.

[36] T.A. Critchley, op. cit., p.243. The exception here was that of Cambridge and Peterborough where the borough had a population larger than that of the county.

[37] *Police Review*, 26 December 1947.

[38] MSJ Committee, 5 October 1948.

[39] Ibid. See also CSJ Committee, 4 February 1949 and Hugh Owen, op. cit., pp.58-59. Those members representing *Anglesey* were Messrs. R.D. Briercliffe, H.R. Evans and Arthur Williams; *Caernarfonshire*, Colonel W.H. Wynne Finch, Captain A. Stanley Davies, Messrs. J.W. Pritchard, and R.W. Williams; *Merioneth*, Sir Evan Jones, Alfred E. Hughes and Richard Thomas Vaughan, together with Mr Hugh J. Owen, Clerk, Mr Richard Jones, Chief Constable and Mr Steven Davies, County Treasurer.

[40] MSJ Committee, 5 February 1946 and CSJ Committee, 6 May 1949.

[41] *Police Review*, 4 February 1949.

[42] T.A. Critchley, op. cit., p.243.

[43] *CDH*, 16 April 1948. Other Welsh amalgamations in the 1940s were Carmarthen Borough Police merged with the County in 1944, and Neath Borough merged with the Glamorgan force in 1947.

[44] *CDH*, May 1950.

[45] CSJ Committee, 6 May 1949.

[46] Hugh Owen, op. cit., p.58.

[47] Ibid., op. cit., p.59. Also CSJ Committee, 3 February 1950.

[48] Ibid.

[49] MSJ Committee, 11 April 1950.

[50] Hugh Owen, op. cit., p.57.

[51] Ibid.

[52] *CDH*, 14 April 1950. Also MSJ Committee, 4 July; 8 and 29 September 1950. See H.K. Birch 'The Merioneth Police 1856-1950', MA University of Wales thesis, 1980, pp.299-302.

[53] *CDH*, 6 December 1906.

[54] T.A. Critchley, op. cit., p.241.

[55] *Y Dydd*, 29 September 1950.

\* The Common Seal of the Gwynedd Police Authority incorporates the Lion of Anglesey, the Goat of Merioneth and the Eagle of Caernarfonshire. As a motto for the Authority Sir Ifor Williams chose a Welsh proverb taken from *Llyfr Du o'r Waun*. However, he concluded that in its original form the language of the proverb was archaic and not readily understandable to the present day Welshman. Sir Ifor then modernised it to read: *Gorau camp cadw* which translated means 'The best feat is to keep the peace'. He also believed it was brief, concise and most apt for a coat of arms, and above all for the coat of arms of *Heddgeidwaid*.

** From information kindly supplied by former Inspector Winston Jones, of the Pembrokeshire Constabulary, who claimed many old records and photographs of the force were destroyed on the orders of the chief constable who wished to make room for documentation which he felt was more important and relevant.

[56] Gwynedd Police Authority, 13 February 1953; 12 February 1954 and 6 February 1959.

[57] FSJ Committee, 12 February 1952; 4 February 1958; 3 February 1959 and (undated) May 1960.

[58] CSJ Committee, 13 February 1948.

[59] Deian Hopkin, 'Social reactions to economic change', *Wales Between the Wars*, ed. by Trevor Herbert and Gareth Elwyn Jones, (Cardiff, 1988), p.57.

[60] Gwynedd Police Authority, 22 February 1952; 13 February 1953; 12 February 1954; 11 February 1955; 10 February 1956; 8 February 1957; 7 February 1958; 6 February 1959; 5 February 1960; 3 February 1961; 2 February 1962; 8 February 1963; 7 February 1964; 5 February 1965; 4 February 1966 and 3 February 1967.

[61] Gwynedd Police Authority, 16 February 1951.

[62] Ibid., 1 August 1952 also 16 February 1951, which states that all police patrol cars were to be fitted with public address systems.

[63] Ibid., 6 November 1959, also 5 February, 1960 which recorded that four motor cycles were also to be equipped with wireless.

[64] Home Office Circular, 285/1965.

[65] *Police Review*, 27 July 1951, also Denbighshire Chief Constable's General Order Book 1951-58, 16 February 1953, which states that the Denbighshire County Council's road safety committee was to introduce school crossing patrols throughout the county.

[66] Ibid., 28 January 1955.

[67] Ibid., 8 June and 20 June 1956.

[68] Ibid., 19 July 1957 and Denbighshire Chief Constable's General Order Book 1951-58, 7 March 1957.

[69] Ibid., also 28 December 1956. Mr A.M. Rees, the newly appointed chief constable, was formerly a superintendent with the Metropolitan Police. The other candidates for the vacant position were: Superintendent H.C. Price, Metropolitan Police; Chief Superintendent Martin, Liverpool City Police; Superintendent and Deputy Chief Constable Owen Jones, Denbighshire Constabulary; Superintendent E.L. Williams, Metropolitan Police; Superintendent T.J. Williams, Gwynedd Constabulary and Superintendent H.G. Woods, Bedfordshire Contabulary.

[70] Ibid., 24 October 1958.

[71] Ibid., 1 November 1957 and 4 February 1955.

[72] *Flintshire Constabulary Centenary Handbook*, op. cit., p.41.
[73] Ibid.
[74] FSJ Committee, 1 February and 6 September 1950; 2 May 1951; 3 November 1953; 3 February 1954; 2 September 1958.
[75] *Police Review*, 13 November 1953.
[76] FSJ Committee, 3 May 1950.
[77] Ibid., 2 February 1955 also *Police Review*, 18 January 1963, where it is reported that police cars were to be less identifiable.
[78] CSJ Committee, 23 November 1945, also Home Office circular No. 72/1952 where increased payments for such use were to take effect from 1 April 1952. See Gwynedd Police Authority, 17 November 1950 and 7 November 1952 and Denbighshire Chief Constable's General Order Book 1951-58, 23 July 1956 and 30 April 1957.
[79] Merioneth Chief Constable's Papers, M/1/201. Letter from Inspector W.D. Williams to the Chairman of the Merioneth standing joint committee dated 27 December 1947.
[80] *Police Review*, 6 October 1950 and Gwynedd Police Authority, 16 February 1951. The enlarged authority had the following acreage for each division: Caernarfonshire 258,858 acres; Anglesey 176,694 acres; Conwy 105,250 acres and Merioneth 422,372 acres. The population in each division was: Caernarfonshire 86,929; Anglesey 50,521; Conwy 36,909; Merioneth 40,848.
[81] *Police Review*, 17 February 1950.
[82] *CDH*, 10 February 1950.
[83] Ibid., 13 May 1949.
[84] *CDH*, 28 July.
[85] Gwynedd Police Authority, 16 July 1954.
[86] *CDH*, 13 March 1953 also Gwynedd Police Authority, 8 May 1953.
[87] Gwynedd Police Authority, 29 November 1957.
[88] Ibid., 7 February 1958. On completion the new extension was officially opened on 6 January 1961 by Brigadier Sir William Wynne Finch.
[89] Roy Ingleton, op. cit., p.377.
[90] Gwynedd Police Authority, 27 July 1951.
[91] Ibid.
[92] Ibid.
[93] Ibid., 4 May 1951.
[94] Ibid., 13 February.
[95] Home Office Circular No. 191/1957 and *CDH*, 28 February 1951, Constable Alun Ross who had been stationed at Holyhead was the first officer of the old Anglesey force to be transferred out of the county to Caernarfon. He was replaced at Holyhead by Constable D.O. Williams, stationed at Four Crosses in Caernarfonshire.
[96] Gwynedd Police Authority, 13 February 1953; 8 February 1957 and 7 February 1964.

[97] Gwynedd Police Authority, 11 June 1965. Also T.A. Critchley op. cit., pp.203-9, in which he discusses the Hendon Police College and the work of Lord Trenchard in the 1930s which included a scheme that allowed men with good educational qualifications to gain direct entry into the officer class.

[98] Ibid., 7 November 1952; 5 November 1954; 11 February 1955; 4 May 1956; 11 July 1958 and 6 February 1959, FSJ Committee, 6 September 1950; 2 May 1951; 2 September 1952; 3 February 1954; 4 November 1958; 5 May 1959, and Denbighshire Chief Constable's General Order Book 1951-58 – 11 July 1951; 10 July 1952; 27 April and 16 July 1953; 18 January 1956; 14 June 1956 and 16 April 1957.

[99] David Ascoli, *The Queen's Peace*, (London, 1979), pp.290-1, and Gwynedd Police Authority, 29 October 1965, it was estimated that in the first year the cost of establishing regional crime squads would amount to £360,785 – the cost to the Gwynedd Constabulary was £7,376, and Home Office Circular No. 249/1964.

[100] Gwynedd Police Authority, 29 October 1965.

[101] Gwynedd Police Authority, 11 February 1955; 6 May 1955; 4 November 1955; 11 May 1958; 3 February 1961 and 5 May 1967. FSJ Committee, 7 May 1957; 5 November 1957; 4 February 1958; 5 May 1959. Also Denbighshire Chief Constable's General Order Book, 1951-58, 24 April and 27 October 1955 and *Police Review*, 30 October 1964.

* The years 1952 and 1954 were particularly memorable for some officers in north Wales. At the coronation in 1953, the total Welsh contingent of 361 officers was under the command of the Deputy Chief Constable of Gwynedd, Superintendent Griffith William Roberts. Of this number at least fifty represented north Wales including two women police officers, one of whom was Mair Elizabeth Jones, stationed at Colwyn Bay. Later, ninety-one officers including forty-nine special constables were recipients of the Coronation Medal. At the Royal Review of police in Hyde Park on 14 July 1954, at least sixty-three officers represented north Wales including one woman police officer Margaret Lorraine Evans, stationed at Wrexham.

[102] T.A. Critchley, op. cit., p.267. This was the fifth Royal Commission on the police in the whole history of the police. The others being in 1839, 1855, 1906 and 1929.

[103] Robert Reiner, op. cit., p.74.

[104] Ibid.

[105] Ibid.

[106] Cmd, 1,728, (May, 1962).

[107] T.A. Critchley, op. cit., p.286.

[108] Richard Cowley, 'Police under Scrutiny: The Inspectors of Constabulary 1856-1990', *Journal of the Police Historiy Society*, No. 11, (1996), pp.25-30, in which he reports that in 1962 Sir William Johnson was appointed to become the first Chief Inspector of Constabulary. Whether he actually took up his office is debatable as other records show that Edward Dodd was appointed Chief Inspector in 1963.

[109] T.A. Critchley, op. cit., p.287. The County and Borough Police Act, 1856 had limited the number of inspectors to three, but this limit had been removed and authority given to appoint a chief inspector by the police (His Majesty's Inspectors of Constabulary) Act, 1945.

[110] Ibid., p.288.

[111] Ibid., p.292. Sir Henry Willink was Master of Magdalen College, Cambridge, and a former minister in Churchill's wartime government. * There was a minority of members on the Commission, headed by Dr Goodheart, who favoured the outright nationalisation of the police.

[112] Ibid.

[113] Ibid., p.295.

[114] Clive Emsley, *The English Police a Political and Social History*, (London, 1966), p.174.

[115] Ibid.

[116] Gwynedd Police Authority, 28 October 1966.

[117] *Police Review*, 13 March 1967.

[118] Ibid., 26 May 1967 and *CDH*, 15 September 1967 also *Police Review*, 4 September 1964. Mr William Stansfield succeeded Mr A.M. Rees, as chief constable of Denbighshire in 1964.

[119] Ibid., 12 August 1967 and *CDH*, 10 February 1967.

[120] Ibid., 18 August 1967.

[121] Ibid., 22 September 1967.

[122] Ibid., 12 January 1968.

[123] Ibid., 23 February 1968. The other officers on the shortlist were Chief Superintendent S. Agnew, Liverpool and Bootle Police; Chief Superintendent K.F. Clarke, Gloucestershire Constabulary; Mr John St David Jones, ACC, Gwynedd Constabulary and Chief Superintendent C.D. Vaughan, Hertfordshire Constabulary.

[124] Ibid., 27 October 1967. The other applicants were Chief Superintendent W.H. Davies, Liverpool and Bootle Police; Superintendent H.S. Edwards, Gwynedd; Superintendent J.E. Evans, Gwynedd; Chief Superintendent H.B. Jones, Gwynedd; Superintendent K.G. Lee, Glamorgan Constabulary and Chief Inspector E.R.M. Thomas, Metropolitan Police.

[125] Ibid., 3 November 1967 and *CDH*, 3 November 1967.

[126] Gwynedd Police Authority, 5 May 1967.

[127] Ibid.

[128] Chief Constable's Annual Report 1969. There were 2,366 police officers from sixteen forces on duty at the investiture.

[129] Ibid. * Although the 1960s were in many ways memorable years for members of the Gwynedd Constabulary, 1961 was a year tinged with much sadness. For on the night of 3 August, Constable Arthur Rees Rowlands was shot and blinded whilst confronting a suspect on Dyfi Bridge, Machynlleth. For his bravery he was later awarded the George Medal. See Gwynedd Police Authority, 3 November 1961; two made by Mr Justice

Hinchcliffe at the trial of John Boynton on 6 October 1961.

[130] Chief Constable's Annual Report 1969.

[131] Ibid., 1971.

[132] Ibid.

[133] Ibid., 1973.

[134] Ibid.

[135] From information kindly supplied by North Wales Police.

[136] Chief Constable's Annual Report, 1975.

[137] Ibid., earlier in the year on 29 January 1974, the Gwynedd Constabulary was given the Freedom of the Borough at Colwyn Bay.

## Chapter XI

# The North Wales Police, 1974-2000

Presenting his annual report to the newly elected members of the North Wales Police Authority on 31 March 1975, the chief constable, Mr Philip Myers, expressed concern about the high incidence of crime within the force area.[1] In expressing this concern, he was not alone, others were equally worried by what they saw as an unacceptable level of violence. Therefore, before examining the position of the police in north Wales during the 1970s, one must look at the way crime was escalating elsewhere.

Writing in a Sunday newspaper, Ernest Millen, former Deputy Assistant Commissioner at New Scotland Yard, suggested a number of reasons why criminal activity was rife. In his opinion, the so-called 'Permissive Society' had run riot.[2] He also believed, that on the one hand there was the vicious and senseless hooliganism of the 'Skin Head' brigade, whilst on the other, there was the 'soaring activity of the dedicated professional criminal'.[3] There was also a tendency for many criminals to be greedy and materialistic, a factor which in his view 'often accompanied a prosperous society'.[4] This was an opinion that a little later was to be echoed by Mr John Alderson, chief constable of Devon and Cornwall, when he stated: 'It is because of man's appetite, for materialism and for the acquisition of goods, that the society of his creation has organic characteristics of a criminogenic nature; in other words it causes crime by its very existence'.[5] Continuing his observations on the criminal, the chief constable went on to relate that: 'the possession of stealable property, cars, household goods, credit cards and so on, not only brings social status, but also makes the thief. Status is increasingly becoming not so much what we are, but what we have'.[6]

A correspondent writing in the *Liverpool Echo* about dangers posed by criminality, felt that the threat to society from muggings, assault and robbery with violence had never been greater.[7] Expressing a similar opinion the Police Superintendents' Association of England and Wales when they met in June 1974 warned that, if the trend to commit crime was allowed to continue, anarchy would prevail.[8] Delegates to the conference were also concerned by a reported suggestion by the former Lord Chancellor, Lord Gardiner, that the time may well have come, 'to have a national police force under a Minister of Justice'.[9] In the opinion of the members of the Association, such an idea would ultimately lead 'to a midnight knock, the gun and lack of public support'.[10] In their belief that anarchy might well occur, delegates were conscious of the miners' strike of 1972, particularly the events at the Saltley Coke Depot in February of that year, when 800 police officers faced 3,000 picketing miners, who had repeated attempts to close the gates thus preventing lorries from either entering or leaving the works.[11] They were also aware of the violence that erupted at a demonstration organised by members of the National Front in Red Lion Square, London, on 15 June 1974, when the police were subjected to a savage attack by members of a rival faction, the International Marxist Group.[12] As a result of the violence fifty-four people were injured, forty-six of whom were police officers. Sadly, a student, in no way a participant in the violence, was killed.[13]

At a meeting of the Police Superintendent's Association in Blackpool in September 1975, when the Home Secretary, Mr Merlyn Rees was in attendance, Chief Superintendent John Wilkinson called for the end of the activities of the 'do-gooders, reformers and certain politicians who helped the criminal, handicapped the police and left the public to suffer'.[14] He believed that law and order was rapidly breaking down and the police were the last to be consulted by reformers.[15] In his view the reformers seemed: 'obsessed with the so-called rights of criminals'.[16] The chief superintendent was extremely critical of the Bail Act of 1976, which came into being as a result of considerable activity by pressure groups calling for reform. The Bill, it seemed, had the effect of frustrating the police and making many officers wonder whether it was worth risking life and limb to arrest violent criminals. In fact, there were numerous reports of criminals on bail committing fresh and sometimes even more serious offences.[17] Writing a little later on the problems created by granting bail, the chief constable of Devon and Cornwall claimed there was a vested interest on the part of the authorities in allowing bail, as the process eased the pressure on the prison service.[18]

It was at this conference, that delegates expressed their disgust at the methods used by many politicians to interfere with the operational control of the police. According to many, the police had more than their fair share of problems without 'constantly defending their position against minor politicians obsessed with a desire for power, a power which can so easily be used in the wrong way if it is taken out of unbiased hands'.[19] In his address to the conference, and hopefully dispelling many fears, the Home Secretary stated that nothing he believed that was more important than the independence of the police service. It would in his opinion 'be a fateful day when the police came under political control, be it local or central'.[20] Adding further to this belief, Mr Rees went on to state that what he wanted was a police service, that is the servant under the law, 'not of a particular government but of society as a whole'.[21]

Addressing a conference at Olympia in London in April 1978, Mr James Anderton, the tough and often outspoken chief constable of the Greater Manchester Police, called for the early establishment of a central crime prevention agency. In his analysis of crime, he believed it was the 'biggest and fastest growing empire in the world, and therefore it was essential that a corporate approach to its prevention was overdue'.[22] Looking to the future, he was strongly of the opinion that the police should shelve their reluctance to give advice and information to firms wishing to improve their security measures. Not to do so was a complete waste of knowledge, experience and expertise. Informing delegates about the growth of crime, the chief constable gave the following figures: in 1900 there were 77,934 recorded crimes; by 1976 the figure had reached 2,135,713.[23] In the same period, convictions rose from 45,259 to 415,471. The number of indictable offences per 100,000 of population in 1976, was four times as high as the figure twenty years previously.[24]

Speaking to members of the security industry at the Café Royale in London in October 1978, Sir Robert Mark, who had recently retired as Commissioner of the Metropolitan Police, believed that a terrible spectre of a Britain virtually defenceless against crimes of burglary, break-in offences and theft had arisen.[25] He was convinced that governments and their police forces could no longer protect people against these offences, certainly in the larger cities. It was time, he believed, to explain frankly 'that each and every citizen must assume the primary responsibility for protecting his own property'.[26] Known for his forthright manner, Sir Robert claimed that recent governments and elements in the legal profession had done much to help the breakdown of law and order. In fact, every change in the law over legal procedures and policy, since 1967, had been favourable to the wrongdoers.[27] According to Sir Robert: 'arrogance, incompetence and prejudice in our legislators, matched only by their failure to research, to consult those who have to enforce and administer the legislation, was the pattern for criminal laws in the 1970s. Serious crime, including armed robbery and even murder, while on bail, had become, through the folly of the government, an increasingly accepted fact of life, as in the United States'.[28] Finally, the system of criminal justice, was, in his opinion, so loaded against conviction of the guilty, that acquittals of criminals had been a powerful encouragement to commit further crime.[29]

Sir Robert's observations painted a depressing picture of a Britain where the growth of crime had become almost unacceptable. Neither was he alone in voicing such views. Experienced chief constables, like James Anderton and John Alderson, and indeed countless others also expressed their alarm. Crime in the seventies was costing Britain's taxpayers more than £500 million a year, yet, it was estimated, that seven out of every ten, of all crimes committed, remained unsolved.[30] It was, therefore, against a background of escalating crime, social disorder and a police service that in many quarters had become despondent, that officers in the newly named North Wales Police Authority confronted in 1974, their ever increasing responsibilities. True, crime within the counties was not as high as in other areas in Britain, nevertheless the mere fact it was rising was a reminder to the authorities that they had to be constantly alert in order to minimise the dangers posed by increasing acts of criminality. Some indication of the number of indictable offences committed in north Wales between 1972-80 is seen in the following table:

### Table 10.1[31]
### Number of Indictable Offences 1972-80

| Year | Reported Crime | Number Substantiated | Detection Rate |
| --- | --- | --- | --- |
| 1972 | 19,777 | 18,956 | 52.8% |
| 1973 | 18,609 | 17,968 | 50.8% |
| 1974 | 22,443 | 21,856 | 58.2% |
| 1975 | 22,600 | 21,950 | 51.3% |
| 1976 | 22,776 | 22,175 | 54.3% |

| 1977 | 26,168 | 25,552 | 56.8% |
| 1978 | 24,121 | 23,562 | 57.6% |
| 1979 | 23,021 | 22,445 | 59.1% |
| 1980 | 23,458 | 22,872 | 53.7% |
|  | 202,973* | 197,336 | Average 51.6% |

* The difference in the figures for reported crime and that which is substantiated, is due to the fact that a number of crimes, on being investigated, were classified under Home Office guidelines 'no crimes'.

Out of a total of 197,336 substantiated offences, which occurred between 1972-80, 127,557 (64.63 per cent) were against property and no violence was used. Where violence against property occurred there were 48,353 such offences (24.5 per cent). Violence against a person over this period amounted to 11,299 (5.7 per cent), the most serious of these being murder, of which there were 42 (6.37 per cent), rape 159 (1.4 per cent), indecent assault on females 1,199 (10.6 per cent) and malicious wounding and assault 8,182 (74.4 per cent).[32] Violence against the person was not restricted to members of the general public. Over this same period 817 attacks were made on officers whilst executing their duties, the worst year being 1976, when 1,123 were assaulted.[33]

As crime increased it was inevitable that the number of officers employed in the Criminal Investigation Department rose accordingly. For example, on 31 December 1974 the number of officers employed in the department, which was headed by a chief superintendent, stood at 136, five of whom were women.[34] There were, however, occasions when the number employed in any one year fluctuated, this was due to officers being seconded, as in 1980, when forty uniformed men, spent up to three months, as aides to the Criminal Investigation Department. The three month attachments were used by senior officers in order to assess potential detective officers.[35] Throughout the 1970s many officers were also sent to various police centres such as Wakefield, Birmingham, Liverpool, Hendon and Bristol which specialised in a particular branch of detective work.[36] Sometimes it was the work of female officers that brought a successful conclusion to a particular case. Detailing a summary of the type of work undertaken by such officers for the benefit of his police committee, the chief constable listed the following.

Table 10.2 [37]
Duties Undertaken by Female Officers 1974

| | |
|---|---:|
| Number of crimes dealt with | 1,796 |
| Number of arrests made | 441 |
| Number of offences etc. | 2,244 |
| Number of care and protection cases | 2 |
| Number of reports sent to and consultations with social services | 389 |
| Number of hours spent on observations and enquiries in connection with drugs | 164 |
| Number of hours spent on observations and enquiries regarding indecency offences | 1,202 |

The actual strength of women police in 1974 stood at fifty-eight, which included one superintendent, two inspectors, four sergeants and fifty-one constables. The establishment of the force also provided for four women police constables to be engaged on motor patrol duties and five women detective constables (including one woman detective constable in the drugs branch). During 1974 a number of policewomen also worked with the Criminal Investigation Department and with the No. 1 Regional Crime Squad on enquiring and observations. In addition, women officers also gave a number of talks to various organisations during the year, on 'The Police as a Career'. They also delivered a number of lectures on the law, which related to children and young persons, at courses which were held at police headquarters in Colwyn Bay.[38]

Recruitment, especially in the large cities like London and Manchester was proving extremely difficult in the 1970s. In the capital, the shortage of officers was so serious that the Commissioner, Sir Robert Mark, had to admit that a large number of criminal offences received only a cursory investigation. Although anxious not to alarm members of the public, he maintained that crimes that involved personal injury or robbery were always fully investigated.[39] Fortunately, in north Wales there was no shortage of applicants during the 1970s. If one examines the three years, 1977, 1979 and 1980 as an example, there were 113, 553 and 801 applicants respectively. To some extent, rising unemployment probably accounted for the increased number applying in 1980. However, despite the large number of applicants in the latter year, only fifty-three were eventually accepted into the force, thus illustrating the high standard expected from those who were successful. Those who failed to gain entrance, were seen either as generally unsuitable for police work, or unable to reach the requisite medical or educational standard required. North Wales was also fortunate in the numbers that applied to be special constables. In his report for 1975, Mr Myers, the chief constable, praised them for their work throughout the year, stating that members of the special constabulary assisted their regular colleagues at every available opportunity.[40] In his report to the police committee a year later, he provided members with the following table, which indicated the Regular/Special Constable ratio in north Wales as compared with other forces in the region:

| Force | Strength of Force | Strength of S.C. [41] |
|---|---|---|
| South Wales | 2,962 | 423 |
| Dyfed Powys | 912 | 180 |
| Gwent | 950 | 350 |
| North Wales | 1,238 | 585 |

During 1976, members of the special constabulary worked a total of 10,891 hours.

Never satisfied that a sufficient number of officers were out patrolling the streets, the chief constable continued, whenever possible, to pursue a policy of civilianising some work by following recommendations laid down by the Home Office as early as the mid 1940s. The chronic shortage of police officers in some areas led to the Home Office encouraging all police authorities and chief constables to 'explore ways of concentrating limited resources of manpower on duties which policemen are uniquely qualified to perform'.[42] An early result was a sustained drive to replace police officers, by civilians with clerical or tradesmen's qualifications, on indoor duties where police training and experience or the authority of a police officer was not required.[43] Later, in February 1965, the Police Federation published a paper entitled *'The Problem'*, which highlighted the fact that the main concern facing the police service was the shortage of manpower and which called for many police duties to be undertaken by a strengthened civilian support structure and an expanded corps of traffic wardens.[44] That the policy of civilianising the police proved successful was confirmed by the following figures: between 1949-59 the numbers engaged went up from 3,881 to 8,082 and by 1975, the number had increased to 20,000 thus releasing many policemen for patrol duties as a consequence.[45]

The number of civilians employed in the North Wales Police rose from 250 in 1972 to 280 in 1980. Most civilians at this time, were either employed as typists, clerks or communications

operators.[46] During the same period, the number of traffic wardens remained static at fifty-nine. On appointment traffic wardens received training in the following: [47]
 a. Functions of traffic wardens.
 b. Relevant local orders and regulations.
 c. Evidence including visits to magistrates courts.
 d. Methods of patrolling with visits to beats and practical exercises.
 e. Instruction in the use of pocket books and various forms with practical exercises.
 f. Correct method of dealing with the public.
 g. Traffic control.

On the whole, the police in north Wales, entered the 1980s with a certain degree of confidence, knowing that although crime had increased it had at least been contained. There were areas, however, that the force viewed as being wholly unacceptable, for example, the number of violent attacks on the person each year, including those made on officers whilst executing their duties. If officers felt at times that they were not appreciated, they were comforted by the fact that between 1975-80 the chief constable received from members of the public, 2,207 letters of appreciation, as against 1,218 from those who complained.[48] Every complaint was fully investigated and if there was doubt about a particular case, it was submitted to the Director of Public Prosecutions, in order to obtain an independent decision. In many instances where a complaint had been laid against an officer or officers, later investigation found that in the majority of cases there were no grounds upon which to proceed.

Presenting the annual report for 1981, to members of the North Wales Police Committee, Mr David Owen, who was appointed on 1 April to succeed Mr Philip Myers as chief constable, praised the work of his predecessor and stated that it was his firm intention to continue the excellent work and uphold reputation of the force.[49] From the outset, the newly appointed chief constable placed great emphasis on the importance of training. Indeed, the training programme for 1981 and 1982, was not only extensive, but also diversified. The innovations of previous years were seen as important and, therefore, were continued and refresher courses for constables and sergeants was substantially increased. Greater use was made of the accommodation available and during the year a total of 874 officers attended a wide variety of courses at headquarters.[50] Neither were senior ranks excluded from training and all officers of superintendent or chief superintendent rank attended a two-day seminar at headquarters. Here the aim was to furnish officers with new developments and allow them to take part in discussions on the many problems that faced the police service in the 1980s.[51]

One area where training was essential, was that provided by the Police Support Unit or PSU, which prepared officers to deal with spontaneous disorders whenever they occurred. The one-day courses resulted in a total of 360 officers being trained over the year.[52] Instruction in the use of firearms was also considered an important part of policing in the 1980s. In September 1981, the force appointed a full-time firearms officer; it was obviously a sign of the times and the policing of Britain was in the process of witnessing great change. As a result of such training, the police in north Wales had eighty officers who were fully trained in the use of weapons.[53] There is little doubt that in preparing officers for any eventuality that might arise, the authorities were fully aware of the tremendous problems the police had faced during the serious rioting in Liverpool, Manchester and London in 1981.[54] In 1982, officers attending courses at headquarters were each issued with a riot helmet and informed that at a later date they would also be provided with shin guards and fire extinguishers.[55] During the summer of 1983, new public order tactics in the event of riots had been devised and detailed in a *Tactical Options Manual* which had been examined and approved by the Home Secretary, the use of which was strictly confined to 270 of the most senior police officers in Britain.[56] The fact that so much secrecy surrounded the reading of the manual, led to a belief in some circles that the police might well be on the road to becoming a paramilitary organisation.[57] That such tactical measures were necessary was borne out during the miners' strike of 1984-85, when hundreds of pickets were confronted by numerous lines of police officers, who were organised and equipped very differently from the time of the dispute at Saltley in 1972.[58]

In a newspaper report on the training methods adopted by the police in north Wales, it was suggested that the use of firearms had become a routine element in the policing of Gwynedd and Clwyd in the late 1980s and that a fifth of the force could be assembled in 'sophisticated riot gear at very short notice'.[59] Such a situation was clearly a sad, hitherto hidden and perhaps shocking reality of the declining standards in social behaviour. Commenting on the situation, Chief Inspector Brian Adams, head of the Force's Operational Unit, formed in 1986, hoped he would never see a situation in which his men would be deployed on the streets of north Wales in riot clothing.[60] The chief inspector had under his command 240 officers specially trained to Home Office guidelines, for quelling public disorder, as well as eighty-two firearms specialists. Each officer had to decide when and how to use his gun in any future confrontation. It was a great responsibility. Apart from frequent periods of refresher training, the specialists continued to perform their regular duties on the beat 'quite indistinguishable from their colleagues'.[61]

Apart from the skirmishes at Wrexham and Point of Ayr collieries, north Wales did not experience the rioting that was witnessed elsewhere during the 1980s. Nevertheless, officers were faced in some ways with a more frightening situation in having to deal with an unseen enemy – the arsonist who seemingly had the ability to strike where and when a suitable occasion presented itself. Reporting to his police committee, Mr David Owen, expressed his continuing concern about arson attacks directed at second homes. Since 1978, fifty-eight houses had either been destroyed or badly damaged and he believed it was just a matter of time before somebody perished in a blaze.[62] Later, in a newspaper article in 1983, the chief constable again expressed his mounting concern, even dismay, at the absence of condemnatory remarks from some leading figures in society and asked 'is it too much to expect those who, lead and represent our society clearly to condemn such criminal behaviour'.[63] He believed that though such condemnation might not actually prevent further attacks, it would certainly give support to the faint hearted who might wish to help the police and deter the misguided idealist.[64] Five years later in 1988, Mr Owen was even more concerned, for he believed the arsonists were becoming increasingly vicious.[65] A newspaper article written in 1992, reporting on the arson campaign of the 1980s fully concurred with the chief constable's earlier remarks. The campaign, led by shadowy figures in a movement which called itself 'Meibion Glyndŵr', had towards the end of the 1980s, become somewhat more vicious and complex. Attacks became more indiscriminate, with bombs being placed under cars, in yachts and on the doorsteps of government buildings. Letter bombs had also been sent to Members of Parliament, including one in June 1990, to David Hunt, Secretary of State for Wales.[66]

Although by the late 1980s, eighteen cottage arsonists had been convicted, the chief constable was convinced that the majority seemed to be sheltering 'behind double standards in certain sections of Welsh society'.[67] What made the task of the police in north Wales even more difficult was the fact that a national opinion poll carried out in the Welsh-speaking areas for HTV, at the height of the campaign, registered 57 per cent support for the bombers' aims, the preservation of the culture and language – if not the means. In Dwyfor, by far the strongest Welsh-speaking area, support was as high as 85 per cent.[68] It was a problem, as the chief constable freely admitted, that the police could not solve on their own.[69]

The lack of co-operation with the police by certain sections of the community during the arson campaign in north Wales, was one also experienced by officers in other forces, whenever they dealt with issues that in many instances were of a particularly sensitive nature. It was to overcome this reluctance to co-operate that led to the appointment of press and public relations officers in a number of forces throughout the United Kingdom during the 1970s and 1980s. Initially, not all police press officers were viewed as helpful by the media, and sometimes, reporters believed that such officers 'far from stimulating the flow of information to the press, were more interested in suppressing it'.[70] Yet, as many were later to concede, public relations with the police were much more than 'a matter of creating a shining branch image through the press'.[71] It was, and still is, essential for the police to seek a close rapport with all sections of the community, particularly with those who out of choice belong to no particular organisation and therefore, generally, have little interest in civic matters, for in the final analysis, it is their opinion that becomes important.[72] Recognising the importance of communicating with the media, led the chief constable to appoint in November 1982, an inspector to serve as the Force's press and public relations officer. According to Mr Owen, such an appointment was most necessary if the Force was to maintain a constant relationship between the police and the media generally, as experience elsewhere had demonstrated that a balanced approach to the two-way process was vital in the interests of all concerned, not least the community who relied on the media for accurate information.[73]

In fact, so successful was the work undertaken by the press and public relations office, that in March 1986, an equally important development in the Force came with the establishment of the Community Liaison Department. This department, from the outset, was administratively controlled from Force headquarters and functional operationally through the Divisional Community Liaison Teams based at each of the four Divisional Headquarters which were: [74]

'A' Division: (Chief Superintendent D.M.I. Griffiths), an area of geographical contrasts, which included the island of Anglesey, and, on the mainland, most of the old county of Caernarfon including the Llŷn Peninsula.

'B' Division: (Chief Superintendent Glyn Roberts), geographically the largest Division in the north Wales police area, comprising as it does 240,091 hectares stretching from the northern coastal strip down the Dyfi estuary. The indigenous population is only some 135,000 but this is increased, many times over, during the holiday season.

'C' Division: (Chief Superintendent J.G. Vickery), covers the Local Authority areas of Rhuddlan, Delyn and Alun and Deeside and is basically the whole of the old county of Flint, apart from the Maelor District, which is now part of 'D' Division. The Division is split into three Sub-Divisions which cover very contrasting areas – i.e. Rhuddlan Sub-Division with headquarters at Rhyl – Deeside Sub-Division with headquarters at Connah's Quay and the adjacent Mold Sub-Division with its headquarters at Mold.

'D' Division: (Chief Superintendent David Thomas), encompasses the Wrexham Maelor and Glyndŵr Administrative areas, together with two very small portions of Colwyn Borough of Trefnant and Pentrefoelas. The Division is divided into two Sub-Divisions, located at Wrexham and Ruabon, which have greatly contrasting geographical, environmental and attendant policing features. Established in March 1986, the Community Liaison Department is headed by a superintendent with overall responsibility for Crime Prevention, Press and Public Relations, liaison with local authorities, voluntary organisations, professional bodies and other similar organisations and more latterly for an Inter-Agency Unit, which was inaugurated on 1 November 1988.[75]

The primary objectives in the liaison role for the Department personnel can be summarised as follows:

- a. To encourage good community relations practices by all members of the force.
- b. To enhance consultation with local communities and to maintain a close liaison with relevant organisations, both statutory and voluntary, as well as the fostering of grass-roots contact with all sections of the public.
- c. To explain to the community the role of the police in society – and in particular, to explain about resources and commitments and what the public can realistically expect from the police: conversely, to explain what the

police feel entitled to expect from the local community.
  d. To train and advise police officers with a view to creating a better individual understanding of the nature and composition of the communities which they serve.
  e. To co-ordinate existing and future divisional efforts in the field of community relations by combining the work of the Crime Prevention Sergeant, School Liaison Officers and Accident Prevention Officers to form a divisional team for community based liaison.
  f. To initiate ideas regarding community involvement which can be utilised in the Divisions.
  g. To ensure that liaison and professional working relationships between police and the relevant agencies involved in dealing with child abuse, women victims of crime and juvenile offenders are of the highest of standards.

In furtherance of the above departmental objectives and community liaison activities – many of which were initiated by the Department at Headquarters, officers of all ranks have continued over the years to increase their involvement in community affairs. Visits to schools and youth clubs included the provision of literature on police related subjects, as well as talks and discussions on a wide variety of issues. Much thought has also gone into the design and production of literature that specifically meets the needs of the north Wales area and this is now freely available in Welsh, English or bilingually.[76]

One area where the police considered it vital to have good communications with the general public was that of road safety. During the 1970s and 1980s, successive chief constables made repeated warnings, particularly to the parents of young children and the elderly, of the dangers posed by the rapid increase in road transport. Such warnings were based on the evidence that between 1970-88, 144,133 road accidents occurred in the north Wales area, of which 1,649 proved fatal.[77] It was to reduce this unacceptable level of accidents and loss of life, that the police introduced a strict road safety policy, whereby, every school attended by children between the ages of five and eleven were visited at least twice in any one year, so as to alert them to the dangers that existed on the roads of north Wales.[78]

Delivering his annual report to the Police Committee in 1984, the chief constable spoke of his concern about the number of road accidents which occurred each year 'seemingly without anyone paying any heed – save the grieving relatives or those who nursed the injured'.[79] Mr Owen believed that it was absolutely essential that his officers operated a strong enforcement policy on road safety which was 'specifically directed at those who cannot accept their fundamental responsibility as vehicle drivers'.[80] It was to press home the importance of road safety that the Force's road traffic officers spent a great deal of their time attending numerous functions so as to display road safety material, yet, despite the many publicity campaigns the police continued to be concerned.

In 1989, the *Liverpool Daily Post* ran a series of articles on the dangers of drinking and driving. Speaking to reports on the subject, the chief constable stated, 'we don't operate a special Christmas campaign against drinking and driving – our vigilance is daily throughout the year'.[81] In an article about the Government's Christmas campaign, the newspaper accused ministers of failing to produce a formula for dealing with drink-driving and was of the opinion that the only remedy was to bring in roadside check point random breath tests as the only effective deterrent.[82] Yet, despite the many calls for legislation, the Home Office amazingly did not consider regulated testing as the answer, believing instead that there should be: [83]

a. No change in police powers.
b. Consolidation of existing powers.
c. Unfettered discretion given to traffic police to test as they considered necessary. However, unfettered discretion given to the traffic police to test as they considered was necessary faced strong opposition because it did not insist that tests were made and, therefore, could be open to abuse by the police.

As the police in north Wales entered the 1990s, the chief constable still concerned, stated in his report that despite all the vigilance, there were no grounds for relaxation in the strict policy adopted by the Force towards those who continue to drink and drive.[84] It was to curb excessive speeding, often by drink-drivers, that the Force made wide use of unmarked police vehicles along with associated technology such as videos, radar and 'vascar' speed devices.[85] Speaking from experience, Superintendent Clive Macgregor, head of the North Wales Traffic Unit who had over the years witnessed the carnage created by traffic accidents, believed it was the duty of members of the public to report to the police, those who drove under the influence of drink.[86]

In their policing plan for 1997 and 1998, the police still maintained that safety on the roads of north Wales was a high priority for the Force. No matter how successful traffic operations strategies had been in the recent past, there were still too many people being killed or injured. Therefore, the Force intended to further enhance its ability to scan and analyse road traffic incident data in partnership with the unitary authorities. It was the intention of the Force to pin-point in future, accident blackspots, which would enable intelligence-led traffic operations to be targeted appropriately and certainly more swiftly. In short, the Force remains resolute in its belief that excessive speed, drinking and driving and lack of appropriate supervision of the vulnerable on the roads of north Wales continues to be the cause of most road accidents and as such, must at all times be positively addressed.[87]

In recognising that the number of road accidents was unacceptable, the police were also keenly aware that they were about to confront a more sinister situation with the rise in offences relating to drug misuse, particularly by the young. What alerted the officers to the problem in the late 1960s was the number of burglary offences committed at pharmacies and drug wholesalers within the Force area.[88] It was to meet this new threat that the then Gwynedd Constabulary established a Drugs Branch, in 1971.[89] By 1 April 1974, the Branch was increased and consisted of one detective inspector, one detective sergeant and four detective constables, one of whom was a female officer.[90] During the early years, cannabis and LSD were the predominant substances of abuse, although there was no real problem at this time in north Wales. In fact, between 1974-80, the annual figures for drug related offences never reached 400, with 1976 being the worst year with 382 offences recorded, 244 of which involved the unlawful possession of cannabis.[91]

However, if the authorities considered the problem of drugs was under control, their confidence was soon shaken by the events of the 1980s. For the first time the number of drug offences topped the 400 mark, when 405 were reported in 1981.[92] Two years later in 1983, 658 offences were recorded, twenty-five of which involved the use of heroin.[93] In view of the fact that in 1973 only 238 drug offences were recorded by the police, the figure for 1983 was disappointing and showed an increase of 176 per cent in a matter of only ten years. According to the chief constable, 'those who contribute most to the abuse of drugs are the suppliers, or pedlars or pushers, who have little or no regard about the potential dangers to others'.[94] So alarmed were the various authorities in north Wales, that in late 1984 the Gwynedd Drugs Council was formed under the chairmanship of the bishop of Bangor.[95] To add to everyone's concern, Dr Cedric Davies, the Gwynedd chief medical officer, was of the opinion, 'that it could also be taken for granted that the number of users was far in excess of the number of cases that had come to the attention of the police'.[96]

In an article, in the *Liverpool Daily Post*, which focused on the drug problem in north Wales, Detective Inspector Humphreys, head of the Drug Squad, which in 1988 had a complement of fourteen officers and two dogs, claimed that heroin addiction had become a matter of great concern for his officers in Deeside, presumably, he believed, as a result of close proximity to Liverpool and Manchester.[97] Holyhead, at the western extremity of north Wales, also had the same problem, which again might have been due to the large influx of people passing through the port each year from Dublin, a known and notorious heroin centre.[98] In the same newspaper, a year later, Mr Owen, the chief constable had an even more chilling message for readers, when he feared that the 'fiercely-addictive crack', the most deadly form of cocaine would soon reach his area.[99] On a fact finding mission to the United States, he had been informed, 'that it only took three smokes to make one an addict for life'.[100]

As the police in north Wales entered the 1990s their relentless campaign against drug misuse continued unabated. Evidence that the problem had not eased, despite the combined efforts of the police, social workers, teachers and church leaders, was highlighted in 1995 when Councillor Hugh Roberts of Barmouth, informed the chief constable, Mr Michael Argent, that every drug from cannabis to cocaine was obtainable in the town.[101] A similar situation also existed in Dwyfor. Constable Ian Williams, the community liaison officer, reported that in 1993, fifty people were arrested for drug related offences but by 1994 the figure had more than doubled and had reached 111.[102] Calling for parents to take a more active role in detecting whether their children were taking drugs, Constable Williams expressed his disappointment that at a meeting convened at Ysgol Glan y Môr, Pwllheli, on drug abuse, only thirty parents out of the school's 580 pupils were present.[103]

In Anglesey, at Llangefni, the drug problem had become so serious that the police supported a plan drawn up by the council and local shopkeepers to install close circuit television cameras in the town centre, particularly in Bulkeley Square, which had become notorious for some suppliers openly selling drugs.[104] As late as August 1998, the chief constable, pleased with the general reduction of crime, had to admit 'that the prevalence of illegal drugs showed little sign of abating, although the force had successfully seized during the year drugs valued at £1.4 million on the streets'.[105] More worrying for the authorities was the Home Office report which stated that heroin abuse was on the increase, and although most new users were described as 'socially deprived', there were clear signs that heroin was also beginning to be used by young people from the more affluent sections of society who were in stable jobs.[106]

Finally, as one of their policing policies for 1998-99 the police in north Wales reiterated that they would, at all times, continue to place considerable emphasis on the enforcement of drugs legislation as part of their comprehensive strategy for tackling the problem. This strategy reflected their belief that only diligent law enforcement disrupts the illegal drugs market, whereby those they arrest for the unlawful possession of drugs, would act as a deterrent and eventually reduce the demand for drugs.[107] In furtherance of this policing strategy, the chief constable appointed seven officers to act as full-time Drug Prevention Officers across the Force area. Their task was to develop initiatives in partnership with other agencies, which it was hoped would further curtail the evil drug trade.[108]

Although much time and effort was devoted by the Force to the problem of drugs, officers were no less active in their determination to curb and contain other forms of criminality. Crime in the 1980s, as elsewhere, was on the increase in north Wales and this called for the police to be extremely vigilant. In his report to the police authority in 1982, the chief constable informed members, that, 'crime seemed to be the only growth industry in present day society'.[109] He reported that there were significant increases in wounding and assaults, burglary, robbery and thefts from vehicles. In his opinion, such offences augured badly for the future and he believed it was extremely difficult for the police alone to control the situation.[110] Adding to his concern he went on 'that unless society in general assists us in all ways possible to combat these trends then the picture was not rosy'.[111] It was to meet this disturbing trend that the chief constable announced that he was to expand and develop the role of crime prevention officers to the full.[112] It was no easy task, for in 1975, the Chief Inspector of Constabulary, in his report, stated: 'the sad fact emerges that more and more people are behaving dishonestly each year and are seemingly prepared to break the law to get what they want – indeed it can be said that we shall not see an appreciable reduction over the whole field of crime unless there is a marked improvement in general standards of behaviour and honesty in the community at large'.[113]

Commenting on the increase in crime in 1983, the chief constable complimented officers on the improvement in the detection rate, although he was quick to point out that there 'was no room for complacency and greater attention had to be paid to the broader rate of crime prevention'.[114] In this field, he stated, the Force had sought at all times to involve the community in as positive a manner as possible. Furthermore, in order to achieve his objective he informed members of the police committee that he had appointed a full-time Crime Prevention Inspector at Headquarters, in order that a more co-ordinating role might be adopted between the Force and the public.[115] In addition, crime prevention panels had been formed and with a great deal of success, for they proved to be a valuable sounding board for regular consultations and ideas.[116] However, three years later, the chief constable had, sadly, to report that the number of crimes continued to rise, from 32,003 in 1985 to 33,817 in 1986, although such a rise was generally reflective of the situation nationally.[117] Of increasing concern to the Force during the 1980s was the number of violent attacks made on officers, and the chief constable called for the courts to be more protective. In 1984, sixty officers were assaulted, in 1985, seventy-six were subjected to attack and the number reached in 1986 was ninety-one. However, even these figures were dwarfed, when in 1987, 207 officers were attacked whilst on duty.[118]

It was to face the increase in violence generally, that the police in north Wales established what were known as Divisional Reserve Units. In effect, they were a mobile squad of officers who, at a moments notice, could be deployed to serious incidents such as public order situations, whenever and wherever they occurred. Six such units operated in the north Wales police area and, as the chief constable regretfully explained, 'their presence was more reminiscent of urban policing than styles normally associated with what is, in essence, a rural force'.[119] That there was a need for such units was a further sad reflection that times were changing and the police had little alternative but to adapt in order to meet what was perceived as a continuing threat to society.

In reviewing the performance of the Force during the 1980s, the assistant chief constable, Mr John Tecwyn Owen, concluded that the strategy adopted by the police had largely been successful, which, in his opinion, was due to the high level of industry and commitment by all the members of the Force.[120]

However, despite what appeared to be a successful decade, there was no time for officers to relax their vigilance. Although drug misuse and drink-driving were always at the forefront of their law enforcement strategy, two other areas of equal concern were the high level of thefts and burglaries, often with violence, and offences that were fast becoming a daily threat to public order.[121]

In the chief constable's report for 1991, Detective Chief Superintendent Gareth Jones, believed that burglary in the home had an effect on victims 'that far outweighed the cost of damage done or the value of property stolen'.[122] This view was borne out a year later when a newspaper article reported the experience of a lady, who, on having her home burgled felt 'the thieves had taken away her happiness, along with precious mementoes of her long life, and perhaps for all time her peace of mind'.[123] What, according to the superintendent, contributed greatly to the increase in this type of offence in north Wales, were the improvements in road communications, thus making the area more accessible and vulnerable to the activities of the travelling criminals. This fact was certainly true, and in the chief constable's report for 1989, the Conwy Valley, Llandudno and Kinmel Bay, were listed as areas where burglaries were particularly prevalent.[124] It was to reduce such burglaries, that the police resorted to operating unmarked crime cars on arterial roads which had the desired effect and resulted in a number of arrests being made.[125]

As a further move in the never-ending battle against crime, the Force, in 1992, purchased a helicopter, a decision not taken lightly. In fact, this was seen by many observers as a complete and utter waste of money, particularly when the authorities already had great difficulty in placing additional officers on the beat.[126] When asked for his opinion on the purchase, a former member of the Police Authority, Councillor Ronnie Madoc Jones said 'he was amazed at the decision'.[127] Commenting further, he believed it would have been better to have spent the money on putting more police feet on pavements'.[128] Explaining to those who doubted the wisdom of buying a helicopter, Chief Superintendent John Cooke stated that the aircraft could reach Dolgellau, Holyhead or Wrexham in a matter of fifteen minutes and added that other forces had operated helicopters: 'for many years extremely successfully and there was no reason at all to believe that it would not also be a success in north Wales'.[129] That his faith in the helicopter was justified came in the chief constable's report for 1993, where it is recorded that the machine had been deployed on 1,229 missions during the year. Of these 80 per cent were crime related and had resulted in the arrest of 240 offenders.[130]

It was not, however, the first time that officers in north Wales had taken to the air. In the chief constable's report for 1983, it is recorded that following an abortive 'smash and grab' raid by two male offenders in Holywell on 17 July 1983, Constable Goronwy Edwards of Buckley, a qualified amateur pilot, accompanied by Sergeant Barry Newman acting as his observer, used a light aircraft in their endeavour to trace the culprits. Although their search was unsuccessful, it illustrated the initiative of the officers in seeking those responsible for the attack.[131] Recognising the importance of a helicopter as the pressures on policing increased led the Police Authority to purchase a more modern and versatile machine which came into service on 31 March 1994.[132] That the Authority was in a position to make such an expensive purchase, stemmed from the receipt of a capital grant of £100,000 from the Home Office. This grant was, in effect, part of a process of encouraging and expanding air support nationally and which coincided with the development of the North West Air Consortium of forces that included Lancashire, Greater Manchester, Merseyside, Cheshire and North Wales, and had as its first chairman, the deputy chief constable, Mr John Tecwyn Owen.[133] However, never content and, whenever possible, always updating its technology, the force in February 1999 took delivery of an even more sophisticated helicopter – the Eurocopter EC 135.[134]

The police in north Wales entered the 1990s with a certain degree of confidence although it was freely admitted, that the high level of crime was still unacceptable. It was felt that greater attention had to be focussed on increasing public awareness of the importance of the crime prevention programmes that were available. For instance, since Neighbourhood Watch schemes were introduced into north Wales in the mid 1980s, greater emphasis seemed to have been placed on the 'growth in the number of householders participating in such schemes, than on the quality of the interaction between the police and the co-ordinators'.[135] Sadly, therefore, many schemes had become inactive and others at best could only be identified as 'stickers only' schemes.[136] In 1991, the police embarked on a campaign that was specifically aimed at changing the public's attitude towards crime and crime prevention generally. This approach was completely in line with the on-going Home Office crime prevention policy.[137] The clear objectives were to heighten the public's awareness, not only of what they could do to secure their homes and properties themselves, but also what they could and should do in the interests of others, particularly the elderly, who were likely to be affected by crime or the fear of crime.[138] That the police were successful in their efforts to expand the Neighbourhood Watch scheme was seen at the end of 1991, when it was recorded that 2,615 schemes were fully operational thus affording protection and care for 47,179 households.[139] By 1993 the number of schemes in operation had reached 2,989, therefore ensuring that 54,000 households would receive added protection. What officers found pleasing, was the fact that the number of schemes in operation in 1993, meant that more than twenty-one households in every hundred, were now protected by the system.[140]

That the police were anxious to see a reduction in crime, was illustrated when a survey conducted in Holyhead, revealed that one in six people were likely to be targeted by criminals.[141] The survey showed, that out of 1,660 people, 278 (17 per cent) were targeted by criminals during the year – ninety-two of them more than once.[142] Burglary, vandalism, serious assaults and threatening behaviour were top of the list.[143] With such frightening statistics, it was somewhat heartening for officers to learn, in April 1994, that the determined campaign to reduce the number of house burglaries in north Wales was beginning to show results.[144] In reporting the success of the campaign to the police authority, Mr John Tecwyn Owen, the acting chief constable informed members 'that the excellent results had not come about without a great deal of dedicated police work and the continuing support of the public'.[145]

In congratulating officers for their dedication, it is sometimes overlooked that a great deal of success in the reduction of crime levels, is often due to the work of the support units. For example, during the period 1 February 1994 to 31 March 1995, the Fingerprint Bureau, made a total of 1,043 identifications, mainly as the result of the computerised Automatic Fingerprint Recognition system, and many of those identified related to offenders residing outside the Force area, who would not have been identified using conventional methods.[146] Similarly, one must also recognise the work undertaken by scene-of-crime officers. This department provides a comprehensive scene examination service to the Force and staff are trained as operators of the computerised 'Electronic Facial Identification System', which assists greatly in the identification of criminal offenders.[147] One must not forget the excellent work provided by the Dog Section. During 1993 the section made 219 arrests and assisted in the arrest of a further 192 offenders.[148] In 1993 the section had fifteen handlers and twenty-one dogs which were deployed at Bodelwyddan, Wrexham and Menai Bridge. German Shepherds (Alsatians) are used for general purpose work, whilst Springer Spaniels are used for certain specialist functions; three for example are used for the detection of drugs, whilst a further five are trained to seek out explosives.[149]

All through the 1990s there had been constant concern expressed by members of the public in north Wales, about the high incidence of public disorder. In the chief constable's report for 1991, Chief Superintendent John Vickery, claimed that there were some difficult areas in his division, which required positive policing to prevent disorder erupting. What had helped, according to the chief superintendent, was the development of the 'Pub Watch' schemes, which were fully operational in the Rhyl and Deeside areas.[150] In the same report, Chief Superintendent David Rowley voiced his deep concern about the number of incidents within his area where firearms were used and cited two places, Wrexham and Gresford, where guns had been used during robberies.[151] On the use of firearms, it was revealed in 1992, that firearms were issued to police officers on forty occasions, as compared to thirty-eight issues in 1991. Twenty-five of the issues related to the criminal use or possession of firearms in such offences as armed robbery, murder and threats to kill, terrorism or drug offences.[152]

In his report to the Police Authority in 1992, Mr David Owen informed members that the discovery of a bomb factory in Llangefni was certainly a success. Literature which ranged from a Meibion Glyndŵr 'hit list' to IRA terrorism was also found on the premises. His report then called upon the general public not to underestimate for one moment the potential of the bombs to cause serious injury or death.[153] In addressing members of the Authority, the chief constable also called upon certain sections of Welsh life to consider carefully their views and attitudes, for he believed that those who contemplated usurping the democratic processes 'had no real or legitimate support'.[154] Mr Owen was also worried about the mass vigilante protest at Newborough in Anglesey against the amount of crime and vandalism in the area.[155] In fact, their protest might well have had the support of Mr John Redwood, Secretary of State for Wales, who when speaking about crime and vandalism and what he termed the 'yobbish tendency' to members of the Cardiff Business Club in 1993, called for offenders not to be seen as 'probation service clients, disadvantaged youngsters or simply young offenders, but what they were, thieves, vandals and hooligans'.[156] Such a view, however, brought an immediate response from Mr Bill Walden-Jones, manager for the National Association for the Care and Resettlement of Offenders, who believed such comments diverted attention from tackling the real causes of crime.[157]

In his report for 1995/1996, the chief constable, Mr Michael Argent, stated that an area of continuing concern, was that of drug related criminality, which was often accompanied by an increasing use of violence by drug offenders.[158] Reporting on crime within the Conwy Division, Chief Superintendent Larry J. Davies stated there had been 483 violent crimes reported during the year and the use of knives and other weapons had become all too prevalent.[159] He also claimed that public disorder 'remained an ugly feature throughout the Division with particularly nasty scenes being experienced in the town centres at Llandudno, Colwyn Bay and Llanrwst'.[160] In the same report, Superintendent Philip Joy, in charge of the Denbighshire Division, stated that police performance during the year had been seriously affected by the demands resulting from the increased amount of late night drinking. The issue certainly affected the levels of violent crime committed and as a consequence were a drain on Divisional resources.[161] In a newspaper article in 1999 it emerged that youths under the age of twenty were committing a third of all crimes in Flintshire. It also reported that a quarter of all calls to the police were concerned with the anti-social behaviour of youths congregating around shopping centres, playing loud music and drinking in public places. In a determined effort to reduce such behaviour, local action teams prepared a strategy which it was hoped would greatly improve the situation, particularly at places like Queensferry, Buckley, Flint, Holywell and Mold.[162] In his report to the Police Authority for 1997/1998, the chief constable stated, that, during the year, there had been 2,688 offences against the person, an increase of 166 on the figure of 2,522, recorded for 1996/1997. There were also, over the same period, twenty cases of violent disorder and 204 incidents of causing an affray.[163] The statistics available for the 1998/1999 period are even more alarming when the figure for violence against the person has risen to 4,703 with the offence of causing an affray rising to 243.[164]

A further sad reflection of the changing times, is that hospital corridors now have to be patrolled and protected from those using violence against members of staff. Today, hospitals once considered the safe havens, are as much at risk from crime and violence as any High Street in north Wales. It is for this reason that the North Wales Police and the Gwynedd Hospitals, NHS Trust, decided to place a full-time officer on the beat in Ysbyty Gwynedd in Bangor. That such a move was necessary, was to be proved when, on his first day on duty, Constable Dewi Thomas arrested a person for theft from the Casualty Department of the 500 bed hospital.[165] Even holidaymakers on the beaches of north Wales are no longer safe. As a result of the menace posed by inconsiderate jet-skiers, the police have been forced to introduce jet-ski patrols as a means of curbing the seaside troublemakers. As a result of this, the citizens of north Wales are now protected on land, sea and in the air.[166]

As the twentieth century drew to a close, other issues, not always entirely linked to crime and its prevention surfaced and the Police Authority, as a consequence, tends to attract a great deal of attention from the media. Firstly, there was the continuing problem of finance, which called for savage and often unpalatable cuts in the police budget. Matters came to a head, when in June 1992, against a background of mounting crime, controversial proposals were introduced which, if implemented, would completely change the pattern of policing in north Wales. The proposals, which were unveiled by the chief constable, Mr David Owen, called for the axing of sixty-two of the ninety-four village police stations.[167] Such proposals, when implemented, would virtually bring to an end the era of the 'individual village policeman, living in a police house in small communities dotted throughout north Wales'.[168] Naturally, such drastic proposals brought a storm of protest and Clwyd County Councillor, Dennis Parry, accused the chief constable of not providing enough evidence to justify such a move.[169] In his opposition to the closure Councillor Parry had the support of Wrexham MP, Dr John Marek, who believed 'the axing of over 60 stations would mean a worse service and hoped that as many people as possible would protest'.[170] However, undaunted, Mr Owen in his annual report for 1992 declared 'that the shortage of manpower required a radical change in the policing arrangements for North Wales'.[171]

In March 1993, it was announced that even though sixty-two rural stations had closed in 1992, plans were afoot to close several more. Support for such action came in an Audit Commission survey, which revealed that officers in the old county stations only spent 53 per cent of their time in their own areas. Under the new policing arrangements, that would be substantially increased to 87 per cent.[172] But reductions were not simply confined to rural police stations as plans were also being studied to reduce the number of superintendents, a rank which generally carries responsibility for all uniform and CID, personnel within a particular area.[173] By 1995 the financial situation had become so serious that several MPs from north Wales went directly to the Home Office, to demand that more money should be provided for the Force.[174] According to Mr Michael Argent, the chief constable, failure to provide the necessary finance would lead to a serious deterioration in the Force's communications network.[175] A sum of £250,000 per annum was required if the Force was to successfully participate in the new National DNA Database, now viewed as a vital aid in crime detection.[176]

In an independent survey conducted by Professor Colin Baker and Alan Waddon of the University College of North Wales Research Centre at Bangor, it was found that 88 per cent of those questioned, believed there should be more officers in north Wales and that the Force was under-resourced.[177] As the financial crisis deepened, it was becoming more and more noticeable that communities throughout north Wales were beginning to react angrily, to any suggestion that would lead to the closure of their police station. At Menai Bridge, the Mayor, Councillor Evans, said that 'the closing of the town's police station would be a major blow to the community at large'.[178] A little earlier, the chief constable had announced that there might well be major changes in the structure of the North Wales Police, in a bid to find savings totalling £4.5 million. However, he was keen to stress that everything would be done to prevent cuts in 'frontline policing'.[179] The situation was extremely serious, especially when one considers that in the mid-1980s north Wales had been served by 153 police stations. Almost every village and town boasted its own station, staffed by familiar friendly faces.[180] Even church leaders began to voice their concern and in an appeal to the chief constable, they asked that no more police stations should be closed, particularly in rural areas where community constables were 'the eyes and ears' of the community.[181] The financial situation, therefore, on the eve of the millennium appeared far from promising and would probably not be resolved for some considerable time, leaving many to contemplate how police budgets in the future should be adequately allocated.

Another issue, was the publication in 1993, of Sir Patrick Sheehy's report. Far too complicated and detailed to be included in this work, it nevertheless has to be mentioned, for many of its proposals, had they been accepted, would have changed completely the structure of the police service as we know it today. It suffices here to record just a few of the proposals, in order that one might better understand the implications of the report. The Inquiry was set up to examine the rank structure, remuneration and conditions of service. The avowed objective of the Inquiry team was to put the police service on a 'businesslike' footing and to this end, all five of its members had business experience, but none of them had any direct knowledge of policing. The recommendations, when published, were strongly criticised by all sections of the police service and many chief officers threatened to resign if the recommendations were implemented in full.[182] On examining the report, the Home Secretary eventually rejected most of the radical recommendations but accepted some of the less contentious points – for example, he accepted that there should be a reduction in police ranks and that chief officers should be appointed on short term, renewable contracts 'associated with the evaluation of their performance'.[183]

In April 1994, Mr David Owen retired after forty-two years service as a policeman and the question on everyone's lips was, who would be his successor?[184] It was to be an issue that in many ways centred around the question of whether the new chief constable should be Welsh-speaking. The Police Authority had no doubt about who they wanted; it was the Deputy Chief Constable, Mr John Tecwyn Owen, a Welsh-speaker, who, because there was a vacancy in the office of chief constable, was appointed acting chief constable of the Force from 1 April 1994. What angered members of the Authority, was the fact that Mr Owen, the most experienced command officer in the North Wales Police, was not to be considered for the Force's top job, because of an outdated rule shortly to be discontinued by the Home Office. The problem was that Mr Owen, if appointed chief constable, would have occupied the top three ranks in the same force and that would have contravened a ruling introduced in 1976, which forbade such an appointment to be made.[185] Initially, the ruling had been intended to encourage senior officers to seek experience in other forces, in order that they would have a wider view of police practice.[186] In an attempt to change the situation, the Police Authority decided to send a deputation to the Home Office to plead its case.[187] Several members voiced their concern about the situation, arguing that not only was Mr Owen's ability to speak Welsh an important consideration, but he was also well qualified for the position.[188] The delegation which included the chief constable, Mr David Owen, and the Police Authority's Chairman, Councillor Elwyn Conway, met the Home Office Minister, Earl Ferrers, to seek clarification of the rule. However, much to the disappointment of the delegation, the Minister made it clear there would be no dispensations.[189] Commenting on the situation, Mr Bill Pierce, of Valley in Anglesey, a former chairman of the North Wales Police Authority said, 'it's a disgraceful state of affairs, when an authority which needs a Welsh speaking chief constable is being disregarded'.[190] Certainly disappointed, the Police Authority had finally to accept that their battle to appoint the acting chief constable to the post, had been lost. On 27 May 1994, Mr Michael Argent, deputy chief constable of Suffolk and a non-Welsh speaker was chosen by the North Wales Police Authority from a short list approved by the Home Office, 'which vetoed all four Welsh-speaking candidates put forward'.[191]

---

[1] C.C. Annual Report, 1975.

[2] *The People*, 12 April 1970.

[3] Ibid.

[4] Ibid.

[5] John Alderson, *Policing Freedom*, (Plymouth, 1979), p.123.

[6] Ibid.

[7] *Liverpool Echo*, 11 June 1973.

[8] *Evening Leader*, 26 June 1974.

[9] Ibid.

[10] Ibid.

[11] Roger Geary, *Policing Industrial Disputes 1893-1985*, (London, 1985), pp.76-7. It was estimated that on 10 February up to 15,000 people were blocking the entrance to the coke depot, and faced with a serious situation, the chief constable, Sir Derrick Capper, announced that in the interests of police safety, the gates would have to be closed. See also A. Scargill, New Unison, *New Left Review*, (July-August 1975), p.18 and *Birmingham Post*, 15 February 1972, which reports that in the main the picketing that had taken place was peaceful and even when scuffles occurred between the police and pickets little more than spirited pushing and shoving seems to have taken place. Also read Clive Emsley, *The English Police*, (London, 1991), pp.183-4, where it is reported that similar mass picketing occurred in the dock strike of 1972, in the dispute at the Grunwick Processing Laboratory in 1977, and in the steel strike of 1980.

[12] Robert Reiner, *The Politics of the Police*, 2nd. ed. (London, 1992), p.86.

[13] Sir Robert Mark, *Policing a Perplexed Society*, (London, 1977), p.101.

[14] *Daily Telegraph*, 27 September 1978.

[15] Ibid.

[16] Ibid.

[17] Ibid. This was not a view shared by the Home Secretary who in his reply to the conference claimed there were more people in prison in Britain than in most other countries in Europe. See also *The Guardian*, 7 March 1977,

where a police officer reported that so many criminals were being allowed bail, it was just like putting sand through a sieve.

[18] John Alderson, op. cit., pp.21-2.

[19] *Daily Telegraph*, 27 September 1978.

[20] Ibid.

[21] Ibid., also T.A. Critchley, *A History of Police in England and Wales*, revised edition (London, 1978), pp.300-1. For an analytical examination of the role of chief constables past and present read David S. Wall, *The Chief Constables of England and Wales – The Socio-legal History of a Criminal Justice Elite*, (Dartmouth, 1998).

[22] *The Guardian*, 26 April 1978.

[23] Ibid.

[24] Ibid. This crime picture was true of the western countries. In fact the growth of crime globally involved hundreds of thousands of professional police officers being employed full-time to combat crime through prevention, protection, investigation, prosecution and detention. As for violent crime in England and Wales it had increased by 100 per cent since 1969, whilst robbery had risen by 92 per cent.

[25] *Manchester Evening News*, 11 October 1978 also *Daily Express*, 13 July 1977.

[26] Ibid.

[27] Ibid.

[28] Ibid.

[29] Ibid.

[30] Clive Borrell and Brian Cashinella, *Crime in Britain Today*, (London, 1975).

[31] C.C. Annual Reports, 1972-80.

[32] Ibid.

[33] C.C. Annual Report 1976. At the end of the year the actual strength of the force was 1,238. In addition thirteen members were seconded to the Regional Crime Squads; eight attached to the Police Training Centre, Cwmbran; one attached to the Central Planning Unit, Pannal Ash, Harrogate and one employed at Hawarden Bridge Steelworks. The total number of members in the Force was, therefore, 1,261. At the end of 1975 the total personnel was 1,243 so that the actual net increase during the year was eighteen.

[34] C.C. Annual Report 1974.

[35] Ibid.

[36] C.C. Annual Reports 1972-80.

[37] C.C. Annual Report 1974.

[38] Ibid. See also C.C. Annual Report 1976 which states that the establishment of women police has been merged with that of the male members following the coming into force of the Sex Discrimination Act, on 29 December 1975. The female members of the force have been integrated into all operational and specialist departments of the force and they are also utilised when it is felt that a particular duty calls for the services of a female officer in preference to a male officer. For a very interesting account of the

early work of policewomen read Mary S. Allen, *Lady in Blue*, (London, 1936).

[39] *Sunday Times*, 9 February 1975 and *Manchester Evening News*, 21 February 1977. It ws claimed that London required another 5,604 officers and Manchester 935 if crime in either city was to be successfully contained.

[40] C.C. Annual Report 1976.

[41] Ibid. That the number of applicants to join the Force was always high, owed much to the excellent work of The Training and Public Relations Department which in conjunction with other Departments within the Force mounted a number of displays at various shows, gala days and the like in the Force area and a recruitment element was always included. Moreover, the recruitment interest was always borne in mind on these occasions when police officers visited teaching and other establishments and organisations for the purpose of delivering talks on police and allied services.

[42] T.A. Critchley, op. cit., p.255.

[43] Ibid. On occasion this policy met with some resistance from chief constables who were keen to keep a few comfortable posts open for policemen nearing retirement or perhaps were recuperating after illness or injury.

[44] *Police Manpower, Equipment Efficiency* (HMSO), 1967.

[45] T.A. Critchley, op. cit., p.255.

[46] C.C. Annual Reports 1972-1980. There was never a shortage of applicants for civilian posts. In 1980 the Force received 529 such applicants of which twenty-six were eventually appointed. The position was the same for those wishing to become traffic wardens, there were 128 applicants of which five were appointed. See *Liverpool Daily Post*, 9 January 1973.

[47] C.C. Annual Report 1980 also Roy Lewis, *A Force for the Future*, (London, 1976), p.40, which claims that in the mid 1970s there were between 6,000 and 7,000 traffic wardens doing work which twenty years previously was reserved for policemen, also J.P. Martin and Gail Wilson, *The Police a Study in Manpower*, (London, 1969), where it is reported that traffic wardens were first introduced in 1960 and between 1962-65 their numbers grew from 456 to 2,396.

[48] C.C. Annual Reports 1975-80.

[49] C.C. Annual Report 1981. Mr P.A. Myers, on retirement was appointed one of Her Majesty's Inspectors of Constabulary on 1 January 1982.

[50] Ibid.

[51] Ibid.

[52] Ibid.

[53] Ibid.

[54] Lord Scarman, *The Scarman Report – The Brixton Disorders 10-12 April 1981*, also *The Guardian*, 16 June 1981; *Observer Review*, 15 November 1981; *Liverpool Echo*, 7, 8 and 25 November 1981; *Manchester Evening News*, 6 and 8 July 1981; *The Observer*, 13 October 1985 and *Liverpool Daily Post*, 26 June 1989 also from information kindly supplied by Chief Superintendent Larry

Davies at Police Headquarters, Colwyn Bay, the police in north Wales were seconded to Liverpool during the rioting at Toxteth.

[55] C.C. Annual Report 1982.

[56] Clive Emsley, *The English Police – A Political and Social History*, (London, 1996), p.183 also Gerry Northam, *Shooting in the Dark*, (London, 1988), pp.38-43, and Anthony Burton, *Urban Terrorism, Theory Practise and Response*, (London, 1975), pp.212-37.

[57] Ibid.

[58] Ibid., also *Liverpool Daily Post*, (undated) August 1986. Also from information kindly supplied by Chief Superintendent Larry Davies (above), police officers from north Wales attended the following collieries during the strike: Wrexham, Point of Ayr, Staffordshire, Leicestershire, Durham, South Yorkshire and Nottinghamshire. Officers from Manchester, Lancashire and Cheshire assisted the North Wales Police at Point of Ayr colliery.

[59] *Liverpool Daily Post*, 18 January 1988.

[60] Ibid.

[61] Ibid.

[62] C.C. Annual Report 1982.

[63] *Cambrian News*, 29 April 1983.

[64] Ibid.

[65] *Liverpool Daily Post*, 22 January 1988.

[66] *The Observer*, 22 November 1992. Here the number of arson attacks carried out between 13 December 1979 and March 1990, are clearly detailed. The chief constable viewed the arsonists as terrorists, but Professor Paul Wilkinson of the University of St Andrews believed the attacks, the targeting of individuals was, 'an act of ethnic cleansing, Celtic Style'.

[67] *Liverpool Daily Post*, 22 April 1988.

[68] *The Observer*, 22 November 1992.

[69] *Liverpool Daily Post*, 22 April 1988.

[70] Anthony Judge, *A Man Apart – The British Policeman and His Job*, (London, 1972), pp.151-2.

[71] Ibid.

[72] Ibid., also Ben Whitaker, *The Police in Society*, (London, 1979), pp.300-4, and Alun Waddon and Colin Baker, *Public Perceptions of the North Wales Police*, (University College of North Wales, Bangor, November 1990).

[73] C.C. Annual Report 1982 and 1988, where it is noted that the post of deputy press officer previously held by a policeman sergeant was civilianised as from July 1988.

[74] C.C. Annual Report 1988.

[75] Ibid.

[76] Ibid.

[77] C.C. Annual Reports 1970-88.

[78] C.C. Annual Reports 1975 and 1980. For example during 1975 police

officers delivered 473 lectures to infant schools, by 1980 this figure had reached 1,072.

[79] C.C. Annual Report 1983 and *Cambrian News*, 20 April 1984.

[80] Ibid.

[81] *Liverpool Daily Post*, 28 November 1989.

[82] Ibid., 6 December 1989.

[83] Ibid., also 1 December 1989 and 15 October 1986.

[84] C.C. Annual Report 1990.

[85] Ibid. See also North Wales Police *'Objectives and Priorities'* 1990 and *Liverpool Daily Post*, 19 January 1988 and 9 August 1989.

[86] *Liverpool Daily Post*, 4 January 1995. During the period 18 December 1994 and 3 January 1995, the North Wales Police tested more drivers than any other Welsh force during a nationwide festive crackdown – in all 2,068 motorists were tested of whom ninety-two were found to be positive.

[87] North Wales Police Annual Policing Plan *'A Total Policing Service'* 1997-1998. See also *Liverpool Daily Post*, 7 August 1999 and *Police Review*, 12 September 1997.

[88] *Cambrian News*, 8 and 15 May 1987.

[89] *Liverpool Daily Post*, 20 January 1988.

[90] C.C. Annual Report 1974.

[91] *Liverpool Daily Post*, 20 January 1988. In the early years the theft of hard drugs such as heroin, morphine and cocaine was virtually unknown in north Wales. Also *Liverpool Echo*, 29 November 1977, which details how drugs pass illegally through the port of Liverpool.

[92] C.C. Annual Report 1981.

[93] C.C. Annual Report 1983.

[94] Ibid.

[95] *Cambrian News*, 8 May 1987.

[96] Ibid., 23 November 1984 and 18 September 1987. Also *Police Review*, 25 April and 17 October 1997; 19 June 1998 and 18 June 1999.

[97] *Liverpool Daily Post*, 20 January 1988.

[98] Ibid.

[99] Ibid., 29 July 1989. Crack cocaine had a street value of between £80 and £100 per gram, although it was usually bought by users at about £10 a 'fix' receiving only a few grains of the drug wrapped in paper.

[100] Ibid., Mr Owen visited the United States in his capacity as chairman of the Crime Committee of the Association of Chief Police Officers. Among the cities he visited were Washington D.C., and New York, both recognised as the joint 'crack cocaine' capitals of America. An illustration of the addictiveness of heroin is also seen in the United States Narcotics Report 1995, which records that in Pakistan there were no reported heroin cases in 1980, yet by 1983 it was estimated there were 'over 100,000 addicts'. See *The Sunday Express*,
17 November 1991 and *The Observer*, 15 November 1992.

[101] *Cambrian News*, 3 March 1995.

[102] *Liverpool Daily Post*, 11 April 1995.

[103] Ibid., also *Police Review*, 18 June 1999; Health Education Council, *What to do About Glue Sniffing* (undated) and Department of Education and Science and Welsh Office, *Drug Misuse and the Young*, (July 1985).

[104] *Liverpool Daily Post*, 24 April 1996. In a survey commissioned by the police, public support for cameras to be installed was overwhelming. Of the 240 persons questioned 232 believed the system would reduce crime and other types of anti-social behaviour and generally make the streets that much safer.

[105] Ibid., 21 August 1998.

[106] Home Office Police Research Group, Crime Detection and Prevention Series, paper 92 (1998) also *The Pharmaceutical Journal* (vol.261), 22 August 1998.

[107] North Wales Police Authority Policing Plan – *Working Together for Safer Communities* 1998-1999.

[108] Ibid.

[109] C.C. Annual Report 1982.

[110] Ibid.

[111] Ibid.

[112] Ibid.

[113] Report of Her Majesty's Chief Inspector of Constabulary (1975), pp.1-2, also T.A. Critchley, op. cit, p.311.

[114] C.C. Annual Report 1986.

[115] C.C. Annual Report 1987.

[116] Ibid., also Colin Moore and John Brown, *Community versus Crime* (London, 1981), pp.1-26.

[117] C.C. Annual Report 1986.

[118] C.C. Annual Report 1987.

[119] Ibid. The background in which such units were first established is well documented in Robert Reiner, *The Politics of the Police* 2 ed. (London, 1992), pp.85-90.

[120] North Wales Police, *Annual Objectives and Performance 1988 and 1989*.

[121] Ibid.

[122] C.C. Annual Report 1991.

[123] *Liverpool Daily Post*, 24 November 1992.

[124] C.C. Annual Report 1989.

[125] Ibid.

[126] *Caernarfon Herald*, 21 February 1992. There was a strong body of opinion that also asked whether the Force could justifiably spend so much of the police budget on the purchase of a helicopter, particularly when a forthcoming Audit Commission Report would question if it was financially viable to continue maintaining ninety-four out-stations.

[127] Ibid.

[128] Ibid., and *Cambrian News*, 26 June 1992.

[129] *Liverpool Daily Post*, 1 October 1992. The five seater aircraft, a 170 mph French built Aerospatiale Squirrell AS 355 F2, took to the air in October 1992 and was the eighteenth helicopter in service in Britain and was based at Kinmel Camp, Bodelwyddan. In an emergency, facilities were also available at Police Headquarters, Colwyn Bay, for the aircraft to land and pick up senior officers in the event of a major incident occurring in north Wales. Initially, the Air Support Unit was under the command of Inspector Nick Snape, and included Constables Stephen Green, Dafydd Evans, Robert Taylor and Kevin Jones, the two civilian pilots were Captains Bruce Stewart and Rob Sleeman, both of whom had seen service with the Army and Royal Navy respectively.

[130] C.C. Annual Report 1993. The helicopter during the year was also used to transport sixty-six casualties, many who were dangerously ill, amongst these were three patients taken to hospitals outside north Wales for life saving transplant surgery. See also *Liverpool Daily Post*, 24 June 1992, 16 November and 14 December 1993; 7 July, 5 and 7 December 1994; 27 May 1998; 28 May, 2 September 1999.

[131] C.C. Annual Report 1983.

[132] C.C. Annual Report 1993.

[133] Ibid. The new helicopter equipped with the latest technological aids, carried a stabilised thermal imaging (heat seeking) camera and a daylight video camera, which enabled the machine and its crew to be deployed on a much wider variety of tasks.

[134] *Liverpool Daily Post*, 29 May 1999. Today the Air Support Unit is under the supervision of Inspector David Curtis, who is assisted by Sergeant Robert Taylor and Constables Mike Cleary, Ann Jones, Geraint Roberts and David Ramessur Williams and Captains Wayne and David Taylor.

[135] C.C. Annual Report 1991.

[136] Ibid.

[137] Ibid.

[138] Ibid., also David J.V. Jones, *Crime and Policing in the Twentieth Century*, (Cardiff 1996), p.257, where he records that the chief constable of Swansea as early as 1911 was actively promoting crime prevention measures.

[139] C.C. Annual Report 1992. As a further measure to protect the public from crime, the police briefed milkmen to pass on to them any incident they regarded as suspicious whilst on their early morning rounds. Officers in the Colwyn Sub-Division also introduced a 'Caramark' property marking scheme which was aimed at drastically reducing the thefts of televisions and other forms of electrical equipment from static caravans along the Towyn coastal belt. Similarly, a 'Hotel Watch' scheme was introduced to reduce the number of thefts from hotels where all too often security was extremely lax.

[140] C.C. Annual Report 1993. See also *Liverpool Daily Post*, 15 April 1995.

[141] *Liverpool Daily Post*, 6 November 1993.
[142] Ibid.
[143] Ibid. See survey also *Liverpool Daily Post*, 18 May 1995.
[144] *Liverpool Daily Post*, 30 April 1994.
[145] Ibid., 20 July 1994 and 24 August 1999.
[146] C.C. Annual Report 1994 – during the year the Bureau examined 14,901 fingerprints.
[147] Ibid.
[148] C.C. Annual Report 1993.
[149] Ibid., also *Liverpool Daily Post*, 12 April 1996 and 18 November 1998, where it is recorded that specially trained labradors in the North Wales Force would soon be leaving Wales to join the police in Moscow, where they will be specifically deployed in sniffing out drugs, explosives and armaments on the city's underground system.
[150] C.C. Annual Report 1981.
[151] Ibid.
[152] C.C. Annual Report 1992.
[153] Ibid.
[154] Ibid. Much of the success achieved by the police in their fight against terrorism owes much to the members of the Special Branch. In north Wales, officers are principally engaged with matters relating to national security. The unit at Holyhead Port has the responsibility of policing one of the primary routes to the Republic of Ireland. In 1994 there were 6,521 ferry movements through the port involving the transit of 2,361,389 passengers. Although it deals mainly with the Special Branch in London, read Rupert Allason, *The Branch, A History of the Metropolitan Police Special Branch 1883-1983*.
[155] *Liverpool Daily Post*, 13 June 1992.
[156] Ibid., 19 October 1993.
[157] Ibid.
[158] C.C. Annual Report 1995/1996.
[159] C.C. Annual Report 1996/1997. Also *Liverpool Daily Post*, 24 August 1999.
[160] Ibid.
[161] Ibid.
[162] *Liverpool Daily Post*, 10 March 1999 and 18 November 1998.
[163] C.C. Annual Report 1997/1998.
[164] C.C. Annual Report 1998/1999.
[165] *Liverpool Daily Post*, 4 February 1999. See also North Wales Police, *Crime and Disorder in Gwynedd Audit Report 1999*, which records that the police receive nearly 300 calls per annum to attend immediately at the hospital, a large proportion of these calls relate to disruptive persons within the hospital and persons missing from wards dealing with mental health cases.

[166] Ibid., 3 May 1999. This initiative, the first of its kind anywhere in UK, follows months of investigations by the North Wales Police and Gwynedd Council into problems caused by a minority of jet-ski users.

[167] *Liverpool Daily Post*, 18 June 1992, and C.C. Annual Report 1993.

[168] Ibid.

[169] Ibid.

[170] Ibid.

[171] C.C. Annual Report 1992, see also *Liverpool Daily Post*, 9 December 1993, where Mr Owen pleads for even more money, explaining to the Police Authority's general purposes committee that costs were bound to rise as a result of providing medical suites and community team bases and an extension to police headquarters.

[172] *Liverpool Daily Post*, 30 March and 12 December 1994.

[173] Ibid., 24 August 1994, also 21 January, 20 July, 5 and 8 December 1994.

[174] Ibid., 4 January 1995.

[175] Ibid., and 21 January 1994.

[176] Ibid., 12 December 1994.

[177] Ibid., 31 August 1996. Also University College of North Wales, Bangor, *Are You Being Served?*

[178] *Liverpool Daily Post*, 31 December 1998. Other police stations due for closure were Benllech, Cemmaes Bay and Gaerwen.

[179] Ibid., 29 October 1998 and 9, 12 and 26 January 1999.

[180] Ibid., 12 January 1999.

[181] Ibid., 26 January 1999.

[182] Arthur Brown, *Police Governance in England and Wales*, (London, 1998), p.173.

[183] Ibid., also *The Observer*, 4 and 25 July 1993, and *Liverpool Daily Post*, 29 July 1993.

[184] Ibid.

[185] *CDH*, 4 March 1994.

[186] Ibid.

[187] *Liverpool Daily Post*, 19 March 1994.

[188] Ibid.

[189] Ibid.

[190] Ibid., 1 March 1994.

[191] Ibid., 28 May 1994.

# Conclusion

As the preceding chapters have sought to demonstrate, the police in north Wales, as indeed elsewhere, have rarely occupied centre stage, yet, despite many obstacles, they have at all times been constant and reassuring background figures, ever watchful while others have gone about their daily lives in comparative safety. In fact, so omnipresent has been the 'bobby' in popular thinking that it has become all too easy to assume 'that there is something inevitable and unproblematic about his existence'.[1] Such an image in part at least, has been encapsulated over the years in television programmes like 'Dixon of Dock Green'. In the series, PC George Dixon, played by the actor Jack Warner, appears on the screen as the 'model beat policeman – avuncular, courageous and honest'.[2] Even as late as the late 1980s and early 1990s, Dixon was still seen as the ideal benchmark for policing.[3] Although it is generally accepted by policemen, journalists and academics that his kind of policing has no place in today's world, it still remains for many, 'the model of a golden age when life appeared much less complicated, and when crime and criminals appeared much more manageable'.[4]

Realistically however, as each chapter in this work unfolds, it has been clearly revealed that the real position of the policeman has been much more complex and contentious. For example, the arrival of a constabulary force in Denbighshire in 1840 proved highly controversial and far from straightforward. The legislative changes that had accompanied the Police Act of 1839 had led to much bitterness being expressed by those who strongly objected to the establishment of a police presence within the county. In fact, resistance to any form of policing was strong and very effective in the first half of the nineteenth century. Even when the idea of policing acquired a greater acceptance, questions were continually raised as to the precise nature and form such a body would take. Interestingly, when the structure of policing eventually came into being, it was considered a product of compromise which, when examined, comprised of three distinct systems and philosophies. When applied to the Metropolitan Police, the borough police and the county forces these clearly illustrated how each should be controlled.[5]

What the authorities encountered in the early years of the new police, particularly after the passing of the Police Act of 1856, were the problems, and there were many, of putting legislative theory into practice. For instance, it was no easy task to create an effective body of men in the boroughs and counties. In some areas it took a little time for forces to be recognised as competent, although in this respect the counties in north Wales seemed to have fared well. Becoming a policeman meant that a man embarked on a life that was different and not only physically demanding but also, at times, dangerous. Once committed to the police, he became quickly aware that his lifestyle as well as that of his family would markedly change. Unfortunately too, the very nature of his work often led to not only himself, but also his family, becoming isolated from the community in which they lived. Adding further to his difficulties, was the fact that his duties not only brought him into conflict with those who committed crime, but also at times with many law abiding citizens who found that parts of their working and leisure lives had become criminalised.[6] Being a policeman did have certain advantages, but when set against what was demanded, the rewards did not seem too great.

By the 1880s there were noticeable improvements; the early harshness of police work was in part ameliorated; pay was increased and even the status of policing began to rise. However, despite obvious progress, what was still missing was the appearance of the career policeman, without whom a stable force could not be created. As Carolyn Steedman explains 'resignations, the voluntary leaving of the force counted throughout the country for the greatest proportion of men leaving'.[7] It was, for many chief constables, a period of great frustration and disappointment as men came and left with some simply failing to make the grade. Whilst a number of police histories record certain triumphs, especially in leadership, the real and often unsung heroes were the constables, who, despite the rigid discipline imposed, remained, and in doing so 'developed an ethos, an *esprit de corps* of their own and made a reality, albeit less than perfect, of the aspirations of their superiors'.[8]

The question of police legitimacy certainly did not come

about easily and in the main proved a long-drawn-out and often painful process. However, despite initial doubts, policing by consent had, by the end of the nineteenth century, become a reality. To some extent, this was achieved as a result of a number of factors in the social order and this included the police, who were now becoming an essential component in any change. Further advancement came with the slow but nevertheless continuing incorporation of the working-classes into the political life of the country. It was a time also, when not only did the living standards of workers improve, but the amount of interpersonal violence began to decline. Important changes in police practices were also a factor, for example, a greater awareness of the meaning of policing by consent, coupled whenever possible with the use of minimal force as well as a greater willingness to use discretion – turning a blind eye on occasion – helped considerably in the creation of better understanding between the police and the policed.

As the police entered the twentieth century, they had largely become an accepted fact of life. On the whole, their presence was positively welcomed by the majority of the upper and middle classes and in fairness there was also considerable support from the working-class, even if at times, it was given begrudgingly. However, despite the improvements outlined, deep-seated hostilities still existed, with roots dating back to the earliest days of the new police, and these were never far below the surface. Violence towards police officers was still an everyday occurrence and when tensions rose, situations became explosive. In many ways, in a society that was still divided in both a material and moral sense, it was difficult not to ignore the fact that the police and those they served were in reality on different sides.

That this observation had much credence, surfaced particularly between 1900-40 when the actions of the police towards those on strike, for example, underwent important changes. There was even, as Jane Morgan records, a move to establish a national police force specifically designed to combat either a local or national threat to public order.[9] It was a concept that met with the approval of chief police officers and one that the Home Office steadily pursued between 1900 and the outbreak of the Second World War in 1939. This drive from the centre, towards a form of greater centralisation, was accompanied by an increase in the operational powers of the police which led eventually to the passing of the Public Order Act 1936. It was as a consequence of these increased powers that the position of the police had to be redefined. There was, for example, a genuine fear that the new powers would lead to an erosion of civil liberties as well as allow the police to become less accountable for their actions at both local and national level.

In order to fully comprehend the full significance of such changes, one has only to examine the years between 1880 and the outbreak of the First World War in 1914, where 'it is possible to trace wave after wave of working-class discontent – discontent which reached a peak in the period 1912-1913'.[10] As John Davies further explains, 'this was the "Great Unrest", it was an international phenomenon that over the years historians have been much exercised in seeking to account for its various aspects'.[11] Prior to this period of unrest, it had been the responsibility' of local police authorities to ensure that law and order within their area was maintained. As far as the Home Office was concerned, their interest at this time was little more than ensuring that the police were efficient in terms of numbers and discipline. However, as industrial unrest became more militant, it was becoming clear that a more co-ordinated and national response by the authorities was required. Urged on by a now more concerned Home Office, local police committees began to increase their reserve manpower and this was largely accomplished by mutual aid agreements, such as they were. Even government support for the military to be involved in certain circumstances was revived, and this process was particularly illustrated during Winston Churchill's time at the Home Office between 1910-11.[12]

With the advent of the First World War, it was noticeable that chief constables became much more accustomed to working under the direction of the Home Office. It was a policy that was to continue, increased even after the war and when industrial tensions rose and violence erupted, the use of troops continued, particularly between the years 1919-26. Vociferous in their demands for greater control of the police, were such prominent Home Office figures as Sir Edward Troup, and later, Sir John Anderson.[13] This call was answered by the Police Act of 1919, which allowed the government to exert even further authority over police affairs. For example, the Home Office now openly encouraged the police to be much more assertive and even aggressive, when faced with serious confrontation. Much more alarming for many, was the attempt by the Home Office to popularize the 'idea of the independence of the office of constable and his accountability to the law, rather than to democratically elected local authorities'.[14]

Such an idea was reinforced by the Emergency Power Act

1920, introduced during the unrest that occurred in 1921 and 1926, which increased even further the powers of the police. These allowed the police to become a formidable force for the government and clearly demonstrated that in a national emergency, law enforcement agencies had to work in close harmony when the security of the state was threatened. That the police now had the ability to co-ordinate and design their operations, was powerfully illustrated during the general strike of 1926, when they worked closely with the military and naval forces employed by the state.[15] What was increasingly apparent during this troublesome period, was a situation whereby local authorities became less able to hold the police accountable for their actions – a situation which was not helped by the strong and independent stance adopted by chief constables with Home Office approval.[16] These actions and changes did much to consolidate the unity of the police in operational matters at a time of crisis. The extra powers also highlighted how, in the course of a few years, the 'Home Office had emerged as their national co-ordinator, and to some extent their leader'.[17]

At the outbreak of the Second World War in 1939, the police, at least theoretically, had a localized character. They were, although to a lesser extent, still under local control. However, there was little doubt, that over the years, the Home Office had certainly strengthened its position and this was especially true in its relationship with county forces like those in north Wales. Therefore, as already illustrated, the effective control as 'exercised by democratically elected representatives inexorably declined'.[18] These new changes in the manner the police were controlled began to alarm, not only those on the left, but also those who championed and cherished the importance of civil liberty. Fears about the future control of the police intensified when chief constables in the boroughs, traditionally under the direction of their respective watch committees, were also being urged to exercise their independence and freedom from accountability and thus assuming a position similar to that enjoyed by chief constables in the counties. The increase in these powers was to lead to the passing of the Police Act of 1964. Former watch committees were abolished and replaced by police committees composed of two-thirds councillors and one-third magistrates. It was a tremendous leap forward for borough chief constables who were now vested with the same authority to appoint, promote and discipline members of their force, as their counterparts in the counties, and the role of chief constable was statutorily defined.

Despite such progress, the question as to whether police authorities could control and influence chief constables in their operational duties is still one that creates concern. Certainly, over the years 'inquiries into police conduct have continued to be singularly difficult to obtain, while the Home Office, under Labour as well as Conservative governments, has invariably upheld the police view-point'.[19] This was certainly the situation during the miners' strike of 1984-85, when attention focussed on the actions of chief constables and the apparent ease with which they could call for assistance in times of serious disorder. In fact, the way the police were deployed during this period led many to accuse them of militarisation and even worse, that they 'were now being employed in a partisan fashion'.[20] In a number of instances, even police officers themselves began questioning their role in the dispute. One thirty-six year old sergeant from a large Midlands urban force with twelve years service, was quoted as saying 'I had some sympathy with the miners. I came from a poor working class family with a mining community background. I know how close-knit they are, and how they must feel when their main source of employment is likely to disappear'.[21] As Clive Emsley explains 'it has always been difficult, if not impossible, for the police to be acknowledged as neutral by both sides in such disputes'.[22]

Sadly, what many critics tended to forget, was that the general improvements in riot drill during the early 1970s sometimes led to accusations in the 1980s that the police were becoming nearer to 'a gendarmerie in their riot equipment and tactics'.[23] What such observers failed to take into account was that the officers involved – both men and women – were ordinary officers whose duties were normally those of beat officers, many of whom, in north Wales at least, were more familiar with patrolling villages than facing large numbers of angry miners who would at times resort to violence. The widespread anxieties raised by the tactics employed by the police during the miners' dispute were further fuelled by the passing in 1985 of the Police and Criminal Evidence Act (Pace), along with the newly enacted legislation that covered offences such as riot, violent disorder, affray and conduct that was likely to evoke violence.[24] This legislation also enabled the police to deal far more effectively with all forms of picketing.[25] The conclusions drawn from these additional police powers depend to a large extent on one's viewpoint during this particular time. On the whole, when the position is compared with the industrial history of some other countries, the police in Britain have successfully managed to bridge 'the gap between an efficient police and democratic accountability'.[26] In fact, if we examine the conduct of the police in north Wales during times of industrial unrest, we find that despite experiencing much provocation at times they have exercised considerable restraint, which in itself is a tribute, not only to them, but also to the leadership of their senior officers. That is not to say, however, that during industrial disputes in Wales strikers have not been killed or severely injured.[27]

Finally, in concluding this research one might well ask, what the future holds for officers serving in the North Wales Police today. It is much easier to chart the past than predict the future. However, there is little doubt, that over the next decade the force will experience many significant changes. One such change, according to the former assistant chief constable, Mr John Cooke, is that the newly elected Welsh Assembly might well advocate that in the future, Wales should be policed by a single force rather than the existing four.[28] Another area, which many believe, could be threatened by changes in the future, is that concerned with the importance and use of the Welsh language within the force. Such fears, probably emanated from the fact that the Police Authority had recently appointed two non-Welsh speaking officers as assistant chief constables.[29] That such fears were groundless, came in an assurance by the newly appointed clerk to the Police Authority, Mr Kevin Dent, that one of his first priorities would be to ensure that the force, given time, would become fully bilingual.[30] Some changes are inevitable and even as this work is being written the Police Authority has announced that the command structure of the force, which at present consists of six divisions, is to be reduced to three, as a means of cutting expenditure.

Later, one senior officer, Superintendent Peter Bolton, on being questioned by the press, explained that, although such a change would ultimately lead to a further reduction in the number of police stations, there was actually no reason for members of the public to be alarmed. For instance, the force had invested heavily in computer technology which enabled rapid communication in support of front line officers. According to the Superintendent, what the change attempted to achieve was, 'a balance between the bobby on the beat and the demands of a fast policing response linked to area cars'.[31]

In allaying fears that might well arise as a result of these changes, Superintendent Peter Williams, the officer responsible for the restructuring process, claimed that what was really changing was the management structure in an effort to cut costs, and that in no circumstances, would service to the public be reduced as a consequence. There is little doubt, that now and in the foreseeable future expenditure will always be the major consideration whenever and wherever police authorities meet.[32] It is, as Mr John Tecwyn Owen, the deputy chief constable, stated on the eve of his retirement, 'everything seems to be viewed from a financial standpoint'.[33] Yet, despite immense difficulties, such as the amount of administrative red tape, and at times, over inspection, he believed, 'that the achievements of the North Wales Police in terms of crime detection and general performance would stand favourable comparison with any other police force in England and Wales'.[34]

As my pen nears that last few lines of this research, I know with confidence, that despite the many changes that will occur over the coming years, the officers serving in the Force today, and indeed their successors, will continue to uphold the great tradition of policing which has now become the hallmark of their service. As an observer of their past history, I cannot help but quote the words of another writer, which equally apply here in north Wales when he wrote, 'that in this service we have something unique and admirable and strong, like a tree that has taken a long time to grow and which, should it ever be cut down, by folly, indifference, or by deliberate evil intent, could never be replaced'.[35]

---

[1] David Taylor, *The New Police in Nineteenth Century England – Crime, Conflict and Control*, (Manchester, 1997), p.136.

[2] Clive Emsley, 'PC Dixon and Commissaire Maigret'. Some myths and realities in the development of English and continental police' – in David W. Howell and Kenneth O. Morgan (ed.), *Crime, Protest and Police in Modern British Society*, (Cardiff, 1999), p.97.

[3] Ibid.

[4] Ibid. See Ben Whitaker, *The Police in Society*, (London, 1979), p.303. Many police officers on watching PC George Dixon, took the view that he appeared 'like an overgrown Boy Scout looking for his good deed – although recognising his performance as a good image, in reality it did not fool anyone'.

[5] David Taylor, op. cit., p.137.

[6] Ibid. For a present day analysis of what life is like for those serving in the various forces in England and Wales read Mike Seabrook, *Coppers – An Inside View of the British Police*, (London, 1987), in which he details that in Britain today the policeman's lot is an increasingly hazardous one.

[7] Carolyn Steedman, *Policing the Victorian Community – The Formation of 'English Provincial Police Forces' 1856-1880*, (London, 1984), p.92.

[8] David Taylor, op. cit., p.137.
[9] Jane Morgan, *Conflict and Order – The Police and Labour Disputes in England and Wales 1900-1939*, (Oxford, 1987), p.276.
[10] John Davies, *A History of Wales*, (Penguin Books, 1993), p.485.
[11] Ibid. As recorded earlier in this work, one such strike occurred in north Wales and proved to be one of the longest disputes in the industrial history of Britain – the Great Strike at the Penrhyn quarry began in November 1900, and did not end until November 1903.
[12] Clive Emsley, *The English Police – A Political History*, (London, 1996), pp.117-19. During the miners' strike at Tarporly in November 1910, Captain Lionel Lindsay, the chief constable of Glamorgan borrowed officers from neighbouring counties and called for the requisitioning of troops. Churchill in this instance, did not sanction such a move and authorised the sending of 300 Metropolitan police officers to the area instead. However, when a similar situation arose in 1911, when striking railwaymen brought the entire railway network to a halt, Churchill acted decisively, dispatching troops around the country, in order to protect vital rail installations. For further reading on this troublesome period consult John Davies, op. cit., pp.489-94 and Roger Geary, *Policing Industrial Disputes 1893-1985*, (London, 1986), pp.39-47.
[13] Jane Morgan, op. cit., p.277.
[14] Ibid., p.278
[15] Ibid., p.277.
[16] Ibid.
[17] T.A. Critchley, *A History of Police in England and Wales*, (London, 1978), revised edition, p.199.
[18] Jane Morgan, op. cit., p.279. Also, Clive Emsley, op. cit., p.164, where he records the celebrated case in 1930 of Fisher v Oldham Corporation. A man called Fisher was mistakenly identified and arrested in London and taken to Oldham. However, it soon emerged that a mistake had been made and Fisher was released, with the result that he took action-seeking damages for false imprisonment. In the belief that the police officers involved would not be able to pay damages, he directed his claim against Oldham Corporation. Ruling on the case Justice McCardie quoted extensively from precedent and came to the decision that 'a police constable is not the servant of the borough. He is a servant of the State, a ministerial officer of the central power, though subject in some respects, to local supervision and local regulations'. In the early 1960s, the Association of Municipal Corporations often disputed the precise meaning of the ruling in its evidence to the Royal Commission on the police. However, those in central government, and subsequent changes by the judiciary, confirmed it as limiting the powers of local authorities over the police, particularly those that appertained to operational matters. See also, Report of the Committee on Police Conditions of Service, PP 1948-9, (Cmd 7831), xix. 385-6.
[19] Jane Morgan, op. cit., p.279. In the Oaksey Report of 1948 it stated that the Police Authority had no right to give the chief constable orders about the disposition of the force or the way in which police duties should be

carried out. The chief officer could not divest himself of responsibility by turning to the watch committee for guidance or instructions on matters of police duty.

[20] Clive Emsley, op. cit., p.257.

[21] Roger Graef, *Talking Blues – the Police in their Own Words*, (London, 1989), p.60.

[22] Clive Emsley, op. cit., p.257.

[23] Ibid.

[24] Jane Morgan, op. cit., p.280.

[25] Peter Hain, *Political Strikes – The State and Trade Unionism in Britain*, (London, 1986), pp.233-5. Also Paul Sieghart, 'Harmless weapons – a threat to liberty', *New Scientist*, 30 March 1978, pp.840-2.

[26] Jane Morgan, op. cit., p.280.

[27] Roger Geary, *Policing Industrial Disputes, 1893-1985*, (London, 1986), pp.40-1, 45-7. Also David J.V. Jones, *Crime and Policing in the Twentieth Century*, (Cardiff, 1996), pp.58 and 132.

[28] *Liverpool Daily Post*, 26 July and 2 December 1999.

[29] Ibid., 26 November 1999. The two newly appointed officers were Richard Brunstrom formerly assistant chief constable of the Cleveland Police and Superintendent Bill Brereton of the Merseyside force. Both officers attended intensive language lessons at the Welsh learning centre at Nant Gwrtheyrn after being appointed.

[30] Ibid., 11 February 2000.

[31] Ibid., 14 and 31 March 2000. The new territorial divisions would comprise of the Western Division, covering Gwynedd and Anglesey, Central Division, which would encompass Conwy and Denbighshire, with Wrexham and Flintshire coming under the new Eastern Division.

[32] Ibid.

[33] Ibid., 30 March 2000.

[34] Ibid. In Mr Owen's view, the Force had been underfunded for several decades, and it was clear it had to reorganise. The above reductions in the number of police divisions had to be completed by 1 April 2000.

[35] William Purcell, *British Police in a Changing Society*, (London, 1974), p.169.

# Bibliography

**Books**

Alderson, John: *Policing Freedom* (Plymouth, 1979).
Allason, Robert: *The Branch, A History of the Metropolitan Police Special Branch 1883-1983*.
Allen, Mary S.: *Lady in Blue* (London, 1936).
Arris, M.; Latham, J.; Pott, J.: *Crime and Punishment – A Welsh Perspective – Nineteenth Century Crime and Protest* (Caernarfon, 1987).
Ascoli, David: *The Queen's Peace, The Origins and Development of the Metropolitan Police 1829-1979* (London, 1979).
Anon, *Kent Police Centenary* (Kent, 1957).
Barton, Michael: *The Policeman in the Community* (London, 1964).
Bate, Islwyn: *History of the Newport Borough Police* (1959).
Block, Eugene, *Fingerprinting* (London, 1969).
Borrell, Clive, and Cashinella, Brian: *Crime in Britain Today* (London, 1975).
Brogden, M.: *The Police – Autonomy and Consent* (London and New York, 1982).
Brophy, John: *The Five Years* (London, 1936).
Brown, Arthur: *Police Governance in England and Wales* (London 1998).
Burton, Anthony: *Urban Terrorism, Theory, Practice and Response* (London, 1975).
Cherrill, Fred: *Cherrill of the Yard* (London, undated).
Coatman, John: *Police* (London, 1959).
Coleman, T.: *The Railway Navvies* (London, 1981).
Collins, P.: *Dickens and Crime* (London, 1962).
Critchley, T.A.: *A History of Police in England and Wales* (Holywell, 1956; London, 1967, 1978 & 1987).
Cromer, James: *The World's Police* (London, 1964).
Davies, John: *A History of Wales* (Hardmansworth, 1993).
Davies, John: *A History of Wales* (London, 1994).
Dilnot, George: *Scotland Yard* (London, 1926).
Dodd, A.H.: *The Industrial Revolution in North Wales*, (Cardiff, 1951 & 1971).
Dodd, A.H.: *A History of Caernarvonshire 1284-1900* (Denbigh, 1968).
Dunabin, J.P.D.: *Rural Discontent in Nineteenth Century Britain* (London, 1974).
Durrant, A.J.: *A Hundred Years of the Surrey Constabulary* (Guildford, 1950).
Eames, Aled: *Ships and Seamen of Gwynedd* (Gwynedd Archives, 1976).
Emsley, Clive: *The English Police – A Political and Social History* (London, 1991 & 1996).
Emsley, Clive: *Crime and Society in England 1750-1900*.
Emsley, Clive: *Policing and its Context 1750-1870* (London, 1983).
Evans, D.G.: *A History of Wales 1815-1906* (Cardiff, 1989).
Evans, H.: *Gorse Glen* (Liverpool, 1948).
*Flintshire Constabulary Centenary Handbook 1956* (Holywell, 1956), Rules and Regulations for the Government and Guidance of the Constabulary (No copy can now be found).
Foster, J.: *Class Struggle and the Industrial Revolution* (London, 1977).

Gatrell, V.A.C.: 'Crime, authority and the police-man state' in F.M.L. Thompson (ed.), *The Cambridge Social History of Britain 1750-1950*, 3 (Cambridge, 1990).
Geary, Roger: *Policing Industrial Disputes 1893-1985* (London, 1985).
Gould, Robert W.: Wuldren, Michael J.: *London's Unarmed Police* (London, 1986).
Hailstone, A.G.: *One Hundred Years of Law Enforcement in Buckinghamshire* (1956).
Hart, J.M.: *The British Police* (London, 1951).
Herbert, T.; Jones, G.E.: *People and Protest: Wales, 1815-80* (Cardiff, 1988).
Hewitt, Eric J.: *A History of Policing Manchester* (Manchester, 1979).
Hibbert, C.: *King Mob* (London, 1958).
Hibbert, Christopher: *The Roots of Evil* (Suffolk, 1963).
Hinksman, A.J.: *The First Hundred Years of the Warwickshire Constabulary* (Rugby, 1957).
Hopkin, Deian: 'Social reactions to economic change' in Trevor Herbert and Gareth Elwyn Jones (eds.), *Wales between the Wars* (Cardiff, 1988).
Howell, David W.: *Land and People in Nineteenth Century Wales* (London, 1978).
Hunt, Walter William: *To Guard My People – A History of the Swansea Police* (Swansea, 1957).
Ingleton, Roy: *The Gentlemen at War – Policing Britain 1939-1945* (Maidstone, 1994).
Jackman, W.T.: *The Development of Transportation in Modern England*, 2nd. edition (London, 1962).
Jefferson, T.; and Grimshaw, R.: *Controlling the Constable* (London, 1984).
Jenkins, G.H.: *The Foundations of Modern Wales* (Oxford, 1993).
Jones, David J.V.: *Before Rebecca – Popular Protests in Wales 1793-1835* (London, 1973).
Jones, David J.V.: *Chartism and Chartists* (London, 1975).
Jones, David J.V.: *Scotch Cattle and Chartism: in People and Protest 1815-1880*, ed. T. Herbert and Gareth Elwyn Jones (Cardiff, 1988).
Jones, David J.V.: *Crime in Nineteenth Century Wales* (Cardiff, 1992).
Jones, David J.V.: *The Last Rising* (Oxford, 1985).
Jones, David J.V.: *Crime and Policing in the Twentieth Century* (Cardiff, 1996).
Jones, E.D.: 'The Methodist revival' in A.J. Roderick (ed.), *Wales through the Ages*, II (Llandybïe, 1960).
Jones, Gareth E.: *Modern Wales – A Concise History*, 2nd. edition (Cambridge, 1984).
Jones, I.G.: *Mid-Vicorian Wales – The Observers and the Observed* (Cardiff, 1992).
Jones, Ivor Wynne: *The Llechwedd Strike of 1893* (Blaenau Ffestiniog, 1993).
Jones, J. Owain: *The History of the Caernarvonshire Constabulary 1856-1950* (Caernarfon, 1963).
Jones, Merfyn: 'Notes from the margin: Class and society in nineteenth century Gwynedd' in David Smith (ed.), *A People and a Proletariat: Essays in the History of Wales 1780-1980* (London, 1980).
Jones, Merfyn: 'Rural and industrial protest in north Wales' in Trevor Herbert and Gareth Elwyn Jones (eds.), *People and Protest: Wales 1815-1880* (Cardiff, 1988).

Jones, R. Merfyn: *The North Wales Quarrymen 1874-1922* (Cardiff, 1982).
Judge, Anthony: *A Man Apart – The British Policeman and his Job* (London, 1972).
Lambert, W.R.: *Drink and Sobriety in Victorian Wales 1820-1895* (Cardiff, 1983).
Lea, L. and Young, J.: *What is to be done about Law and Order – Crisis in the Eighties* (Penguin Books, 1984).
Lee, W.L. Melville: *A History of Police in England* (London, 1901).
Lerry, George: *The Policemen of Denbighshire.*
Lewis, Roy: *A Force for the Future* (London, 1976).
Lindsay, Jean: *The Great Strike – A History of the Penrhyn Quarry Dispute 1900-1903* (Newton Abbot, 1987).
Lloyd, Lewis: *The Port of Caernarfon 1793-1900* (Caernarfon, 1989).
Lloyd, Lewis: *Sails on the Mawddach* (Caernarfon, 1981).
Lock, Joan: *The British Policewoman* (London, 1979).
Maddox, W.C.: *A History of the Montgomeryshire Constabulary 1840-1948* (Carmarthen, 1982).
Maitland, F.W.: *Justice and Police* (London, 1885).
Mannheim, Hermann: *War and Crime* (London, 1941).
Martin, J.R. and Wilson, Gail: *The Police a Study in Manpower* (London, 1969).
Mark, Sir Robert: *Policing a Perplexed Society* (London, 1977).
Marshall, J.D.: *The Old Poor Law 1795-1834*, 2nd. edition (London, 1985).
Martiensson, Anthony: *Crime and the Public* (Penguin, 1951).
McNee, Sir David: *McNee's Law* (London, 1983).
*Monmouthshire Constabulary Centenary Handbook* (1957).
Moore, Colin and Brown, John: *Community versus Crime* (London, 1981).
Morgan, D.W.: *Brief Glory* (Liverpool, 1948).
Morgan, Jane: *Conflict and Order, The Police and Labour Disputes in England and Wales 1900-1939* (Oxford, 1987).
Morgan, Kenneth O.: *Wales in British Politics 1868-1922* (Cardiff, 1991).
Morris, A.: *Merionethshire* (Cambridge, 1915).
Morris, R.J.: 'Clubs, societies and associations' in F.M.L. Thompson (ed.), *The Cambridge Social History of Britain 1750-1950*, 3 (Cambridge, 1990).
Morton, James: *Bent Coppers* (London, 1993).
Moylan, Sir John: *Scotland Yard and the Metropolitan Police* (London, 1929).
Northam, Gerry: *Shooting in the Dark* (London, 1988).
Owen, Hugh: *The History of the Anglesey Constabulary* (Llangefni, 1952).
Owen, Hugh J.: *The Treasures of the Mawddach* (Bala, 1950).
Palmer, S.: *Police and Protest in England and Ireland 1780-1850* (Cambridge, 1988).
Phillips, David: *Crime and Authority in Victorian England* (London, 1977).
Phillips, Sir Thomas: *Wales, the Language, Social Conditions, Moral Character and Religious Opinions of the People, Considered in their Relation to Education* (London, 1849)
Pulling, Christopher: *Mr Punch and the Police* (London, 1964).
Purcell, William: *British Police in a Changing Society* (London, 1974).
Radford, A.: *The Economic History of England 1760-1860*, 2nd. edition (London, 1960).
Radzinowicz, Leon and King, Joan: *The Growth of Crime – The International Experience* (Pelican Books, 1979).

Renier, Robert: *The Politics of the Police*, 2nd. edition (Harvester and Wheatsheaf, London, 1992).
Reiner, Robert: *Chief Constables* (Oxford, 1991).
Reith, Charles: *The Blind Eye of History – A Study of the Present Police Era* (London, 1952).
Reynolds, S.; Wooley, B. and T.: *Seems So! A Working Class View of Politics* (London, 1911).
Ribton-Turner, C.J.: *A History of Vagrants and Vagrancy* (London, 1887).
Roberts, R.: *The Classic Slum* (London, 1973).
Royle, Edward: *Modern Britain – A Social History* (London, 1987).
Scarman, Lord: *The Scarman Report – The Brixton Disorders 10-12 April 1981* (London, 1981).
Scott, Sir Harold: *Scotland Yard* (London, 1955).
Seth, Ronald: *The Specials – The Story of the Special Constabulary* (London, 1961).
Sharpe, J.A.: *Crime in Early Modern England 1550-1750* (London, 1984).
Stallion, Martin, and Wall, David S.: *The British Police – Police Forces and Chief Officers 1829-2000* (Police History Society, Bramshill, Hampshire, 1999).
Steedman, Carolyn: *Policing the Victorian Community – The Formation of English Provincial Police Forces 1851-1880* (London, 1984).
Stern, W.M.: *Britain Yesterday and Today* (London, 1962).
Tames, R.: *Economy and Society in Nineteenth Century Britain* (London, 1972).
Taylor, David: *The New Police in Nineteenth Century England – Crime, Conflict and Control* (Manchester, 1997).
Taylor, David: *Mastering Economic and Social History* (London, 1988).
Taylor, M.B. and Wilkinson, V.L.: *Badges of Office 1829-1989* (Oxford, 1989).
Tobias, J.J.: *Nineteenth Century Crime, Prevention and Treatment* (Newton Abbot, 1972).
*The Tithe War*, a Clwyd Record Office Publication (Hawarden, 1975)
Veysey, A.G.: *Annual Report of the County Archivist – Clwyd Record Office* (Hawarden, 1975).
Waddon, Alun, and Baker, Colin: *Public Perceptions of the North Wales Police* (University College of Wales, Bangor, November 1990).
Wall, David S.: *The Chief Constables of England and Wales the Socio-legal History of a Criminal Justice Elite* (Dartmouth, 1998).
Wallace, Ryland: *Organise! Organise! Organise! – A Study of Reform Agitations in Wales 1840-1886* (Cardiff, 1991).
Whitaker, Ben: *The Police* (Penguin, 1964).
Whitaker, Ben: *The Police Society* (London, 1979).
Williams, David: *A History of Modern Wales* (London, 1950).
Williams, David: *Keeping the Peace – The Police and Public Order* (London, 1967).
Williams, Gwyn A.: *The Merthyr Rising* (Cardiff, 1988).
Williams, John: *Digest of Welsh Historical Statistics*, Vol. 1 (Cardiff, 1985).

**Articles**

Burge, Alun, 'The Mold riots of 1869' *Llafur*, 3 (3), 1982.
Cowley, Richard, 'Police under scrutiny – the inspectors of constabulary 1856-1990', *Journal of the Police History Society*, 11, 1996.
Ellis, Susan C., 'Observations of Anglesey life through quarter sessions rolls 1860-1869', *Transactions of the Anglesey Antiquarian Society and Field Club*, 1986.
Hart, Jenifer, 'Reform of the borough police, 1835-1856', *English Historical Review*, LXX, 1955.
Jenkins, J. Geraint, 'Rural industry in Anglesey', *Transactions of the Anglesey Antiquarian Society and Field Club*, 1967.
Jones, David J. V., "'A dead loss to the community': the criminal vagrant in mid-nineteenth century Wales', *Welsh History Review*, 8 (3), 1977.
Jones, David J. V., 'The poacher: a study in Victorian crime and protest', *The Historical Journal*, XXII (4), 1979.
Jones, G. Penrhyn, 'Cholera in Wales', *National Library of Wales Journal*, X (III),1958.
Jones, Ieuan Gwynedd, 'Merioneth politics in mid-nineteenth century: the politics of a rural economy', *Journal of the Merioneth Historical and Record Society*, V (IV), 1968.
Jones, W. Hugh, 'A strike at Talargoch lead-mine one hundred years ago', *Flintshire Historical Society Publications*, 16, 1956.
Lerry, George, 'The policemen of Denbighshire', *Transactions of the Denbighshire Historical Society*, 2, 1953.
O'Leary, Paul, 'Anti-Irish riots in Wales, 1826-1882', *Llafur*, 5 (4), 1991.
Parry-Jones, Brenda, 'The journals of H. J. Reveley (1812-1889) of Bryn-y-gwin, Dolgellau', *Journal of the Merioneth Historical and Record Society*, VI (III), 1971.
Richter, Donald, 'The Welsh Police, the Home Office and the Welsh tithe war of 1886-91', *Welsh History Review*, 12 (1), 1984.
Scargill, Arthur, 'The new unionism', *New Left Review*, 92, 1975.
Storch, Robert D., 'The plague of blue locusts: police reform and popular resistance in Northern England 1840-57', *International Review of Social History*, 20, 1975.
Storch, Robert D., 'The policeman as domestic missionary: urban discipline and popular culture in Northern England, 1850-1880', *Journal of Social History*, 9, 1976.
Thomas, David, 'Anglesey shipbuilding down to 1840', *Transactions of the Anglesey Antiquarian Society and Field Club*, 1932.
Troup, Sir Edward, 'Police administration, local and national', *Police Journal*, 1, 1928.
Williams, J. Roose, 'Quarryman's champion: the life and activities of William John Parry of Coetmor', *Transactions of the Caernarvonshire Historical Society*, 29, 1968.

## Newspapers and Periodicals

*Birmingham Post*
*Cambrian News*
*Carnarvon and Denbigh Herald*
*Chester Chronicle*
*Chester Courant*
*Daily Express*
*Daily Mail*
*Daily Telegraph*
*Evening Leader*
*Flintshire Observer*
*Liverpool Daily Post*
*Liverpool Echo*
*Liverpool Mercury*
*Llanelli and County Guardian*
*Merionethshire Standartd*
*Manchester Evening News*
*Manchester Guardian*
*Mold Distric Chronicle*
*Montgomeryshire County Times*
*North Wales Chronicle*
*North Wales Gazette*
*Observer*
*Observer Review*
*Police Guardian*
*Police Review*
*Police Service Advertiser*
*Sunday Express*
*Sunday Times*
*The Denbigh Free Press*
*The Guardian*
*The People*
*The Pharmaceutical Journal*
*The Times*
*Wrexham Advertiser*
*Y Dydd*


## Parliamentary Papers

PP 1816 (510) v, Report on the State of the Police Metropolis
PP 1828 vi, Police of the Metropolis
PP 1837 xxxii, Reports of the Inspectors of Prisons, North Wales
PP 1842 xxxii, Returns of Police Establishments in each County or Division of a County
PP 1847 xvii
PP 1852-3 xxxvi, Report of Select Committee on Police
PP 1857-8 xlvii, Report of Select Committee on Police
PP 1860 lii, Report of Her Majesty's Inspectors of Constabulary
PP 1862 xiv, Reports of the Inspectors of Constabulary, North Wales

PP 1867-68 xvii, Employment of Women and Children in Agriculture – First Report of Commissioners
PP 1877 xv, Report of Select Committee on Police Superannuation Funds and Minutes of Evidence
PP 1887 xxxviii, Report of an Inquiry as to Disturbances Connected with the Levying of Tithe Rent Charge in Wales, Q1061, Q3343
PP 1908 ix, Report of the Select Committee on the Police Force's Weekly Rest Day and Minutes of Evidence
PP 1908 Qn 2012

## Hansard's Parliamentary Debates

NS Vol. xviii, February 1828
2nd. series. Peel and Wellington 1829. Speeches on the Metropolis Police Bill, House of Commons April 1829, and House of Lords June 1829
NS Vol. xviii, February 1828
3rd. series, cxl March 1856

## National Library of Wales

Glynllifon MSS 1961-84

## Anglesey Record Office, Llangefni

Quarter Session Rolls 1858, 1874, 1877, 1878, 1879, 1886
Chief Constable's General Order Books 1911-18. WH/1/62
Correspondence of Chief Constable of Anglesey 1915-18. WH/1/67
Home Office letters to the Chief Constable 1913-19. WH/73
Statement of Pay of Police, North Wales Counties, Chief Constable's Office, Llangefni 1912
Standing Joint Committee 1886, 1889, 1891, 1894, 1896, 1901, 1903, 1914, 1944

## Denbighshire Record Office, Ruthin

Quarter Session Rolls 1840, 1841, 1844, 1845, 1846, 1847, 1848, 1850, 1851, 1852, 1853, 1854, 1856, 1857, 1862, 1865, 1868, 1870, 1874, 1876, 1880, 1881, 1888
Chief Constable's Papers 1817-1922. DPD/2/1
Chief Constable's General Order Books 1929-1942, 1942-1950, 1951-1958
Standing Joint Committee 1891, 1893, 1895, 1896, 1897, 1898, 1903, 1909, 1913

## Flintshire Record Office, Hawarden

Quarter Session Rolls 1857, 1865, 1868, 1869, 1871, 1873, 1874, 1875, 1882
Chief Constable's General Order Book 1877-1902, 1907, 1909, FP/2/8

Constabulary Records 1865-1876, PS/3/9, FP/2/29-31
Constabulary General Orders 1903-1921, FP/2/9
Overton Divisional Letterbook
Standing Joint Committee 1893, 1895, 1896, 1945, 1946, 1950, 1951, 1952, 1953, 1954, 1957, 1958, 1959, 1960

**Gwynedd Archives Service**

1. **Caernarfon Record Office**

    Quarter Session Rolls 1857, 1864, 1870, 1877, 1878, 1879, 1882, 1883, 1885
    Standing Joint Committee 1894, 1895, 1896, 1900, 1901, 1902, 1903, 1909, 1911, 1940, 1941, 1942, 1944, 1946, 1948, 1949, 1950
    Constabulary Records xj/462
    Reports of HM Inspectors of Constabulary 1863-4
    Pwllheli Minute Book, August 1879

2. **Meirionnydd Record Office, Dolgellau**

    Quarter Session Rolls 1855, 1857, 1858, 1861, 1863, 1866, 1859, 1873, 1874, 1876, 1877, 1878, 1880, 1882, 1883, 1884, 1888, 1890, 1891, 1901, 1906, 1904, 1907, 1908, 1909, 1911, 1912, 1914, 1918, 1936, 1939, 1940
    Standing Joint Committee 1915, 1943, 1946, 1948, 1950
    Constabulary Records Z/H/4/20 and Z/H/2/1/, Journal of Constable John Hughes
    Corwen Occurrence Book 1884
    Chief Constable's Papers M/1/201
    Tywyn Occurrence Book, 1884

**Unpublished thesis**

H.K. Birch, 'The Merioneth Police 1856-1950', University of Wales MA thesis, 1980.

**Others**

Hansard lxiii, June 1914
The Police (Expenses) Act 1874
Home Office, HO 82356-20
HO 65/4
HO 45/05, 5276, Letter to Lord Palmerston from Chief Constable of Essex
Reports of HM Inspectors of Constabulary for 1856-7, 1940-5
The Rural Constabulary Act 1839 (2 and 3 Vict., c 93)
Interim Report on the Royal Commission on Police (November 1960)
Home Office Circular 189/1945; 191/1957; 249/1964; 285/1965.
HMSO 1967 Police Manpower, Equipment Efficiency

Justice of the Peace lxxx March 1916
Jones, J.V.: Cites PRO HO 45/6812. Letter from Thomas Mostyn
Home Office Police Research Group, Crime Detection and Prevention Series, paper 92 (1998)
North Wales Police, Annual Objectives and Performance 1988 and 1989
North Wales Police, Objectives and Priorities 1990
North Wales Police Annual Policing Plan, A Total Policing Service 1997-98
North Wales Police Authority Policing Plan – Working Together for Safer Communities 1998-1999
North Wales Police, Crime and Disorder in Gwynedd Audit Report 1999
Health Education Council, What to do about glue sniffing (undated)
Dept. of Education and Science and Welsh Office, Drug Misuse and the Young (July 1985)
Gwynedd Police Authority 1951-67
Gwynedd Chief Constable's Annual Report 1969-99
Cmd 1222; 7674; 7831; 7070 (1947); 7321 (January 1948), 1728 (May 1962).
10 Geo iv, c 44

# INDEX

Accountability, 14,15,16,17,18,21
Additional duties, 116
Agriculture, 51-53
ALDERSON, John, 13
Aliens Order, 279
ARCHER, Lord, 18
Arson, 335
ASCOLI, David, 13,15
ASSHETON SMITH, 28,145
*Autocar*, 193
Automobile Association, 194

Bail Act 1976, 327
BANTON, Michael, 13,18
Bicycles, 185-6,265
BIDDULPH, R.M., Lord Lieut., 65, 72,117
Blackpool, 19
'Blue Books' 1847, 55
BOATENG, Paul, 17
BRADSHAW, Supt. J., 76,78
Brighton, 19,312
Brixton riots, 14,17,21
Brymbo and Bersham Ironworks, 31
BULKELEY family, 51,79,126,147

C.N.D., 18
Canals, 31
Cardigan, 19,312
Carrier pigeons, 239
Cavalry, 244
CHADWICK, Edwin, 57
Chartism, 54,63,64
Chief Constables, 64,91,116,120,131, 147-155,165, 188-91,298,351
Children's Act 1908, 183
Chirk Aqueduct, 31
City of London Police, 17
Civil disorder, 125,126,127
Civilian staff, 317,332
COLQUHOUN, Patrick, 56
Community Liaison Department, 336
CONDON, Sir Paul, 18,21
Consent, 14,15
Conwy Suspension Bridge, 28
Conwy Tubular Bridge, 49
Corn Laws 1815, 51
Corn Riots, 56

CORNWALLIS WEST, Major, 148
County and Borough Police Act 1856, 80,81,85,88,132
Crime Prevention, 342
Criminal investigation, 266
CRITCHLEY, T.A., 13,15,288,295
CUTLER, Sir Horace, 16

Defence of the Realm, 245
Defence Regulations, 279
Denbighshire Constabulary, 58, 62-84,148-151
Denbighshire Yeomanry, 53
DENMAN, John, 66,68,74,75,92,117, 148
Desborough Committee, 19,225,252, 255,257,298
Detectives, 267,311,330
Discipline, 155,257,269
Divisional Reserve Units, 343
Dogs Act 1906, 178
Drink-driving, 339
Drug misuse, 340-2
Drunkenness, 158-161,245

Education, 257,262
Ellesmere Canal, 31
EMSLEY, Clive, 12,238,366

Ffrwd Colliery, 31
Firearms, 334,347
First World War 1914-18, 238-247
Food riots, 53
Forensic science, 267
FOSTER, 15,16

GEARY, Roger, 13
GEE, Thomas, 205, 210
General Strike 1926, 260,365
GLADSTONE, W.E., 49,164,205
Good conduct awards, 71
Gordon Riots 1780, 56
Greater London Council, 16
GREY, Earl, 64
GRIEVE, D.A.C. John, 21

HEATH, Mr, 20
HEATON, John, 65,77
Helicopter, 344-5
Holyhead Road, 27,28

Home Guard, 280
Home Office, 17,19,20,21,64,86,95,
 132,178,180,208,262
Home Secretary, 16,17,19,57,64,67,
 76,132,181,184,254,256,301,313
HOSKER, Thomas, 29
Housing, 310
HUGHES, Thomas, 75

Identification markings, 308
Identity cards, 279
Incendiarism, 53
Indictable offences, 329
Industrialisation, 26,31,50
Inspectors of Constabulary, 85,93,
 94,126,130,180,246,266,288
Investiture 1911, 227
Investiture 1969, 316
Irish navvies, 49

JONES, David J.V., 13,121
JONES, Michael D., 55
JONES, R. Humphrey, 78

KING, Supt. G.M., 76,77,78
King's Police Medal, 288

Leave, 183,239
Licensing and Game Laws, 124,159
LIVINGSTONE, Ken, 17
Local Government Act 1888, 166,177
Lock-ups, 69,76,85,113,144-6

MacPherson Report of 1999, 21
Magistrates, 50,56,62,64,67,75,79,86,
 154,166,306
MAINWARING, Townshend M.P., 72,
 77,150
Manchester Yeomanry, 56
MANSFIELD, Michael, QC, 21
MARK, Sir Robert, 13-14,20,328,331
Marshall Inquiry Report, 16
MAUDLING, Reginald, 20
MAYNE, Richard, 15
McNEE, David, 13,16,17
Menai Suspension Bridge, 28
Menai Tubular Bridge, 49
Mergers, 131,153,261,295,301-5,
 314-5

Metropolitan Police, 15,21,57,90,
 133,227,252-3
Military, 129,212,214,218,221,225,
 364
Miners' strikes, 15,20,62,327,334,366
Montgomeryshire Canal, 31
MORGAN, Jane, 13,15,21,363
Mostyn Estates 125,146
Motor Car Act 1903, 192
Motor cars, 191-5,240,264
Motor cycles, 261,265,307
Municipal Corporations Act 1835, 57
Mutual aid, 225-6,283,364

National Eisteddfod 1898, 226
National Insurance Act 1911, 184
National Police Fund, 261
Neighbourhood Watch, 345
New Scotland Yard, 19,20

NEWBOROUGH, Lord, 87,115,126
Nonconformity, 55
Notting Hill, 18
Nottingham, 18

Oaksey Committee, 19,299-300

PALMER, John, 29
PALMERSTON, Lord, 80
Parish Constables, 56,57,80,88
PEEL, Sir Robert, 57,80
PENRHYN family, 51,126,131,157,
 217
Penrhyn Quarry Strike, 217-26
Personnel numbers, 278,297,332
Peterloo Riots, 56
Photography, 132
Poaching, 125,162
Police Act 1890, 134,174,180,225
Police Act 1919, 253,364
Police Act 1946, 301
Police Act of 1964, 17,19,365
Police and Citizens' Association 1894,
 175
Police and Firemen's (War Reserve)
 Act 1939, 284
Police Authority, 17
Police College, 296
Police Council, 253-6,266,300

Police Federation, 95,253,256,263, 299,332
Police Force's (Weekly Rest Day) Act 1910, 184-5
Police Rates, 120
*Police Review*, 175
Police Stations, 85,113,114,144-46, 296, 349
Police Superintendent's Association, 327
Police Support Unit, 334
*Police Service Advertiser*, 118
Police vehicles, 265,283,307-9
Police Widows Pension Act 1918, 254
Political Reform, 63
Poor Law Amendment Act 1834, 51,63
Population, 25
Post Office, 27
Private Constables, 180
Public Health, 55

Queen's Police Medal, 316

Racism, 21
RADZINOWICZ, Leon, 18
Railway Act 1844, 49
Railways, 30,49,50,73,163,229
Raven and Bell Hotel, Shrewsbury, 29
Rebecca Riots, 64
Recruitment, 73,89,331
Reform Bill 1832, 63
REINER, Robert, 13,16,21,312
REITH, Charles, 13,15
RENNIE, John, 28
Rewards, 126,163
Riot Act, 130,213
Road accidents, 306, 338-40
ROWAN, Charles, 15
Royal Automobile Club, 193
Royal Commission, 19
Royal Mail, 29,30
Royal Visits, 226
RSPCA, 179
Rural Police Act 1839, 64,65,67
Ruthin Gaol, 63

Salaries, 65,74,75,76,85,90,94,119, 143-4,154,181-2,252,254-6,263-4, 286,298-300
Scandals, 18

SCARMAN, Lord, 14,17,20,21
Search and Arrest, 119
Second World War, 276-93
Shipbuilding, 32,49
Shooting, 260
Shop Act 1912, 183
Sick Pay, 69
Slate, 32
*Snowden's Police Constable's Guide for 1862*, 117
Social Changes, 26,50
Southend, 19
Special Constables, 127,206,238,241, 276,296,317,332
St John's Ambulance Brigade, 184
Stagecoaches, 29,30,31
Standing Joint Committees, 166
STANLEY, Hon. W.O., 146
STEVENS, John, 18
Stocks, 77
STORCH, Robert D., 12,15,16
Sunday Closing Act 1881, 160
Superannuation Fund, 69,75,96,133, 150,174-6
Support Units, 346
SWAFFIELD, Sir James, 16

TAYLOR, David, 15
Telegraphy, 164,239,283,308
Telephones, 187,244,258,263,283,308
TELFORD, Thomas, 28
Thames River Police, 56
THATCHER, Mrs, 20
*The New Police*, 15
*The Times*, 14
Tithe Commutation Act 1836, 206
Tithe Rent Charge Act 1891, 216
Tithe Wars, 157,205-17
Trade unions, 218
Traffic census 1925, 265
Traffic Wardens, 333
Training, 267,296,311,333
Turnpike Trusts, 26,27,28,29,30
Types of offences, 119,121,122

Uniformity of prosecutions, 122
Uniforms, 69,71,76,85,96,285
Unsolved Crimes, 259
Utilitarians, 57

Vagrancy, 123-4,161-2

War bonus payments, 243
Watch Committees, 58
WELLINGTON, Duke of, 57
Welsh Guards, 241
Welsh language, 90,93,147,351-2,367
Welsh Webs, 32
WHITAKER, Ben, 13
White Lion Hotel, Chester, 29
WILLIAMSON, Frank, 20
Women police, 268,277,281-2,331
Woollen industry, 52,53
Worcester, 19,312

YALE, Col., 65,72,74
YOUNG, Arthur, 26